The Huguenots in France

Also from Westphalia Press
westphaliapress.org

The Idea of the Digital University

Dialogue in the Roman-Greco World

The History of Photography

International or Local Ownership?: Security Sector Development in Post-Independent Kosovo

Lankes, His Woodcut Bookplates

Opportunity and Horatio Alger

The Role of Theory in Policy Analysis

The Little Confectioner

Non Profit Organizations and Disaster

The Idea of Neoliberalism: The Emperor Has Threadbare Contemporary Clothes

Social Satire and the Modern Novel

Ukraine vs. Russia: Revolution, Democracy and War: Selected Articles and Blogs, 2010-2016

James Martineau and Rebuilding Theology

A Strategy for Implementing the Reconciliation Process

Issues in Maritime Cyber Security

A Different Dimension: Reflections on the History of Transpersonal Thought

Iran: Who Is Really In Charge?

Contracting, Logistics, Reverse Logistics: The Project, Program and Portfolio Approach

Unworkable Conservatism: Small Government, Freemarkets, and Impracticality

Springfield: The Novel

Lariats and Lassos

Ongoing Issues in Georgian Policy and Public Administration

Growing Inequality: Bridging Complex Systems, Population Health and Health Disparities

Designing, Adapting, Strategizing in Online Education

Pacific Hurtgen: The American Army in Northern Luzon, 1945

Natural Gas as an Instrument of Russian State Power

New Frontiers in Criminology

Feeding the Global South

Beijing Express: How to Understand New China

The Rise of the Book Plate: An Exemplative of the Art

The Huguenots in France

After the Revocation of the
Edict of Nantes
with Memoirs of Distinguished
Huguenot Refugees,
and A Visit to the
Country of Voudois

by Samuel Smiles

WESTPHALIA PRESS
An Imprint of Policy Studies Organization

The Huguenots in France, After the Revocation of the Edict of Nantes
with Memoirs of Distinguished Huguenot Refugees,
and A Visit to the Country of Voudois
All Rights Reserved © 2018 by Policy Studies Organization

Westphalia Press
An imprint of Policy Studies Organization
1527 New Hampshire Ave., NW
Washington, D.C. 20036
info@ipsonet.org

ISBN-13: 978-1-63391-644-9
ISBN-10: 1-63391-644-8

Cover design by Jeffrey Barnes:
jbarnesbook.design

Daniel Gutierrez-Sandoval, Executive Director
PSO and Westphalia Press

Updated material and comments on this edition
can be found at the Westphalia Press website:
www.westphaliapress.org

THE HUGUENOTS IN FRANCE.

THE HUGUENOTS IN FRANCE

After the Revocation of the Edict of Nantes

WITH MEMOIRS OF DISTINGUISHED HUGUENOT REFUGEES

AND

A VISIT TO THE COUNTRY OF THE VAUDOIS

By SAMUEL SMILES

AUTHOR OF "THE HUGUENOTS: THEIR SETTLEMENTS, CHURCHES, AND INDUSTRIES IN ENGLAND AND IRELAND," "SELF-HELP," "CHARACTER," ETC.

"Plus à me frapper on s'amuse,
Tant plus de marteaux on y use."
THÉODORE DE BÈZE

"They maintained their faith in the noble way of persecution, and served God in the fire, whereas we honour him in the sunshine."
SIR THOMAS BROWNE

NEW EDITION.

LONDON
GEORGE ROUTLEDGE AND SONS, LIMITED
BROADWAY, LUDGATE HILL
MANCHESTER AND NEW YORK
1893

DR. SMILES'S WORKS.

JASMIN: Barber, Poet, Philanthropist. Post 8vo. 6s. 4th Thousand.

"What Jasmin did for himself in poetry Dr. Smiles has now done for him in prose, doing full justice to that part of his life which Jasmin's simple modesty forbade him to record, namely, his unceasing philanthropic efforts. The story is noble as well as touching, and is told by Dr. Smiles with abundance of sympathy and appreciation."—*The Times*

"Il a fait un livre bien personnel et aussi complet que possible. Voilà Jasmin 'raconté' en anglais pour la posterité. C'est M. Smiles qui est la coupable, et son élégant volume nous a tout à fait charmé."—*Revue Littéraire.*

"One of the most touching and charming biographies we have ever read."—*Critic* (New York).

LIFE AND LABOUR; or, Characteristics of Men of Talent and Genius. 6s.

MEN OF INVENTION AND INDUSTRY. 6s.

THE HUGUENOTS: Their Settlements, Churches, and Industries in England and Ireland. Crown 8vo. 7s. 6d.

SIX SHILLINGS EACH.

SELF-HELP.	**THRIFT.**
CHARACTER.	**DUTY.**

INDUSTRIAL BIOGRAPHY. 6s.

LIVES OF THE ENGINEERS. Illustrated. 5 Vols. 7s. 6d. each.

LIFE OF GEORGE STEPHENSON. With Illustrations. 21s.; 7s. 6d.; or 2s. 6d.

JAMES NASMYTH, ENGINEER: An Autobiography. With Portrait and 90 Illustrations. 16s. and 6s.

LIFE OF THOMAS EDWARD, Scotch Naturalist. Illustrated by Sir George Reid, P.R.S.A. 6s.

LIFE OF ROBERT DICK, Geologist and Botanist. Illustrated. 12s.

JOHN MURRAY, Albemarle Street.

PREFACE.

IN preparing this edition for the press, I have ventured to add three short memoirs of distinguished Huguenot Refugees and their descendants.

Though the greatest number of Huguenots banished from France at the Revocation of the Edict of Nantes were merchants and manufacturers, who transferred their skill and arts to England, which was not then a manufacturing country; a large number of nobles and gentry emigrated to this and other countries, leaving their possessions to be confiscated by the French king.

The greater number of the nobles entered the armies of the countries in which they took refuge. In Holland, they joined the army of the Prince of Orange, afterwards William III., King of England. After driving the armies of Louis XIV. out of Ireland, they met the French at Ramilies, Blenheim, and Malplacquet, and other battles in the Low Countries. A Huguenot engineer directed the operations at the siege of Namur, which ended in its capture. Another conducted the siege of Lille, which was also taken.

But perhaps the greatest number of Huguenot nobles entered the Prussian service. Their descendants revisited France on more than one occasion. They overran the northern and eastern parts of France in 1814 and 1815; and last of all they vanquished the descendants of their former persecutors at Sedan in 1870. Sedan was, prior to the Revocation of the Edict of Nantes, the renowned seat of Protestant learning; while now it is known as the scene of the greatest military catastrophe which has occurred in modern history.

The Prime Minister of France, M. Jules Simon, not long ago recorded the fateful effects of Louis XIV.'s religious intolerance. In discussing the perpetual ecclesiastical questions which still disturb France, he recalled the fact that not less than eighty of the German staff in the late war were representatives of Protestant families, driven from France by the Revocation of the Edict of Nantes.

The first of the appended memoirs is that of Samuel de Péchels, a noble of Languedoc, who, after enduring great privations, reached England through Jamaica, and served as a lieutenant in Ireland under William III. Many of his descendants have been distinguished soldiers in the service of England. The second is Captain Rapin, who served faithfully in Ireland, and was called away to be tutor to the young Duke of Portland. He afterwards spent his time at Wesel on the Rhine, where he wrote his "History of England." The third is Captain Riou, "the gallant and the good," who was killed at the battle of Copenhagen. These memoirs might be multiplied to any extent; but those given are enough to show the good work which the Huguenots and their descendants have done in the service of England.

INTRODUCTION.

SIX years since, I published a book entitled *The Huguenots: their Settlements, Churches, and Industries, in England and Ireland*. Its object was to give an account of the causes which led to the large migrations of foreign Protestants from Flanders and France into England, and to describe their effects upon English industry as well as English history.

It was necessary to give a brief *résumé* of the history of the Reformation in France down to the dispersion of the Huguenots, and the suppression of the Protestant religion by Louis XIV. under the terms of the Revocation of the Edict of Nantes.

Under that Act, the profession of Protestantism was proclaimed to be illegal, and subject to the severest penalties. Hence, many of the French Protestants who refused to be "converted," and had the means of emigrating, were under the necessity of leaving France and endeavouring to find personal freedom and religious liberty elsewhere.

The refugees found protection in various countries. The principal portion of the emigrants from Languedoc and the south-eastern provinces of France crossed the frontier into Switzerland, and settled there, or afterwards proceeded into the states of Prussia, Holland, and Denmark, as well as into England and Ireland. The chief number of emigrants from the northern and western seaboard provinces of France, emigrated directly into England, Ireland, America, and the Cape of Good Hope. In my previous work, I endeavoured to give as accurate a description as was possible of the emigrants who settled in England and Ireland, to which the American editor of the work (the Hon. G. P. Disosway) has added an account of those who settled in the United States of America.

But besides the Huguenots who contrived to escape from France during the dragonnades which preceded and the persecutions which followed the Revocation of the Edict of Nantes, there was still a very large number of Huguenots remaining in France who had not the means wherewith to fly from their country. These were the poorer people, the peasants, the small farmers, the small manufacturers, many of whom were spoiled of their goods for the very purpose of preventing them from emigrating. They were consequently under the necessity of remaining in their native country, whether they changed their religion by force or not. It is to give an account of these people, as a supplement to my former book, that the present work is written.

It is impossible to fix precisely the number of the

INTRODUCTION. ix

Huguenots who left France to avoid the cruelties of Louis XIV., as well as of those who perforce remained to endure them. It shakes one's faith in history to observe the contradictory statements published with regard to French political or religious facts, even of recent date. A general impression has long prevailed that there was a Massacre of St. Bartholemew in Paris in the year 1572; but even that has recently been denied, or softened down into a mere political squabble. It is not, however, possible to deny the fact that there was a Revocation of the Edict of Nantes in 1685, though it has been vindicated as a noble act of legislation, worthy even of the reputation and character of Louis the Great.

No two writers agree as to the number of French citizens who were driven from their country by the Revocation. A learned Roman Catholic, Mr. Charles Butler, states that only 50,000 persons "retired" from France; whereas M. Capefigue, equally opposed to the Reformation, who consulted the population tables of the period (although the intendants made their returns as small as possible in order to avoid the reproach of negligence), calculates the emigration at 230,000 souls, namely, 1,580 ministers, 2,300 elders, 15,000 gentlemen, the remainder consisting almost entirely of traders and artisans.

These returns, quoted by M. Capefigue, were made only a few years after the Revocation, although the emigration continued without intermission for many years later. M. Charles Coquerel says that whatever horror may be felt for the Massacre of St. Bartholomew of 1572, the persecutions which preceded and followed the Act of Revocation in 1685, "kept France under a perpetual St. Bartholomew for about sixty years." During that time it is believed that more than 1,000,000 Frenchmen either left the kingdom, or were killed, imprisoned, or sent to the galleys in their efforts to escape.

The Intendant of Saintonge, a King's officer, not likely to exaggerate the number of emigrants, reported in 1698, long before the emigration had ceased, that his province had lost 100,000 Reformers. Languedoc suffered far more; whilst Boulainvilliers reports that besides the emigrants who succeeded in making their escape, the province lost not fewer than 100,000 persons by premature death, the sword, strangulation, and the wheel.

The number of French emigrants who resorted to England may be inferred from the fact that at the beginning of last century there were not fewer than *thirty-five* French Protestant churches in London alone, at a time when the population of the metropolis was not one-fourth of what it is now; while there were other large French settlements at Canterbury, Norwich, Southampton, Bristol, Exeter, &c., as well as at Dublin, Lisburn, Portarlington, and other towns in Ireland.

Then, with respect to the much larger number of Protestants who remained in France after the Revocation of the Edict of Nantes, there is the same difference of opinion. A deputation of Huguenot pastors and elders, who waited upon the Duc de Noailles in 1682, informed him that there were then 1,800,000 Protestant *families* in France. Thirty years after that date, Louis XIV. proclaimed that there were no Protestants whatever in France; that Protestantism had been entirely suppressed, and that any one found professing that faith must be considered as a "relapsed heretic," and sentenced to imprisonment, the galleys, or the other punishments to which Protestants were then subject.

After an interval of about seventy-five years, during which Protestantism (though suppressed by the law) contrived to lead a sort of underground life—the Protestants meeting by night, and sometimes by day, in caves, valleys, moors, woods, old quarries, hollow beds of rivers, or, as they themselves called it, "in the Desert"—they at length contrived to lift their heads into the light of day, and then Rabaut St. Etienne stood up in the Constituent Assembly at Paris, in 1787, and claimed the rights of his Protestant fellow-countrymen—the rights of "2,000,000 useful citizens." Louis XVI. granted them an Edict of Tolerance, about a hundred years after Louis XIV. had revoked the Edict of Nantes; but the measure proved too late for the King, and too late for France, which had already been sacrificed to the intolerance of Louis XIV. and his Jesuit advisers.

After all the sufferings of France — after the cruelties to which her people have been subjected by the tyranny of her monarchs and the intolerance of her priests,—it is doubtful whether she has yet learnt wisdom from her experience and trials. France was brought to ruin a century ago by the Jesuits who held the entire education of the country in their hands. They have again recovered their ground, and the Congreganistes are now what the Jesuits were before. The Sans-Cullotes of 1793 were the pupils of the priests; so were the Communists of 1871.* M. Edgar Quinet has recently said to his countrymen: "The Jesuitical and clerical spirit which has sneaked in among you and all your affairs has ruined you. It has corrupted the spring of life; it has delivered you over to the enemy ... Is this to last for ever? For heaven's sake spare us at least the sight of a Jesuits' Republic as the coronation of our century."

In the midst of these prophecies of ruin, we have M. Veuillot frankly avowing his Ultramontane policy in the *Univers*. He is quite willing to go back to the old burnings, hangings, and quarterings, to prevent any freedom of opinion about religious matters. "For my part," he says, "I frankly avow my regret not only that John Huss was not burnt sooner, but that Luther was not burnt too. And I regret further that there has not been some prince sufficiently pious and politic to have made a crusade against the Protestants."

M. Veuillot is perhaps entitled to some respect for boldly speaking out what he means and thinks

* M. Simiot's speech before the National Assembly, 16th March, 1873

There are many amongst ourselves who mean the same thing, without having the courage to say so —who hate the Reformation quite as much as M. Veuillot does, and would like to see the principles of free examination and individual liberty torn up root and branch.

With respect to the proposed crusade against Protestantism, it will be seen from the following work what the " pious and politic" Louis XIV. attempted, and how very inefficient his measures eventually proved in putting down Protestantism, or in extending Catholicism. Louis XIV. found it easier to make martyrs than apostates; and discovered that hanging, banishment, the galleys, and the sword were not amongst the most successful of " converters."

The history of the Huguenots during the time of their submergence as an "underground church" is scarcely treated in the general histories of France. Courtly writers blot them out of history as Louis XIV. desired to blot them out of France. Most histories of France published in England contain little notice of them. Those who desire to pursue the subject further, will obtain abundant information, more particularly from the following works :—

    ELIE BÉNOÎT : *Histoire de l'Edit de Nantes.*
    CHARLES COQUEREL : *Histoire des Eglises du Désert.*
    NAPOLEON PEYRAT : *Histoire des Pasteurs de Désert.*
    ANTOINE COURT : *Histoire des Troubles de Cevennes.*
    EDMUND HUGHES : *Histoire de la Restauration du Protestantisme en France au xviii. Siècle.*
    A. BONNEMÈRE : *Histoire des Camisardes.*
    ADOLPHE MICHEL : *Louvois et Les Protestantes.*
    ATHANASE COQUEREL FILS : *Les Forçats pour La Foi, &c., &c.*

It remains to be added that part of this work—viz., the "Wars of the Camisards," and the "Journey in the Country of the Vaudois"—originally appeared in *Good Words*.

S. S.

LONDON, *October*, 1873.

CONTENTS.

THE HUGUENOTS IN FRANCE AFTER THE REVOCATION OF THE EDICT OF NANTES.

CHAPTER	PAGE
I. REVOCATION OF THE EDICT OF NANTES	1
II. EFFECTS OF THE REVOCATION—CHURCH IN THE DESERT	12
III. CLAUDE BROUSSON, THE HUGUENOT ADVOCATE	30
IV. CLAUDE BROUSSON, PASTOR AND MARTYR	50
V. OUTBREAK IN LANGUEDOC	75
VI. INSURRECTION OF THE CAMISARDS	99
VII. EXPLOITS OF CAVALIER	130
VIII. END OF THE CAMISARD INSURRECTION	166
IX. GALLEY-SLAVES FOR THE FAITH	190
X. ANTOINE COURT	205
XI. REORGANIZATION OF THE CHURCH IN THE DESERT	218
XII. THE CHURCH IN THE DESERT—PAUL RABAUT	235
XIII. END OF THE PERSECUTIONS—THE FRENCH REVOLUTION	253

MEMOIRS OF DISTINGUISHED HUGUENOT REFUGEES.

I. STORY OF SAMUEL DE PÉCHELS	285
II. CAPTAIN RAPIN, AUTHOR OF THE "HISTORY OF ENGLAND"	316
III. CAPTAIN RIOU, R.N.	368

A VISIT TO THE COUNTRY OF THE VAUDOIS.

I. INTRODUCTORY—EARLY PERSECUTIONS OF THE VAUDOIS	383
II. THE VALLEY OF THE ROMANCHE—BRIANÇON	401
III. VAL LOUISE—HISTORY OF FELIX NEFF	420
IV. THE VAUDOIS MOUNTAIN-REFUGE OF DORMILHOUSE	437
V. GUILLESTRE AND THE VALLEY OF QUEYRAS	455
VI. THE VALLEY OF THE PELICE—LA TOUR—ANGROGNA—THE PRA DE TOUR	472
VII. THE GLORIOUS RETURN: AN EPISODE IN THE HISTORY OF THE ITALIAN VAUDOIS	493

MAPS.

	PAGE
THE COUNTRY OF THE CEVENNES	98
"THE COUNTRY OF FELIX NEFF" (DAUPHINY)	382
THE VALLEY OF LUSERNE	472

THE HUGUENOTS IN FRANCE.

CHAPTER I.

REVOCATION OF THE EDICT OF NANTES.

THE Revocation of the Edict of Nantes was signed by Louis XIV. of France, on the 18th of October, 1685, and published four days afterwards.

Although the Revocation was the personal act of the King, it was nevertheless a popular measure, approved by the Catholic Church of France, and by the great body of the French people.

The King had solemnly sworn, at the beginning of his reign, to maintain the tolerating Edict of Henry IV. —the Huguenots being amongst the most industrious, enterprising, and loyal of his subjects. But the advocacy of the King's then Catholic mistress, Madame de Maintenon, and of his Jesuit Confessor, Père la Chaise, overcame his scruples, and the deed of Revocation of the Edict was at length signed and published.

The aged Chancellor, Le Tellier, was so overjoyed at the measure, that on affixing the great seal of France to the deed, he exclaimed, in the words of Simeon, " Lord, now lettest thou thy servant depart in peace, for mine eyes have seen thy salvation."

Three months later, the great Bossuet, the eagle of Meaux, preached the funeral sermon of Le Tellier; in the course of which he testified to the immense joy of the Church at the Revocation of the Edict. "Let us," said he, "expand our hearts in praises of the piety of Louis. Let our acclamations ascend to heaven, and let us say to this new Constantine, this new Theodosius, this new Marcian, this new Charlemagne, what the thirty-six fathers formerly said in the Council of Chalcedon: 'You have affirmed the faith, you have exterminated the heretics; it is a work worthy of your reign, whose proper character it is. Thanks to you, heresy is no more. God alone can have worked this marvel. King of heaven, preserve the King of earth: it is the prayer of the Church, it is the prayer of the Bishops.'"*

Madame de Maintenon also received the praises of the Church. "All good people," said the Abbé de Choisy, "the Pope, the bishops, and all the clergy, rejoice at the victory of Madame de Maintenon." Madame enjoyed the surname of Director of the Affairs of the Clergy; and it was said by the ladies of St. Cyr (an institution founded by her), that "the cardinals and the bishops knew no other way of approaching the King save through her."

It is generally believed that her price for obtaining the King's consent to the Act of Revocation, was the withdrawal by the clergy of their opposition to her marriage with the King; and that the two were privately united by the Archbishop of Paris at Versailles, a few days after, in the presence of Père la Chaise and two more witnesses. But Louis XIV. never publicly recognised De Maintenon as his wife—never rescued

* Bossuet, "Oraison Funèbre du Chancellier Letellier."

her from the ignominious position in which she originally stood related to him.

People at court all spoke with immense praises of the King's intentions with respect to destroying the Huguenots. "Killing them off" was a matter of badinage with the courtiers. Madame de Maintenon wrote to the Duc de Noailles, "The soldiers are killing numbers of the fanatics—they hope soon to free Languedoc of them."

That picquante letter-writer, Madame de Sévigné, often referred to the Huguenots. She seems to have classed them with criminals or wild beasts. When residing in Low Brittany during a revolt against the Gabelle, a friend wrote to her, "How dull you must be!" "No," replied Madame de Sévigné, "we are not so dull—hanging is quite a refreshment to me! They have just taken twenty-four or thirty of these men, and are going to throw them off."

A few days after the Edict had been revoked, she wrote to her cousin Bussy, at Paris: "You have doubtless seen the Edict by which the King revokes that of Nantes. There is nothing so fine as that which it contains, and never has any King done, or ever will do, a more memorable act." Bussy replied to her: "I immensely admire the conduct of the King in destroying the Huguenots. The wars which have been waged against them, and the St. Bartholomew, have given some reputation to the sect. His Majesty has gradually undermined it; and the edict he has just published, maintained by the dragoons and by Bourdaloue,* will soon give them the *coup de grâce*."

---

* Bourdaloue had just been sent from the Jesuit Church of St Louis at Paris, to Montpelier, to aid the dragoons in converting the Protestants, and bringing them back to the Church.

In a future letter to Count Bussy, Madame de Sévigné informed him of "a dreadfully fatiguing journey which her son-in-law M. de Grignan had made in the mountains of Dauphiny, to pursue and punish the miserable Huguenots, who issued from their holes, and vanished like ghosts to avoid extermination."

De Baville, however, the Lieutenant of Languedoc, kept her in good heart. In one of his letters, he said, "I have this morning condemned seventy-six of these wretches (Huguenots), and sent them to the galleys." All this was very pleasant to Madame de Sévigné.

Madame de Scuderi, also, more moderately rejoiced in the Act of Revocation. "The King," she wrote to Bussy, "has worked great marvels against the Huguenots; and the authority which he has employed to unite them to the Church will be most salutary to themselves and to their children, who will be educated in the purity of the faith; all this will bring upon him the benedictions of Heaven."

Even the French Academy, though originally founded by a Huguenot, publicly approved the deed of Revocation. In a discourse uttered before it, the Abbé Tallemand exclaimed, when speaking of the Huguenot temple at Charenton, which had just been destroyed by the mob, "Happy ruins, the finest trophy France ever beheld!" La Fontaine described heresy as now "reduced to the last gasp." Thomas Corneille also eulogized the zeal of the King in "throttling the Reformation." Barbier D'Aucourt heedlessly, but truly, compared the emigration of the Protestants "to the departure of the Israelites from Egypt." The Academy afterwards proposed, as the subject of a poem, the Revocation of the Edict of Nantes, and Fontenelle had the fortune, good or bad, of winning the prize.

The philosophic La Bruyère contributed a maxim in praise of the Revocation. Quinault wrote a poem on the subject; and Madame Deshoulières felt inspired to sing "The Destruction of Heresy." The Abbé de Rancé spoke of the whole affair as a prodigy: "The Temple of Charenton destroyed, and no exercise of Protestantism within the kingdom; it is a kind of miracle, such as we had never hoped to have seen in our day."

The Revocation was popular with the lower class, who went about sacking and pulling down the Protestant churches. They also tracked the Huguenots and their pastors, where they found them evading or breaking the Edict of Revocation; thus earning the praises of the Church and the fines offered by the King for their apprehension. The provosts and sheriffs of Paris represented the popular feeling, by erecting a brazen statue of the King who had rooted out heresy; and they struck and distributed medals in honour of the great event.

The Revocation was also popular with the dragoons. In order to "convert" the Protestants, the dragoons were unduly billeted upon them. As both officers and soldiers were then very badly paid, they were thereby enabled to live at free quarters. They treated everything in the houses they occupied as if it were their own, and an assignment of billets was little less than the consignment of the premises to the military, to use for their own purposes, during the time they occupied them.*

The Revocation was also approved by those who wished to buy land cheap. As the Huguenots were prevented holding their estates unless they conformed to the Catholic religion, and as many estates were

* Sir John Reresby's Travels and Memoirs.

accordingly confiscated and sold, land speculators, as well as grand seigneurs who wished to increase their estates, were constantly on the look-out for good bargains. Even before the Revocation, when the Huguenots were selling their land in order to leave the country, Madame de Maintenon wrote to her nephew, for whom she had obtained from the King a grant of 800,000 francs, "I beg of you carefully to use the money you are about to receive. Estates in Poitou may be got for nothing; the desolation of the Huguenots will drive them to sell more. You may easily acquire extensive possessions in Poitou."

The Revocation was especially gratifying to the French Catholic Church. The Pope, of course, approved of it. *Te Deums* were sung at Rome in thanksgiving for the forced conversion of the Huguenots. Pope Innocent XI. sent a brief to Louis XIV., in which he promised him the unanimous praises of the Church. "Amongst all the proofs," said he, "which your Majesty has given of natural piety, not the least brilliant is the zeal, truly worthy of the most Christian King, which has induced you to revoke all the ordinances issued in favour of the heretics of your kingdom."[*]

The Jesuits were especially elated by the Revocation. It had been brought about by the intrigues of their party, acting on the King's mind through Madame de Maintenon and Père la Chaise. It enabled them to fill their schools and nunneries with the children of Protestants, who were compelled by law to pay for their education by Jesuit priests. To furnish the required accommodation, nearly the whole of the Protestant temples that had not been pulled down were

[*] Pope Innocent XI.'s Letter of November 13th, 1685.

made over to the Jesuits, to be converted into monastic schools and nunneries. Even Bossuet, the "last father of the Church," shared in the spoils of the Huguenots. A few days after the Edict had been revoked, Bossuet applied for the materials of the temples of Nauteuil and Morcerf, situated in his diocese; and his Majesty ordered that they should be granted to him.*

Now that Protestantism had been put down, and the officers of Louis announced from all parts of the kingdom that the Huguenots were becoming converted by thousands, there was nothing but a clear course before the Jesuits in France. For their religion was now the favoured religion of the State.

It is true there were the Jansenists—declared to be heretical by the Popes, and distinguished for their opposition to the doctrines and moral teaching of the Jesuits—who were suffering from a persecution which then drove some of the members of Port Royal into exile, and eventually destroyed them. But even the Jansenists approved the persecution of the Protestants. The great Arnault, their most illustrious interpreter, though in exile in the Low Countries, declared that though the means which Louis XIV. had employed had been "rather violent, they had in nowise been unjust."

But Protestantism being declared destroyed, and Jansenism being in disgrace, there was virtually no legal religion in France but one—that of the Roman Catholic Church. Atheism, it is true, was tolerated, but then Atheism was not a religion. The Atheists did not, like the Protestants, set up rival churches, or appoint rival ministers, and seek to draw people to their assemblies. The Atheists, though they tacitly approved the religion of the King, had no opposition

* "Louvois et les Protestants," par Adolphe Michel, p. 286.

to offer to it—only neglect, and perhaps concealed contempt.

Hence it followed that the Court and the clergy had far more toleration for Atheism than for either Protestantism or Jansenism. It is authentically related that Louis XIV. on one occasion objected to the appointment of a representative on a foreign mission on account of the person being supposed to be a Jansenist; but on its being discovered that the nominee was only an Atheist, the objection was at once withdrawn.*

At the time of the Revocation, when the King and the Catholic Church were resolved to tolerate no religion other than itself, the Church had never seemed so powerful in France. It had a strong hold upon the minds of the people. It was powerful in its leaders and its great preachers; in fact, France has never, either before or since, exhibited such an array of preaching genius as Bossuet, Bourdaloue, Flechier, and Massillon.

Yet the uncontrolled and enormously increased power conferred upon the French Church at that time, most probably proved its greatest calamity. Less than a hundred years after the Revocation, the Church had lost its influence over the people, and was despised. The Deists and Atheists, sprung from the Church's bosom, were in the ascendant; and Voltaire, Rousseau, Diderot, and Mirabeau, were regarded as greater men than either Bossuet, Bourdaloue, Flechier, or Massillon.

Not one of the clergy we have named, powerful orators though they were, ever ventured to call in question the cruelties with which the King sought to compel the Protestants to embrace the dogmas of their Church. There were no doubt many Catholics who deplored the force practised on the

* *Quarterly Review.*

Huguenots; but they were greatly in the minority, and had no power to make their opposition felt. Some of them considered it an impious sacrilege to compel the Protestants to take the Catholic sacrament—to force them to accept the host, which Catholics believed to be the veritable body of Christ, but which the Huguenots could only accept as bread, over which some function had been performed by the priests, in whose miraculous power of conversion they did not believe.

Fénélon took this view of the forcible course employed by the Jesuits; but he was in disgrace as a Jansenist, and what he wrote on the subject remained for a long time unknown, and was only first published in 1825. The Duc de Saint-Simon, also a Jansenist, took the same view, which he embodied in his "Memoirs;" but these were kept secret by his family, and were not published for nearly a century after his death.

Thus the Catholic Church remained triumphant. The Revocation was apparently approved by all, excepting the Huguenots. The King was flattered by the perpetual conversions reported to be going on throughout the country—five thousand persons in one place, ten thousand in another, who had abjured and taken the communion—at once, and sometimes "instantly."

"The King," says Saint-Simon, "congratulated himself on his power and his piety. He believed himself to have renewed the days of the preaching of the Apostles, and attributed to himself all the honour. The Bishops wrote panegyrics of him; the Jesuits made the pulpits resound with his praises. . . . . He swallowed their poison in deep draughts."*

---

* "Memoirs of the Duke of Saint-Simon," translated by **Bayle St. John,** vol. iii. p. 260.

Louis XIV. lived for thirty years after the Edict of Nantes had been revoked. He had therefore the fullest opportunity of observing the results of the policy he had pursued. He died in the hands of the Jesuits, his body covered with relics of the true cross. Madame de Maintenon, the "famous and fatal witch," as Saint-Simon called her, abandoned him at last; and the King died, lamented by no one.

He had banished, or destroyed, during his reign, about a million of his subjects, and those who remained did not respect him. Many regarded him as a self-conceited tyrant, who sought to save his own soul by inflicting penance on the backs of others. He loaded his kingdom with debt, and overwhelmed his people with taxes. He destroyed the industry of France, which had been mainly supported by the Huguenots. Towards the end of his life he became generally hated; and while his heart was conveyed to the Grand Jesuits, his body, which was buried at St. Denis, was hurried to the grave accompanied by the execrations of the people.

Yet the Church remained faithful to him to the last. The great Massillon preached his funeral sermon; though the message was draped in the livery of the Court. "How far," said he, "did Louis XIV. carry his zeal for the Church, that virtue of sovereigns who have received power and the sword only that they may be props of the altar and defenders of its doctrine! Specious reasons of State! In vain did you oppose to Louis the timid views of human wisdom, the body of the monarchy enfeebled by the flight of so many citizens, the course of trade slackened, either by the deprivation of their industry, or by the furtive removal of their wealth! Dangers fortify his zeal. The work of God fears not man. He believes even that he strengthens his throne by overthrowing that of error. The profane temples are destroyed, the pulpits of seduction are cast down. The prophets of falsehood are torn from their flocks. At the first blow dealt to it by Louis, heresy falls, disappears, and is reduced either to hide itself in the obscurity whence it issued, or to cross the seas, and to bear with it into foreign lands its false gods, its bitterness, and its rage." *

Whatever may have been the temper which the Huguenots displayed when they were driven from France by persecution, they certainly carried with them something far more valuable than rage. They carried with them their virtue, piety, industry, and valour, which proved the source of wealth, spirit, freedom, and character, in all those countries—Holland, Prussia, England, and America—in which these noble exiles took refuge.

We shall next see whether the Huguenots had any occasion for entertaining the "rage" which the great Massillon attributed to them.

* Funeral Oration on Louis XIV.

CHAPTER II.

EFFECTS OF THE REVOCATION.

THE Revocation struck with civil death the entire Protestant population of France. All the liberty of conscience which they had enjoyed under the Edict of Nantes, was swept away by the act of the King. They were deprived of every right and privilege; their social life was destroyed; their callings were proscribed; their property was liable to be confiscated at any moment; and they were subjected to mean, detestable, and outrageous cruelties.

From the day of the Revocation, the relation of Louis XIV. to his Huguenot subjects was that of the Tyrant and his Victims. The only resource which remained to the latter was that of flying from their native country; and an immense number of persons took the opportunity of escaping from France.

The Edict of Revocation proclaimed that the Huguenot subjects of France must thenceforward be of "the King's religion;" and the order was promulgated throughout the kingdom. The Prime Minister, Louvois, wrote to the provincial governors, "His Majesty desires that the severest rigour shall be shown to those who will not conform to His Religion, and those who seek the foolish glory of wishing to be the last, must be pushed to the utmost extremity."

EFFECTS OF THE REVOCATION.

The Huguenots were forbidden, under the penalty of death, to worship publicly after their own religious forms. They were also forbidden, under the penalty of being sent to the galleys for life, to worship privately in their own homes. If they were overheard singing their favourite psalms, they were liable to fine, imprisonment, or the galleys. They were compelled to hang out flags from their houses on the days of Catholic processions; but they were forbidden, under a heavy penalty, to look out of their windows when the Corpus Domini was borne along the streets.

The Huguenots were rigidly forbidden to instruct their children in their own faith. They were commanded to send them to the priest to be baptized and brought up in the Roman Catholic faith, under the penalty of five hundred livres fine in each case. The boys were educated in Jesuit schools, the girls in nunneries, the parents being compelled to pay the required expenses; and where the parents were too poor to pay, the children were at once transferred to the general hospitals. A decree of the King, published in December, 1685, ordered that every child of *five years* and upwards was to be taken possession of by the authorities, and removed from its Protestant parents. This decree often proved a sentence of death, not only to the child, but to its parents.

The whole of the Protestant temples throughout France were subject to demolition. The expelled pastors were compelled to evacuate the country within fifteen days. If, in the meantime, they were found performing their functions, they were liable to be sent to the galleys for life. If they undertook to marry Protestants, the marriages were declared illegal, and the children bastards. If, after the expiry of the fifteen days, they were found lingering in France, the pastors were then liable to the penalty of death.

Protestants could neither be born, nor live, nor die, without state and priestly interference. Protestant *sages-femmes* were not permitted to exercise their functions; Protestant doctors were prohibited from practising; Protestant surgeons and apothecaries were suppressed; Protestant advocates, notaries, and lawyers were interdicted; Protestants could not teach, and all their schools, public and private, were put down. Protestants were no longer employed by the Government in affairs of finance, as collectors of taxes, or even as labourers on the public roads, or in any other office. Even Protestant grocers were forbidden to exercise their calling.

There must be no Protestant librarians, booksellers, or printers. There was, indeed, a general raid upon Protestant literature all over France. All Bibles, Testaments, and books of religious instruction, were collected and publicly burnt. There were bonfires in almost every town. At Metz, it occupied a whole day to burn the Protestant books which had been seized, handed over to the clergy, and condemned to be destroyed.

Protestants were even forbidden to hire out horses, and Protestant grooms were forbidden to give riding lessons. Protestant domestics were forbidden to hire themselves as servants, and Protestant mistresses were forbidden to hire them under heavy penalties. If they engaged Protestant servants, they were liable to be sent to the galleys for life. They were even prevented employing "new converts."

Artisans were forbidden to work without certificates that their religion was Catholic. Protestant apprenticeships were suppressed. Protestant washerwomen were excluded from their washing-places on the river. In fact, there was scarcely a degradation that could be invented, or an insult that could be perpetrated, that was not practised upon those poor Huguenots who refused to be of "the King's religion."

Even when Protestants were about to take refuge in death, their troubles were not over. The priests had the power of forcing their way into the dying man's house, where they presented themselves at his bedside, and offered him conversion and the viaticum. If the dying man refused these, he was liable to be seized after death, dragged from the house, pulled along the streets naked, and buried in a ditch, or thrown upon a dunghill.*

For several years before the Revocation, while the persecutions of the Huguenots had been increasing, many had realised their means, and fled abroad into Switzerland, Germany, Holland, and England. But after the Revocation, emigration from France was strictly forbidden, under penalty of confiscation of the whole goods and property of the emigrant. Any person found attempting to leave the country, was liable to the seizure of all that belonged to him, and to perpetual imprisonment at the galleys; one half the amount realised by the sale of the property being paid to the informers, who thus became the most active agents of the Government. The Act also ordered that all landed proprietors who had left France before the

---

* Such was, in fact, the end of a man so distinguished as M. Paul Chenevix, Councillor of the Court of Metz, who died in 1686, the year after the Revocation. Although of the age of eighty, and so illustrious for his learning, his dead body was dragged along the streets on a hurdle and thrown upon a dunghill. See "Huguenot Refugees and their Descendants," under the name *Chenevix*. The present Archbishop of Dublin is descended from his brother Philip Chenevix, who settled in England shortly after the Revocation.

Revocation, should return within four months, under penalty of confiscation of all their property.

Amongst those of the King's subjects who were the most ready to obey his orders were some of the old Huguenot noble families, such as the members of the houses of Bouillon, Coligny, Rohan, Tremouille, Sully, and La Force. These great vassals, whom a turbulent feudalism had probably in the first instance induced to embrace Protestantism, were now found ready to change their profession of religion in servile obedience to the monarch.

The lesser nobility were more faithful and consistent. Many of them abandoned their estates and fled across the frontier, rather than live a daily lie to God by forswearing the religion of their conscience. Others of this class, on whom religion sat more lightly, as the only means of saving their property from confiscation, pretended to be converted to Roman Catholicism; though, we shall find, that these "new converts," as they were called, were treated with as much suspicion on the one side as they were regarded with contempt on the other.

There were also the Huguenot manufacturers, merchants, and employers of labour, of whom a large number closed their workshops and factories, sold off their goods, converted everything into cash, at whatever sacrifice, and fled across the frontier into Switzerland—either settling there, or passing through it on their way to Germany, Holland, or England.

It was necessary to stop this emigration, which was rapidly diminishing the population, and steadily impoverishing the country. It was indeed a terrible thing for Frenchmen to tear themselves away from their country—Frenchmen, who have always clung so close to their soil that they have rarely been able to form colonies of emigration elsewhere—it was breaking so many living fibres to leave France, to quit the homes of their fathers, their firesides, their kin, and their race. Yet, in a multitude of cases, they were compelled to tear themselves by the roots out of the France they so loved.

Yet it was so very easy for them to remain. The King merely required them to be "converted." He held that loyalty required them to be of "his religion." On the 19th of October, 1685, the day after he had signed the Act of Revocation, La Reynée, lieutenant of the police of Paris, issued a notice to the Huguenot tradespeople and working-classes, requiring them to be converted instantly. Many of them were terrified, and conformed accordingly. Next day, another notice was issued to the Huguenot bourgeois, requiring them to assemble on the following day for the purpose of publicly making a declaration of their conversion.

The result of these measures was to make hypocrites rather than believers, and they took effect upon the weakest and least-principled persons. The strongest, most independent, and high-minded of the Huguenots, who would *not* be hypocrites, resolved passively to resist them, and if they could not be allowed to exercise freedom of conscience in their own country, they determined to seek it elsewhere. Hence the large increase in the emigration from all parts of France immediately after the Act of Revocation had been proclaimed.* All the roads leading to the frontier

* It is believed that 400,000 emigrants left France through religious persecution during the twenty years previous to the Revocation, and that 600,000 escaped during the twenty years after that event. M. Charles Coquerel estimates the number of Protestants in France at that time to have been two millions of *men* (" Eglises du Désert," i. 497) The number of Protestant pastors was about one thousand—

or the sea-coast streamed with fugitives. They went in various forms and guises—sometimes in bodies of armed men, at other times in solitary parties, travelling at night and sleeping in the woods by day. They went as beggars, travelling merchants, sellers of beads and chaplets, gipsies, soldiers, shepherds, women with their faces dyed and sometimes dressed in men's clothes, and in all manner of disguises.

To prevent this extensive emigration, more violent measures were adopted. Every road out of France was posted with guards. The towns, highways, bridges, and ferries, were all watched; and heavy rewards were promised to those who would stop and bring back the fugitives. Many were taken, loaded with irons, and dispatched by the most public roads through France—as a sight to be seen by other Protestants—to the galleys at Marseilles, Brest, and other ports. As they went along they were subject to every sort of indignity in the towns and villages through which they passed. They were hooted, stoned, spit upon, and loaded with insult.

Many others went by sea, in French as well as in foreign ships. Though the sailors of France were prohibited the exercise of the reformed religion, under the penalty of fines, corporal punishment, and seizure of the vessels where the worship was allowed, yet many of the emigrants contrived to get away by the help of French ship captains, masters of sloops, fishing-boats, and coast pilots—who most probably sympathized with the views of those who wished to fly their country rather than become hypocrites and forswear their religion. A large number of emigrants, who went

of whom six hundred went into exile, one hundred were executed or sent to the galleys, and the rest are supposed to have accepted pensions as " new converts."

hurriedly off to sea in little boats, must have been drowned, as they were never afterwards heard of.

There were also many English ships that appeared off the coast to take the flying Huguenots away by night. They also escaped in foreign ships taking in their cargoes in the western harbours. They got cooped up in casks or wine barraques, with holes for breathing places; others contrived to get surreptitiously into the hold, and stowed themselves away among the goods. When it became known to the Government that many Protestants were escaping in this way, provision was made to meet the case; and a Royal Order was issued that, before any ship was allowed to set sail for a foreign port, the hold should be fumigated with deadly gas, so that any hidden Huguenot who could not otherwise be detected, might thus be suffocated! *

In the meantime, however, numerous efforts were being made to convert the Huguenots. The King, his ministers, the dragoons, the bishops, and clergy used all due diligence. "Everybody is now missionary," said the fascinating Madame de Sévigné; "each has his mission—above all the magistrates and governors of provinces, *helped by the dragoons*. It is the grandest and finest thing that has ever been imagined and executed." †

The conversions effected by the dragoons were much more sudden than those effected by the priests. Sometimes a hundred or more persons were converted by a single troop within an hour. In this way Murillac converted thousands of persons in a week. The regi-

---

* We refer to "The Huguenots: their Settlements, Churches, and Industries in England and Ireland," where a great many incidents are given relative to the escape of refugees by land and sea, which need not here be repeated.

† Letter to the President de Moulceau, November 24th, 1685.

ment of Ashfeld converted the whole province of Poitou in a month.

De Noailles was very successful in his conversions. He converted Nismes in twenty-four hours; the day after he converted Montpellier; and he promised in a few weeks to deliver all Lower Languedoc from the leprosy of heresy. In one of his dispatches soon after the Revocation, he boasted that he had converted 350 nobility and gentry, 54 ministers, and 25,000 individuals of various classes.

The quickness of the conversions effected by the dragoons is easily to be accounted for. The principal cause was the free quartering of soldiers in the houses of the Protestants. The soldiers knew what was the object for which they were thus quartered. They lived freely in all ways. They drank, swore, shouted, beat the heretics, insulted their women, and subjected them to every imaginable outrage and insult.

One of their methods of making converts was borrowed from the persecutions of the Vaudois. It consisted in forcing the feet of the intended converts into boots full of boiling grease, or they would hang them up by the feet, sometimes forgetting to cut them down until they were dead. They would also force them to drink water perpetually, or make them sit under a slow dripping upon their heads until they died of madness. Sometimes they placed burning coals in their hands, or used an instrument of torture resembling that known in Scotland as the thumbscrews.[*] Many of their attempts at conversion were accompanied by details too hideous to be recorded.

[*] Thumbscrews were used in the reign of James II. Louis and James borrowed from each other the means of converting heretics; but whether the origin of the thumbscrew be French or Scotch is not known.

Of those who would not be converted, the prisons were kept full. They were kept there without the usual allowance of straw, and almost without food. In winter they had no fire, and at night no lamp. Though ill, they had no doctors. Besides the gaoler, their only visitors were priests and monks, entreating them to make abjuration. Of course many died in prison—feeble women, and aged and infirm men. In the society of obscene criminals, with whom many were imprisoned, they prayed for speedy deliverance by death, and death often came to their help.

More agreeable, but still more insulting, methods of conversion were also attempted. Louis tried to bribe the pastors by offering them an increase of annual pay beyond their former stipends. If there were a Protestant judge or advocate, Louvois at once endeavoured to bribe him over. For instance, there was a heretical syndic of Strasburg, to whom Louvois wrote, " Will you be converted? I will give you 6,000 livres of pension.—Will you not? I will dismiss you."

Of course many of the efforts made to convert the Huguenots proved successful. The orders of the Prime Minister, the free quarters afforded to the dragoons, the preachings and threatenings of the clergy, all contributed to terrify the Protestants. The fear of being sent to the galleys for life—the threat of losing the whole of one's goods and property—the alarm of seeing one's household broken up, the children seized by the priests and sent to the nearest monkery or nunnery for maintenance and education—all these considerations doubtless had their effect in increasing the number of conversions.

Persecution is not easy to bear. To have all the public powers and authorities employed against one's life, interests, and faith, is what few can persistently oppose. And torture, whether it be slow or sudden, is what many persons, by reason of their physical capacity, have not the power to resist. Even the slow torment of dragoons quartered in the houses of the heretics—their noise and shoutings, their drinking and roistering, the insults and outrages they were allowed to practise—was sufficient to compel many at once to declare themselves to be converted.

Indeed, pain is, of all things, one of the most terrible of converters. One of the prisoners condemned to the galleys, when he saw the tortures which the victims about him had to endure by night and by day, said that sufferings such as these were "enough to make one conform to Buddhism or Mahommedanism as well as to Popery"; and doubtless it was force and suffering which converted the Huguenots, far more than love of the King or love of the Pope.

By all these means—forcible, threatening, insulting, and bribing—employed for the conversion of the Huguenots, the Catholics boasted that in the space of three months they had received an accession of five hundred thousand new converts to the Church of Rome.

But the "new converts" did not gain much by their change. They were forced to attend mass, but remained suspected. Even the dragoons who converted them, called them dastards and deniers of their faith. They tried, if they could, to avoid confession, but confess they must. There was the fine, confiscation of goods, and imprisonment at the priest's back.

Places were set apart for them in the churches, where they were penned up like lepers. A person was stationed at the door with a roll of their names, to which they were obliged to answer. During the service, the most prominent among them were made to carry the lights, the holy water, the incense, and such things, which to Huguenots were an abomination. They were also required to partake of the Host, which Protestants regarded as an awful mockery of the glorious Godhead.

The Duc de Saint-Simon, in his memoirs, after referring to the unmanly cruelties practised by Louis XIV. on the Huguenots, "without the slightest pretext or necessity," characterizes this forced participation in the Eucharist as sacrilegious and blasphemous folly, notwithstanding that nearly all the bishops lent themselves to the practice. "From simulated abjuration," he says, " they [the Huguenots] are dragged to endorse what they do not believe in, and to receive the divine body of the Saint of saints whilst remaining persuaded that they are only eating bread which they ought to abhor. Such is the general abomination born of flattery and cruelty. From torture to abjuration, and from that to the communion, there were only twenty-four hours' distance; and the executioners were the conductors of the converts, and their witnesses. Those who in the end appeared to have become reconciled, when more at leisure did not fail, by their flight or their behaviour, to contradict their pretended conversion."*

Indeed, many of the new converts, finding life in France to be all but intolerable, determined to follow the example of the Huguenots who had already fled, and took the first opportunity of disposing of their goods and leaving the country. One of the first things they did on reaching a foreign soil, was to attend a congre-

* "Memoirs of the Duke of Saint-Simon," Bayle St. John's Translation, iii. 259.

gation of their brethren, and make "reconnaisances," or acknowledgment of their repentance for having attended mass and pretended to be converted to the Roman Catholic Church.* At one of the sittings of the Threadneedle Street Huguenot Church in London, held in May, 1687—two years after the Revocation—not fewer than 497 members were again received into the Church which, by force, they had pretended to abandon.

Not many pastors abjured. A few who yielded in the first instance through terror and stupor, almost invariably returned to their ancient faith. They were offered considerable pensions if they would conform and become Catholics. The King promised to augment their income by one-third, and if they became advocates or doctors in law, to dispense with their three years' study, and with the right of diploma.

At length, most of the pastors had left the country. About seven hundred had gone into Switzerland, Holland, Prussia, England, and elsewhere. A few remained going about to meetings of the peasantry, at the daily risk of death; for every pastor taken was hung. A reward of 5,500 livres was promised to whoever should take a pastor, or cause him to be taken. The punishment of death was also pronounced against all persons who should be discovered attending such meetings.

Nevertheless, meetings of the Protestants continued to be held, with pastors or without. They were, for the most part, held at night, amidst the ruins of their pulled-down temples. But this exposed them to great danger, for spies were on the alert to inform upon them and have them apprehended.

* See "The Huguenots: their Settlements, &c., in England and Ireland," chap. xvi.

At length they selected more sheltered places in remote quarters, where they met for prayer and praise, often resorting thither from great distances. They were, however, often surprised, cut to pieces by the dragoons, who hung part of the prisoners on the neighbouring trees, and took the others to prison, from whence they were sent to the galleys, or hung on the nearest public gibbet.

Fulcran Rey was one of the most celebrated of the early victims. He was a native of Nismes, twenty-four years old. He had just completed his theological studies; but there were neither synods to receive him to pastoral ordination, nor temples for him to preach in. The only reward he could earn by proceeding on his mission was death, yet he determined to preach. The first assemblies he joined were in the neighbourhood of Nismes, where his addresses were interrupted by assaults of the dragoons. The dangers to his co-religionaries were too great in the neighbourhood of this populous town; and he next went to Castres and the Vaunage; after which he accepted an invitation to proceed into the less populous districts of the Cevennes.

He felt the presentiment of death upon him in accepting the invitation; but he went, leaving behind him a letter to his father, saying that he was willing, if necessary, to give his life for the cause of truth. "Oh! what happiness it would give me," he said, "if I might be found amongst the number of those whom the Lord has reserved to announce his praise and to die for his cause!"

His apostolate was short but glorious. He went from village to village in the Cevennes, collected the old worshippers together, prayed and preached to them, encouraging all to suffer in the name of Christ. He remained at this work for about six weeks, when a spy who accompanied him—one whom he had regarded as sincere a Huguenot as himself—informed against him for the royal reward, and delivered him over to the dragoons.

Rey was at first thrown into prison at Anduze, when, after a brief examination by the local judge, he was entrusted to thirty soldiers, to be conveyed to Alais. There he was subjected to further examination, avowing that he had preached wherever he had found faithful people ready to hear him. At Nismes, he was told that he had broken the law, in preaching contrary to the King's will. "I obey the law of the King of kings," he replied; "it is right that I should obey God rather than man. Do with me what you will; I am ready to die."

The priests, the judges, and other persons of influence endeavoured to induce him to change his opinions. Promises of great favours were offered him if he would abjure; and when the intendant Baville informed him of the frightful death before him if he refused, he replied, "My life is not of value to me, provided I gain Christ." He remained firm. He was ordered to be put to the torture. He was still unshaken. Then he was delivered over to the executioner. "I am treated," he said, "more mildly than my Saviour."

On his way to the place of execution, two monks walked by his side to induce him to relent, and to help him to die. "Let me alone," he said, "you annoy me with your consolations." On coming in sight of the gallows at Beaucaire, he cried, "Courage, courage! the end of my journey is at hand. I see before me the ladder which leads to heaven."

The monks wished to mount the ladder with him. "Return," said he, "I have no need of your help. I have assistance enough from God to take the last step of my journey." When he reached the upper platform, he was about, before dying, to make public his confession of faith. But the authorities had arranged beforehand that this should be prevented. When he opened his mouth, a roll of military drums muffled his voice. His radiant look and gestures spoke for him. A few minutes more, and he was dead; and when the paleness of death spread over his face, it still bore the reflex of joy and peace in which he had expired. "There is a veritable martyr," said many even of the Catholics who were witnesses of his death.

It was thought that the public hanging of a pastor would put a stop to all further ministrations among the Huguenots. But the sight of the bodies of their brethren hung on the nearest trees, and the heads of their pastors rolling on the scaffold, did not deter them from continuing to hold religious meetings in solitary places, more especially in Languedoc, Viverais, and the provinces in the south-east of France.

Between the year 1686, when Fulcran Rey was hanged at Beaucaire, and the year 1698, when Claude Brousson was hanged at Montpellier, not fewer than seventeen pastors were publicly executed; namely, three at Nismes, two at St. Hippolyte and Marsillargues in the Cevennes, and twelve on the Peyrou at Montpellier—the public place on which Protestant Christians in the South of France were then principally executed.

There has been some discussion lately as to the

massacre of the Huguenots about a century before this period. It has been held that the St. Bartholomew Massacre was only a political squabble, begun by the Huguenots, in which they got the worst of it. The number of persons killed on the occasion has been reduced to a very small number. It has been doubted whether the Pope had anything to do with the medal struck at Rome, bearing the motto *Ugonottorum Strages* ("Massacre of the Huguenots"), with the Pope's head on one side, and an angel on the other pursuing and slaying a band of flying heretics.

Whatever may be said of the massacre of St. Bartholomew, there can be no mistake about the persecutions which preceded and followed the Revocation of the Edict of Nantes. They were continued for more than half a century, and had the effect of driving from France about a million of the best, most vigorous, and industrious of Frenchmen. In the single province of Languedoc, not less than a hundred thousand persons (according to Boulainvillers) were destroyed by premature death, one-tenth of whom perished by fire, strangulation, or the wheel.

It could not be said that Louis XIV. and the priests were destroying France and tearing its flesh, and that Frenchmen did not know it. The proclamations, edicts and laws published against the Huguenots were known to all Frenchmen. Bénoît* gives a list of three hundred and thirty-three issued by Louis XIV. during the ten years subsequent to the Revocation, and they were continued, as we shall find, during the succeeding reign.

"We have," says M. Charles Coquerel, "a horror of

---

* "Histoire de l'Edit de Nantes," par Elie Bénoît.

St. Bartholomew! Will foreigners believe it, that France observed a code of laws framed in the same infernal spirit, which maintained *a perpetual St. Bartholomew's day in this country for about sixty years!* If they cannot call us the most barbarous of people, their judgment will be well founded in pronouncing us the most inconsistent."*

M. De Felice, however, will not believe that the Revocation of the Edict of Nantes was popular in France. He takes a much more patriotic view of the French people. He cannot believe them to have been wilfully guilty of the barbarities which the French Government committed upon the Huguenots. It was the King, the priests, and the courtiers only! But he forgets that these upper barbarians were supported by the soldiers and the people everywhere. He adds, however, that if the Revocation *were* popular, "it would be the most overwhelming accusation against the Church of Rome, that it had thus educated and fashioned France."† There is, however, no doubt whatever that the Jesuits, during the long period that they had the exclusive education of the country in their hands, *did* thus fashion France; for, in 1793, the people educated by them treated King, Jesuits, priests, and aristocracy, in precisely the same manner that they had treated the Huguenots about a century before.

* "Histoire des Eglises du Désert," par Charles Coquerel, i. 498.
† De Felice's "History of the Protestants of France," book iii. sect. 17.

CHAPTER III.

CLAUDE BROUSSON, THE HUGUENOT ADVOCATE.

TO give an account in detail of the varieties of cruelty inflicted on the Huguenots, and of the agonies to which they were subjected for many years before and after the passing of the Act of Revocation, would occupy too much space, besides being tedious through the mere repetition of like horrors. But in order to condense such an account, we think it will be more interesting if we endeavour to give a brief history of the state of France at that time, in connection with the biography of one of the most celebrated Huguenots of his period, both in his life, his piety, his trials, and his endurance —that of Claude Brousson, the advocate, the pastor, and the martyr of Languedoc.

Claude Brousson was born at Nismes in 1647. He was designed by his parents for the profession of the law, and prosecuted his studies at the college of his native town, where he graduated as Doctor of Laws.

He commenced his professional career about the time when Louis XIV. began to issue his oppressive edicts against the Huguenots. Protestant advocates were not yet forbidden to practise, but they already laboured under many disabilities. He continued, however, for some time to exercise his profession, with much ability, at

Castres, Castelnaudry, and Toulouse. He was frequently employed in defending Protestant pastors, and in contesting the measures for suppressing their congregations and levelling their churches under existing edicts, some time before the Revocation of the Edict of Nantes had been finally resolved upon.

Thus, in 1682, he was engaged in disputing the process instituted against the ministers and elders of the church at Nismes, with the view of obtaining an order for the demolition of the remaining Protestant temple of that city.* The pretext for suppressing this church was, that a servant girl from the country, being a Catholic, had attended worship and received the sacrament from the hands of M. Peyrol, one of the ministers.

Brousson defended the case, observing, at the conclusion of his speech, that the number of Protestants was very great at Nismes; that the ministers could not be personally acquainted with all the people, and especially with occasional visitors and strangers; that the ministers were quite unacquainted with the girl, or that she professed the Roman Catholic religion: "facts which rendered it probable that she was sent to the temple for the purpose of furnishing an occasion for the prosecution." Sentence was for the present suspended.

Another process was instituted during the same year

---

* John Locke passed through Nismes about this time. "The Protestants at Nismes," he said, "have now but one temple, the other being pulled down by the King's order about four years since. The Protestants had built themselves an hospital for the sick, but that is taken from them; a chamber in it is left for the sick, but never used, because the priests trouble them when there. Notwithstanding these discouragements [this was in 1676, *before* the Revocation], I do not find many go over; one of them told me, when I asked them the question, that the Papists did nothing but by force or by money."—KING's *Life of Locke*, i. 100.

for the suppression of the Protestant church at Uzes, and another for the demolition of the large Protestant temple at Montpellier. The pretext for destroying the latter was of a singular character.

A Protestant pastor, M. Paulet, had been bribed into embracing the Roman Catholic religion, in reward for which he was appointed counsellor to the Presidial Court of Montpellier. But his wife and one of his daughters refused to apostatize with him. The daughter, though only between ten and eleven years old, was sent to a convent at Teirargues, where, after enduring considerable persecution, she persisted in her steadfastness, and was released after a twelvemonth's confinement. Five years later she was again seized and sent to another convent; but, continuing immovable against the entreaties and threats of the abbess and confessor, she was again set at liberty.

An apostate priest, however, who had many years before renounced the Protestant faith, and become director and confessor of the nuns at Teirargues, forged two documents; the one to show that while at the convent, Mdlle. Paulet had consented to embrace the Catholic religion, and the other containing her formal abjuration. It was alleged that her abjuration had been signified to Isaac Dubourdieu, of Montpellier, one of the most distinguished pastors of the French Church; but that, nevertheless, he had admitted her to the sacrament. This, if true, was contrary to law; upon which the Catholic clergy laid information against the pastor and the young lady before the Parliament of Toulouse, when they obtained sentence of imprisonment against the former, and the penance of *amende honorable* against the latter.

The demolition of temples was the usual consequence

of convictions like these. The Duc de Noailles, lieutenant-general of the province, entered the city on the 16th of October, 1682, accompanied by a strong military force; and at a sitting of the Assembly of the States which shortly followed, the question of demolishing the Protestant temple at Montpellier was brought under consideration. Four of the Protestant pastors and several of the elders had before waited upon De Noailles to claim a respite until they should have submitted their cause to the King in Council.

The request having been refused, one of the deputation protested against the illegality of the proceedings, and had the temerity to ask his excellency whether he was aware that there were eighteen hundred thousand Protestant families in France? Upon which the Duke, turning to the officer of his guard, said, "Whilst we wait to see what will become of these eighteen hundred thousand Protestant families, will you please to conduct these gentlemen to the citadel?"*

The great temple of Montpellier was destroyed immediately on receipt of the King's royal mandate. It required the destruction of the place within twenty-four hours; "but you will give me pleasure," added the King, in a letter to De Noailles, "if you accomplish it in two."

It was, perhaps, scarcely necessary, after the temple had been destroyed, to make any effort to justify these high-handed proceedings. But Mdlle. Paulet, on whose pretended conversion to Catholicism the proceedings had been instituted, was now requested to admit the authenticity of the documents. She was still

---

* When released from prison, Gaultier escaped to Berlin and became minister of a large Protestant congregation there. Isaac Dubourdieu escaped to England, and was appointed one of the ministers of the Savoy Church in London.

imprisoned in Toulouse; and although entreated and threatened by turns to admit their truth, she steadfastly denied their genuineness, and asking for a pen, she wrote under each of them, " I affirm that the above signature was not written by my hand.—Isabeau de Paulet."

Of course the documents were forged; but they had answered their purpose. The Protestant temple of Montpellier lay in ruins, and Isabeau de Paulet was re-committed to prison. On hearing of this incident, Brousson remarked, "This is what is called instituting a process against persons *after* they have been condemned "—a sort of " Jedwood justice."

The repetition of these cases of persecution—the demolition of their churches, and the suppression of their worship—led the Protestants of the Cevennes, Viverais, and Dauphiny to combine for the purpose of endeavouring to stem the torrent of injustice. With this object, a meeting of twenty-eight deputies took place in the house of Brousson, at Toulouse, in the month of May, 1683. As the Assembly of the States were about to take steps to demolish the Protestant temple at Montauban and other towns in the south, and as Brousson was the well-known advocate of the persecuted, the deputies were able to meet at his house to conduct their deliberations, without exciting the jealousy of the priests and the vigilance of the police.

What the meeting of Protestant deputies recommended to their brethren was embodied in a measure, which was afterwards known as "The Project." The chief objects of the project were to exhort the Protestant people to sincere conversion, and the exhibition of the good life which such conversion implies; constant prayer to the Holy Spirit to enable them to remain steadfast in their profession and in the reading and meditation of the Scriptures; encouragements to them to hold together as congregations for the purpose of united worship; "submitting themselves unto the common instructions and to the yoke of Christ, in all places wheresoever He shall have established the true discipline, although the edicts of earthly magistrates be contrary thereto."

At the same time, Brousson drew up a petition to the Sovereign, humbly requesting him to grant permission to the Huguenots to worship God in peace after their consciences, copies of which were sent to Louvois and the other ministers of State. On this and other petitions, Brousson observes, "Surely all the world and posterity will be surprised, that so many respectful petitions, so many complaints of injuries, and so many solid reasons urged for their removal, produced no good result whatever in favour of the Protestants."

The members of the churches which had been interdicted, and whose temples had been demolished, were accordingly invited to assemble in private, in the neighbouring fields or woods—not in public places, nor around the ruins of their ancient temples—for the purpose of worshipping God, exciting each other to piety by prayer and singing, receiving instruction, and celeating the Lord's Supper.

Various meetings were accordingly held, in the llowing month of July, in the Cevennes and Viverais. t St. Hypolite, where the temple of the Protestants had een destroyed, about four thousand persons met in a field near the town, when the minister preached to them from the text—"Render unto Cæsar the things which are Cæsar's, and unto God the things which are God's." The meeting was conducted with the utmost solemnity; and a Catholic priest who was present, on giving information to the Bishop of Nismes of the transaction, admitted that the preacher had advanced nothing but what the bishop himself might have spoken.

The dragoons were at once sent to St. Hypolite to put an end to these meetings, and to "convert" the Protestants. The town was almost wholly Protestant. The troops were quartered in numbers in every house; and the people soon became "new converts."

The losses sustained by the inhabitants of the Cevennes from this forced quartering of the troops upon them—and Anduze, Sauve, St. Germain, Vigan, and Ganges were as full of them as St. Hypolite—may be inferred from the items charged upon the inhabitants of St. Hypolite alone* :—

To the regiment of Montpezat, for a billet for sixty-five days	50,000 livres.
To the three companies of Red Dragoons, for ninety-five days	30,000 ,,
To three companies of Villeneuve's Dragoons, for thirty days	6,000 ,,
To three companies of the Blue Dragoons of Languedoc, for three months and nine days	37,000 ,,
To a company of Cravates (troopers) for fourteen days	1,400 ,,
To the transport of three hundred and nine companies of cavalry and infantry	10,000 ,,
To provisions for the troops	60,000 ,,
To damage sustained by the destruction done by the soldiers, of furniture, and losses by the seizure of property, &c.	50,000 ,,
Total	244,400

Meetings of the persecuted were also held, under the terms of "The Project," in Viverais and Dauphiny. These meetings having been repeated for several weeks, the priests of the respective districts called upon their bishops for help to put down this heretical display. The

* Claude Brousson, "Apologie du Projet des Réformé."

Bishop of Valence (Daniel de Cosmac) accordingly informed them that he had taken the necessary steps, and that he had been apprised that twenty thousand soldiers were now on their march to the South to put down the Protestant movement.

On their arrival, the troops were scattered over the country, to watch and suppress any meetings that might be held. The first took place on the 8th of August, at Chateaudouble, a manufacturing village in Drome. The assembly was surprised by a troop of dragoons; but most of the congregation contrived to escape. Those who were taken were hung upon the nearest trees.

Another meeting was held about a fortnight later at Bezaudun, which was attended by many persons from Bourdeaux, a village about half a league distant. While the meeting was at prayer, intelligence was brought that the dragoons had entered Bourdeaux, and that it was a scene of general pillage. The Bourdeaux villagers at once set out for the protection of their families. The troopers met them, and suddenly fell upon them. A few of the villagers were armed, but the principal part defended themselves with stones. Of course they were overpowered; many were killed by the sword, and those taken prisoners were immediately hanged.

A few, who took to flight, sheltered themselves in a barn, where the soldiers found them, set fire to the place, and murdered them as they endeavoured to escape from the flames. One young man was taken prisoner, David Chamier,* son of an advocate, and

* The grandfather of this Chamier drew up for Henry IV. the celebrated Edict of Nantes. The greater number of the Chamiers left France. Several were ministers in London and Maryland, U.S. Captain Chamier is descended from the family.

related to some of the most eminent Protestants in France. He was taken to the neighbouring town of Montelimar, and, after a summary trial, he was condemned to be broken to death upon the wheel. The sentence was executed before his father's door; but the young man bore his frightful tortures with astonishing courage.

The contumacious attitude of the Protestants after so many reports had reached Louis XIV. of their entire "conversion," induced him to take more active measures for their suppression. He appointed Marshal Saint-Ruth commander of the district—a man who was a stranger to mercy, who breathed only carnage, and who, because of his ferocity, was known as "The Scourge of the Heretics."

Daniel de Cosmac, Bishop of Valence, had now the help of Saint-Ruth and his twenty thousand troops. The instructions Saint-Ruth received from Louvois were these: "Amnesty has no longer any place for the Viverais, who continue in rebellion after having been informed of the King's gracious designs. In one word, you are to cause such a desolation in that country that its example may restrain all other Huguenots, and may teach them how dangerous it is to rebel against the King."

This was a work quite congenial to Saint-Ruth*—

* Saint-Ruth was afterwards, in 1691, sent to Ireland to take the command of the army fighting for James II. against William III. There, Saint-Ruth had soldiers, many of them Huguenots banished from France, to contend with; and he was accordingly somewhat less successful than in Viverais, where his opponents were mostly peasants and workmen, armed (where armed at all) with stones picked from the roads. Saint-Ruth and his garrison were driven from Athlone, where a Huguenot soldier was the first to mount the breach. The army of William III., though eight thousand fewer in number, followed Saint-Ruth and his Irish army to the field of Aughrim. His host was there drawn up in an almost impregnable position—along the heights of Kilcommeden, with the Castle of Aughrim on his left wing, a deep bog on his right, and another bog of about two

rushing about the country, scourging, slaughtering, laying waste, and suppressing the assemblies—his soldiers rushing upon their victims with cries of "Death or the Mass!"

Tracking the Protestants in this way was like "a hunt in a great enclosure." When the soldiers found a meeting of the people going on, they shot them down at once, though unarmed. If they were unable to fly, they met death upon their knees. Antoine Court recounts meetings in which as many as between three and four hundred persons, old men, women, and children, were shot dead on the spot.

De Cosmac, the bishop, was very active in the midst of these massacres. When he went out to convert the people, he first began by sending out Saint-Ruth with the dragoons. Afterwards he himself followed to give instructions for their "conversion," partly through favours, partly by money. "My efforts," he himself admitted, "were not always without success; yet I must avow that the fear of the dragoons, and of their being quartered in the houses of the heretics, contributed much more to their conversion than anything that I did."

The same course was followed throughout the Cevennes. It would be a simple record of cruelty to describe in detail the military proceedings there: the dispersion of meetings; the hanging of persons

---

miles extending along the front, and apparently completely protecting the Irish encampment. Nevertheless, the English and Huguenot army under Ginckle, bravely attacked it, forced the pass to the camp, and routed the army of Saint-Ruth, who himself was killed by a cannon-ball. The principal share of this victory was attributed to the gallant conduct of the three regiments of Huguenot horse, under the command of the Marquess de Ruvigny (himself a banished Huguenot nobleman) who, in consequence of his services, was raised to the Irish peerage, under the title of Earl of Galway.

found attending them; the breaking upon the wheel of the pastors captured, amidst horrible tortures; the destruction of dwellings and of the household goods which they contained. But let us take the single instance of Homel, formerly pastor of the church at Soyon.

Homel was taken prisoner, and found guilty of preaching to his flock after his temple had been destroyed. For this offence he was sentenced to be broken to death upon the wheel. To receive this punishment he was conducted to Tournon, in Viverais, where the Jesuits had a college. He first received forty blows of the iron bar, after which he was left to languish with his bones broken, for forty hours, until he died. During his torments, he said: "I count myself happy that I can die in my Master's service. What! did my glorious Redeemer descend from heaven and suffer an ignominious death for my salvation, and shall I, to prolong a miserable life, deny my blessed Saviour and abandon his people?" While his bones were being broken on the wheel, he said to his wife: "Farewell, once more, my beloved spouse! Though you witness my bones broken to shivers, yet is my soul filled with inexpressible joy." After life was finally extinct, his heart was taken to Chalençon to be publicly exhibited, and his body was exposed in like manner at Beauchatel.

De Noailles, the governor, when referring in one of his dispatches to the heroism displayed by the tortured prisoners, said: "These wretches go to the wheel with the firm assurance of dying martyrs, and ask no other favour than that of dying quickly. They request pardon of the soldiers, but there is not one of them that will ask pardon of the King."

To return to Claude Brousson. After his eloquent

defence of the Huguenots of Montauban—the result of which, of course, was that the church was ordered to be demolished—and the institution of processes for the demolition of fourteen more Protestant temples, Brousson at last became aware that the fury of the Catholics and the King was not to be satisfied until they had utterly crushed the religion which he served.

Brousson was repeatedly offered the office of counsellor of Parliament, equivalent to the office of judge, if he would prove an apostate; but the conscience of Brousson was not one that could be bought. He also found that his office of defender of the doomed Huguenots could not be maintained without personal danger, whilst (as events proved) his defence was of no avail to them; and he resolved, with much regret, to give up his profession for a time, and retire for safety and rest to his native town of Nismes.

He resided there, however, only about four months. Saint-Ruth and De Noailles were now overawing Upper Languedoc with their troops. The Protestants of Nismes had taken no part in "The Project;" their remaining temple was still open. But they got up a respectful petition to the King, imploring his consideration of their case. Roman Catholics and Protestants, they said, had so many interests in common, that the ruin of the one must have the effect of ruining the other, —the flourishing manufactures of the province, which were mostly followed by the Protestants, being now rapidly proceeding to ruin. They, therefore, implored his Majesty to grant them permission to prosecute their employments unmolested on account of their religious profession; and lastly, they conjured the King, by his piety, by his paternal clemency, and by every law of equity, to grant them freedom of religious worship.

It was of no use. The hearts of the King, his clergy, and his ministers, were all hardened against them. A copy of the above petition was presented by two ministers of Nismes and several influential gentlemen of Lower Languedoc to the Duke de Noailles, the governor of the province. He treated the deputation with contempt, and their petition with scorn. Writing to Louvois, the King's prime minister, De Noailles said: "Astonished at the effrontery of these wretched persons, I did not hesitate to send them all prisoners to the Citadel of St. Esprit (in the Cevennes), telling them that if there had been *petites maisons** enough in Languedoc I should not have sent them there."

Nismes was now placed under the same ban as Vivarais, and denounced as "insurrectionary." To quell the pretended revolt, as well as to capture certain persons who were supposed to have been accessory to the framing of the petition, a detachment of four hundred dragoons was ordered into the place. One of those to be apprehended was Claude Brousson. Hundreds of persons knew of his abode in the city, but notwithstanding the public proclamation (which he himself heard from the window of the house where he was staying), and the reward offered for his apprehension, no one attempted to betray him.

After remaining in the city for three days, he adopted a disguised dress, passed out of the Crown Gate, and in the course of a few days found a safe retreat in Switzerland.

Peyrol and Icard, two of the Protestant ministers whom the dragoons were ordered to apprehend, also escaped into Switzerland, Peyrol settling at

---

* The prisons of Languedoc were already crowded with Protestants, and hundreds had been sent to the galleys at Marseilles.

Lausanne, and Icard becoming the minister of a Huguenot church in Holland. But although the ministers had escaped, all the property they had left behind them was confiscated to the Crown. Hideous effigies of them were prepared and hung on gibbets in the market-place of Nismes by the public executioner, the magistrates and dragoons attending the sham proceeding with the usual ceremony.

At Lausanne, where Claude Brousson settled for a time, he first attempted to occupy himself as a lawyer; but this he shortly gave up to devote himself to the help of the persecuted Huguenots. Like Jurieu and others in Holland, who flooded Europe with accounts of the hideous cruelties of Louis XIV. and his myrmidons the clergy and dragoons, he composed and published a work, addressed to the Roman Catholic party as well as to the Protestants of all countries, entitled, " The State of the Reformed Church of France." He afterwards composed a series of letters specially addressed to the Roman Catholic clergy of France.

But expostulation was of no use. With each succeeding year the persecution became more bitter, until at length, in 1685, the Edict was revoked. In September of that year Brousson learnt that the Protestant church of his native city had been suppressed, and their temple given over to a society of female converters; that the wives and daughters of the Protestants who refused to abjure their faith had been seized and imprisoned in nunneries and religious seminaries; and that three hundred of their husbands and fathers were chained together and sent off in one day for confinement in the galleys at Marseilles.

The number of Huguenots resorting to Switzerland

being so great,* and they often came so destitute, that a committee was formed at Lausanne to assist the emigrants, and facilitate their settlement in the canton, or enable them to proceed elsewhere. Brousson was from the first an energetic member of this committee. Part of their work was to visit the Protestant states of the north, and find out places to which the emigrants might be forwarded, as well as to collect subscriptions for their conveyance.

In November 1685, a month after the Revocation, Brousson and La Porte set out for Berlin with this object. La Porte was one of the ministers of the Cevennes, who had fled before a sentence of death pronounced against him for having been concerned in "The Project." At Berlin they were received very cordially by the Elector of Brandenburg, who had already given great assistance to the Huguenot emigrants, and expressed himself as willing to do all that he could for their protection. Brousson and La Porte here met the Rev. David Ancillon, who had been for thirty-three years pastor at Metz,† and

---

* Within about three weeks no fewer than seventeen thousand five hundred French emigrants passed into Lausanne. Two hundred Protestant ministers fled to Switzerland, the greater number of whom settled in Lausanne, until they could journey elsewhere.

† Ancillon was an eminently learned man. His library was one of the choicest that had ever been collected, and on his expulsion from Metz it was pillaged by the Jesuits. Metz, now part of German Lorraine, was probably not so ferociously dragooned as other places. Yet the inhabitants were under the apprehension that the massacre of St. Bartholomew was about to be repeated upon them on Christmas Day, 1685, the soldiers of the garrison having been kept under arms all night. The Protestant churches were all pulled down, the ministers were expelled, and many of their people followed them into Germany. There were numerous Protestant soldiers in the Metz garrison, and the order of the King was that, like the rest of his subjects, they should become converted. Many of the officers resigned and entered the service of William of Orange, and many of the soldiers deserted. The bribe offered for the conversion of privates was as follows: Common soldiers and dragoons,

was now pastor of the Elector at Berlin; Gaultier, banished from Montpellier; and Abbadie, banished from Saumur—all ministers of the Huguenot Church there; with a large number of banished ministers and emigrant Protestants from all the provinces of France.

The Elector suggested to Brousson that while at Berlin he should compose a summary account of the condition of the French Protestants, such as should excite the interest and evoke the help of the Protestant rulers and people of the northern States. This was done by Brousson, and the volume was published, entitled "Letters of the Protestants of France who have abandoned all for the cause of the Gospel, to other Protestants; with a particular Letter addressed to Protestant Kings, Electors, Rulers, and Magistrates." The Elector circulated this volume, accompanying it with a letter written in his name, to all the princes of the Continent professing the Augsburg Confession; and it was thus mainly owing to the Elector's intercession that the Huguenots obtained the privilege of establishing congregations in several of the states of Germany, as well as in Sweden and Denmark.

Brousson remained nearly five months at Berlin, after which he departed for Holland to note the progress of the emigration in that country, and there he met a large number of his countrymen. Nearly two hundred and fifty Huguenot ministers had taken refuge in

---

two pistoles per head; troopers, three pistoles per head. The Protestants of Alsace were differently treated. They constituted a majority of the population; Alsace and Strasburg having only recently been seized by Louis XIV. It was therefore necessary to be cautious in that quarter; for violence would speedily have raised a revolution in the province which would have driven them over to Germany, whose language they spoke. Louvois could therefore only proceed by bribing; and he was successful in buying over some of the most popular and influential men.

Holland; there were many merchants and manufacturers who had set up their branches of industry in the country; and there were many soldiers who had entered the service of William of Orange. While in Holland, Brousson resided principally with his brother, a banished Huguenot, who had settled at Amsterdam as a merchant.

Having accomplished all that he could for his Huguenot brethren in exile, Brousson returned to Lausanne, where he continued his former labours. He bethought him very much of the Protestants still remaining in France, wandering like sheep without shepherds, deprived of guidance, books, and worship—the prey of ravenous wolves,—and it occurred to him whether the Protestant pastors had done right in leaving their flocks, even though by so doing they had secured the safety of their own lives. Accordingly, in 1686, he wrote and published a "Letter to the Pastors of France at present in Protestant States, concerning the Desolation of their own Churches, and their own Exile."

In this letter he says:—"If, instead of retiring before your persecutors, you had remained in the country; if you had taken refuge in forests and caverns; if you had gone from place to place, risking your lives to instruct and rally the people, until the first shock of the enemy was past; and had you even courageously exposed yourselves to martyrdom—as in fact those have done who have endeavoured to perform your duties in your absence—perhaps the examples of constancy, or zeal, or of piety you had discovered, might have animated your flocks, revived their courage, and arrested the fury of your enemies." He accordingly exhorted the Protestant ministers who had left France to return to their flocks at all hazards.

This advice, if acted on, was virtually condemning the pastors to death. Brousson was not a pastor. Would *he* like to return to France at the daily risk of the rack and the gibbet? The Protestant ministers in exile defended themselves. Bénoît, then residing in Germany, replied in a "History and Apology for the Retreat of the Pastors." Another, who did not give his name, treated Brousson's censure as that of a fanatic, who meddled with matters beyond his vocation. "You who condemn the pastors for not returning to France at the risk of their lives," said he, "*why do you not first return to France yourself?*"

Brousson was as brave as his words. He was not a pastor, but he might return to the deserted flocks, and encourage and comfort them. He could no longer be happy in his exile at Lausanne. He heard by night the groans of the prisoners in the Tower of Constance, and the noise of the chains borne by the galley slaves at Toulon and Marseilles. He reproached himself as if it were a crime with the repose which he enjoyed. Life became insupportable to him and he fell ill. His health was even despaired of; but one day he suddenly rose up and said to his wife, "I must set out; I will go to console, to relieve, to strengthen my brethren, groaning under their oppressions."

His wife threw herself at his feet. "Thou wouldst go to certain death," she said; "think of me and thy little children." She implored him again and again to remain. He loved his wife and children, but he thought a higher duty called him away from them. When his friends told him that he would be taken prisoner and hung, he said, "When God permits his servants to die for the Gospel, they preach louder from the grave than they did during life." He remained unshaken. He would go to the help of the oppressed with the love of a brother, the faith of an apostle, and the courage of a martyr.

Brousson knew the danger of the office he was about to undertake. There had, as we have seen, been numerous attempts made to gather the Protestant people together, and to administer consolation to them by public prayers and preaching. The persons who conducted these services were not regular pastors, but only private members of their former churches. Some of them were very young men, and they were nearly all uneducated as regards clerical instruction. One of the most successful was Isaac Vidal, a lame young man, a mechanic of Colognac, near St. Hypolite, in the Cevennes. His self-imposed ministrations were attended by large numbers of people. He preached for only six months and then died—a natural death, for nearly all who followed him were first tortured and then hung.

We have already referred to Fulcran Rey, who preached for about nine months, and was then executed. In the same year were executed Meyrueis, by trade a woolcarder, and Rocher, who had been a reader in one of the Protestant churches. Emanuel Dalgues, a respectable inhabitant of Salle, in the Cevennes, also received the crown of martyrdom. Ever since the Revocation of the Edict, he had proclaimed the Gospel o'er hill and dale, in woods and caverns, to assemblies of the people wherever he could collect them. He was executed in 1687. Three other persons—Gransille, Mercier, and Esclopier—who devoted themselves to preaching, were transported as slaves to America; and David Mazel, a boy twelve years of age, who had a wonderful memory, and preached sermons which he had learned by heart, was transported, with his father and other frequenters of the assemblies, to the Carribee Islands.

At length Brousson collected about him a number of Huguenots willing to return with him into France, in order to collect the Protestant people together again, to pray with them, and even to preach to them if the opportunity occurred. Brousson's companions were these: Francis Vivens, formerly a schoolmaster in the Cevennes; Anthony Bertezene, a carpenter, brother of a preacher who had recently been condemned to death; and seven other persons named Papus, La Pierrè, Serein, Dombres, Poutant, Boisson, and M. de Bruc, an aged minister, who had been formerly pastor of one of the churches in the Cevennes. They prepared to enter France in four distinct companies, in the month of July, 1689.

CHAPTER IV.

CLAUDE BROUSSON, PASTOR AND MARTYR.

BROUSSON left Lausanne on the 22nd of July, accompanied by his dear friend, the Rev. M. de Bruc. The other members of the party had preceded them, crossing the frontier at different places. They all arrived in safety at their destination, which was in the mountain district of the Cevennes. They resorted to the neighbourhood of the Aigoual, the centre of a very inaccessible region—wild, cold, but full of recesses for hiding and worship. It was also a district surrounded by villages, the inhabitants of which were for the most part Protestant.

The party soon became diminished in number. The old pastor, De Bruc, found himself unequal to the fatigue and privations attending the work. He was ill and unable to travel, and was accordingly advised by his companions to quit the service and withdraw from the country.

Persecution also destroyed some of them. When it became known that assemblies for religious observances were again on foot, an increased force of soldiers was sent into the district, and a high price was set on the heads of all the preachers that could be apprehended. The soldiers scoured the country, and, helped by the paid spies, they shortly succeeded in apprehending Boisson and Dombres, at St. Paul's, north of Anduze, in the Cevennes. They were both executed at Nismes, being first subjected to torture on the rack, by which their limbs were entirely dislocated. They were then conveyed to the place of execution, praying and singing psalms on the way, and finished their course with courage and joy.

When Brousson first went into the Cevennes, he did not undertake to preach to the people. He was too modest to assume the position of a pastor; he merely undertook, as occasion required, to read the Scriptures in Protestant families and in small companies, making his remarks and exhortations thereupon. He also transcribed portions of his own meditations on the Scriptures, and gave them away for distribution from hand to hand amongst the people.

When it was found that his instructions were much appreciated, and that numbers of people assembled to hear him read and exhort, he was strongly urged to undertake the office of public instructor amongst them, especially as their ministers were being constantly diminished by execution.

He had been about five months in the Cevennes, and was detained by a fall of snow on one of the mountains, where his abode was a sheepcote, when the proposal that he should become a preacher was first made to him. Vivens was one of those who most strongly supported the appeal made to Brousson. He spent many hours in private prayer, seeking the approval of God for the course he was about to undertake. Vivens also prayed in the several assemblies that Brousson might be confirmed, and that God would be pleased to pour upon him his Holy Spirit, and strengthen him so that he might become a faithful and successful labourer in this great calling.

Brousson at length consented, believing that duty and conscience alike called upon him to give the best of his help to the oppressed and persecuted Protestants of the mountains. "Brethren," he said to them, when they called upon him to administer to them the Holy Sacrament of the Eucharist—"Brethren, I look above you, and hear the most High God calling me through your mouths to this most responsible and sacred office; and I dare not be disobedient to his heavenly call. By the grace of God I will comply with your pious desires: dedicate and devote myself to the work of the ministry, and spend the remainder of my life in unwearied pains and endeavours for promoting God's glory, and the consolation of precious souls."

Brousson received his call to the ministry in the Cevennes amidst the sound of musketry and grapeshot which spread death among the ranks of his brethren. He was continuously tracked by the spies of the Jesuits, who sought his apprehension and death; and he was hunted from place to place by the troops of the King, who followed him in his wanderings into the most wild and inaccessible places.

The perilous character of his new profession was exhibited only a few days after his ordination, by the apprehension of Olivier Souverain at St. Jean de Gardonenque, for preaching the Gospel to the assemblies. He was at once conducted to Montpellier and executed on the 15th of January, 1690.

During the same year, Dumas, another preacher in the Cevennes, was apprehended and fastened by the troopers across a horse in order to be carried to Montpellier. His bowels were so injured and his body so crushed by this horrible method of conveyance, that Dumas died before he was half way to the customary place of martyrdom.

Then followed the execution of David Quoite, a wandering and hunted pastor in the Cevennes for several years. He was broken on the wheel at Montpellier, and then hanged. "The punishment," said Louvreleuil, his tormentor, " which broke his bones, did not break his hardened heart: he died in his heresy." After Quoite, M. Bonnemere, a native of the same city, was also tortured and executed in like manner on the Peyrou.

All these persons were taken, executed, destroyed, or imprisoned, during the first year that Brousson commenced his perilous ministry in the Cevennes.

About the same time three women, who had gone about instructing the families of the destitute Protestants, reading the Scriptures and praying with them, were apprehended by Baville, the King's intendant, and punished. Isabeau Redothiere, eighteen years of age, and Marie Lintarde, about a year younger, both the daughters of peasants, were taken before Baville at Nismes.

"What! are you one of the preachers, forsooth?" said he to Redothiere. "Sir," she replied, "I have exhorted my brethren to be mindful of their duty towards God, and when occasion offered, I have sought God in prayer for them; and, if your lordship calls that preaching, I have been a preacher." "But," said the Intendant, "you know that the King has forbidden this." "Yes, my lord," she replied, "I know it very well, but the King of kings, the God of heaven and earth, He hath commanded it." "You deserve death," replied Baville.

But the Intendant awarded her a severer fate. She was condemned to be imprisoned for life in the Tower of Constance, a place echoing with the groans of women, most of whom were in chains, perpetually imprisoned there for worshipping God according to conscience.

Lintarde was in like manner condemned to imprisonment for life in the castle of Sommieres, and it is believed she died there. Nothing, however, is known of the time when she died. When a woman was taken and imprisoned in one of the King's torture-houses, she was given up by her friends as lost.

A third woman, taken at the same time, was more mercifully dealt with. Anne Montjoye was found assisting at one of the secret assemblies. She was solicited in vain to abjure her faith, and being condemned to death, was publicly executed.

Shortly after his ordination, Brousson descended from the Upper Cevennes, where the hunt for Protestants was becoming very hot, into the adjacent valleys and plains. There it was necessary for him to be exceedingly cautious. The number of dragoons in Languedoc had been increased so as to enable them regularly to patrol the entire province, and a price had been set upon Brousson's head, which was calculated to quicken their search for the flying pastor.

Brousson was usually kept informed by his Huguenot friends of the direction taken by the dragoons in their patrols, and hasty assemblies were summoned in their absence. The meetings were held in some secret place—some cavern or recess in the rocks. Often they were held at night, when a few lanterns were hung on the adjacent trees to give light. Sentinels were set in the neighbourhood, and all the adjoining roads were watched. After the meeting was over the assemblage dispersed in different directions, and Brousson immediately left for another district, travelling mostly by night, so as to avoid detection. In this manner he usually presided at three or four assemblies each week, besides two on the Sabbath day—one early in the morning and another at night.

At one of his meetings, held at Boucoiran on the Gardon, about half way between Nismes and Anduze, a Protestant nobleman—a *nouveau convertis*, who had abjured his religion to retain his estates—was present, and stood near the preacher during the service. One of the Government spies was present, and gave information. The name of the Protestant nobleman was not known. But the Intendant, to strike terror into others, seized six of the principal landed proprietors in the neighbourhood — though some of them had never attended any of the assemblies since the Revocation— and sent two of them to the galleys, and the four others to imprisonment for life at Lyons, besides confiscating the estates of the whole to the Crown.

Brousson now felt that he was bringing his friends into very great trouble, and, out of consideration for them, he began to think of again leaving France. The dragoons were practising much cruelty on the Protestant population, being quartered in their houses, and at liberty to plunder and extort money to any extent. They were also incessantly on the look out for the assemblies, being often led by mounted priests and spies to places where they had been informed that meetings were about to be held. Their principal object, besides hanging the persons found attending, was to seize the preachers, more especially Brousson and Vivens, believing that the country would be more effectually "converted," provided they could be seized and got out of the way.

Brousson, knowing that he might be seized and taken prisoner at any moment, had long considered whether he ought to resist the attempts made to capture him. He had at first carried a sword, but at length ceased to wear it, being resolved entirely to cast himself on Providence; and he also instructed all who resorted to his meetings to come to them unarmed.

In this respect Brousson differed from Vivens, who thought it right to resist force by force; and in the event of any attempt being made to capture him, he considered it expedient to be constantly provided with arms. Yet he had only once occasion to use them, and it was the first and last time. The reward of ten thousand livres being now offered for the apprehension of Brousson and Vivens, or five thousand for either, an active search was made throughout the province. At length the Government found themselves on the track of Vivens. One of his known followers, Valderon, having been apprehended and put upon the rack, was driven by torture to reveal his place of concealment. A party of soldiers went in pursuit, and found Vivens with three other persons, concealed in a cave in the neighbourhood of Alais.

Vivens was engaged in prayer when the soldiers came upon him. His hand was on his gun in a moment. When asked to surrender he replied with a shot, not knowing the number of his opponents. He followed up with two other shots, killing a man each time, and then exposing himself, he was struck by a volley, and fell dead. The three other persons in the cave being in a position to hold the soldiers at defiance for some time, were promised their lives if they would sur render. They did so, and with the utter want of truth, loyalty, and manliness that characterized the persecutors, the promise was belied, and the three prisoners were hanged, a few days after, at Alais. Vivens' body was taken to the same place. The Intendant sat in judgment upon it, and condemned it to be drawn through the streets upon a hurdle and then burnt to ashes.

Brousson was becoming exhausted by the fatigues and privations he had encountered during his two years' wanderings and preachings in the Cevennes; and he not only desired to give the people a relaxation from their persecution, but to give himself some absolutely necessary rest. He accordingly proceeded to Nismes, his birthplace, where many people knew him; and where, if they betrayed him, they might easily have earned five thousand livres. But so much faith was kept by the Protestants amongst one another, that Brousson felt that his life was quite as safe amongst his townspeople as it had been during the last two years amongst the mountaineers of the Cevennes.

It soon became known to the priests, and then to the Intendant, that Brousson was resident in concealment at Nismes; and great efforts were accordingly made for his apprehension. During the search, a letter of Brousson's was found in the possession of M. Guion, an aged minister, who had returned from Switzerland to resume his ministry, according as he might find it practicable. The result of this discovery was, that Guion was apprehended, taken before the Intendant, condemned to be executed, and sent to Montpellier, where he gave up his life at seventy years old—the drums beating, as usual, that nobody might hear his last words. The house in which Guion had been taken at Nismes was ordered to be razed to the ground, in punishment of the owner who had given him shelter.

After spending about a month at Nismes, Brousson was urged by his friends to quit the city. He accordingly succeeded in passing through the gates, and went to resume his former work. His first assembly was held in a commodious place on the Gardon, between Valence, Brignon, and St. Maurice, about ten miles distant from Nismes. Although he had requested that only the Protestants in the immediate neighbourhood should attend the meeting, so as not to excite the apprehensions of the authorities, yet a multitude of persons came from Uzes and Nismes, augmented by accessions from upwards of thirty villages. The service was commenced about ten o'clock, and was not completed until midnight.

The concourse of persons from all quarters had been so great that the soldiers could not fail to be informed of it. Accordingly they rode towards the place of assemblage late at night, but they did not arrive until the meeting had been dissolved. One troop of soldiers took ambush in a wood through which the worshippers would return on their way back to Uzes. The command had been given to "draw blood from the conventicles." On the approach of the people the soldiers fired, and killed and wounded several. About forty others were taken prisoners. The men were sent to the galleys for life, and the women were thrown into gaol at Carcassone—the Tower of Constance being then too full of prisoners.

After this event, the Government became more anxious in their desire to capture Brousson. They published far and wide their renewed offer of reward for his apprehension. They sent six fresh companies of soldiers specially to track him, and examine the woods and search the caves between Uzes and Alais. But Brousson's friends took care to advise him of the approach of danger, and he sped away to take shelter in another quarter. The soldiers were, however, close upon his heels; and one morning, in attempting to enter a village for the purpose of drying himself—having been exposed to the winter's rain and cold all night—he suddenly came upon a detachment of soldiers! He avoided them by taking shelter in a thicket, and while there, he observed another detachment pass in file, close to where he was concealed. The soldiers were divided into four parties, and sent out to search in different directions, one of them proceeding to search every house in the village into which Brousson had just been about to enter.

The next assembly was held at Sommieres, about eight miles west of Nismes. The soldiers were too late to disperse the meeting, but they watched some of the people on their return. One of these, an old woman, who had been observed to leave the place, was shot on entering her cottage; and the soldier, observing that she was attempting to rise, raised the butt end of his gun and brained her on the spot.

The hunted pastors of the Cevennes were falling off one by one. Bernard Saint Paul, a young man, who had for some time exercised the office of preacher, was executed in 1692. One of the brothers Du Plans was executed in the same year, having been offered his life if he would conform to the Catholic religion. In the following year Paul Colognac was executed, after being broken to death on the wheel at Masselargais, near to which he had held his last assembly. His arms, thighs, legs, and feet were severally broken with the iron bar some hours before the *coup de grace,* or death-blow, was inflicted. Colognac endured his sufferings with heroic fortitude. He was only twenty-four. He had commenced to preach at twenty, and laboured at the work for only four years.

Brousson's health was fast giving way. Every place that he frequented was closely watched, so that he had often to spend the night under the hollow of a rock, or under the shelter of a wood, exposed to rain and snow,—and sometimes he had even to contend with a wolf for the shelter of a cave. Often he was almost perishing for want of food; and often he found himself nearly ready to die for want of rest. And yet, even in the midst of his greatest perils, his constant thought was of the people committed to him, and for whose eternal happiness he continued to work.

As he could not visit all who wished to hear him, he wrote out sermons that might be read to them. His friend Henry Poutant, one of those who originally accompanied him from Switzerland and had not yet been taken prisoner by the soldiers, went about holding meetings for prayer, and reading to the people the sermons prepared for them by Brousson.

For the purpose of writing out his sermons, Brousson carried about with him a small board, which he called his "Wilderness Table." With this placed upon his knees, he wrote the sermons, for the most part in woods and caves. He copied out seventeen of these sermons, which he sent to Louis XIV., to show him that what "he preached in the deserts contained nothing but the pure word of God, and that he only exhorted the people to obey God and to give glory to Him."

The sermons were afterwards published at Amsterdam, in 1695, under the title of "The Mystic Manna of the Desert." One would have expected that, under the bitter persecutions which Brousson had suffered during so many years, they would have been full of denunciation; on the contrary, they were only full of love. His words were only burning when he censured his hearers for not remaining faithful to their Church and to their God.

At length, the fury of Brousson's enemies so increased, and his health was so much impaired, that he again thought of leaving France. His lungs were so much injured by constant exposure to cold, and his voice had become so much impaired, that he could not preach. He also heard that his family, whom he had left at Lausanne, required his assistance. His only son was growing up, and needed education. Perhaps Brousson had too long neglected those of his own household; though he had every confidence in the prudence and thoughtfulness of his wife.

Accordingly, about the end of 1693, Brousson made arrangements for leaving the Cevennes. He set out in the beginning of December, and arrived at Lausanne about a fortnight later, having been engaged on his extraordinary mission of duty and peril for four years and five months. He was received like one rescued from the dead. His health was so injured, that his wife could scarcely recognise her husband in that wan, wasted, and weatherbeaten creature who stood before her. In fact, he was a perfect wreck.

He remained about fifteen months in Switzerland, during which he preached in the Huguenots' church; wrote out many of his pastoral letters and sermons; and, when his health had become restored, he again proceeded on his travels into foreign countries. He first went into Holland. He had scarely arrived there, when intelligence reached him from Montpellier of the execution, after barbarous torments, of his friend Papus, —one of those who had accompanied him into the Cevennes to preach the Gospel some six years before. There were now very few of the original company left.

On hearing of the martydom of Papus, Brousson, in a pastoral letter which he addressed to his followers, said: "He must have died some day; and as he could not have prolonged his life beyond the term appointed, how could his end have been more happy and more glorious? His constancy, his sweetness of temper, his patience, his humility, his faith, his hope, and his piety, affected even his judges and the false pastors who endeavoured to seduce him, as also the soldiers and all that witnessed his execution. He could not have preached better than he did by his martyrdom; and I doubt not that his death will produce abundance of fruit."

While in Holland, Brousson took the opportunity of having his sermons and many of his pastoral letters printed at Amsterdam; after which he proceeded to make a visit to his banished Huguenot friends in England. He also wished to ascertain from personal inquiry the advisability of forwarding an increased number of French emigrants—then resident in Switzerland—for settlement in this country. In London, he met many of his friends from the South of France— for there were settled there as ministers, Graverol of Nismes, Satur of Moutauban, four ministers from Montpellier for whom he had pleaded in the courts at Toulouse—the two Dubourdieus and the two Berthaus—fathers and sons. There were also La Coux from Castres, De Joux from Lyons, Roussillon from

Montredon, Mestayer from St. Quentin, all settled in London as ministers of Huguenot churches.

After staying in England for only about a month, Brousson was suddenly recalled to Holland to assume the office to which he was appointed without solicitation, of preacher to the Walloon church at the Hague. Though his office was easy—for he had several colleagues to assist him in the duties—and the salary was abundant for his purposes, while he was living in the society of his wife and family—Brousson nevertheless very soon began to be ill at ease. He still thought of the abandoned Huguenots "in the Desert"; without teachers, without pastors, without spiritual help of any kind. When he had undertaken the work of the ministry, he had vowed that he would devote his time and talents to the support and help of the afflicted Church; and now he was living at ease in a foreign country, far removed from those to whom he considered his services belonged. These thoughts were constantly recurring and pressing upon his mind; and at length he ceased to have any rest or satisfaction in his new position.

Accordingly, after only about four months' connection with the Church at the Hague, Brousson decided to relinquish the charge, and to devote himself to the service of the oppressed and afflicted members of his native Church in France. The Dutch Government, however, having been informed of his perilous and self-sacrificing intention, agreed to continue his salary as a pastor of the Walloon Church, and to pay it to his wife, who henceforth abode at the Hague.

Brousson determined to enter France from the north, and to visit districts that were entirely new to him. For this purpose he put himself in charge of a guide.

At that time, while the Protestants were flying from France, as they continued to do for many years, there were numerous persons who acted as guides for those not only flying from, but entering the country. Those who guided Protestant pastors on their concealed visits to France, were men of great zeal and courage—known to be faithful and self-denying—and thoroughly acquainted with the country. They knew all the woods, and fords, and caves, and places of natural shelter along the route. They made the itinerary of the mountains and precipices, of the byways and deserts, their study. They also knew of the dwellings of the faithful in the towns and villages where Huguenots might find relief and shelter for the night. They studied the disguises to be assumed, and were prepared with a stock of phrases and answers adapted for every class of inquiries.

The guide employed by Brousson was one James Bruman—an old Huguenot merchant, banished at the Revocation, and now employed in escorting Huguenot preachers back to France, and escorting flying Huguenot men, women, and children from it.* The pastor and his guide started about the end of August, 1695. They proceeded by way of Liége; and travelling south, they crossed the forest of Ardennes, and entered France near Sedan.

Sedan, recently the scene of one of the greatest calamities that has ever befallen France, was, about two centuries ago, a very prosperous place. It was the seat of a great amount of Protestant learning and Protestant industry. One of the four principal Huguenot academies of France was situated in that town. It was

* Many of these extraordinary escapes are given in the author's "Huguenots: their Settlements, Churches, and Industries, in England and Ireland."

suppressed in 1681, shortly before the Revocation, and its professors, Bayle, Abbadie, Basnage, Brazy, and Jurieu, expelled the country. The academy buildings themselves had been given over to the Jesuits—the sworn enemies of the Huguenots.

At the same time, Sedan had been the seat of great woollen manufactures, originally founded by Flemish Protestant families, and for the manufacture of arms, implements of husbandry, and all kinds of steel and iron articles.* At the Revocation, the Protestants packed up their tools and property, suddenly escaped across the frontier, near which they were, and went and established themselves in the Low Countries, where they might pursue their industries in safety. Sedan was ruined, and remained so until our own day, when it has begun to experience a little prosperity from the tourists desirous of seeing the place where the great French Army surrendered.

When Brousson visited the place, the remaining Protestants resided chiefly in the suburban villages of Givonne and Daigny. He visited them in their families, and also held several private meetings, after which he was induced to preach in a secluded place near Sedan at night.

This assembly, however, was reported to the authorities, who immediately proceeded to make search for the heretic preacher. A party of soldiers, informed by the spies, next morning invested the house in which Brousson slept. They first apprehended Bruman, the guide, and thought that in him they had secured the

* There were from eighty to ninety establishments for the manufacture of broadcloth in Sedan, giving employment to more than two thousand persons. These, together with the iron and steel manufactures, were entirely ruined at the Revocation, when the whole of the Protestant mechanics went into exile, and settled for the most part in Holland and England.

pastor. They next rummaged the house, in order to find the preacher's books. But Brousson, hearing them coming in, hid himself behind the door, which, being small, hardly concealed his person.

After setting a guard all round the house, ransacking every room in it, and turning everything upside down, they left it; but two of the children, seeing Brousson's feet under the door, one of them ran after the officer of the party, and exclaimed to him, pointing back, "Here, sir, here!" But the officer, not understanding what the child meant, went away with his soldiers, and Brousson's life was, for the time, saved.

The same evening, Brousson changed his disguise to that of a wool-comber, and carrying a parcel on his shoulder, he set out on the same evening with another guide. He visited many places in which Protestants were to be found—in Champagne, Picardy, Normandy, Nevernois, and Burgundy. He also visited several of his friends in the neighbourhood of Paris.

We have not many details of his perils and experiences during his journey. But the following passage is extracted from a letter addressed by him to a friend in Holland: "I assure you that in every place through which I passed, I witnessed the poor people truly repenting their fault (*i.e.* of having gone to Mass), weeping day and night, and imploring the grace and consolations of the Gospel in their distress. Their persecutors daily oppress them, and burden them with taxes and imposts; but the more discerning of the Roman Catholics acknowledge that the cruelties and injustice done towards so many innocent persons, draw down misery and distress upon the kingdom. And truly it is to be apprehended that God will abandon its inhabitants to their wickedness, that he may afterwards pour down his most terrible judgments upon that ungrateful and vaunting country, which has rejected his truth and despised the day of visitation."

During the twelve months that Brousson was occupied with his perilous journey through France, two more of his friends in the Cevennes suffered martyrdom—La Porte on the 7th of February, 1696, and Henri Guerin on the 22nd of June following. Both were broken alive on the wheel before receiving the *coup de grace*.

Towards the close of the year, Brousson arrived at Basle, from whence he proceeded to visit his friends throughout the cantons of Switzerland, and then he returned to Holland by way of the Rhine, to rejoin his family at the Hague.

At that time, the representatives of the Allies were meeting at Ryswick the representatives of Louis XIV., who was desirous of peace. Brousson and the French refugee ministers resident in Holland endeavoured to bring the persecutions of the French Protestants under the notice of the Conference. But Louis XIV. would not brook this interference. He proposed going on dealing with the heretics in his own way. "I do not pretend," he said, "to prescribe to William III. rules about his subjects, and I expect the same liberty as to my own."

Finding it impossible to obtain redress for his fellow-countrymen under the treaty of Ryswick, which was shortly after concluded, Brousson at length prepared to make his third journey into France in the month of August 1697. He set out greatly to the regret of his wife, who feared it might be his last journey, as indeed it proved to be. In a letter which he wrote to console her, from some remote place where he was snowed up about the middle of the following December, he said:

"I cannot at present enter into the details of the work the Lord has given me grace to labour in; but it is the source of much consolation to a large number of his poor people. It will be expedient that you do not mention where I am, lest I should be traced. It may be that I cannot for some time write to you; but I walk under the conduct of my God, and I repeat that I would not for millions of money that the Lord should refuse me the grace which renders it imperative for me to labour as I now do in His work."*

When the snow had melted sufficiently to enable Brousson to escape from the district of Dauphiny, near the High Alps, where he had been concealed, he made his way across the country to the Viverais, where he laboured for some time. Here he heard of the martyrdom of the third of the brothers Du Plans, broken on the wheel and executed like the others on the Peyrou at Montpellier.

During the next nine months, Brousson laboured in the north-eastern provinces of Languedoc (more particularly in the Cevennes and Viverais), Orange, and Dauphiny. He excited so much interest amongst the Protestants, who resorted from a great distance to attend his assemblies, that the spies (who were usually pretended Protestants) soon knew of his presence in the neighbourhood, and information was at once forwarded to the Intendant or his officers.

Persecution was growing very bitter about this time. By orders of the bishops the Protestants were led by force to Mass before the dragoons with drawn swords, and the shops of merchants who refused to go to Mass

---

* The following was the portraiture of Brousson, issued to the spies and police: "Brousson is of middle stature, and rather spare, aged forty to forty-two, nose large, complexion dark, hair black, heads well formed."

regularly were ordered to be closed. Their houses were also filled with soldiers. "The soldiers or militia," said Brousson to a friend in Holland, "frequently commit horrible ravages, breaking open the cabinets, removing every article that is saleable, which are often purchased by the priests at insignificant prices; the rest they burn and break up, after which the soldiers are removed; and when the sufferers think themselves restored to peace, fresh billets are ordered upon them. Many are consequently induced to go to Mass with weeping and lamentation, but a great number remain inflexible, and others fly the kingdom."

When it became known that Brousson, in the course of his journeyings, had arrived, about the end of August, 1698, in the neighbourhood of Nismes, Baville was greatly mortified; and he at once offered a reward of six hundred louis d'or for his head. Brousson nevertheless entered Nismes, and found refuge amongst his friends. He had, however, the imprudence to post there a petition to the King, signed by his own hand, which had the effect of at once setting the spies upon his track. Leaving the city itself, he took refuge in a house not far from it, whither the spies contrived to trace him, and gave the requisite information to the Intendant. The house was soon after surrounded by soldiers, and was itself entered and completely searched

Brousson's host had only had time to make him descend into a well, which had a niche in the bottom in which he could conceal himself. The soldiers looked down the well a dozen times, but could see nothing. Brousson was not in the house; he was not in the chimneys; he was not in the outhouses. He *must* be in the well! A soldier went down the well to make a personal examination. He was let down close to the surface of the water, and felt all about. There was nothing! Feeling awfully cold, and wishing to be taken out, he called to his friends, "There is nothing here, pull me up." He was pulled up accordingly, and Brousson was again saved.

The country about Nismes being beset with spies to track the Protestants and prevent their meetings, Brousson determined to go westward and visit the scattered people in Rouerge, Pays de Foix, and Bigorre, proceeding as far as Bearn, where a remnant of Huguenots still lingered, notwithstanding the repeated dragooning to which the district had been subjected. It was at Oberon that he fell into the hands of a spy, who bore the same name as a Protestant friend to whom his letter was addressed. Information was given to the authorities, and Brousson was arrested. He made no resistance, and answered at once to his name.

When the Judas who had betrayed him went to M. Pénon, the intendant of the province, to demand the reward set upon Brousson's head, the Intendant replied with indignation, "Wretch! don't you blush to look upon the man in whose blood you traffic? Begone! I cannot bear your presence!"

Brousson was sent to Pau, where he was imprisoned in the castle of Foix, at one time the centre of the Reformation movement in the South of France—where Calvin had preached, where Jeanne d'Albret had lived, and where Henry IV. had been born.

From Pau, Brousson was sent to Montpellier, escorted by dragoons. At Toulouse the party took passage by the canal of Languedoc, which had then been shortly open. At Somail, during the night, Brousson saw that all the soldiers were asleep. He had but to step on shore to regain his liberty; but he had promised to the Intendant of Bearn, who had allowed him to go unfettered, that he would not attempt to escape. At Agade there was a detachment of a hundred soldiers, ready to convey the prisoner to Baville, Intendant of Languedoc. He was imprisoned in the citadel of Montpellier, on the 30th October, 1698.

Baville, who knew much of the character of Brousson—his peacefulness, his piety, his self-sacrifice, and his noble magnanimity—is said to have observed on one occasion, "I would not for a world have to judge that man." And yet the time had now arrived when Brousson was to be judged and condemned by Baville and the Presidial Court. The trial was a farce, because it had been predetermined that Brousson should die. He was charged with preaching in France contrary to the King's prohibition. This he admitted; but when asked to whom he had administered the Sacrament, he positively refused to disclose, because he was neither a traitor nor informer to accuse his brethren. He was also charged with having conspired to introduce a foreign army into France under the command of Marshal Schomberg. This he declared to be absolutely false, for he had throughout his career been a man of peace, and sought to bring back Christ's followers by peaceful means only.

His defence was of no avail. He was condemned to be racked, then to be broken on the wheel, and afterwards to be executed. He received the sentence without a shudder. He was tied on the rack, but when he refused to accuse his brethren he was released from it. Attempts were made by several priests and friars to add him to the number of "new converts," but these were altogether fruitless. All that remained was to execute him finally on the public place of execution—the Peyrou.

The Peyrou is the pride of modern Montpellier. It is the favourite promenade of the place, and is one of the finest in Europe. It consists of a broad platform elevated high above the rest of the town, and commanding extensive views of the surrounding country. In clear weather, Mont Ventoux, one of the Alpine summits, may be seen across the broad valley of the Rhone on the east, and the peak of Mont Canizou in the Pyrenees on the west. Northward stretches the mountain range of the Cevennes, the bold Pic de Saint-Loup the advanced sentinel of the group; while in the south the prospect is bounded by the blue line of the Mediterranean.

The Peyrou is now pleasantly laid out in terraced walks and shady groves, with gay parterres of flowers—the upper platform being surrounded with a handsome stone balustrade. An equestrian statue of Louis XIV. occupies the centre of the area; and a triumphal arch stands at the entrance to the promenade, erected to commemorate the "glories" of the same monarch, more particularly the Revocation by him of the Edict of Nantes—one of the entablatures of the arch displaying a hideous figure, intended to represent a Huguenot, lying trampled under foot of the "Most Christian King."

The Peyrou was thus laid out and ornamented in the reign of his successor, Louis XV., "the Well-beloved," during which the same policy for which Louis XIV. was here glorified by an equestrian statue and a triumphal arch continued to be persevered in—of imprisoning, banishing, hanging, or sending to the galleys such of the citizens of France as were not of "the King's religion."

But during the reign of Louis XIV. himself, the Peyrou was anything but a pleasure-ground. It was the infamous place of the city—the *place de Grève*—a desert, barren, blasted table-land, where sometimes half-a-dozen decaying corpses might be seen swinging from the gibbets on which they had been hung. It was specially reserved, because of its infamy, for the execution of heretics against Rome; and here, accordingly, hundreds of Huguenot martyrs—whom power, honour, and wealth failed to bribe or to convert—were called upon to seal their faith with their blood.

Brousson was executed at this place on the 4th of November, 1698. It was towards evening, while the sun was slowly sinking behind the western mountains, that an immense multitude assembled on the Peyrou to witness the martyrdom of the devoted pastor. Not fewer than twenty thousand persons were there, including the principal nobility of the city and province, besides many inhabitants of the adjoining mountain district of the Cevennes, some of whom had come from a great distance to be present. In the centre of the plateau, near where the equestrian statue of the great King now stands, was a scaffold, strongly surrounded by troops to keep off the crowd. Two battalions, drawn up in two lines facing each other, formed an avenue of bayonets between the citadel, near at hand, and the place of execution.

A commotion stirred the throng; and the object of the breathless interest excited shortly appeared in the person of a middle-sized, middle-aged man, spare, grave, and dignified in appearance, dressed in the ordinary garb of a pastor, who walked slowly towards the scaffold, engaged in earnest prayer, his eyes and hands lifted towards heaven. On mounting the platform, he stood forward to say a few last words to the people, and give to many of his friends, whom he knew to be in the crowd, his parting benediction. But his voice was instantly stifled by the roll of twenty drums, which continued to beat a quick march until the hideous ceremony was over, and the martyr, Claude Brousson, had ceased to live.*

Strange are the vicissitudes of human affairs! Not a hundred years passed after this event, before the great grandson of the monarch, at whose instance Brousson had laid down his life, appeared upon a scaffold in the Place Louis XIV. in Paris, and implored permission to say his few last words to the people. In vain! His voice was drowned by the drums of Santerre!

* The only favour which Brousson's judges showed him at death was as regarded the manner of carrying his sentence into execution. He was condemned to be broken alive on the wheel, and then strangled; whereas by special favour the sentence was commuted into strangulation first and the breaking of his bones afterwards. So that while Brousson's impassive body remained with his persecutors to be broken, **his pure unconquered spirit mounted in triumph towards heaven.**

CHAPTER V.

OUTBREAK IN LANGUEDOC.

ALTHOUGH the arbitrary measures of the King were felt all over France, they nowhere excited more dismay and consternation than in the province of Languedoc. This province had always been inhabited by a spirited and energetic people, born lovers of liberty. They were among the earliest to call in question the despotic authority over mind and conscience claimed by the see of Rome. The country is sown with the ashes of martyrs. Long before the execution of Brousson, the Peyrou at Montpellier had been the Calvary of the South of France.

As early as the twelfth century, the Albigenses, who inhabited the district, excited the wrath of the Popes. Simple, sincere believers in the Divine providence, they rejected Rome, and took their stand upon the individual responsibility of man to God. Count de Foix said to the legate of Innocent III.: "As to my religion, the Pope has nothing to do with it. Every man's conscience must be free. My father has always recommended to me this liberty, and I am content to die for it."

A crusade was waged against the Albigenses, which lasted for a period of about sixty years. Armies were concentrated upon Languedoc, and after great slaughter the heretics were supposed to be exterminated.

But enough of the people survived to perpetuate the love of liberty in their descendants, who continued to exercise a degree of independence in matters of religion and politics almost unknown in other parts of France. Languedoc was the principal stronghold of the Huguenots in the sixteenth and seventeenth centuries; and when, in 1685, Louis XIV. revoked the Edict of Nantes, which interdicted freedom of worship under penalty of confiscation, banishment, and death, it is not surprising that such a policy should have occasioned widespread consternation, if not hostility and open resistance.

At the period of the Revocation there were, according to the Intendant of the province, not fewer than 250,000 Protestants in Languedoc, and these formed the most skilled, industrious, enterprising, and wealthy portion of the community. They were the best farmers, vine-dressers, manufacturers, and traders. The valley of Vaunage, lying to the westward of Nismes, was one of the richest and most highly cultivated parts of France. It contained more than sixty temples, its population being almost exclusively Protestant; and it was known as "The Little Canaan," abounding as it did in corn, and wine, and oil.

The greater part of the commerce of the South of France was conducted by the Protestant merchants of Nismes, of whom the Intendant wrote to the King in 1699, "If they are still bad Catholics, at any rate they have not ceased to be very good traders."

The Marquis d'Aguesseau bore similar testimony to the intelligent industry of the Huguenot population "By an unfortunate fatality," said he, "in nearly every

OUTBREAK IN LANGUEDOC.

kind of art the most skilful workmen, as well as the richest merchants, belong to the pretended reformed religion."

The Marquis, who governed Languedoc for many years, was further of opinion that the intelligence of the Protestants was in a great measure due to the instructions of their pastors. "It is certain," said he, "that one of the things which holds the Huguenots to their religion is the amount of information which they receive from their instructors, and which it is not thought necessary to give in ours. The Huguenots *will* be instructed, and it is a general complaint amongst the new converts not to find in our religion the same mental and moral discipline they find in their own."

Baville, the intendant, made an observation to a similar effect in a confidential communication which he made to the authorities at Paris in 1697, in which he boasted that the Protestants had now all been converted, and that there were 198,483 new converts in Languedoc. "Generally speaking," he said, "the new converts are much better off, being more laborious and industrious than the old Catholics of the province. The new converts must not be regarded as Catholics; they almost all preserve in their heart their attachment to their former religion. They may confess and communicate as much as you will, because they are menaced and forced to do so by the secular power. But this only leads to sacrilege. To gain them, *their hearts must be won*. It is there that religion resides, and it can only be solely established by effecting that conquest."

From the number, as well as the wealth and education, of the Protestants of Languedoc, it is reasonable to suppose that the emigration from this quarter of France should have been very considerable during the persecutions which followed the Revocation. Of course nearly all the pastors fled, death being their punishment if they remained in France. Hence many of the most celebrated French preachers in Holland, Germany, and England were pastors banished from Languedoc. Claude and Saurin both belonged to the province; and among the London preachers were the Dubourdieus, the Bertheaus, Graverol, and Pégorier.

It is also interesting to find how many of the distinguished Huguenots who settled in England came from Languedoc. The Romillys and Layards came from Montpellier; the Saurins from Nismes; the Gaussens from Lunel; and the Bosanquets from Caila;* besides the Auriols, Arnauds, Pechels, De Beauvoirs, Durands, Portals, Boileaus, D'Albiacs, D'Oliers, Rious, and Vignoles, all of whom belonged to the Huguenot landed gentry of Languedoc, who fled and sacrificed everything rather than conform to the religion of Louis XIV.

When Brousson was executed at Montpellier, it was believed that Protestantism was finally dead. At all events, it was supposed that those of the Protestants who remained, without becoming converted, were at length reduced to utter powerlessness. It was not believed that the smouldering ashes contained any sparks that might yet be fanned into flames. The Huguenot landed proprietors, the principal manufacturers, the best of the artisans, had left for other countries. Protestantism was now entirely without leaders. The

* There are still Gaussens at St. Mamert, in the department of Gard; and some of the Bosanquet family must have remained on their estates or returned to Protestantism, as we find a Bosanquet of Caila broken alive at Nismes, because of his religion, on the 7th September, 1702, after which his corpse was publicly exposed on the Montpellier high road.

very existence of Protestantism in any form was denied by the law; and it might perhaps reasonably have been expected that, being thus crushed out of sight, it would die.

But there still remained another important and vital element—the common people—the peasants, the small farmers, the artisans, and labouring classes—persons of slender means, for the most part too poor to emigrate, and who remained, as it were, rooted to the soil on which they had been born. This was especially the case in the Cevennes, where, in many of the communes, almost the entire inhabitants were Protestants; in others, they formed a large proportion of the population; while in all the larger towns and villages they were very numerous, as well as widely spread over the whole province.

The mountainous district of the Cevennes is the most rugged, broken, and elevated region in the South of France. It fills the department of Lozère, as well as the greater part of Gard and Herault. The principal mountain-chain, about a hundred leagues in length, runs from north-east to south-west, and may almost be said to unite the Alps with the Pyrenees. From the centre of France the surface rises with a gradual slope, forming an inclined plane, which reaches its greatest height in the Cevennic chain, several of the summits of which are about five thousand five hundred feet above the sea level. Its connection with the Alpine range is, however, broken abruptly by the deep valley of the Rhone, running nearly due north and south.

The whole of this mountain district may be regarded as a triangular plateau rising gradually from the north-west, and tilted up at its south-eastern angle. It is composed for the most part of granite, overlapped by strata belonging to the Jurassic-system; and in many places, especially in Auvergne, the granitic rocks have been burst through by volcanoes, long since extinct, which rise like enormous protuberances from the higher parts of the platform. Towards the southern border of the district, the limestone strata overlapping the granite assume a remarkable development, exhibiting a series of flat-topped hills bounded by perpendicular cliffs some six or eight hundred feet high.

"These plateaux," says Mr. Scrope, in his interesting account of the geology of Central France, "are called 'causses' in the provincial dialect, and they have a singularly dreary and desert aspect from the monotony of their form and their barren and rocky character. The valleys which separate them are rarely of considerable width. Winding, narrow, and all but impassable clift-like glens predominate, giving to the Cevennes that peculiarly intricate character which enabled its Protestant inhabitants, in the beginning of the last century, to offer so stubborn and gallant a resistance to the atrocious persecutions of Louis XIV."

Such being the character of this mountain district—rocky, elevated, and sterile—the people inhabiting it, though exceedingly industrious, are for the most very poor. Sheep-farming is the principal occupation of the people of the hill country; and in the summer season, when the lower districts are parched with drought, tens of thousands of sheep may be seen covering the roads leading to the Upper Cevennes, whither they are driven for pasture. There is a comparatively small breadth of arable land in the district. The mountains in many places contain only soil enough to grow juniper-bushes. There is very little verdure to relieve the eye—few turf-clad slopes or earth-covered ledges to repay the tillage of the farmer. Even the mountains of lower elevation are for the most part stony deserts. Chestnut-trees, it is true, grow luxuriantly in the sheltered places, and occasionally scanty crops of rye on the lower mountain-sides. Mulberry-trees also thrive in the valleys, their leaves being used for the feeding of silkworms, the rearing of which forms one of the principal industries of the district.

Even in the immediate neighbourhood of Nismes—a rich and beautiful town, abounding in Roman remains, which exhibit ample evidences of its ancient grandeur —the country is arid, stony, and barren-looking, though here the vine, the olive, and the fig-tree, wherever there is soil enough, grow luxuriantly in the open air. Indeed, the country very much resembles in its character the land of Judea, being rocky, parched, and in many places waste, though in others abounding in corn and wine and oil. In the interior parts of the district the scenery is wild and grand, especially in the valleys lying under the lofty mountain of Lozère. But the rocks and stones are everywhere in the ascendant.

A few years ago we visited the district; and while proceeding in the old-fashioned diligence which runs between Alais and Florac—for the district is altogether beyond the reach of railways—a French contractor, accompanying a band of Italian miners, whom he was taking into the mountains to search for minerals, pointing to the sterile rocks, exclaimed to us, "Messieurs, behold the very poorest district in France! It contains nothing but juniper-bushes! As for its agriculture, it produces nothing; manufactures, nothing; commerce, nothing! *Rien, rien, rien!*"

The observation of this French *entrepreneur* reminds

us of an anecdote that Telford, the Scotch engineer, used to relate of a countryman with reference to his appreciation of Scotch mountain beauty. An English artist, enraptured by the scenery of Ben MacDhui, was expatiating on its magnificence, and appealed to the native guide for confirmation of his news. "I dinna ken aboot the scenery," replied the man, "but there's plenty o' big rocks and stanes; an' the kintra's awfu' puir." The same observation might doubtless apply to the Cevennes. Yet, though the people may be poor, they are not miserable or destitute, for they are all well-clad and respectable-looking peasants, and there is not a beggar to be seen in the district.

But the one country, as the other, grows strong and brave men. These barren mountain districts of the Cevennes have bred a race of heroes; and the men are as simple and kind as they are brave. Hospitality is a characteristic of the people, which never fails to strike the visitor accustomed to the exactions which are so common along the hackneyed tourist routes.

As in other parts of France, the peasantry here are laborious almost to excess. Robust and hardy, they are distinguished for their perseverance against the obstacles which nature constantly opposes to them. Out-door industry being suspended in winter, during which they are shut up in their cabins for nearly six months by the ice and snow, they occupy themselves in preparing their wool for manufacture into cloth. The women card, the children spin, the men weave; and each cottage is a little manufactory of drugget and serge, which is taken to market in spring, and sold in the low-country towns. Such was the industry of the Cevennes nearly two hundred years since, and such it remains to the present day.

The people are of a contented nature, and bear their poverty with cheerfulness and even dignity. While they partake of the ardour and strong temper which characterize the inhabitants of the South of France, they are probably, on the whole, more grave and staid than Frenchmen generally, and are thought to be more urbane and intelligent; and though they are unmanageable by force, they are remarkably accessible to kindess and moral suasion.

Such, in a few words, are the more prominent characteristics of the country and people of the Cevennes.

When the popular worship of the mountain district of Languedoc—in which the Protestants constituted the majority of the population—was suppressed, great dismay fell upon the people; but they made no signs of resistance to the royal authority. For a time they remained comparatively passive, and it was at first thought they were indifferent. Their astonished enemies derisively spoke of them as displaying "the patience of a Huguenot,"—the words having passed into a proverb.

But their persecutors did not know the stuff of which these mountaineers were made. They had seen their temples demolished one after another, and their pastors banished, leaving them "like poor starved sheep looking for the pasture of life." Next they heard that such of their pastors as had been apprehended for venturing to minister to them in "the Desert" had been taken to Nismes and Montpellier and hanged. Then they began to feel excited and indignant. For they could not shake off their own belief and embrace another man's, even though that man was their king. If Louis XIV. had ordered them to believe that two and two make six, they could not possibly believe, though they might pretend to do so, that it made any other number than four. And so it was with the King's order to them to profess a faith which they could not bring their minds to believe in.

These poor people entertained the conviction that they possessed certain paramount rights as men. Of these they held the right of conscience to be one of the principal. They were willing to give unto Cæsar the things that were Cæsar's; but they could not give him those which belonged unto God. And if they were forced to make a choice, then they must rather disobey their King than the King of kings.

Though deprived of their leaders and pastors, the dispossessed Huguenots emerged by degrees from their obscurity, and began to recognise each other openly. If their temples were destroyed, there remained the woods and fields and mountain pastures, where they might still meet and worship God, even though it were in defiance of the law. Having taken counsel together, they resolved " not to forsake the assembling of themselves together ; " and they proceeded, in all the Protestant districts in the South of France—in Viverais, Dauphiny, and the Cevennes—to hold meetings of the people, mostly by night, for worship—in woods, in caves, in rocky gorges, and in hollows of the hills. Then began those famous assemblies of "the Desert," which were the nightmare of Louvois and the horror of Louis XIV.

When it came to the knowledge of the authorities that such meetings were being held, large bodies of troops were sent into the southern provinces, with orders to disperse them and apprehend the ringleaders. These orders were carried out with much barbarity. Amongst various assemblies which were discovered and attacked in the Cevennes, were those of Auduze and Vigan, where the soldiers fell upon the defenceless people, put the greater number to the sword, and hanged upon the nearest trees those who did not succeed in making their escape.

The authorities waited to see the effect of these "vigorous measures;" but they were egregiously disappointed. The meetings in the Desert went on as before, and even increased in number. Then milder means were tried. Other meetings were attacked in like manner, and the people found attending them taken prisoners. They were then threatened with death unless they became converted, and promised to attend Mass. They declared that they preferred death. A passion for martyrdom even seemed to be spreading amongst the infatuated people!

Then the peasantry began secretly to take up arms for their defence. They had thus far been passive in their resistance, and were content to brave death provided they could but worship together. At length they felt themselves driven in their despair to resist force by force—acting, however, in the first place, entirely on the defensive—"leaving the issue," to use the words of one of their solemn declarations, "to the providence of God."

They began—these poor labourers, herdsmen, and woolcarders—by instituting a common fund for the purpose of helping their distressed brethren in surrounding districts. They then invited such as were disposed to join them to form themselves into companies, so as to be prepared to come together and give their assistance as occasion required. When meetings in the Desert were held, it became the duty of these enrolled men to post themselves as sentinels on the surrounding heights, and give notice of the approach of their enemies. They also constituted a sort of voluntary police for their respective districts, taking notice of the changes of the royal troops, and dispatching information by trusty emissaries, intimating the direction of their march.

The Intendant, Baville, wrote to Louvois, minister of Louis XIV. during the persecutions, expressing his surprise and alarm at the apparent evidences of organization amongst the peasantry. "I have just learned," said he in one letter,* " that last Sunday there was an assembly of nearly four hundred men, many of them armed, at the foot of the mountain of Lozère. I had thought," he added, " that the great lesson taught them at Vigan and Anduze would have restored tranquillity to the Cevennes, at least for a time. But, on the contrary, the severity of the measures heretofore adopted seems only to have had the effect of exasperating and hardening them in their iniquitous courses."

As the massacres had failed, the question next arose whether the inhabitants might not be driven into exile, and the country entirely cleared of them. "They pretend," said Louvois, " to meet in ' the Desert ; ' why not take them at their word, and make the Cevennes *really* a Desert ? " But there were difficulties in the way of executing this plan. In the first place, the Protestants of Languedoc were a quarter of a million in number. And, besides, if they were driven out of it, what would become of the industry and the wealth of this great province—what of the King's taxes ?

The Duke de Noailles advised that it would be neces-

* October 20, 1686.

sary to proceed with some caution in the matter. "If his Majesty," he wrote to Baville, "thinks there is no other remedy than changing the whole people of the Cevennes, it would be better to begin by expelling those who are not engaged in commerce, who inhabit inaccessible mountain districts, where the severity of the climate and the poverty of the soil render them rude and barbarous, as in the case of those people who recently met at the foot of the Lozère. Should the King consent to this course, it will be necessary to send here at least four additional battalions of foot to execute his orders."*

An attempt was made to carry out this measure of deportation of the people, but totally failed. With the aid of spies, stimulated by high rewards, numerous meetings in the Desert were fallen upon by the troops, and those who were not hanged were transported—some to Italy, some to Switzerland, and some to America. But transportation had no terrors for the people, and the meetings continued to be held as before.

Baville then determined to occupy the entire province with troops, and to carry out a general disarmament of of the population. Eight regiments of regular infantry were sent into the Cevennes, and fifty regiments of militia were raised throughout the province, forming together an army of some forty thousand men. Strong military posts were established in the mountains, and new forts and barracks were erected at Alais, Anduze, St. Hypolyte, and Nismes. The mountain-roads being almost impassable, many of them mere mule paths, Baville had more than a hundred new high-roads and branch-roads constructed and made practicable for the passage of troops and transport of cannon.

* Noailles to Baville, 29th October, 1686.

By these means the whole country became strongly occupied, but still the meetings in the Desert went on. The peasantry continued to brave all risks—of exile, the galleys, the rack, and the gibbet—and persevered in their assemblies, until the very ferocity of their persecutors became wearied. The people would not be converted either by the dragoons or the priests who were stationed amongst them. In the dead of the night they would sally forth to their meetings in the hills; though their mountains were not too steep, their valleys not too secluded, their defiles not too impenetrable to protect them from pursuit and attack, for they were liable at any moment to be fallen upon and put to the sword.

The darkness, the dangers, the awe and mystery attending these midnight meetings invested them with an extraordinary degree of interest and even fascination. It is not surprising that under such circumstances the devotion of these poor people should have run into fanaticism and superstition. Singing the psalms of Marot by night, under the shadow of echoing rocks, they fancied they heard the sounds of heavenly voices filling the air. At other times they would meet amidst the ruins of their fallen sanctuaries, and mysterious sounds of sobbing and wailing and groaning would seem as if to rise from the tombs of their fathers.

Under these distressing circumstances—in the midst of poverty, suffering, and terror—a sort of religious hysteria suddenly developed itself amongst the people, breaking out and spreading like many other forms of disease, and displaying itself chiefly in the most persecuted quarters of Dauphiny, Viverais, and the Cevennes. The people had lost their pastors; they had not the guidance of sober and intelligent persons; and they were left merely to pray and to suffer. The terrible raid of the priests against the Protestant books had even deprived most of the Huguenots of their Bibles and psalm-books, so that they were in a great measure left to profit by their own light, such as it was.

The disease to which we refer, had often before been experienced, under different forms, amongst uneducated people when afflicted by terror and excitement; such, for instance, as the Brotherhood of the Flagellants, which followed the attack of the plague in the Middle Ages; the Dancing Mania, which followed upon the Black Death; the Child's Pilgrimages, the Convulsionaires, the Revival epilepsies and swoons, which have so often accompanied fits of religious devotion worked up into frenzy; these diseases being merely the result of excitement of the senses, which convulse the mind and powerfully affect the whole nervous system.

The "prophetic malady," as we may call it, which suddenly broke out amongst the poor Huguenots, began with epileptic convulsions. They fell to the ground senseless, foamed at the mouth, sobbed, and eventually revived so far as to be able to speak and "prophesy," like a mesmerised person in a state of *clairvoyance*. The disease spread rapidly by the influence of morbid sympathy, which, under the peculiar circumstances we have described, exercises an amazing power over human minds. Those who spoke with power were considered "inspired." They prayed and preached extatically, the most inspired of the whole being women, boys, and even children.

One of the first "prophets" who appeared was Isabel Vincent, a young shepherdess of Crest, in Dauphiny, who could neither read nor write. Her usual speech was the patois of her country, but when she became inspired she spoke perfectly, and, according to Michelet, with great eloquence. "She chanted," he says, "at first the Commandments, then a psalm, in a low and fascinating voice. She meditated a moment, then began the lamentation of the Church, tortured, exiled, at the galleys, in the dungeons: for all those evils she blamed our sins only, and called all to penitence. Then, starting anew, she spoke angelically of the Divine goodness."

Boucher, the intendant of the province, had her apprehended and examined. She would not renounce. "You may take my life," she said, "but God will raise up others to speak better things than I have done." She was at last imprisoned at Grenoble, and afterwards in the Tower of Constance.

As Isabel Vincent had predicted, many prophets followed in her steps, but they did not prophesy so divinely as she. They denounced "Woe, woe" upon their persecutors. They reviled Babylon as the oppressor of the House of Israel. They preached the most violent declamations against Rome, drawn from the most lugubrious of the prophets, and stirred the minds of their hearers into the most furious indignation.

The rapidity with which the contagion of convulsive prophesying spread was extraordinary. The adherents were all of the poorer classes, who read nothing but the Bible, and had it nearly by heart. It spread from Dauphiny to Viverais, and from thence into the Cevennes. "I have seen," said Marshal Villars, "things that I could never have believed if they had not passed under my own eyes—an entire city, in which all the women and girls, without exception, appeared possessed by the devil: they quaked and prophesied publicly in the streets."*

Flottard says there were eight thousand persons in one province who had inspiration. All were not, however, equally inspired. There were four degrees of ecstasy: first, the being called; next, the inspiration; then, the prophesy; and, lastly, the gift, which was the inspiration in the highest degree.

All this may appear ludicrous to some. And yet the school of credulity is a very wide one. Even in these enlightened times in which we live, we hear of tables turning, spelling out words, and "prophesying" in their own way. There are even philosophers, men of science, and literati who believe in spiritualists that rise on sofas and float about in the air, who project themselves suddenly out of one window and enter by another, and do many other remarkable things. And though our spiritual table-rapping and floating about may seem to be of no possible use, the "prophesying" of the Camisards was all but essential to the existence of the movement in which they were engaged.

The population became intensely excited by the prevalence of this enthusiasm or fanaticism. "When a Huguenot assembly," says Brueys, "was appointed, even before daybreak, from all the hamlets round, the men, women, boys, girls, and even infants, came in crowds, hurrying from their huts, pierced through the woods, leapt over the rocks, and flew to the place of appointment."†

Mere force was of no avail against people who supposed themselves to be under supernatural influences. The meetings in the Desert, accordingly, were attended

* " Vie du Maréchal de Villars," i. 125.
† Brueys, " Histoire du Fanaticisme de Notre Temps."

with increased and increasing fascination, and Baville, who had reported to the King the entire pacification and conversion of Languedoc, to his dismay found the whole province bursting with excitement, which a spark at any moment might fire into frenzy. And that spark was shortly afterwards supplied by the archpriest Chayla, director of missions at Pont-de-Montvert.

Although it was known that many of the peasantry attended the meetings armed, there had as yet been no open outbreak against the royal authority in the Cevennes. At Cheilaret, in the Vivarais, there had been an encounter between the troops and the peasantry; but the people were speedily dispersed, leaving three hundred dead and fifty wounded on the field.

The Intendant Baville, after thus pacifying the Vivarais, was proceeding on his way back to Montpellier, escorted by some companies of dragoons and militia, passing through the Cevennes by one of the new roads he had caused to be constructed along the valley of the Tarn, by Pont-de-Montvert to Florac. What was his surprise, on passing through the village of Pont-de-Montvert, to hear the roll of a drum, and shortly after to perceive a column of rustics, some three or four hundred in number, advancing as if to give him battle. Baville at once drew up his troops and charged the column, which broke and fled into an adjoining wood. Some were killed and others taken prisoners, who were hanged next day at St. Jean-du-Gard. A reward of five hundred louis d'or was advertised for the leader, who was shortly after tracked to his hiding-place in a cavern situated between Anduze and Alais, and was there shot, but not until after he had killed three soldiers with his fusil.

After this event persecution was redoubled throughout the Cevennes. The militia ran night and day after the meetings in the Desert. All persons found attending them, who could be captured, were either killed on the spot or hanged. Two companies of militia were quartered in Pont-de-Montvert at the expense of the inhabitants; and they acted under the direction of the archpriest Du Chayla. This priest, who was a native of the district, had been for some time settled as a missionary in Siam engaged in the conversion of Buddhists, and on his return to France he was appointed to undertake the conversion of the people of the Cevennes to the faith of Rome.

The village of Pont-de-Montvert is situated in the hollow of a deep valley formed by the mountain of Lozère on the north, and of Bougès on the south, at the point at which two streams, descending from their respective summits, flow into the Tarn. The village is separated by these streams into three little hamlets, which are joined together by the bridge which gives its name to the place. The addition of "Mont Vert," however, is a misnomer; for though seated at the foot of a steep mountain, it is not green, but sterile, rocky, and verdureless. The village is best reached from Florac, from which it is about twenty miles distant. The valley runs east and west, and is traversed by a tolerably good road, which at the lower part follows the windings of the Tarn, and higher up runs in and out along the mountain ledges, at every turn presenting new views of the bold, grand, and picturesque scenery which characterizes the wilder parts of the Cevennes. Along this route the old mule-road is still discernible in some places—a difficult, rugged, mountain path, which must have kept the district sealed up during the greater part of the year, until Baville constructed the new road for the purpose of opening up the country for the easier passage of troops and munitions of war.

A few poor hamlets occur at intervals along the road, sometimes perched on apparently inaccessible rocks, and at the lower part of the valley an occasional chateau is to be seen, as at Miral, picturesquely situated on a height. But the country is too poor by nature—the breadth of land in the bottom of the ravine being too narrow and that on the mountain ledges too stony and sterile—ever to have enabled it to maintain a considerable population. On all sides little is to be seen but rocky mountain sides, stony and precipitous, with bold mountain peaks extending beyond them far away in the distance.

Pont-de-Montvert is the centre of a series of hamlets, the inhabitants of which were in former times almost exclusively Protestant, as they are now; and where meetings in the Desert were of the most frequent occurrence. Strong detachments of troops were accordingly stationed there and at Florac for the purpose of preventing the meetings and overawing the population. Besides soldiers, the authorities also established missions throughout the Cevennes, and the principal inspector of these missions was the archpriest Chayla. The house in which he resided at Pont-de-Montvert is still pointed out. It is situated near the north end of the bridge over the Tarn; but though the lower part of the building remains as it was in his time, the upper portion has been for the most part rebuilt.

Chayla was a man of great force of character—zealous, laborious, and indefatigable—but pitiless, relentless, and cruel. He had no bowels of compassion. He was deaf to all appeals for mercy. With nim the penalty of non-belief in the faith of Rome was imprisonment, torture, death. Eight young priests lived with him, whose labours he directed; and great was his annoyance to find that the people would not attend his ministrations, but continued to flock after their own prophet-preachers in the Desert.

Moral means having failed, he next tried physical. He converted the arched cellars of his dwelling into dungeons, where he shut up those guilty of contumacy; and day by day he put them to torture. It seems like a satire on religion to say that, in his attempt to convert souls, this vehement missionary made it one of his principal studies to find out what amount of agony the bodies of those who differed from him would bear short of actual death. He put hot coals into their hands, which they were then made to clench; wrapped round their fingers cotton steeped in oil, which was then set on fire; besides practising upon them the more ordinary and commonplace tortures. No wonder that the archpriest came to be detested by the inhabitants of Pont-de-Montvert.

At length, a number of people in the district, in order to get beyond reach of Chayla's cruelty, determined to emigrate from France and take refuge in Geneva. They assembled one morning secretly, a cavalcade of men and women, and set out under the direction of a guide who knew the mountain paths towards the east. When they had travelled a few hours, they fell into an ambuscade of militia, and were marched back to the archpriest's quarters at Pont-de-Montvert. The women were sent to Mende to be immured in convents, and the men were imprisoned in the archpriest's dungeons. The parents of some of the captives ran to throw themselves at his feet, and implored mercy for their sons; but Chayla was inexorable. He declared harshly that the prisoners must suffer according to the law—that the fugitives must go the galleys, and their guide to the gibbet.

On the following Sunday, the 23rd of July, 1702, one of the preaching prophets, Pierre Seguier of Magistavols, a hamlet lying to the south of Pont-de-Montvert, preached to an assembly on the neighbouring mountain of Bougès; and there he declared that the Lord had ordered him to take up arms to deliver the captives and exterminate the archpriest of Moloch. Another and another preacher followed in the same strain, the excited assembly encouraging them by their cries, and calling upon them to execute God's vengeance on the persecutors of God's people.

That same night Seguier and his companions went round amongst the neighbouring hamlets to summon an assemblage of their sworn followers for the evening of the following day. They met punctually in the Altefage Wood, and under the shadow of three gigantic beech trees, the trunks of which were standing but a few years ago, they solemnly swore to deliver their companions and destroy the archpriest.

When night fell, a band of fifty determined men marched down the mountain towards the bridge, led by Seguier. Twenty of them were armed with guns and pistols. The rest carried scythes and hatchets. As they approached the village, they sang Marot's version of the seventy-fourth Psalm. The archpriest heard the unwonted sound as they came marching along. Thinking it was a nocturnal assembly, he cried to his soldiers, "Run and see what this means." But the doors of the house were already invested by the mountaineers, who shouted out for "The prisoners! the prisoners!" "Back, Huguenot canaille!" cried Chayla from the window. But they only shouted the louder for "The prisoners!"

The archpriest then directed the militia to fire, and one of the peasants fell dead. Infuriated, they seized the trunk of a tree, and using it as a battering-ram, at once broke in the door. They next proceeded to force the entrance to the dungeon, in which they succeeded, and called upon the prisoners to come forth. But some of them were so crippled by the tortures to which they had been subjected, that they could not stand. At sight of their sufferings the fury of the assailants increased, and, running up the staircase, they called out for the archpriest. "Burn the priest and the satellites of Baal!" cried their leader; and heaping together the soldiers' straw beds, the chairs, and other combustibles, they set the whole on fire.

Chayla, in the hope of escaping, jumped from a window into the garden, and in the fall broke his leg. The peasants discovered him by the light of the blazing dwelling. He called for mercy. "No," said Seguier, "only such mercy as you have shown to others;" and he struck him the first blow.

The others followed. "This for my father," said the next, "whom you racked to death!"

"This for my brother," said another, "whom you sent to the galleys!"

"This for my mother, who died of grief!"

This for my sister, my relatives, my friends, in exile, in prison, in misery!

And thus blow followed blow, fifty-two in all, half of which would probably have been mortal, and the detested Chayla lay a bleeding mass at their feet!

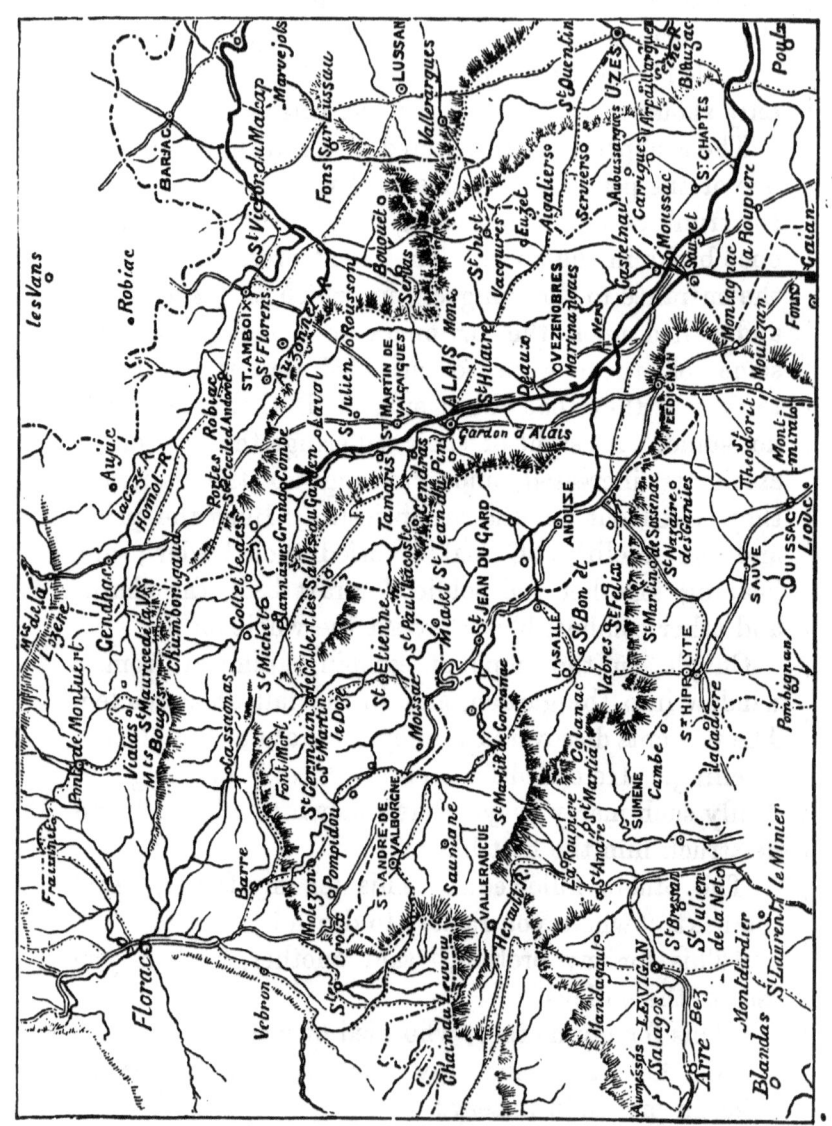

Map of the Country of the Cevennes.

CHAPTER VI.

INSURRECTION OF THE CAMISARDS.

THE poor peasants, wool-carders, and neatherds of the Cevennes, formed only a small and insignificant section of the great body of men who were about the same time engaged in different countries of Europe in vindicating the cause of civil and religious liberty. For this cause, a comparative handful of people in the Low Countries, occupying the Dutch United Provinces, had banded themselves together to resist the armies of Spain, then the most powerful monarchy in the world. The struggle had also for some time been in progress in England and Scotland, where it culminated in the Revolution of 1688; and it was still raging in the Vaudois valleys of Piedmont.

The object contended for in all these cases was the same. It was the vindication of human freedom against royal and sacerdotal despotism. It could only have been the direst necessity that drove a poor, scattered, unarmed peasantry, such as the people of the Cevennes, to take up arms against so powerful a sovereign as Louis XIV. Their passive resistance had lasted for fifteen long years, during which many of them had seen their kindred racked, hanged, or sent to the galleys; and at length their patience was exhausted, and the inevitable outburst took place. Yet they were at any moment ready to lay down their arms and return to their allegiance, provided only a reasonable degree of liberty of worship were assured to them. This, however, their misguided and bigoted monarch would not tolerate; for he had sworn that no persons were to be suffered in his dominions save those who were of "the King's religion."

The circumstances accompanying the outbreak of the Protestant peasantry in the Cevennes in many respects resembled those which attended the rising of the Scotch Covenanters in 1679. Both were occasioned by the persistent attempts of men in power to enforce a particular form of religion at the point of the sword. The resisters of the policy were in both cases Calvinists;* and they were alike indomitable and obstinate in their assertion of the rights of conscience. They held that religion was a matter between man and his God, and not between man and his sovereign or the Pope. The peasantry in both cases persevered in their

* Whether it be that Calvinism is electic as regards races and individuals, or that it has (as is most probably the case) a powerful formative influence upon individual character, certain it is that the Calvinists of all countries have presented the strongest possible resemblance to each other—the Calvinists of Geneva and Holland, the Huguenots of France, the Covenanters of Scotland, and the Puritans of Old and New England, seeming, as it were, to be but members of the same family. It is curious to speculate on the influence which the religion of Calvin—himself a Frenchman—might have exercised on the history of France, as well as on the individual character of Frenchmen, had the balance of forces carried the nation bodily over to Protestantism (as was very nearly the case) towards the end of the sixteenth century. Heinrich Heine has expressed the opinion that the western races contain a large proportion of men for whom the moral principle of Judaism has a strong elective affinity; and in the sixteenth and seventeenth centuries, the Old Testament certainly seems to have exercised a much more powerful influence on the minds of religious reformers than the New. "The Jews," says Heine, "were the Germans of the East, and nowadays the Protestants in German countries (England, Scotland, America, Germany, Holland) are nothing more nor less than ancient Oriental Jews."

own form of worship. In Languedoc, the mountaineers of the Cevennes held their assemblies in "The Desert;" and in Scotland, the "hill-folk" of the West held their meetings on the muirs. In the one country as in the other, the monarchs sent out soldiers as their missionaries—Louis XIV. employing the dragoons of Louvois and Baville, and Charles II. those of Claverhouse and Dalzell. These failing, new instruments of torture were invented for their "conversion." But the people, in both cases, continued alike stubborn in their adherence to their own simple and, as some thought, uncouth form of faith.

The French Calvinist peasantry, like the Scotch, were great in their preachers and their prophets. Both devoted themselves with enthusiasm to psalmody, insomuch that "psalm-singers" was their nickname in both countries. The one had their Clement Marot by heart, the other their Sternhold and Hopkins. Huguenot prisoners in chains sang psalms in their dungeons, galley slaves sang them as they plied at the oar, fugitives in the halting-places of their flight, the condemned as they marched to the gallows, and the Camisards as they rushed into battle. It was said of the Covenanters that "they lived praying and preaching, and they died praying and fighting;" and the same might have been said of the Huguenot peasantry of the Cevennes.

The immediate cause of the outbreak of the insurrection in both countries was also similar. In the one case, it was the cruelty of the archpriest Chayla, the inventor of a new machine of torture called "the Squeezers,"* and in the other the cruelty of Arch-

---

* The instrument is thus described by Cavalier, in his "Memoirs of the Wars of the Cevennes," London, 1726 : "This inhuman man

bishop Sharpe, the inventor of that horrible instrument called "the Iron Boot," that excited the fury of the people; and the murder of the one by Seguier and his band at Pont-de-Montvert, as of the other by Balfour of Burley and his companions on Magus Muir, proved the signal for a general insurrection of the peasantry in both countries. Both acts were of like atrocity; but they corresponded in character with the cruelties which had provoked them. Insurrections, like revolutions, are not made of rose-water. In such cases, action and reaction are equal; the violence of the oppressors usually finding its counterpart in the violence of the oppressed.

The insurrection of the French peasantry proved by far the most determined and protracted of the two; arising probably from the more difficult character of the mountain districts which they occupied and the quicker military instincts of the people, as well as because several of their early leaders and organizers were veteran soldiers who had served in many campaigns. The Scotch insurgents were suppressed by the English army under the Duke of Monmouth in less than two months after the original outbreak, though their cause eventually triumphed in the Revolution of 1688; whereas the peasantry of the Cevennes, though deprived of all extraneous help, continued to maintain a heroic struggle for several years, but were under the necessity of at last succumbing to the overpowering military force of Louis XIV., after which the Hugue-

---

had invented a rack (more cruel, if it be possible, than that usually made use of) to torment these poor unfortunate gentlemen and ladies; which was a beam he caused to be split in two, with vices at each end. Every morning he would send for these poor people, in order to examine them, and if they refused to confess what he desired, he caused their legs to be put in the slit of the beam, and there squeezed them till the bones cracked," &c., &c. (p. 35).

nots of France continued to be stamped out of sight, and apparently out of existence, for nearly a century.

In the preceding chapter, we left the archpriest Chayla a corpse at the feet of his murderers. Several of the soldiers found in the château were also killed, as well as the cook and house-steward, who had helped to torture the prisoners. But one of the domestics, and a soldier, who had treated them with kindness, were, at their intercession, pardoned and set at liberty. The corpses were brought together in the garden, and Seguier and his companions, kneeling round them—a grim and ghastly sight—sang psalms until daybreak, the uncouth harmony mingling with the crackling of the flames of the dwelling overhead, and the sullen roar of the river rushing under the neighbouring bridge.

When the grey of morning appeared, the men rose from their knees, emerged from the garden, crossed the bridge, and marched up the main street of the village. The inhabitants had barricaded themselves in their houses, being in a state of great fear lest they should be implicated in the murder of the archpriest. But Seguier and his followers made no further halt in Pont-de-Montvert, but passed along, still singing psalms, towards the hamlet of Frugères, a little further up the valley of the Tarn.

Seguier has been characterised as "the Danton of the Cevennes." This fierce and iron-willed man was of great stature—bony and dark-visaged, without upper teeth, his hair hanging loose over his shoulders—and of a wild and mystic appearance, occasioned probably by the fits of ecstasy to which he was subject, and the wandering life he had for so many years led as a prophet-preacher in the Desert. This terrible man had resolved upon a general massacre of the priests, and he now threw himself upon Frugères for the purpose of carrying out the enterprise begun by him at Pont-de-Montvert. The curé of the hamlet, who had already heard of Chayla's murder, fled from his house at sound of the approaching psalm-singers, and took refuge in an adjoining rye-field. He was speedily tracked thither, and brought down by a musket-ball; and a list of twenty of his parishioners, whom he had denounced to the archpriest, was found under his cassock.

From Frugères the prophet and his band marched on to St. Maurice de Ventalong, so called because of the winds which at certain seasons blow so furiously along the narrow valley in which it is situated; but the prior of the convent, having been warned of the outbreak, had already mounted his horse and taken to flight. Here Seguier was informed of the approach of a body of militia who were on his trail; but he avoided them by taking refuge on a neighbouring mountain-side, where he spent the night with his companions in a thicket.

Next morning, at daybreak, he descended the mountain, crossed the track of his pursuers, and directed himself upon St. André de Lancèze. The whole country was by this time in a state of alarm; and the curé of the place, being on the outlook, mounted the clock-tower and rang the tocsin. But his parishioners having joined the insurgents, the curé was pursued, captured in the belfry, and thrown from its highest window. The insurgents then proceeded to gut the church, pull down the crosses, and destroy all the emblems of Romanism on which they could lay their hands.

INSURRECTION OF THE CAMISARDS.

Seguier and his band next hurried across the mountains towards the south, having learnt that the curés of the neighbourhood had assembled at St. Germain to assist at the obsequies of the archpriest Chayla, whose body had been brought thither from Pont-de-Montvert on the morning after his murder. When Seguier was informed that the town and country militia were in force in the place, he turned aside and went in another direction. The curés, however, having heard that Seguier was in the neighbourhood, fled panic-stricken, some to the château of Portes, others to St. André, while a number of them did not halt until they had found shelter within the walls of Alais, some twenty miles distant.

Thus four days passed. On the fifth night Seguier appeared before the château of Ladevèze, and demanded the arms which had been deposited there at the time of the disarmament of the peasantry. The owner replied by a volley of musketry, which killed and wounded several of the insurgents, at the same time ringing the alarm-bell. Seguier, furious at this resistance, at once burst open the gates, and ordered a general massacre of the household. This accomplished, he ransacked the place of its arms and ammunition, and before leaving set the castle on fire, the flames throwing a lurid glare over the surrounding country. Seguier's band then descended the mountain on which the château is situated, and made for the north in the direction of Cassagnas, arriving at the elevated plateau of Font-Morte a little before daybreak.

In the meantime, Baville, the intendant of the province, was hastening to Pont-de-Montvert to put down the insurrection and avenge the death of the archpriest. The whole country was roused. Troops were dispatched in hot haste from Alais; the militia were assembled from all quarters and marched upon the disturbed district. The force was placed under the orders of Captain Poul, an old soldier of fortune, who had distinguished himself in the German wars, and in the recent crusade against the Italian Vaudois. It was because of the individual prowess which Captain Poul had displayed in his last campaign, that, at the peace of Ryswick, Baville requested that he should be attached to the army of Languedoc, and employed in putting down the insurgents of the Cevennes.

Captain Poul was hastening with his troops to Florac when, having been informed of the direction in which Seguier and his band had gone, he turned aside at Barre, and after about an hour's march eastward, he came up with them at Font-Morte. They suddenly started up from amongst the broom where they had lain down to sleep, and, firing off their guns upon the advancing host, without offering any further resistance, fled in all directions. Poul and his men spurred after them, cutting down the fugitives. Coming up with Seguier, who was vainly trying to rally his men, Poul took him prisoner with several others, and they were forthwith chained and marched to Florac. As they proceeded along the road, Poul said to Seguier, "Well, wretch! now I have got you, how do you expect to be treated after the crimes you have committed?" "As I would myself have treated you, had I taken you prisoner," was the reply.

Seguier stood before his judges calm and fearless. "What is your name?" he was asked. "Pierre Seguier." "Why do they call you Esprit?" "Because the Spirit of God is in me." "Your abode?" "In the Desert, and shortly in heaven." "Ask pardon of the King!" "We have no other King but the Eternal." "Have you no feeling of remorse for your crimes?" "My soul is as a garden full of shady groves and of peaceful fountains."

Seguier was condemned to have his hands cut off at the wrist, and be burnt alive at Pont-de-Montvert. Nouvel, another of the prisoners, was broken alive at Ladevèze, and Bonnet, a third, was hanged at St. André. They all suffered without flinching. Seguier's last words, spoken amidst the flames, were, "Brethren, wait, and hope in the Eternal. The desolate Carmel shall yet revive, and the solitary Lebanon shall blossom as the rose!" Thus perished the grim, unflinching prophet of Magistavols, the terrible avenger of the cruelties of Chayla, the earliest leader in the insurrection of the Camisards!

It is not exactly known how or when the insurgents were first called Camisards. They called themselves by no other name than "The Children of God" (*Enfants de Dieu*); but their enemies variously nicknamed them "The Barbets," "The Vagabonds," "The Assemblers," "The Psalm-singers," "The Fanatics," and lastly, "The Camisards." This name is said to have been given them because of the common blouse or camisole which they wore—their only uniform. Others say that it arose from their wearing a white shirt, or camise, over their dress, to enable them to distinguish each other in their night attacks; and that this was not the case, is partly countenanced by the fact that in the course of the insurrection a body of peasant royalists took the field, who designated themselves the "*White Camisards*," in contradistinction from the others. Others say the word is derived from *camis*, signifying a road-runner. But whatever the origin of the word may be, the Camisards was the name most commonly applied to the insurgents, and by which they continue to be known in local history.

Captain Poul vigorously followed up the blow delivered at Font-Morte. He apprehended all suspected persons in the Upper Cevennes, and sent them before the judges at Florac. Unable to capture the insurgents who had escaped, he seized their parents, their relations, and families, and these were condemned to various punishments. But what had become of the insurgents themselves? Knowing that they had nothing but death to expect, if taken, they hid themselves in caves known only to the inhabitants of the district, and so secretly that Poul thought they had succeeded in making their escape from France. The Intendant Baville arrived at the same conclusion, and he congratulated himself accordingly on the final suppression of the outbreak. Leaving sundry detachments of troops posted in the principal villages, he returned to Alais, and invited the fugitive priests at once to return to their respective parishes.

After remaining in concealment for several days, the surviving insurgents met one night to consult as to the steps they were to take, with a view to their personal safety. They had by this time been joined by several sympathizers, amongst others by three veteran soldiers —Laporte, Espérandieu, and Rastelet—and by young Cavalier, who had just returned from Geneva, where he had been in exile, and was now ready to share in the dangers of his compatriots. The greater number of those present were in favour of bidding a final adieu to France, and escaping across the frontier into Switzerland, considering that the chances of their offering any successful resistance to their oppressors. were altogether hopeless. But against this craven course Laporte raised his voice.

"Brethren," said he, "why depart into the land of the stranger? Have we not a country of our own, the country of our fathers? It is, you say, a country of slavery and death! Well! Free it! and deliver your oppressed brethren. Never say, 'What can we do? we are few in number, and without arms!' The God of armies shall be our strength. Let us sing aloud the psalm of battles, and from the Lozère even to the sea Israel will arise! As for arms, have we not our hatchets? These will bring us muskets! Brethren, there is only one course worthy to be pursued. It is to live for our country; and, if need be, to die for it. Better die by the sword than by the rack or the gallows!"

From this moment, not another word was said of flight. With one voice, the assembly cried to the speaker, "Be our chief! It is the will of the Eternal!" "The Eternal be the witness of your promises," replied Laporte; "I consent to be your chief!" He assumed forthwith the title of "Colonel of the Children of God," and named his camp "The camp of the Eternal!"

Laporte belonged to an old Huguenot family of the village of Massoubeyran, near Anduze. They were respectable peasants, some of whom lived by farming and others by trade. Old John Laporte had four sons, of whom the eldest succeeded his father as a small farmer and cattle-breeder, occupying the family dwelling at Massoubeyran, still known there as the house of "Laporte-Roland." It contains a secret retreat, opening from a corner of the floor, called the "Cachette de

Roland," in which the celebrated chief of this name, son of the owner, was accustomed to take refuge; and in this cottage, the old Bible of Roland's father, as well as the halbert of Roland himself, continue to be religiously preserved.

Two of Laporte's brothers were Protestant ministers. One of them was the last pastor of Collet-de-Deze in the Cevennes. Banished because of his faith, he fled from France at the Revocation, joined the army of the Prince of Orange in Holland, and came over with him to England as chaplain of one of the French regiments which landed at Torbay in 1688. Another brother, also a pastor, remained in the Cevennes, preaching to the people in the Desert, though at the daily risk of his life, and after about ten years' labour in this vocation, he was apprehended, taken prisoner to Montpellier, and strangled on the Peyrou in the year 1696.

The fourth brother was the Laporte whom we have just described as undertaking the leadership of the hunted insurgents remaining in the Upper Cevennes. He had served as a soldier in the King's armies, and at the peace of Ryswick returned to his native village, the year after his elder brother had suffered martyrdom at Montpellier. He settled for a time at Collet-de-Deze, from which his other brother had been expelled, and there he carried on the trade of an ironworker and blacksmith. He was a great, brown, brawny man, of vehement piety, a constant frequenter of the meetings in the Desert, and a mighty psalm-singer—one of those strong, massive, ardent-natured men who so powerfully draw others after them, and in times of revolution exercise a sort of popular royalty amongst the masses. The oppression which had raged so furiously in the district excited his utmost indignation, and when he sought out the despairing insurgents in the mountains, and found that they were contemplating flight, he at once gave utterance to the few burning words we have cited, and fixed their determination to strike at least another blow for the liberty of their country and their religion.

The same evening on which Laporte assumed the leadership (about the beginning of August, 1702) he made a descent on three Roman Catholic villages in the neighbourhood of the meeting-place, and obtained possession of a small stock of powder and balls. When it became known that the insurgents were again drawing together, others joined them. Amongst these were Castonet, a forest-ranger of the Aigoal mountain district in the west, who brought with him some twelve recruits from the country near Vebron. Shortly after, there arrived from Vauvert the soldier Catinet, bringing with him twenty more. Next came young Cavalier, from Ribaute, with another band, armed with muskets which they had seized from the prior of St. Martin, with whom they had been deposited.

Meanwhile Laporte's nephew, young Roland, was running from village to village in the Vaunage, holding assemblies and rousing the people to come to the help of their distressed brethren in the mountains. Roland was a young man of bright intelligence, gifted with much of the preaching power of his family. His eloquence was of a martial sort, for he had been bred a soldier, and though young, had already fought in many battles. He was everywhere received with open arms in the Vaunage.

"My brethren," said he, "the cause of God and the deliverance of Israel is at stake. Follow us to the mountains. No country is better suited for war—we have the hill-tops for camps, gorges for ambuscades, woods to rally in, caves to hide in, and, in case of flight, secret tracts trodden only by the mountain goat. All the people there are your brethren, who will throw open their cabins to you, and share their bread and milk and the flesh of their sheep with you, while the forests will supply you with chestnuts. And then, what is there to fear? Did not God nourish his chosen people with manna in the desert? And does He not renew his miracles day by day? Will not his Spirit descend upon his afflicted children? He consoles us, He strengthens us, He calls us to arms, He will cause his angels to march before us! As for me, I am an old soldier, and will do my duty!"*

These stirring words evoked an enthusiastic response. Numbers of the people thus addressed by Roland declared themselves ready to follow him at once. But instead of taking with him all who were willing to join the standard of the insurgents, he directed them to enrol and organize themselves, and await his speedy return; selecting for the present only such as were in his opinion likely to make efficient soldiers, and with these he rejoined his uncle in the mountains.

The number of the insurgents was thus raised to about a hundred and fifty—a very small body of men, contemptible in point of numbers compared with the overwhelming forces by which they were opposed, but all animated by a determined spirit, and commanded by fearless and indomitable leaders. The band was divided into three brigades of fifty each; Laporte taking the command of the companions of Seguier; the new-comers

* Brueys, "Histoire de Fanatisme;" Peyrat, "Histoire des Pasteurs du Désert."

being divided into two bodies of like number, who elected Roland and Castanet as their respective chiefs.

Laporte occupied the last days of August in drilling his troops, and familiarising them with the mountain district which was to be the scene of their operations. While thus engaged, he received an urgent message from the Protestant herdsmen of the hill-country of Vebron, whose cattle, sheep, and goats a band of royalist militia, under Colonel Miral, had captured, and were driving northward towards Florac. Laporte immediately ran to their help, and posted himself to intercept them at the bridge of Tarnon, which they must cross. On the militia coming up, the Camisards fell upon them furiously, on which they took to flight, and the cattle were driven back in triumph to the villages.

Laporte then led his victorious troops towards Collet, the village in which his brother had been pastor. The temple in which he ministered was still standing—the only one in the Cevennes that had not been demolished, the Seigneur of the place intending to convert it into a hospital. Collet was at present occupied by a company of fusiliers, commanded by Captain Cabrières. On nearing the place, Laporte wrote to this officer, under an assumed name, intimating that a religious assembly was to be held that night in a certain wood in the neighbourhood. The captain at once marched thither with his men, on which Laporte entered the village, and reopened the temple, which had continued unoccupied since the day on which his brother had gone into exile. All that night Laporte sang psalms, preached, and prayed by turns, solemnly invoking the help of the God of battles in this holy war in which he was engaged for the liberation of his country. Shortly before daybreak, Laporte and his companions retired from the temple, and after setting fire to the Roman Catholic church, and the houses of the consul, the captain, and the curé, he left the village, and proceeded in a northerly direction.

That same morning, Captain Poul arrived at the neighbouring valley of St. Germain, for the purpose of superintending the demolition of certain Protestant dwellings, and then he heard of Laporte's midnight expedition. He immediately hastened to Collet, assembled all the troops he could muster, and put himself on the track of the Camisards. After a hot march of about two hours in the direction of Coudouloux, Poul discerned Laporte and his band encamped on a lofty height, from the scarped foot of which a sloping grove of chestnuts descended into the wide grassy plain, known as the "Champ Domergue."

The chestnut grove had in ancient times been one of the sacred places of the Druids, who celebrated their mysterious rites in its recesses, while the adjoining mountains were said to have been the honoured haunts of certain of the divinities of ancient Gaul. It was therefore regarded as a sort of sacred place, and this circumstance was probably not without its influence in rendering it one of the most frequent resorts of the hunted Protestants in their midnight assemblies, as well as because it occupied a central position between the villages of St. Frézal, St. Andéol, Dèze, and Violas. Laporte had now come hither with his companions to pray, and they were so engaged when the scouts on the look-out announced the approach of the enemy.

Poul halted his men to take breath, while Laporte held a little council of war. What was to be done? Laporte himself was in favour of accepting battle on the spot, while several of his lieutenants advised immediate flight into the mountains. On the other hand, the young and impetuous Cavalier, who was there, supported the opinion of his chief, and urged an immediate attack; and an attack was determined on accordingly.

The little band descended from their vantage-ground on the hill, and came down into the chestnut wood, singing the sixty-eighth Psalm—"Let God arise, let his enemies be scattered." The following is the song itself, in the words of Marot. When the Huguenots sang it, each soldier became a lion in courage.

> "Que Dieu se montre seulement
> Et l'on verra dans un moment
>   Abandonner la place;
> Le camp des ennemies épars,
> Epouvanté de toutes parts,
>   Fuira devant sa face.
>
> On verra tout ce camp s'enfuir,
> Comme l'on voit s'évanouir
>   Une épaisse fumée;
> Comme la cire fond au feu,
> Ainsi des méchants devant Dieu,
>   La force est consumée.
>
> L'Eternel est notre recours :
> Nous obtenons par son secours,
>   Plus d'une deliverance.
> C'est Lui qui fut notre support,
> Et qui tient les clefs de la mort,
>   Lui seul en sa puissance.
>
> A nous défendre toujours prompt,
> Il frappe le superbe front
>   De la troupe ennemie;
> On verra tomber sous ses coups
> Ceux qui provoquent son courroux
>   Par leur méchante vie.

This was the "Marseillaise" of the Camisards, their war-song in many battles, sung by them as a *pas de charge* to the music of Goudimal. Poul, seeing them approach from under cover of the wood, charged them at once, shouting to his men, "Charge, kill, kill the Barbets!"* But "the Barbets," though they were only as one to three of their assailants, bravely held their ground. Those who had muskets kept up a fusilade, whilst a body of scythemen in the centre repulsed Poul, who attacked them with the bayonet. Several of these terrible scythemen were, however, slain, and three were taken prisoners.

Laporte, finding that he could not drive Poul back, retreated slowly into the wood, keeping up a running fire, and reascended the hill, whither Poul durst not follow him. The Royalist leader was satisfied with remaining master of the hard-fought field, on which many of his soldiers lay dead, together with a captain of militia.

The Camisard chiefs then separated, Laporte and his band taking a westerly direction. The Royalists, having received considerable reinforcements, hastened from different directions to intercept him, but he slipped through their fingers, and descended to Pont-de-Montvert, from whence he threw himself upon the villages situated near the sources of the western Gardon. At the same time, to distract the attention of the Royalists, the other Camisard leaders descended, the one towards the south, and the other towards the east, disarming the Roman Catholics, carrying off their arms, and spreading consternation wherever they went.

Meanwhile, Count Broglie, Captain Poul, Colonel Miral, and the commanders of the soldiers and militia all over the Cevennes, were hunting the Protestants and their families wherever found, pillaging their houses, driving away their cattle, and burning their

* The "Barbets" (or "Water-dogs") was the nickname by which the Vaudois were called, against whom Poul had formerly been employed in the Italian valleys.

huts; and it was evident that the war on both sides was fast drifting into one of reprisal and revenge. Brigands, belonging to neither side, organized themselves in bodies, and robbed Protestants and Catholics with equal impartiality.

One effect of this state of things was rapidly to increase the numbers of the disaffected. The dwellings of many of the Protestants having been destroyed, such of the homeless fugitives as could bear arms fled into the mountains to join the Camisards, whose numbers were thus augmented, notwithstanding the measures taken for their extermination.

Laporte was at last tracked by his indefatigable enemy, Captain Poul, who burned to wipe out the disgrace which he conceived himself to have suffered at Champ-Domergue. Information was conveyed to him that Laporte and his band were in the neighbourhood of Molezon on the western Gardon, and that they intended to hold a field-meeting there on Sunday, the 22nd of October.

Poul made his dispositions accordingly. Dividing his force into two bodies, he fell upon the insurgents impetuously from two sides, taking them completely by surprise. They hastily put themselves in order of battle, but their muskets, wet with rain, would not fire, and Laporte hastened with his men to seek the shelter of a cliff near at hand. While in the act of springing from one rock to another, he was seen to stagger and fall. He had been shot dead by a musket bullet, and his career was thus brought to a sudden close. His followers at once fled in all directions.

Poul cut off Laporte's head, as well as the heads of the other Camisards who had been killed, and sent them in two baskets to Count Broglie. Next day the heads were exposed on the bridge of Anduze; the day after on the castle wall of St. Hypolite; after which these ghastly trophies of Poul's victory were sent to Montpellier to be permanently exposed on the Peyrou.

Such was the end of Laporte, the second leader of the Camisards. Seguier, the first, had been chief for only six days; Laporte, the second, for only about two months. Again Baville supposed the pacification of the Cevennes to be complete. He imagined that Poul, in cutting off Laporte's head, had decapitated the insurrection. But the Camisard ranks had never been so full as now, swelled as they were by the persecutions of the Royalists, who, by demolishing the homes of the peasantry, had in a measure forced them into the arms of the insurgents. Nor were they ever better supplied with leaders, even though Laporte had fallen. No sooner did his death become known, than the "Children of God" held a solemn assembly in the mountains, at which Roland, Castanet, Salomon, Abraham, and young Cavalier were present; and after lamenting the death of their chief, they with one accord elected Laporte's nephew, Roland, as his successor.

A few words as to the associates of Roland, whose family and origin have already been described. André Castanet of Massavaque, in the Upper Cevennes, had been a goatherd in his youth, after which he worked at his father's trade of a wool-carder. An avowed Huguenot, he was, shortly after the peace of Ryswick, hunted out of the country because of his attending the meetings in the Desert; but in 1700 he returned to preach and to prophesy, acting also as a forest-ranger in the Aigoal Mountains. Of all the chiefs he was the greatest controversialist, and in his capacity of preacher he distinguished himself from his companions by wearing a wig. There must have been something comical in his appearance, for Brueys describes him as a little, squat, bandy-legged man, presenting "the figure of a little bear." But it was an enemy who drew the picture.

Next there was Salomon Conderc, also a wool-carder, a native of the hamlet of Mazelrode, south of the mountain of Bougès. For twenty years the Condercs, father and son, had been zealous worshippers in the Desert—Salomon having acted by turns as Bible-reader, precentor, preacher, and prophet. We have already referred to the gift of prophesying. All the leaders of the Camisards were prophets. Elie Marion, in his "Théâtre Sacre de Cevennes," thus describes the influence of the prophets on the Camisard War :—

"We were without strength and without counsel," says he; "but our inspirations were our succour and our support. They elected our leaders, and conducted them; they were our military discipline. It was they who raised us, even weakness itself, to put a strong bridle upon an army of more than twenty thousand picked soldiers. It was they who banished sorrow from our hearts in the midst of the greatest peril, as well as in the deserts and the mountain fastnesses, when cold and famine oppressed us. Our heaviest crosses were but lightsome burdens, for this intimate communion that God allowed us to have with Him bore up and consoled us; it was our safety and our happiness."

Many of the Condercs had suffered for their faith. The archpriest Chayla had persecuted them grievously. One of their sisters was seized by the soldiery and carried off to be immured in a convent at Mende, but was rescued on the way by Salomon and his brother Jacques. Of the two, Salomon, though deformed, had the greatest gift in prophesying, and hence the choice of him as a leader.

Abraham Mazel belonged to the same hamlet as Conderc. They were both of the same age—about twenty-five—of the same trade, and they were as inseparable as brothers. They had both been engaged with Seguier's band in the midnight attack on Pont-de-Montvert, and were alike committed to the desperate enterprise they had taken in hand. The tribe of Mazel abounds in the Cevennes, and they had already given many martyrs to the cause. Some emigrated to America, some were sent to the galleys; Oliver Mazel, the preacher, was hanged at Montpellier in 1690, Jacques Mazel was a refugee in London in 1701, and in all the combats of the Cevennes there were Mazels leading as well as following.

Nicholas Joany, of Genouilliac, was an old soldier, who had seen much service, having been for some time quartermaster of the regiment of Orleans. Among other veterans who served with the Camisards, were Espérandieu and Rastelet, two old sub-officers, and Catinat and Ravenel, two thorough soldiers. Of these Catinat achieved the greatest notoriety. His proper name was Mauriel—Abdias Mauriel; but having served as a dragoon under Marshal Catinat in Italy, he conceived such an admiration for that general, and was so constantly eulogizing him, that his comrades gave him the nickname of Catinat, which he continued to bear all through the Camisard war.

But the most distinguished of all the Camisard chiefs, next to Roland, was the youthful John Cavalier, peasant boy, baker's apprentice, and eventually insurgent leader, who, after baffling and repeatedly defeating the armies of Louis XIV., ended his remarkable career as governor of Jersey and major-general in the British service.

Cavalier was a native of Rîbaute, a village on the Gardon, a little below Anduze. His parents were persons in humble circumstances, as may be inferred from the fact that when John was of sufficient age he was sent into the mountains to herd cattle, and when a little older he was placed apprentice to a baker at Anduze.

His father, though a Protestant at heart, to avoid persecution, pretended to be converted to Romanism, and attended Mass. But his mother, a fervent Calvinist, refused to conform, and diligently trained her sons in her own views. She was a regular attender of meetings in the Desert, to which she also took her children.

Cavalier relates that on one occasion, when a very little fellow, he went with her to an assembly which was conducted by Claude Brousson; and when he afterwards heard that many of the people had been apprehended for attending it, of whom some were hanged and others sent to the galleys, the account so shocked him that he felt he would then have avenged them if he had possessed the power.

As the boy grew up, and witnessed the increasing cruelty with which conformity was enforced, he determined to quit the country; and, accompanied by twelve other young men, he succeeded in reaching Geneva after a toilsome journey of eight days. He had not been at Geneva more than two months, when—heart-sore, solitary, his eyes constantly turned towards his dear Cevennes—he accidentally heard that his father and mother had been thrown into prison because of his flight—his father at Carcassone, and his mother in the dreadful tower of Constance, near Aiguesmortes, one of the most notorious prisons of the Huguenots.

He at once determined to return, in the hope of being able to get them set at liberty. On his reaching Ribaute, to his surprise he found them already released, on condition of attending Mass. As his presence in his father's house might only serve to bring fresh trouble upon them—he himself having no intention of conforming—he went up for refuge into the mountains of the Cevennes.

The young Cavalier was present at the midnight meeting on the Bougès, at which it was determined to slay the archpriest Chayla. He implored leave to accompany the band; but he was declared to be too young for such an enterprise, being a boy of only sixteen, so he was left behind with his friends.

Being virtually an outlaw, Cavalier afterwards joined the band of Laporte, under whom he served as lieutenant during his short career. At his death the insurrection assumed larger proportions, and recruits flocked apace to the standard of Roland, Laporte's successor. Harvest-work over, the youths of the Lower Cevennes hastened to join him, armed only with bills and hatchets. The people of the Vaunage more than fulfilled their promise to Roland, and sent him five hundred men. Cavalier also brought with him from Ribaute a further number of recruits, and by the end of autumn the Camisards under arms, such as they were, amounted to over a thousand men.

Roland, unable to provide quarters or commissariat for so large a number, divided them into five bodies, and sent them into their respective cantonments (so to speak) for the winter. Roland himself occupied the district known as the Lower Cevennes, comprising the Gardonnenque and the mountain district situated between the rivers Vidourle and the western Gardon. That part of the Upper Cevennes, which extends between the Anduze branch of the Gardon and the river Tarn, was in like manner occupied by a force commanded by Abraham Mazel and Solomon Conderc, while Andrew Castanet led the people of the western Cevennes, comprising the mountain region of the Aigoal and the Esperou, near the sources of the Gardon d'Anduze and the Tarnon. The rugged mountain district of the Lozére, in which the Tarn, the Ceze, and the Alais branch of the Gardon have their origin, was placed under the command of Joany. And, finally, the more open country towards the south, extending from Anduze to the sea-coast, including the districts around Alais, Uzés, Nismes, as well as the populous valley of the Vaunage, was placed under the direction of young Cavalier, though he had scarcely yet completed his seventeenth year.

These chiefs were all elected by their followers, who chose them, not because of any military ability they might possess, but entirely because of their "gifts" as preachers and "prophets." Though Roland and Joany had been soldiers, they were also preachers, as were Castanet, Abraham, and Salomon; and young Cavalier had already given remarkable indications of the prophetic gift. Hence, when it became the duty of the band to which he belonged to select a chief, they passed over the old soldiers, Espérandieu, Raslet, Catinat, and Ravenel, and pitched upon the young baker lad of Ribaute, not because he could fight, but because he could preach; and the old soldiers cheerfully submitted themselves to his leadership.

The portrait of this remarkable Camisard chief represents him as a little handsome youth, fair and ruddy complexioned, with lively and prominent blue eyes, and a large head, from whence his long fair hair hung floating over his shoulders. His companions recognised in him a supposed striking resemblance to the scriptural portrait of David, the famous shepherd of Israel.

The Camisard legions, spread as they now were over the entire Cevennes, and embracing Lower Languedoc as far as the sea, were for the most part occupied during the winter of 1702-3 in organizing themselves, obtaining arms, and increasing their forces. The respective districts which they occupied were so many recruiting-grounds, and by the end of the season they had enrolled nearly three thousand men. They were still, however, very badly armed. Their weapons included fowling-pieces, old matchlocks, muskets taken from the militia, pistols, sabres, scythes, hatchets, billhooks, and even ploughshares. They were very short of powder, and what they had was mostly bought surreptitiously from the King's soldiers, or by messengers sent for the purpose to Nismes and Avignon. But Roland, finding that such sources of supply could not be depended upon, resolved to manufacture his own powder.

A commissariat was also established, and the most spacious caves in the most sequestered places were sought out and converted into magazines, hospitals, granaries, cellars, arsenals, and powder factories. Thus Mialet, with its extensive caves, was the headquarters of Roland; Bouquet and the caves at Euzet, of Cavalier; Cassagnacs and the caves at Magistavols, of Salomon; and so on with the others. Each chief had his respective canton, his granary, his magazine, and his arsenal. To each retreat was attached a special body of tradesmen—millers, bakers, shoemakers, tailors, armourers, and other mechanics; and each had its special guards and sentinels.

We have already referred to the peculiar geological features of the Cevennes, and to the limestone strata which embraces the whole granitic platform of the southern border almost like a frame. As is almost invariably the case in such formations, large caves, occasioned by the constant dripping of water, are of frequent occurrence; and those of the Cevennes, which are in many places of great extent, constituted a peculiar feature in the Camisard insurrection. There is one of such caves in the neighbourhood of the Protestant town of Ganges, on the river Herault, which often served as a refuge for the Huguenots, though it is now scarcely penetrable because of the heavy falls of stone from the roof. This cavern has two entrances, one from the river Herault, the other from the Mendesse, and it extends under the entire mountain, which separates the two rivers. It is still known as the "Camisards' Grotto." There are numerous others of a like character all over the district; but as those of Mialet were of special importance—Mialet, "the Metropolis of the Insurrection," being the head-quarters of Roland—it will be sufficient if we briefly describe a visit paid to them in the month of June, 1870.

The town of Anduze is the little capital of the Gardonnenque, a district which has always been exclusively Protestant. Even at the present day, of the 5,200 inhabitants of Anduze, 4,600 belong to that faith; and these include the principal proprietors, cultivators, and manufacturers of the town and neighbourhood. During the wars of religion, Anduze was one of the Huguenot strongholds. After the death of Henry IV. the district continued to be held by the Duc de Rohan, the ruins of whose castle are still to be seen on the summit of a pyramidal hill on the north of the town. Anduze is jammed in between the precipitous mountain of St. Julien, which rises behind it, and the river Gardon, along which a modern quay-wall extends, forming a pleasant promenade as well as a barrier against the furious torrents which rush down from the mountains in winter.

A little above the town, the river passes through a rocky gorge formed by the rugged grey cliffs of Peyremale on the one bank and St. Julien on the other. The bare precipitous rocks rise up on either side like two cyclopean towers, flanking the gateway of the Cevennes. The gorge is so narrow at bottom that there is room only for the river running in its rocky bed below, and a roadway along either bank—that on the eastern side having been partly formed by blasting out the cliff which overhangs it.

After crossing the five-arched bridge which spans the Gardon, the road proceeds along the eastern bank, up the valley towards Mialet. It being market-day at Anduze, well-clad peasants were flocking into the town, some in their little pony-carts, others with their baskets or bundles of produce, and each had his "Bon jour, messieurs!" for us as we passed. So long as the road held along the bottom of the valley, passing through the scattered hamlets and villages north of the town, our little springless cart got along cleverly enough. But after we had entered the narrower valley higher up, and the cultivated ground became confined to a little strip along either bank, then the mountain barriers seemed to rise in front of us and on all sides, and the road became winding, steep, and difficult.

A few miles up the valley, the little hamlet of Massoubeyran, consisting of a group of peasant cottages—one of which was the birthplace of Roland, the Camisard chief—was seen on a hill-side to the right; and about two miles further on, at a bend of the road, we came in sight of the village of Mialet, with its whitewashed, flat-roofed cottages—forming a little group of peasants' houses lying in the hollow of the hills. The principal building in it is the Protestant temple, which continues to be frequented by the inhabitants; the *Annuaire Protestante* for 1868-70, stating the Protestant population of the district to be 1,325. Strange to say, the present pastor, M. Seguier, bears the name of the first leader of the Camisard insurrection; and one of the leading members of the consistory, M. Laporte, is a lineal descendant of the second and third leaders.

From its secluded and secure position among the hills, as well as because of its proximity to the great Temelac road constructed by Baville, which passed from Anduze by St. Jean-de-Gard into the Upper Cevennes, Mialet was well situated as the headquarters of the Camisard chief. But it was principally because of the numerous limestone caves abounding in the locality, which afforded a ready hiding-place for the inhabitants in the event of the enemies' approach, as well as because they were capable of being adapted for the purpose of magazines, stores, and hospitals, that Mialet became of so much importance as the citadel of the insurgents. One of such caverns or grottoes is still to be seen about a mile below Mialet, of extraordinary magnitude. It extends under the hill which rises up on the right-hand side of the road, and is entered from behind, nearly at the summit. The entrance is narrow and difficult, but the interior is large and spacious, widening out in some places into dome-shaped chambers, with stalactites hanging from the roof. The whole extent of this cavern cannot be much less than a quarter of a mile, judging from the time it took to explore it and to return from the furthest point in the interior to the entrance. The existence of this place had been forgotten until a few years ago, when it was rediscovered by a man of Anduze, who succeeded in entering it, but, being unable to find his way out, he remained there for three days without food, until the alarm was given and his friends came to his rescue and delivered him.

Immediately behind the village of Mialet, under the side of the hill, is another large cavern, with other grottoes branching out of it, capable, on an emergency, of accommodating the whole population. This was used by Roland as his principal magazine. But perhaps the most interesting of these caves is the one used as a hospital for the sick and wounded. It is situated about a mile above Mialet, in a limestone cliff almost overhanging the river. The approach to it is steep and difficult, up a footpath cut in the face of the rock. At length a little platform is reached, about a hundred feet above the level of the river, behind which is a low wall extending across the entrance to the cavern. This wall is pierced with two openings, intended for two culverins, one of which commanded the road leading down the pass, and the other the road up the valley from the direction of the village. The outer vault is large and roomy, and extends back into a lofty dome-shaped cavern about forty feet high, behind which a long tortuous vault extends for several hundred feet.

The place is quite dry, and sufficiently spacious to accommodate a large number of persons; and there can be do doubt as to the uses to which it was applied during the wars of the Cevennes.

The person who guided us to the cave was an ordinary working man of the village—apparently a blacksmith—a well-informed, intelligent person—who left his smithy, opposite the Protestant temple at which our pony-cart drew up, to show us over the place; and he took pride in relating the traditions which continue to be handed down from father to son relating to the great Camisard war of the Cevennes.

CHAPTER VII.

EXPLOITS OF CAVALIER.

THE country round Nismes, which was the scene of so many contests between the Royalists and the Camisard insurgents at the beginning of last century, presents nearly the same aspect as it did then, excepting that it is traversed by railways in several directions. The railway to Montpellier on the west, crosses the fertile valley of the Vaunage, "the little Canaan," still rich in vineyards as of old. That to Alais on the north, proceeds for the most part along the valley of the Gardon, the names of the successive stations reminding the passing traveller of the embittered contests of which they were the scenes in former times: Nozières, Boucoiran, Ners, Vezenobres, and Alais itself, now a considerable manufacturing town, and the centre of an important coal-mining district.

The country in the neighbourhood of Nismes is by no means picturesque. Though undulating, it is barren, arid, and stony. The view from the Tour Magne, which is very extensive, is over an apparently skeleton landscape, the bare rocks rising on all sides without any covering of verdure. In summer the grass is parched and brown. There are few trees visible; and these mostly mulberry, which, when cropped, have a blasted look. Yet, wherever soil exists, in the bottoms, the land is very productive, yielding olives, grapes, and chestnuts in great abundance.

As we ascend the valley of the Gardon, the country becomes more undulating and better wooded. The villages and farmhouses have all an old-fashioned look; not a modern villa is to be seen. We alight from the train at the Ners station—Ners, where Cavalier drove Montrevel's army across the river, and near which, at the village of Martinargues, he completely defeated the Royalists under Lajonquière. We went to see the scene of the battle, some three miles to the south-east, passing through a well-tilled country, with the peasants busily at work in the fields. From the high ground behind Ners a fine view is obtained of the valley of the Gardon, overlooking the junction of its two branches descending by Alais and Anduze, the mountains of the Cevennes rising up in the distance. To the left is the fertile valley of Beaurivage, celebrated in the Pastorals of Florian, who was a native of the district.

Descending the hill towards Ners, we were overtaken by an aged peasant of the village, with a scythe over his shoulder, returning from his morning's work. There was the usual polite greeting and exchange of salutations—for the French peasant is by nature polite— and a ready opening was afforded for conversation. It turned out that the old man had been a soldier of the first empire, and fought under Soult in the desperate battle of Toulouse in 1814. He was now nearly eighty, but was still able to do a fair day's work in the fields. Inviting us to enter his dwelling and partake of his hospitality, he went down to his cellar and fetched therefrom a jug of light sparkling wine, of which we partook. In answer to an inquiry whether there were any Protestants in the neighbourhood, the old man replied that Ners was "all Protestant." His grandson, however, who was present, qualified this sweeping statement by the remark, *sotto voce*, that many of them were "nothing."

The conversation then turned upon the subject of Cavalier and his exploits, when our entertainer launched out into a description of the battle of Martinargues, in which the Royalists had been "toutes abattus." Like most of the Protestant peasantry of the Cevennes, he displayed a very familiar acquaintance with the events of the civil war, and spoke with enthusiasm and honest pride of the achievements of the Camisards.

We have in previous chapters described the outbreak of the insurrection and its spread throughout the Upper Cevennes; and we have now rapidly to note its growth and progress to its culmination and fall.

While the Camisards were secretly organizing their forces under cover of the woods and caves of the mountain districts, the governor of Languedoc was indulging in the hope that the insurrection had expired with the death of Laporte and the dispersion of his band. But, to his immense surprise, the whole country was suddenly covered with insurgents, who seemed as if to spring from the earth in all quarters simultaneously. Messengers brought him intelligence at the same time of risings in the mountains of the Lozère and the Aigoal, in the neighbourhoods of Anduze and Alais, and even in the open country about Nismes and Calvisson, down almost to the sea-coast.

Wherever the churches had been used as garrisons and depositories of arms, they were attacked, stormed, and burnt. Cavalier says he never meddled with any church which had not been thus converted into a "den of thieves;" but the other leaders were less scrupulous. Salomon and Abraham destroyed all the establishments and insignia of their enemies on which they could lay hands—crosses, churches, and presbyteries. The curé of Saint-Germain said of Castanet in the Aigoal that he was "like a raging torrent." Roland and Joany ran from village to village ransacking dwellings, châteaux, churches, and collecting arms. Knowing every foot of the country, they rapidly passed by mountain tracks from one village to another; suddenly appearing in the least-expected quarters, while the troops in pursuit of them had passed in other directions.

Cavalier had even the hardihood to descend upon the low country, and to ransack the Catholic villages in the neighbourhood of Nismes. By turns he fought, preached, and sacked churches. About the middle of November, 1702, he preached at Aiguevives, a village not far from Calvisson, in the Vaunage. Count Broglie, commander of the royal troops, hastened from Nismes to intercept him. But pursuing Cavalier was like pursuing a shadow; he had already made his escape into the mountains. Broglie assembled the inhabitants of the village in the church, and demanded to be informed who had been present with the Camisard preacher. "All!" was the reply: "we are all guilty." He seized the principal persons of the place and sent them to Baville. Four were hanged, twelve were sent to the galleys, many more were flogged, and a heavy fine was levied on the entire village.

Meanwhile, Cavalier had joined Roland near Mialet, and again descended upon the low country, marching through the villages along the valley of the Vidourle, carrying off arms and devastating churches. Broglie sent two strong bodies of troops to intercept them; but the light-footed insurgents had already crossed the Gardon.

A few days later (December 5th), they were lying concealed in the forest of Vaquières, in the neighbourhood of Cavalier's head-quarters at Euzet. Their retreat having been discovered, a strong force of soldiers and militia was directed upon them, under the command of the Chevalier Montarnaud (who, being a new convert, wished to show his zeal), and Captain Bimard of the Nismes militia.

They took with them a herdsman of the neighbourhood for their guide, not knowing that he was a confederate of the Camisards. Leading the Royalists into the wood, he guided them along a narrow ravine, and hearing no sound of the insurgents, it was supposed that they were lying asleep in their camp.

Suddenly three sentinels on the outlook fired off their pieces. At this signal Ravenel posted himself at the outlet of the defile, and Cavalier and Catinat along its two sides. Raising their war-song, the sixty-eighth psalm, the Camisards furiously charged the enemy. Captain Bimard fell at the first fire. Montarnaud turned and fled with such of the soldiers and militia as could follow him; and not many of them succeeded in making their escape from the wood.

"After which complete victory," says Cavalier, "we returned to the field of battle to give our hearty thanks to Almighty God for his extraordinary assistance, and afterwards stripped the corpses of the enemy, and secured their arms. We found a purse of one hundred pistoles in Captain Bimard's pocket, which was very acceptable, for we stood in great need thereof, and expended part of it in buying hats, shoes, and stockings for those who wanted them, and with the remainder bought six great mule loads of brandy, for our winter's supply, from a merchant who was sending it to be sold at Anduze market."*

On the Sunday following, Cavalier held an assembly for public worship near Monteze on the Gardon, at which about five hundred persons were present. The governor of Alais, being informed of the meeting, resolved to put it down with a strong hand; and he set out for the purpose at the head of a force of about six hundred horse and foot. A mule accompanied him, laden with ropes with which to bind or hang the rebels. Cavalier had timely information, from scouts posted on the adjoining hills, of the approach of the governor's force, and though the number of fighting men in the Camisard assembly was comparatively small, they resolved to defend themselves.

Sending away the women and others not bearing arms, Cavalier posted his little band behind an old entrenchment on the road along which the governor was approaching, and awaited his attack. The horsemen came on at the charge; but the Camisards, firing over the top of the entrenchment, emptied more than a dozen saddles, and then leaping forward, saluted them with a general discharge. At this, the horsemen turned and fled, galloping through the foot coming up behind them, and throwing them into complete disorder. The Camisards pulled off their coats, in order the better to pursue the fugitives.

The Royalists were in full flight, when they were met by a reinforcement of two hundred men of Marsilly's regiment of foot. But these, too, were suddenly seized by the panic, and turned and fled with the rest, the

* "Memoirs of the Wars of the Cevennes," p. 74.

Camisards pursuing them for nearly an hour, in the course of which they slew more than a hundred of the enemy. Besides the soldiers' clothes, of which they stripped the dead, the Camisards made prize of two loads of ammunition and a large quantity of arms, which they were very much in need of, and also of the ropes with which the governor had intended to hang them.

Emboldened by these successes, Cavalier determined on making an attack on the strong castle of Servas, occupying a steep height on the east of the forest of Bouquet. Cavalier detested the governor and garrison of this place because they too closely watched his movements, and overlooked his head-quarters, which were in the adjoining forest; and they had, besides, distinguished themselves by the ferocity with which they attacked and dispersed recent assemblies in the Desert.

Cavalier was, however, without the means of directly assaulting the place, and he waited for an opportunity of entering it, if possible, by stratagem. While passing along the road between Alais and Lussan one day, he met a detachment of about forty men of the royal army, whom he at once attacked, killing a number of them, and putting the rest to flight. Among the slain was the commanding officer of the party, in whose pockets was found an order signed by Count Broglie directing all town-majors and consuls to lodge him and his men along their line of march. Cavalier at once determined on making use of this order as a key to open the gates of the castle of Servas.

He had twelve of his men dressed up in the clothes of the soldiers who had fallen, and six others in their ordinary Camisard dress bound with ropes as prisoners of war. Cavalier himself donned the uniform of the fallen officer; and thus disguised and well armed, the party moved up the steep ascent to the castle. On reaching the outer gate Cavalier presented the order of Count Broglie, and requested admittance for the purpose of keeping his pretended Camisard prisoners in safe custody for the night. He was at once admitted with his party. The governor showed him round the ramparts, pointing out the strength of the place, and boasting of the punishments he had inflicted on the rebels.

At supper Cavalier's soldiers took care to drop into the room one by one, apparently for orders, and suddenly, on a signal being given, the governor and his attendants were seized and bound. At the same time the guard outside was attacked and overpowered. The outer gates were opened, the Camisards rushed in, the castle was taken, and the garrison put to the sword.

Cavalier and his band carried off with them to their magazine at Bouquet all the arms, ammunition, and provisions they could find, and before leaving they set fire to the castle. There must have been a large store of gunpowder in the vaults of the place besides what the Camisards carried away, for they had scarcely proceeded a mile on their return journey when a tremendous explosion took place, shaking the ground like an earthquake, and turning back, they saw the battlements of the detested Château Servas hurled into the air.

Shortly after, Roland repeated at Sauvé, a little fortified town hung along the side of a rocky hill a few miles to the south of Anduze, the stratagem which Cavalier had employed at Servas, and with like success. He disarmed the inhabitants, and carried off the arms and provisions in the place; and though he released the commandant and the soldiers whom he had taken prisoners, he shot a persecuting priest and a Capuchin monk, and destroyed all the insignia of Popery in Sauvé.

These terrible measures caused a new stampede of the clergy all over the Cevennes. The nobles and gentry also left their châteaux, the merchants their shops and warehouses, and took refuge in the fortified towns. Even the bishops of Mende, Uzès, and Alais barricaded and fortified their episcopal palaces, and organized a system of defence as if the hordes of Attila had been at their gates.

With each fresh success the Camisards increased in daring, and every day the insurrection became more threatening and formidable. It already embraced the whole mountain district of the Cevennes, as well as a considerable extent of the low country between Nismes and Montpellier. The Camisard troops, headed by their chiefs, marched through the villages with drums beating in open day, and were quartered by billet on the inhabitants in like manner as the royal regiments. Roland levied imposts and even tithes throughout his district, and compelled the farmers, at the peril of their lives, to bring their stores of victual to the "Camp of the Eternal." In the midst of all, they held their meetings in the Desert, at which the chiefs preached, baptized, and administered the sacrament to their flocks.

The constituted authorities seemed paralyzed by the extent of the insurrection, and the suddenness with which it spread. The governor of the province had so repeatedly reported to his royal master the pacification of Languedoc, that when this last and worst outbreak occurred he was ashamed to announce it. The peace of Ryswick had set at liberty a large force of soldiers, who had now no other occupation than to "convert" the Protestants and force them to attend Mass. About five hundred thousand men were now under arms for this purpose—occupied as a sort of police force, very much to their own degradation as soldiers.

A large body of this otherwise unoccupied army had been placed under the direction of Baville for the purpose of suppressing the rebellion—an army of veteran horse and foot, whose valour had been tried in many hard-fought battles. Surely it was not to be said that this immense force could be baffled and defied by a few thousand peasants, cowherds, and wool-carders, fighting for what they ridiculously called their "rights of conscience!" Baville could not believe it; and he accordingly determined again to apply himself more vigorously than ever to the suppression of the insurrection, by means of the ample forces placed at his disposal.

Again the troops were launched against the insurgents, and again and again they were baffled in their attempts to overtake and crush them. The soldiers became worn out by forced marches, in running from one place to another to disperse assemblies in the Desert. They were distracted by the number of places in which the rebels made their appearance. Cavalier ran from town to town, making his attacks sometimes late at night, sometimes in the early morning; but before the troops could come up he had done all the mischief he intended, and was perhaps fifty miles distant on another expedition. If the Royalists divided themselves into small bodies, they were in danger of being overpowered; and if they kept together in large bodies, they moved about with difficulty, and could not overtake the insurgents, "by reason," said Cavalier, "we could go further in three hours than they could in a whole day; regular troops not being used to march through woods and mountains as we did."

At length the truth could not be concealed any longer. The States of Languedoe were summoned to meet at Montpellier, and there the desperate state of affairs was fully revealed. The bishops of the principal dioceses could with difficulty attend the meeting, and were only enabled to do so by the assistance of strong detachments of soldiers—the Camisards being masters of the principal roads. They filled the assembly with their lamentations, and declared that they had been betrayed by the men in power. At their urgent solicitation, thirty-two more companies of Catholic fusiliers and another regiment of dragoons were ordered to be immediately embodied in the district. The governor also called to his aid an additional regiment of dragoons from Rouergue; a battalion of marines from the ships-of-war lying at Marseilles and Toulon; a body of Miguelets from Roussillon, accustomed to mountain warfare; together with a large body of Irish officers and soldiers, part of the Irish Brigade.

And how did it happen that the self-exiled Irish patriots were now in the Cevennes, helping the army of Louis XIV. to massacre the Camisards by way of teaching them a better religion? It happened thus: The banishment of the Huguenots from France, and their appearance under William III. in Ireland to fight at the Boyne and Augrhim, contributed to send the Irish Brigade over to France—though it must be confessed that the Irish Brigade fought much better for Louis XIV. than they had ever done for Ireland.

After the surrender of Limerick in 1691, the prin-

EXPLOITS OF CAVALIER.

cipal number of the Irish followers of James II. declared their intention of abandoning Ireland and serving their sovereign's ally the King of France. The Irish historians allege that the number of the brigade at first amounted to nearly thirty thousand men.* Though they fought bravely for France, and conducted themselves valiantly in many of her great battles, they were unfortunately put forward to do a great deal of dirty work for Louis XIV. One of the first campaigns they were engaged in was in Savoy, under Catinat, in repressing the Vaudois or Barbets.

The Vaudois peasantry were for the most part unarmed, and their only crime was their religion. The regiments of Viscount Clare and Viscount Dillon, principally distinguished themselves against the Vaudois. The war was one of extermination, in which many of the Barbets were killed. Mr. O'Connor states that between the number of the Alpine mountaineers cut off, and the extent of devastation and pillage committed amongst them by the Irish, Catinat's commission was executed with terrible fidelity; the memory of which "has rendered their name and nation odious to the Vaudois. Six generations," he remarks, "have since passed away, but neither time nor subsequent calamities have obliterated the impression made by the waste and desolation of this military incursion."† Because of the outrages and destruction committed upon the women and children in the valleys in the absence of their natural defenders, the Vaudois still speak of the Irish as "the foreign assassins."

The Brigade having thus faithfully served Louis XIV.

* O'Callaghan's "History of the Irish Brigades in the service of France," p. 29.
† Ibid., p. 180.

in Piedmont, were now occupied in the same work in the Cevennes. The historian of the Brigade does not particularise the battles in which they were engaged with the Camisards, but merely announces that "on several occasions, the Irish appear to have distinguished themselves, especially their officers."

When Cavalier heard of the vast additional forces about to be thrown into the Cevennes, he sought to effect a diversion by shifting the theatre of war. Marching down towards the low country with about two hundred men, he went from village to village in the Vaunage, holding assemblies of the people. His whereabouts soon became known to the Royalists, and Captain Bonnafoux, of the Calvisson militia, hearing that Cavalier was preaching one day at the village of St. Comes, hastened to capture him.

Bonnafoux had already distinguished himself in the preceding year, by sabring two assemblies surprised by him at Vauvert and Caudiac, and his intention now was to serve Cavalier and his followers in like manner. Galloping up to the place of meeting, the Captain was challenged by the Camisard sentinel; and his answer was to shoot the man dead with his pistol. The report alarmed the meeting, then occupied in prayer; but rising from their knees, they at once formed in line and advanced to meet the foe, who turned and fled at their first discharge.

Cavalier next went southward to Caudiac, where he waited for an opportunity of surprising Aimargues, and putting to the sword the militia, who had long been the scourge of the Protestants in that quarter. He entered the latter town on a fair day, and walked about amongst the people; but, finding that his intention was known, and that his enterprise was not likely to succeed, he turned aside and resolved upon another course. But first it was necessary that his troops should be supplied with powder and ammunition, of which they had run short. So, disguising himself as a merchant, and mounted on a horse with capacious saddlebags, he rode off to Nismes, close at hand, to buy gunpowder. He left his men in charge of his two lieutenants, Ravanel and Catinat, who prophesied to him that during his absence they would fight a battle and win a victory.

Count Broglie had been promptly informed by the defeated Captain Bonnafoux that the Camisards were in the neighbourhood; and he set out in pursuit of them with a strong body of horse and foot. After several days' search amongst the vineyards near Nismes and the heathery hills about Milhaud, Broglie learnt that the Camisards were to be found at Caudiac. But when he reached that place he found the insurgents had already left, and taken a northerly direction. Broglie followed their track, and on the following day came up with them at a place called Mas de Gaffarel, in the Val de Bane, about three miles west of Nismes. The Royalists consisted of two hundred militia, commanded by the Count and his son, and two troops of dragoons, under Captain la Dourville and the redoubtable Captain Poul.

The Camisards had only time to utter a short prayer, and to rise from their knees and advance singing their battle psalm, when Poul and his dragoons were upon them. Their charge was so furious that Ravanel and his men were at first thrown into disorder; but rallying, and bravely fighting, they held their ground. Captain Poul was brought to the ground by a stone hurled from a sling by a young Vauvert miller named Samuelet; Count Broglie himself was wounded by a musket-ball, and many of his dragoons lay stretched on the field. Catinat observing the fall of Poul, rushed forward, cut off his head with a sweep of his sabre, and mounting Poul's horse, almost alone chased the Royalists, now flying in all directions. Broglie did not draw breath until he had reached the secure shelter of the castle of Bernis.

While these events were in progress, Cavalier was occupied on his mission of buying gunpowder in Nismes. He was passing along the Esplanade—then, as now, a beautiful promenade—when he observed from the excitement of the people, running about hither and thither, that something alarming had occurred. On making inquiry he was told that "the Barbets" were in the immediate neighbourhood, and it was even feared they would enter and sack the city. Shortly after, a trooper was observed galloping towards them at full speed along the Montpellier Road, without arms or helmet. He was almost out of breath when he came up, and could only exclaim that "All is lost! Count Broglie and Captain Poul are killed, and the Barbets are pursuing the remainder of the royal troops into the city!"

The gates were at once ordered to be shut and barricaded; the *générale* was beaten; the troops and militia were mustered; the priests ran about in the streets crying, "We are undone!" Some of the Roman Catholics even took shelter in the houses of the Protestants, calling upon them to save their lives. But the night passed, and with it their alarm, for the Camisards did not make their appearance. Next morning a message arrived from Count Broglie, shut up in the castle of Bernis, ordering the garrison to come to his relief.

In the meantime, Cavalier, with the assistance of his friends in Nismes, had obtained the articles of which he was in need, and prepared to set out on his return journey. The governor and his detachment were issuing from the western gate as he left, and he accompanied them part of the way, still disguised as a merchant, and mounted on his horse, with a large portmanteau behind him, and saddle-bags on either side full of gunpowder and ammunition. The Camisard chief mixed with the men, talking with them freely about the Barbets and their doings. When he came to the St. Hypolite road he turned aside; but they warned him that if he went that way he would certainly fall into the hands of the Barbets, and lose not only his horse and his merchandise, but his life. Cavalier thanked them for their advice, but said he was not afraid of the Barbets, and proceeded on his way, shortly rejoining his troop at the appointed rendezvous.

The Camisards crossed the Gardon by the bridge of St. Nicholas, and were proceeding towards their headquarters at Bouquet, up the left bank of the river, when an attempt was made by the Chevalier de St. Chaptes, at the head of the militia of the district, to cut off their retreat. But Ravanel charged them with such fury as to drive the greater part into the Gardon, then swollen by a flood, and those who did not escape by swimming were either killed or drowned.

Thus the insurrection seemed to grow, notwithstanding all the measures taken to repress it. The number of soldiers stationed in the province was from time to time increased; they were scattered in detachments all over the country, and the Camisards took care to give them but few opportunities of exhibiting their force, and then only when at a comparative disadvantage. The Royalists, at their wits' end, considered what was next to be done in order to the pacification of the country. The simple remedy, they knew, was to allow these poor simple people to worship in their own way without molestation. Grant them this privilege, and they were at any moment ready to lay down their arms, and resume their ordinary peaceful pursuits.

But this was precisely what the King would not allow. To do so would be an admission of royal fallibility which neither he nor his advisers were prepared to make. To enforce conformity on his subjects, Louis XIV. had already driven some half-a-million of the best of them into exile, besides the thousands who had perished on gibbets, in dungeons, or at the galleys. And was he now to confess, by granting liberty of worship to these neatherds, carders, and peasants, that the vigorous policy of "the Most Christian King" had been an entire mistake?

It was resolved, therefore, that no such liberty should be granted, and that these peasants, like the rest of the King's subjects, were to be forced, at the sword's point if necessary, to worship God in *his* way, and not in theirs. Viewed in this light, the whole proceeding would appear to be a ludicrous absurdity, but for its revolting impiety and the abominable cruelties with which it was accompanied. Yet the Royalists even blamed themselves for the mercy which they had hitherto shown to the Protestant peasantry; and the more virulent amongst them urged that the whole of the remaining population that would not at once conform to the Church of Rome, should forthwith be put to the sword!

Brigadier Julien, an apostate Protestant, who had served under William of Orange in Ireland, and afterwards under the Duke of Savoy in Piedmont, disappointed with the slowness of his promotion, had taken service under Louis XIV., and was now employed as a partizan chief in the suppression of his former co-religionists in Languedoc. Like all renegades, he was a bitter and furious persecutor; and in the councils of Baville his voice was always raised for the extremest measures. He would utterly exterminate the insurgents, and, if necessary, reduce the country to a desert. "It is not enough," said he, "merely to kill those bearing arms; the villages which supply the combatants, and which give them shelter and sustenance, ought to be burnt down: thus only can the insurrection be suppressed."

In a military point of view Julien was probably right; but the savage advice startled even Baville. "Nothing can be easier," said he, "than to destroy the towns and villages; but this would be to make a desert of one of the finest and most productive districts of Languedoc." Yet Baville himself eventually adopted the very policy which he now condemned.

In the first place, however, it was determined to pursue and destroy Cavalier and his band. Eight hundred men, under the Count de Touman, were posted at Uzès; two battalions of the regiment of Hainault, under Julien, at Anduze; while Broglie, with a strong body of dragoons and militia, commanded the passes at St. Ambrose. These troops occupied, as it were, the three sides of a triangle, in the centre of which Cavalier was known to be in hiding in the woods of Bouquet. Converging upon him simultaneously, they hoped to surround and destroy him.

But the Camisard chief was well advised of their movements. To draw them away from his magazines, Cavalier marched boldly to the north, and slipping through between the advancing forces, he got into Broglie's rear, and set fire to two villages inhabited by Catholics. The three bodies at once directed themselves upon the burning villages; but when they reached them Cavalier had made his escape, and was nowhere to be heard of. For four days they hunted the country between the Gardon and the Ceze, beating the woods and exploring the caves; and then they returned, harassed and vexed, to their respective quarters.

While the Royalists were thus occupied, Cavalier fell upon a convoy of provisions which Colonel Marsilly was leading to the castle of Mendajols, scattered and killed the escort, and carried off the mules and their loads to the magazines at Bouquet. During the whole of the month of January, the Camisards, notwithstanding the inclemency of the weather, were constantly on the move, making their appearance in the most unexpected quarters; Roland descending from Mialet on Anduze, and rousing Broglie from his slumbers by a midnight fusillade; Castanet attacking St. André, and making a bonfire of the contents of the church; Joany disarming Genouillac; and Lafleur terrifying the villages of the Lozère almost to the gates of Mende.

Although the winters in the South of France, along the shores of the Mediterranean, are comparatively mild and genial, it is very different in the mountain districts of the interior, where the snow lies thick upon the ground, and the rivers are bound up by frost. Cavalier, in his Memoirs, describes the straits to which his followers were reduced in that inclement season, being " destitute of houses or beds, victuals, bread, or money, and left to struggle with hunger, cold, snow, misery, and poverty."

"General Broglie," he continues, "believed and hoped that though he had not been able to destroy us with the sword, yet the insufferable miseries of the winter would do him that good office. Yet God Almighty prevented it through his power, and by unexpected means his Providence ordered the thing so well that at the end of the winter we found ourselves in being, and in a better condition than we expected. . . . . As for our retiring places, we were used in the night-time to go into hamlets or sheepfolds built in or near the woods, and thought ourselves happy when we lighted upon a stone or piece of timber to make our pillows withal, and a little straw or dry leaves to lie upon in our clothes. We did in this condition sleep as gently and soundly as if we had lain upon a down bed. The weather being extremely cold, we had a great occasion for fire ; but residing mostly in woods, we used to get great quantity of faggots and kindle them, and so sit round about them and warm ourselves. In this manner we spent a quarter of a year, running up and down, sometimes one way and sometimes another, through great forests and upon high mountains, in deep snow and upon ice. And notwithstanding the sharpness of the weather, the small stock of our provisions, and the marches and counter-marches we were continually obliged to make, and which gave us but seldom the opportunity of washing the only shirt we had upon our back, not one amongst us fell sick. One might have perceived in our visage a complexion as fresh as if we had fed upon the most delicious meats, and at the end of the season we found ourselves in a good disposition heartily to commence the following campaign."*

The campaign of 1703, the third year of the insurrection, began unfavourably for the Camisards. The ill-success of Count Broglie as commander of the royal forces in the Cevennes, determined Louis XIV.—from whom the true state of affairs could no longer be concealed—to supersede him by Marshal Montrevel, one of the ablest of his generals. The army of Languedoc was again reinforced by ten thousand of the best soldiers of France, drawn from the armies of Germany and Italy. It now consisted of three regiments of dragoons and twenty-four battalions of foot—of the Irish Brigade, the Miguelets, and the Languedoc fusiliers—which, with

* Cavalier's "Memoirs of the Wars of the Cevennes," pp. 111—114.

the local militia, constituted an effective force of not less than sixty thousand men!

Such was the irresistible army, commanded by a marshal of France, three lieutenant-generals, three major-generals, and three brigadier-generals, now stationed in Languedoc, to crush the peasant insurrection. No wonder that the Camisard chiefs were alarmed when the intelligence reached them of this formidable force having been set in motion for their destruction.

The first thing they determined upon was to effect a powerful diverson, and to extend, if possible, the area of the insurrection. For this purpose, Cavalier, at the head of eight hundred men, accompanied by thirty baggage mules, set out in the beginning of February, with the object of raising the Viverais, the north-eastern quarter of Languedoc, where the Camisards had numerous partizans. The snow was lying thick upon the ground when they set out; but the little army pushed nôrthward, through Rochegude and Barjac. At the town of Vagnas they found their way barred by a body of six hundred militia, under the Count de Roure. These they attacked with great fury and speedily put to flight.

But behind the Camisards was a second and much stronger royalist force, eighteen hundred men, under Brigadier Julien, who had hastened up from Lussan upon Cavalier's track, and now hung upon his rear in the forest of Vagnas. Next morning the Camisards accepted battle, fought with their usual bravery, but having been trapped into an ambuscade, they were overpowered by numbers, and at length broke and fled in disorder, leaving behind them their mules, baggage, seven drums, and a quantity of arms, with some two hundred dead and wounded. Cavalier himself escaped with difficulty, and, after having been given up for lost, reached the rendezvous at Bouquet in a state of complete exhaustion, Ravanel and Catinat having preceded him thither with the remains of his broken army.

Roland and Cavalier now altered their tactics. They resolved to avoid pitched battles such as that at Vagnas, where they were liable to be crushed at a blow, and to divide their forces into small detachments constantly on the move, harassing the enemy, interrupting their communications, and falling upon detached bodies whenever an opportunity for an attack presented itself.

To the surprise of Montrevel, who supposed the Camisards finally crushed at Vagnas, the intelligence suddenly reached him of a multitude of attacks on fortified posts, burning of châteaux and churches, captures of convoys, and defeats of detached bodies of Royalists.

Joany attacked Genouillac, cut to pieces the militia who defended it, and carried off their arms and ammunition, with other spoils, to the camp at Faux-des-Armes, Shortly after, in one of his incursions, he captured a convoy of forty mules laden with cloth, wine, and provisions for Lent; and, though hotly pursued by a much superior force, he succeeded in making his escape into the mountains.

Castanet was not less active in the west—sacking and burning Catholic villages, and putting their inhabitants to the sword by way of reprisal for similar atrocities committed by the Royalists. At the same time, Montrevel pillaged and burned Euzet and St. Jean de Ceirarges, villages inhabited by Protestants; and there was not a hamlet but was liable at any moment to be sacked and destroyed by one or other of the contending parties.

Nor was Roland idle. Being greatly in want of arms and ammunition, as well as of shoes and clothes for his men, he collected a considerable force, and made a descent, for the purpose of obtaining them, on the rich and populous towns of the south; more particularly on the manufacturing town of Ganges, where the Camisards had many friends. Although Roland, to divert the attention of Montrevel from Ganges, sent a detachment of his men into the neighbourhood of Nismes to raise the alarm there, it was not long before a large royalist force was directed against him.

Hearing that Montrevel was marching upon Ganges, Roland hastily left for the north, but was overtaken near Pompignan by the marshal at the head of an army of regular horse and foot, including several regiments of local militia, Miguelets, marines, and Irish. The Royalists were posted in such a manner as to surround the Camisards, who, though they fought with their usual impetuosity, and succeeded in breaking through the ranks of their enemies, suffered a heavy loss in dead and wounded. Roland himself escaped with difficulty, and with his broken forces fled through Durfort to his stronghold at Mialet.

After the battle, Marshal Montrevel returned to Ganges, where he levied a fine of ten thousand livres on the Protestant population, giving up their houses to pillage, and hanging a dozen of those who had been the most prominent in abetting the Camisards during their recent visit. At the same time, he reported to headquarters at Paris that he had entirely destroyed the rebels, and that Languedoc was now "pacified."

Much to his surprise, however, not many weeks

elapsed before Cavalier, who had been laid up by the small-pox during Roland's expedition to Ganges, again appeared in the field, attacking convoys, entering the villages and carrying off arms, and spreading terror anew to the very gates of Nismes. He returned northwards by the valley of the Rhône, driving before him flocks and herds for the provisioning of his men, and reached his retreat at Bouquet in safety. Shortly after, he issued from it again, and descended upon Ners, where he destroyed a detachment of troops under Colonel de Jarnaud; next day he crossed the Gardon, and cut up a reinforcement intended for the garrison of Sommières; and the day after he was heard of in another place, attacking a convoy, and carrying off arms, ammunition, and provisions.

Montrevel was profoundly annoyed at the failure of his efforts thus far to suppress the insurrection. It even seemed to increase and extend with every new measure taken to crush it. A marshal of France, at the head of sixty thousand men, he feared lest he should lose credit with his friends at court unless he were able at once to root out these miserable cowherds and woolcarders who continued to bid defiance to the royal authority which he represented; and he determined to exert himself with renewed vigour to exterminate them root and branch.

In this state of irritation the intelligence was one day brought to the marshal while sitting over his wine after dinner at Nismes, that an assembly of Huguenots was engaged in worship in a mill situated on the canal outside the Port-des-Carmes. He at once ordered out a battalion of foot, marched on the mill, and surrounded it. The soldiers burst open the door, and found from two to three hundred women, children, and old men engaged in prayer; and proceeded to put them to the sword. But the marshal, impatient at the slowness of the butchery, ordered the men to desist and to fire the place. This order was obeyed, and the building, being for the most part of wood, was soon wrapped in flames, from amidst which rose the screams of women and children. All who tried to escape were bayoneted, or driven back into the burning mill. Every soul perished —all excepting a girl, who was rescued by one of Montrevel's servants. But the pitiless marshal ordered both the girl and her deliverer to be put to death. The former was hanged forthwith, but the lackey's life was spared at the intercession of some sisters of mercy accidentally passing the place.

In the same savage and relentless spirit, Montrevel proceeded to extirpate the Huguenots wherever found. He caused all suspected persons in twenty-two parishes in the diocese of Nismes to be seized and carried off. The men were transported to North America, and the women and children imprisoned in the fortresses of Roussillon.

But the most ruthless measures were those which were adopted in the Upper Cevennes: there nothing short of devastation would satisfy the marshal. Thirty-two parishes were completely laid waste; the cattle, grain, and produce which they contained were seized and carried into the towns of refuge garrisoned by the Royalists—Alais, Anduze, Florac, St. Hypolite, and Nismes—so that nothing should be left calculated to give sustenance to the rebels. Four hundred and sixty-six villages and hamlets were reduced to mere heaps of ashes and blackened ruins, and such of their inhabitants as were not slain by the soldiery fled with their families into the wilderness.

All the principal villages inhabited by the Protestants were thus completely destroyed, together with their mills and barns, and every building likely to give them shelter. Mialet was sacked and burnt—Roland, still suffering from his wounds, being unable to strike a blow in defence of his stronghold. St. Julien was also plundered and levelled, and its inhabitants carried captive to Montpellier, where the women and children were imprisoned, and the men sent to the galleys.

When Cavalier heard of the determination of Montrevel to make a desert of the country, he sent word to him that for every Huguenot village destroyed he would destroy two inhabited by the Romanists. Thus the sacking and burning on the one side was immediately followed by increased sacking and burning on the other. The war became one of mutual destruction and extermination, and the unfortunate inhabitants on both sides were delivered over to all the horrors of civil war.

So far, however, from the Camisards being suppressed, the destruction of the dwellings of the Huguenots only served to swell their numbers, and they descended from their mountains upon the Catholics of the plains in increasing force and redoubled fury. Montlezan was utterly destroyed — all but the church, which was strongly barricaded, and resisted Cavalier's attempts to enter it. Aurillac, also, was in like manner sacked and gutted, and the destroying torrent swept over all the towns and villages of the Cevennes.

Cavalier was so ubiquitous, so daring, and often so successful in his attacks, that of all the Camisard leaders he was held to be the most dangerous, and a high price was accordingly set upon his head by the governor. Hence many attempts were made to betray him. He was haunted by spies, some of whom even succeeded in obtaining admission to his ranks. More than once the spies were detected—it was pretended through prophetic influence—and immediately shot. But on one occasion Cavalier and his whole force narrowly escaped destruction through the betrayal of a pretended follower.

While the Royalists were carrying destruction through the villages of the Upper Cevennes, Cavalier, Salomon, and Abraham, in order to divert them from their purpose, resolved upon another descent into the low country, now comparatively ungarrisoned. With this object they gathered together some fifteen hundred men, and descended from the mountains by Collet, intending to cross the Gardon at Beaurivage. On Sunday, the 29th of April, they halted in the wood of Malaboissière, a little north of Mialet, for a day's preaching and worship; and after holding three services, which were largely attended, they directed their steps to the Tower of Belliot, a deserted farmhouse on the south of the present high road between Alais and Anduze.

The house had been built on the ruins of a feudal castle, and took its name from one of the old towers still standing. It was surrounded by a dry stone wall, forming a court, the entrance to which was closed by hurdles. On their arrival at this place late at night, the Camisards partook of the supper which had been prepared for them by their purveyor on the occasion —a miller of the neighbourhood, named Guignon— whose fidelity was assured not only by his apparent piety, but by the circumstance that two of his sons belonged to Cavalier's band.

No sooner, however, had the Camisards lain down to sleep than the miller, possessed by the demon of gold, set out directly for Alais, about three miles distant, and, reaching the quarters of Montrevel, sold the secret of Cavalier's sleeping-place to the marshal for fifty pieces of gold, and together with it the lives of his own sons and their fifteen hundred companions.

The marshal forthwith mustered all the available troops in Alais, consisting of eight regiments of foot (of which one was Irish) and two of dragoons, and set out at once for the Tower of Belliot, taking the precaution to set a strict guard upon all the gates, to prevent the possibility of any messenger leaving the place to warn Cavalier of his approach. The Royalists crept towards the tower in three bodies, so as to cut off their retreat in every direction. Meanwhile, the Camisards, unapprehensive of danger, lay wrapped in slumber, filling the tower, the barns, the stables, and outhouses.

The night was dark, and favoured the Royalists' approach. Suddenly, one of their divisions came upon the advanced Camisard sentinels. They fired, but were at once cut down. Those behind fled back to the sleeping camp, and raised the cry of alarm. Cavalier started up, calling his men "to arms," and, followed by about four hundred, he precipitated himself on the heads of the advancing columns. Driven back, they rallied again, more troops coming up to their support, and again they advanced to the attack.

To his dismay, Cavalier found the enemy in overwhelming force, enveloping his whole position. By great efforts he held them back until some four or five hundred more of his men had joined him, and then he gave way and retired behind a ravine or hollow, probably forming part of the fosse of the ancient château. Having there rallied his followers, he recrossed the ravine to make another desperate effort to relieve the remainder of his troop shut up in the tower.

A desperate encounter followed, in the midst of which two of the royalist columns, mistaking each other for enemies in the darkness, fired into each other and increased the confusion and the carnage. The moon rose on this dreadful scene, and revealed to the Royalists the smallness of the force opposed to them. The struggle was renewed again and again; Cavalier still seeking to relieve those shut up in the tower, and the Royalists, now concentrated and in force, to surround and destroy him.

At length, after the struggle had lasted for about five hours, Cavalier, in order to save the rest of his men, resolved on retiring before daybreak; and he succeeded in effecting his retreat without being pursued by the enemy.

The three hundred Camisards who continued shut up in the tower refused to surrender. They transformed the ruin into a fortress, barricading every entrance, and firing from every loophole. When their ammunition was expended, they hurled stones, joists, and tiles down upon their assailants from the summit of the tower. For four more hours they continued to hold out. Cannon were sent for from Alais, to blow in the doors; but before they arrived all was over. The place had been set on fire by hand grenades, and the imprisoned Camisards, singing psalms amidst the flames to their last breath, perished to a man.

This victory cost Montrevel dear. He lost some twelve hundred dead and wounded before the fatal Tower of Belliot; whilst Cavalier's loss was not less than four hundred dead, of whom a hundred and eighteen were found at daybreak along the brink of the ravine. One of these was mistaken for the body of Cavalier; on which Montrevel, with characteristic barbarity, ordered the head to be cut off and sent to *Cavalier's mother* for identification!

From the slight glimpses we obtain of the *man* Montrevel in the course of these deplorable transactions, there seems to have been something ineffably mean and spiteful in his nature. Thus, on another occasion, in a fit of rage at having been baffled by the young Camisard leader, he dispatched a squadron of dragoons to Ribaute for the express purpose of pulling down the house in which Cavalier had been born!

A befitting sequel to this sanguinary struggle at the Tower of Belliot was the fate of Guignon, the miller, who had betrayed the sleeping Camisards to Montrevel. His crime was discovered. The gold was found upon him. He was tried, and condemned to death. The Camisards, under arms, assembled to see the sentence carried out. They knelt round the doomed man, while the prophets by turn prayed for his soul, and implored the clemency of the Sovereign Judge. Guignon professed the utmost contrition, besought the pardon of his brethren, and sought leave to embrace for the last time his two sons—privates in the Camisard ranks. The two young men, however, refused the proffered embrace with a gesture of apparent disgust; and they looked on, the sad and stern spectators of the traitor's punishment.

Again Montrevel thought he had succeeded in crushing the insurrection, and that he had cut off its head with that of the Camisard chief. But his supposed discovery of the dead body proved an entire mistake; and not many days elapsed before Cavalier made his appearance before the gates of Alais, and sent in a challenge to the governor to come out and fight him. And it is to be observed that by this time a fiercely combative spirit, of fighting for fighting's sake, began to show itself among the Camisards. Thus, Castanet appeared one day before the gates of Meyreuis, where the regiment of Cordes was stationed, and challenged the colonel to come out and fight him in the open; but the challenge was declined. On another occasion, Cavalier in like manner challenged the commander of Vic to bring out thirty of his soldiers and fight thirty Camisards. The challenge was accepted, and the battle took place; they fought until ten men only remained alive on either side, but the Camisards were masters of the field.

Montrevel only redoubled his efforts to exterminate the Camisards. He had no other policy. In the summer of 1703 the Pope (Clement XI.) came to his assistance, issuing a bull against the rebels as being of "the execrable race of the ancient Albigenses," and promising "absolute and general remission of sins" to all such as should join the holy militia of Louis XIV. in "exterminating the cursed heretics and miscreants, enemies alike of God and of Cæsar."

A special force was embodied with this object—the Florentines, or "White Camisards"—distinguished by the white cross which they wore in front of their hats. They were for the most part composed of desperadoes and miscreants, and went about pillaging and burning, with so little discrimination between friend and foe, that the Catholics themselves implored the marshal to suppress them. These Florentines were the perpetrators of such barbarities that Roland determined to raise a body of cavalry to hunt them down; and with that object, Catinat, the old dragoon, went down to the

Camargues—a sort of island-prairies lying between the mouths of the Rhône—where the Arabs had left a hardy breed of horses; and there he purchased some two hundred steeds wherewith to mount the Camisard horse, to the command of which Catinat was himself appointed.

It is unnecessary to particularise the variety of combats, of marchings and countermarchings, which occurred during the progress of the insurrection. Between the contending parties, the country was reduced to a desert. Tillage ceased, for there was no certainty of the cultivator reaping the crop; more likely it would be carried off or burnt by the conflicting armies. Beggars and vagabonds wandered about robbing and plundering without regard to party or religion; and social security was entirely at an end.

Meanwhile, Montrevel still called for more troops. Of the twenty battalions already entrusted to him, more than one-third had perished; and still the insurrection was not suppressed. He hoped, however, that the work was now accomplished; and, looking to the wasted condition of the country, that the famine and cold of the winter of 1703-4 would complete the destruction of such of the rebels as still survived.

During the winter, however, the Camisard chiefs had not only been able to keep their forces together, but to lay up a considerable store of provisions and ammunition, principally by captures from the enemy; and in the following spring they were in a position to take the field in even greater force than ever. They, indeed, opened the campaign by gaining two important victories over the Royalists; but though they were their greatest, they were also nearly their last.

The battle of Martinargues was the Cannæ of the Camisards. It was fought near the village of that name, not far from Ners, early in the spring of 1704. The campaign had been opened by the Florentines, who, now that they had made a desert of the Upper Cevennes, were burning and ravaging the Protestant villages of the plain. Cavalier had put himself on their track, and pursued and punished them so severely, that in their distress they called upon Montrevel to help them, informing him of the whereabouts of the Camisards.

A strong royalist force of horse and foot was immediately sent in pursuit, under the command of Brigadier Lajonquière. He first marched upon the Protestant village of Lascours, where Cavalier had passed the previous night. The brigadier severely punished the inhabitants for sheltering the Camisards, putting to death four persons, two of them girls, whom he suspected to be Cavalier's prophetesses. On the people refusing to indicate the direction in which the Camisards had gone, he gave the village up to plunder, and the soldiers passed several hours ransacking the place, in the course of which they broke open and pillaged the wine-cellars.

Meanwhile, Cavalier and his men had proceeded in a northerly direction, along the right bank of the little river Droude, one of the affluents of the Gardon. A messenger from Lascours overtook him, telling him of the outrages committed on the inhabitants of the village; and shortly after, the inhabitants of Lascours themselves came up—men, women, and children, who had been driven from their pillaged homes by the royalist soldiery. Cavalier was enraged at the recital of their woes; and though his force was not one-sixth the strength of the enemy, he determined to meet their advance and give them battle.

Placing the poor people of Lascours in safety, the Camisard leader took up his position on a rising ground at the head of a little valley close to the village of Martinargues. Cavalier himself occupied the centre, his front being covered by a brook running in the hollow of a ravine. Ravanel and Catinat, with a small body of men, were posted along the two sides of the valley, screened by brushwood. The approaching Royalists, seeing before them only the feeble force of Cavalier, looked upon his capture as certain.

"See!" cried Lajonquière, "at last we have hold of the Barbets we have been so long looking for!" With his dragoons in the centre, flanked by the grenadiers and foot, the Royalists advanced with confidence to the charge. At the first volley, the Camisards prostrated themselves, and the bullets went over their heads. Thinking they had fallen before his fusillade, the commander ordered his men to cross the ravine and fall upon the remnant with the bayonet. Instantly, however, Cavalier's men started to their feet, and smote the assailants with a deadly volley, bringing down men and horses. At the same moment, the two wings, until then concealed, fired down upon the Royalists and completed their confusion. The Camisards, then raising their battle-psalm, rushed forward and charged the enemy. The grenadiers resisted stoutly, but after a few minutes the entire body—dragoons, grenadiers, marines, and Irish—fled down the valley towards the Gardon, and the greater number of those who were not killed were drowned, Lajonquière himself escaping with difficulty.

In this battle perished a colonel, a major, thirty-three captains and lieutenants, and four hundred and fifty men, while Cavalier's loss was only about twenty killed and wounded. A great booty was picked up on the field, of gold, silver, jewels, ornamented swords, magnificent uniforms, scarfs, and clothing, besides horses, as well as the plunder brought from Lascours.

The opening of the Lascours wine-cellars proved the ruin of the Royalists, for many of the men were so drunk that they were unable either to fight or fly. After returning thanks to God on the battle-field, Cavalier conducted the rejoicing people of Lascours back to their village, and proceeded to his head-quarters at Bouquet with his booty and his trophies.

Another encounter shortly followed at the Bridge of Salindres, about midway between Auduze and St. Jean du Gard, in which Roland inflicted an equally decisive defeat on a force commanded by Brigadier Lalande. Informed of the approach of the Royalists, Roland posted his little army in the narrow, precipitous, and rocky valley, along the bottom of which runs the river Gardon. Dividing his men into three bodies, he posted one on the bridge, another in ambuscade at the entrance to the defile, and a third on the summit of the precipice overhanging the road.

The Royalists had scarcely advanced to the attack of the bridge, when the concealed Camisards rushed out and assailed their rear, while those stationed above hurled down rocks and stones, which threw them into complete disorder. They at once broke and fled, rushing down to the river, into which they threw themselves; and but for Roland's neglect in guarding the steep footpath leading to the ford at the mill, the whole body would have been destroyed. As it was, they suffered heavy loss, the general himself escaping with difficulty, leaving his white-plumed hat behind him in the hands of the Camisards.

CHAPTER VIII.

END OF THE CAMISARD INSURRECTION.

THE insurrection in the Cevennes had continued for more than two years, when at length it began to excite serious uneasiness at Versailles. It was felt to be a source of weakness as well as danger to France, then at war with Portugal, England, and Savoy. What increased the alarm of the French Government was the fact that the insurgents were anxiously looking abroad for help, and endeavouring to excite the Protestant governments of the North to strike a blow in their behalf.

England and Holland had been especially appealed to. Large numbers of Huguenot soldiers were then serving in the English army; and it was suggested that if they could effect a landing on the coast of Languedoc, and co-operate with the Camisards, it would at the same time help the cause of religious liberty, and operate as a powerful diversion in favour of the confederate armies, then engaged with the armies of France in the Low Countries and on the Rhine.

In order to ascertain the feasibility of the proposed landing, and the condition of the Camisard insurgents, the ministry of Queen Anne sent the Marquis de Miremont, a Huguenot refugee in England, on a mission to the Cevennes; and he succeeded in reaching the insurgent camp at St. Felix, where he met Roland and the other leaders, and arranged with them for the descent of a body of Huguenot soldiers on the coast.

In the month of September, 1703, the English fleet was descried in the Gulf of Lyons, off Aiguesmortes, making signals, which, however, were not answered. Marshal Montrevel had been warned of the intended invasion; and, summoning troops from all quarters, he so effectually guarded the coast, that a landing was found impracticable. Though Cavalier was near at hand, he was unable at any point to communicate with the English ships; and after lying off for a few days, they spread their sails, and the disheartened Camisards saw their intended liberators disappear in the distance.

The ministers of Louis XIV. were greatly alarmed by this event. The invasion had been frustrated for the time, but the English fleet might return, and eventually succeed in effecting a landing. The danger, therefore, had to be provided against, and at once. It became clear, even to Louis XIV. himself, that the system of terror and coercion which had heretofore been exclusively employed against the insurgents, had proved a total failure. It was accordingly determined to employ some other means, if possible, of bringing this dangerous insurrection to an end. In pursuance of this object, Montrevel, to his intense mortification, was recalled, and the celebrated Marshal Villars, the victor of Hochstadt and Friedlingen, was appointed in his stead, with full powers to undertake and carry out the pacification of Languedoc.

Villars reached Nismes towards the end of August, 1704; but before his arrival, Montrevel at last succeeded in settling accounts with Cavalier, and wiped out many old scores by inflicting upon him the severest defeat the Camisard arms had yet received. It was his first victory over Cavalier, and his last.

Cavalier's recent successes had made him careless. Having so often overcome the royal troops against great odds, he began to think himself invincible, and to despise his enemy. His success at Martinargues had the effect of greatly increasing his troops; and he made a descent upon the low country in the spring of 1704, at the head of about a thousand foot and two hundred horse.

Appearing before Bouciran, which he entered without resistance, he demolished the fortifications, and proceeded southwards to St. Géniès, which he attacked and took, carrying away horses, mules, and arms. Next day he marched still southward to Caveirac, only about three miles east of Nismes.

Montrevel designedly published his intention of taking leave of his government on a certain day, and proceeding to Montpellier with only a very slender force—pretending to send the remainder to Beaucaire, in the opposite direction, for the purpose of escorting Villars, his successor, into the city. His object in doing this was to deceive the Camisard leader, and to draw him into a trap.

The intelligence became known to Cavalier, who now watched the Montpellier road, for the purpose of inflicting a parting blow upon his often-baffled enemy. Instead, however, of Montrevel setting out for Monpellier with a small force, he mustered almost the entire troops belonging to the garrison of Nismes—over six thousand horse and foot—and determined to overwhelm Cavalier, who lay in his way. Montrevel divided his force into several bodies, and so disposed them as completely to surround the comparatively small Camisard force, near Langlade. The first encounter was with the royalist regiment of Firmarcon, which Cavalier completely routed; but while pursuing them too keenly, the Camisards were assailed in flank by a strong body of foot posted in vineyards along the road, and driven back upon the main body. The Camisards now discovered that a still stronger battalion was stationed in their rear; and, indeed, wherever they turned, they saw the Royalists posted in force. There was no alternative but cutting their way through the enemy; and Cavalier, putting himself at the head of his men, led the way, sword in hand.

A terrible struggle ensued, and the Camisards at last reached the bridge at Rosni; but there, too, the Royalists were found blocking the road, and crowding the heights on either side. Cavalier, to avoid recognition, threw off his uniform, and assumed the guise of a simple Camisard. Again he sought to force his way through the masses of the enemy. His advance was a series of hand-to-hand fights, extending over some six miles, and the struggle lasted for nearly the entire day. More than a thousand dead strewed the roads, of whom one half were Camisards. The Royalists took five drums, sixty-two horses, and four mules laden with provisions, but not one prisoner.

When Villars reached Nismes and heard of this battle, he went to see the field, and expressed his admiration at the skill and valour of the Camisard chief. "Here is a man," said he, "of no education, without any experience in the art of war, who has conducted himself under the most difficult and delicate circumstances as if he had been a great general. Truly, to fight such a battle were worthy of Cæsar!"

Indeed, the conduct of Cavalier in this struggle so impressed Marshal Villars, that he determined, if possible, to gain him over, together with his brave followers, to the ranks of the royal army. Villars was no bigot, but a humane and honourable man, and a thorough soldier. He deplored the continuance of this atrocious war, and proceeded to take immediate steps to bring it, if possible, to a satisfactory conclusion.

In the meantime, however, the defeat of the Camisards had been followed by other reverses. During the absence of Cavalier in the South, the royalist general Lalande, at the head of five thousand troops, fell upon the joint forces of Roland and Joany at Brenoux, and completely defeated them. The same general lay in wait for the return of Cavalier with his broken forces, to his retreat near Euzet; and on his coming up, the Royalists, in overpowering numbers, fell upon the dispirited Camisards, and inflicted upon them another heavy loss.

But a greater calamity, if possible, was the discovery and capture of Cavalier's magazines in the caverns near Euzet. The royalist soldiers, having observed an old woman frequently leaving the village for the adjoining wood with a full basket and returning with an empty one, suspected her of succouring the rebels, arrested her, and took her before the general. When questioned at first she would confess nothing; on which she was ordered forthwith to be hanged. When taken to the gibbet in the market-place, however, the old woman's resolution gave way, and she entreated to be taken back to the general, when she would confess everything. She then acknowledged that she had the care of an hospital in the adjoining wood, and that her daily errands had been thither. She was promised pardon if she led the soldiers at once to the place; and she did so, a battalion following at her heels.

Advancing into the wood, the old woman led the soldiers to the mouth of a cavern, into which she pointed, and the men entered. The first sight that met their eyes was a number of sick and wounded Camisards lying upon couches along ledges cut in the rock. They were immediately put to death. Entering further into the cavern, the soldiers were surprised to find in an inner vault an immense magazine of grain, flour, chestnuts, beans, barrels of wine and brandy; farther in, stores of drugs, ointment, dressings, and hospital furnishings; and finally, an arsenal containing a large store of sabres, muskets, pistols, and gunpowder, together with the materials for making it; all of which the Royalists seized and carried off.

Lalande, before leaving Euzet, inflicted upon it a terrible punishment. He gave it up to pillage, then burnt it to the ground, and put the inhabitants to the sword—all but the old woman, who was left alone amidst the corpses and ashes of the ruined village. Lalande returned in triumph to Alais, some of his soldiers displaying on the points of their bayonets the ears of the slain Camisards.

Other reverses followed in quick succession. Salomon was attacked near Pont-de-Montvert, the birthplace of the insurrection, and lost some eight hundred of his men. His magazines at Magistavols were also discovered and ransacked, containing, amongst other stores, twenty oxen and a hundred sheep.

Thus, in four combats, the Camisards lost nearly half their forces, together with a large part of their arms, ammunition, and provisions. The country occupied by them had been ravaged and reduced to a state of desert, and there seemed but little prospect of their again being able to make head against their enemies.

The loss of life during the last year of the insurrection had been frightful. Some twenty thousand men had perished—eight thousand soldiers, four thousand of the Roman Catholic population, and from seven to eight thousand Protestants.

Villars had no sooner entered upon the functions of his office than he set himself to remedy this dreadful state of things. He was encouraged in his wise intentions by the Baron d'Aigalliers, a Protestant nobleman of high standing and great influence, who had emigrated into England at the Revocation, but had since returned. This nobleman entertained the ardent desire of reconciling the King with his Protestant subjects; and he was encouraged by the French Court to endeavour to bring the rebels of the Cevennes to terms.

One of the first things Villars did, was to proceed on a journey through the devastated districts; and he could not fail to be horrified at the sight of the villages in ruins, the wasted vineyards, the untilled fields, and the deserted homesteads which met his eyes on every side. Wherever he went, he gave it out that he was ready to pardon all persons—rebels as well as their chiefs—who should lay down their arms and submit to the royal clemency; but that, if they continued obstinate and refused to submit, he would proceed against them to the last extremity. He even offered to put arms in the hands of such of the Protestant population as would co-operate with him in suppressing the insurrection.

In the meantime, the defeated Camisards under Roland were reorganizing their forces, and preparing again to take the field. They were unwilling to submit themselves to the professed clemency of Villars, without some sufficient guarantee that their religious rights— in defence of which they had taken up arms—would be respected. Roland was already establishing new magazines in place of those which had been destroyed; he was again recruiting his brigades from the Protestant communes, and many of those who had recovered from their wounds again rallied under his standard.

At this juncture, D'Aigalliers suggested to Villars that a negotiation should be opened directly with the Camisard chiefs to induce them to lay down their arms. Roland refused to listen to any overtures; but Cavalier was more accessible, and expressed himself willing to negotiate for peace provided his religion was respected and recognised.

And Cavalier was right. He saw clearly that longer resistance was futile, that it could only end in increased devastation and destruction; and he was wise in endeavouring to secure the best possible terms under the circumstances for his suffering co-religionists. Roland, who refused all such overtures, was the more uncompromising and tenacious of purpose; but Cavalier, notwithstanding his extreme youth, was by far the more practical and politic of the two.

There is no doubt also that Cavalier had begun to weary of the struggle. He became depressed and sad, and even after a victory he would kneel down amidst the dead and wounded, and pray to God that He would turn the heart of the King to mercy, and help to reestablish the ancient temples throughout the land.

An interview with Cavalier was eventually arranged by Lalande. The brigadier invited him to a conference, guaranteeing him safe conduct, and intimating that if he refused the meeting, he would be regarded as the enemy of peace, and held responsible before God and man for all future bloodshed. Cavalier replied to Lalande's invitation, accepting the interview, indicating the place and the time of meeting.

Catinat, the Camisard general of horse, was the bearer of Cavalier's letter, and he rode on to Alais to deliver it, arrayed in magnificent costume. Lalande was at table when Catinat was shown in to him. Observing the strange uniform and fierce look of the intruder, the brigadier asked who he was. "Catinat!" was the reply. "What," cried Lalande, "are you the Catinat who killed so many people in Beaucaire?" "Yes, it is I," said Catinat, "and I only endeavoured to do my duty." "You are hardy, indeed, to dare to show yourself before me." "I have come," said the Camisard, "in good faith, persuaded that you are an honest man, and on the assurance of my brother Cavalier that you would do me no harm. I come to deliver you his letter." And so saying, he handed it to the brigadier. Hastily perusing the letter, Lalande said, "Go back to Cavalier, and tell him that in two hours I shall be at the Bridge of Avène with only ten officers and thirty dragoons."

The interview took place at the time appointed, on the bridge over the Avène, a few miles south of Alais. Cavalier arrived, attended by three hundred foot and sixty Camisard dragoons. When the two chiefs recognised each other, they halted their escorts, dismounted, and, followed by some officers, proceeded on foot to meet each other.

Lalande had brought with him Cavalier's younger brother, who had been for some time a prisoner, and presented him, saying, "The King gives him to you in token of his merciful intentions." The brothers, who had not met since their mother's death, embraced and wept. Cavalier thanked the general; and then, leaving their officers, the two went on one side, and conferred together alone.

"The King," said Lalande, "wishes, in the exercise of his clemency, to terminate this war amongst his subjects; what are your terms and your demands?" "They consist of three things," replied Cavalier: "liberty of worship; the deliverance of our brethren who are in prison and at the galleys; and, if the first condition be refused, then free permission to leave France." "How many persons would wish to leave the kingdom?" asked Lalande. "Ten thousand of various ages and both sexes." "Ten thousand! It is impossible! Leave might possibly be granted for two, but certainly not for ten." "Then," said Cavalier, "if the King will not allow us to leave the kingdom, he will at least re-establish our ancient edicts and privileges?"

Lalande promised to report the result of the conference to the marshal, though he expressed a doubt whether he could agree to the terms proposed. The brigadier took leave of Cavalier by expressing the desire to be of service to him at any time; but he made a gross and indelicate mistake in offering his purse to the Camisard chief. "No, no!" said Cavalier, rejecting it with a look of contempt, "I wish for none of your gold, but only for religious liberty, or, if that be refused, for a safe conduct out of the kingdom."

Lalande then asked to be taken up to the Camisard troop, who had been watching the proceedings of their leader with great interest. Coming up to them in the ranks, he said, "Here is a purse of a hundred louis with which to drink the King's health." Their reply was like their leader's, "We want no money, but liberty of conscience." "It is not in my power to grant you that," said the general, "but you will do well to submit to the King's will." "We are ready," said they, "to obey his orders, provided he grants our just demands; but if not, we are prepared to die arms in hand." And thus ended this memorable interview, which lasted for about two hours; Lalande and his followers returning to Alais, while Cavalier went with his troop in the direction of Vezenobres.

Cavalier's enemies say that in the course of his interview with Lalande he was offered honours, rewards, and promotion, if he would enter the King's service; and it is added that Cavalier was tempted by these offers, and thereby proved false to his cause and followers. But it is more probable that Cavalier was sincere in his desire to come to fair terms with the King, observing the impossibility, under the circumstances, of prolonging the struggle against the royal armies with any reasonable prospect of success. If Cavalier were really bribed by any such promises of promotion, at all events such promises were never fulfilled; nor did the French monarch reward him in any way for his endeavours to bring the Camisard insurrection to an end.

It was characteristic of Roland to hold aloof from these negotiations, and refuse to come to any terms whatever with "Baal." As if to separate himself entirely from Cavalier, he withdrew into the Upper Cevennes to resume the war. At the very time that Cavalier was holding the conference with the royalist general at the Bridge of the Avène, Roland and Joany, with a body of horse and foot, waylaid the Count de Tournou at the plateau of Font-morte—the place where Seguier, the first Camisard leader, had been

END OF THE CAMISARD INSURRECTION. 177

defeated and captured—and suddenly fell upon the Royalists, putting them to flight.

A rich booty fell into the hands of the Camisards, part of which consisted of the quarter's rental of the confiscated estate of Salgas, in the possession of the King's collector, Viala, whom the royalist troops were escorting to St. Jean de Gard. The collector, who had made himself notorious for his cruelty, was put to death after frightful torment, and his son and nephew were also shot. So far, therefore, as Roland and his associates were concerned, there appeared to be no intention of surrender or compromise; and Villars was under the necessity of prosecuting the war against them to the last extremity.

In the meantime, Cavalier was hailed throughout the low country as the pacificator of Languedoc. The people on both sides had become heartily sick of the war, and were glad to be rid of it on any terms that promised peace and security for the future. At the invitation of Marshal Villars, Cavalier proceeded towards Nismes, and his march from town to town was one continuous ovation. He was eagerly welcomed by the population; and his men were hospitably entertained by the garrisons of the places through which they passed. Every liberty was allowed him; and not a day passed without a religious meeting being held, accompanied with public preaching, praying, and psalm-singing. At length Cavalier and his little army approached the neighbourhood of Nismes, where his arrival was anticipated with extraordinary interest.

The beautiful old city had witnessed many strange sights; but probably the entry of the young Camisard chief was one of the most remarkable of all. This herd-boy and baker's apprentice of the Cevennes, after holding at bay the armies of France for nearly three years, had come to negotiate a treaty of peace with its most famous general. Leaving the greater part of his cavalry and the whole of his infantry at St. Césaire, a few miles from Nismes, Cavalier rode towards the town attended by eighteen horsemen commanded by Catinat. On approaching the southern gate, he found an immense multitude waiting his arrival. "He could not have been more royally welcomed," said the priest of St. Germain, "had he been a king."

Cavalier rode at the head of his troop gaily attired; for fine dress was one of the weaknesses of the Camisard chiefs. He wore a tight-fitting doeskin coat ornamented with gold lace, scarlet breeches, a muslin cravat, and a large beaver with a white plume; his long fair hair hanging over his shoulders. Catinat rode by his side on a high-mettled charger, attracting all eyes by his fine figure, his martial air, and his magnificent costume. Cavalier's faithful friend, Daniel Billard, rode on his left; and behind followed his little brother in military uniform, between the Baron d'Aigalliers and Lacombe, the agents for peace.

The cavalcade advanced through the dense crowd, which could with difficulty be kept back, past the Roman Amphitheatre, and along the Rue St. Antoine, to the Garden of the Récollets, a Franciscan convent, nearly opposite the elegant Roman temple known as the Maison Carée.* Alighting from his horse at the gate, and stationing his guard there under the charge of Catinat, Cavalier entered the garden, and was conducted to Marshal Villars, with whom was Baville, intendant of the province; Baron Sandricourt, governor

* The Nismes Theatre now occupies part of the Jardin des Récollets.

END OF THE CAMISARD INSURRECTION.

of Nismes; General Lalande, and other dignitaries. Cavalier looked such a mere boy, that Villars at first could scarcely believe that it was the celebrated Camisard chief who stood before him. The marshal, however, advanced several steps, and addressed some complimentary words to Cavalier, to which he respectfully replied.

The conference then began and proceeded, though not without frequent interruptions from Baville, who had so long regarded Cavalier as a despicable rebel, that he could scarcely brook the idea of the King's marshal treating with him on anything like equal terms. But the marshal checked the intendant by reminding him that he had no authority to interfere in a matter which the King had solely entrusted to himself. Then turning to Cavalier, he asked him to state his conditions for a treaty of peace.

Cavalier has set forth in his memoirs the details of the conditions proposed by him, and which he alleges were afterwards duly agreed to and signed by Villars and Baville, on the 17th of May, 1704, on the part of the King. The first condition was liberty of conscience, with the privilege of holding religious assemblies in country places. This was agreed to, subject to the Protestant temples not being rebuilt. The second—that all Protestants in prison or at the galleys should be set at liberty within six weeks from the date of the treaty—was also agreed to. The third—that all who had left the kingdom on account of their religion should have liberty to return, and be restored to their estates and privileges—was agreed to, subject to their taking the oath of allegiance. The fourth—as to the re-establishment of the parliament of Languedoc on its ancient footing—was promised consideration. The fifth and sixth—that the province should be free from capitation tax for ten years, and that the Protestants should hold Montpellier, Cette, Perpignan, and Aiguemortes, as cautionary towns—were refused. The seventh—that those inhabitants of the Cevennes whose houses had been burnt during the civil war should pay no imposts for seven years—was granted. And the eighth—that Cavalier should raise a regiment of dragoons to serve the King in Portugal—was also granted.

These conditions are said to have been agreed to on the distinct understanding that the insurrection should forthwith cease, and that all persons in arms against the King should lay them down and submit themselves to his majesty's clemency.

The terms having been generally agreed to, Cavalier respectfully took his leave of the marshal, and returned to his comrades at the gate. But Catinat and the Camisard guard had disappeared. The conference had lasted two hours, during which Cavalier's general of horse had become tired of waiting, and gone with his companions to refresh himself at the sign of the Golden Cup. On his way thither, he witched the world of Nismes with his noble horsemanship, making his charger bound and prance and curvet, greatly to the delight of the immense crowd that followed him.

On the return of the Camisard guard to the Récollets, Cavalier mounted his horse, and, escorted by them, proceeded to the Hôtel de la Poste, where he rested. In the evening, he came out on the Esplanade, and walked freely amidst the crowd, amongst whom were many ladies, eager to see the Camisard hero, and happy if they could but hear him speak, or touch his dress. He then went to visit the mother of Daniel, his favourite prophet, a native of Nismes, whose father and brother were both prisoners because of their religion. Returning to the hotel, Cavalier mustered his guard, and set out for Calvisson, followed by hundreds of people, singing together as they passed through the town gate the 133rd Psalm—"Behold, how good and how pleasant it is for brethren to dwell together in unity!"

Cavalier remained with his companions at Calvisson for eight days, during which he enjoyed the most perfect freedom of action. He held public religious services daily, at first amidst the ruins of the demolished Protestant temple, and afterwards, when the space was insufficient, in the open plain outside the town walls. People came from all quarters to attend them—from the Vaunage, from Sommières, from Lunel, from Nismes, and even from Montpellier. As many as forty thousand persons are said to have resorted to the services during Cavalier's sojourn at Calvisson. The plains resounded with preaching and psalmody from morning until evening, sometimes until late at night, by torchlight.

These meetings were a great cause of offence to the more bigoted of the Roman Catholics, who saw in them the triumph of their enemies. They muttered audibly against the policy of Villars, who was tolerating if not encouraging heretics—worthy, in their estimation, only of perdition. Fléchier, Bishop of Nismes, was full of lamentations on the subject, and did not scruple to proclaim that war, with all its horrors, was even more tolerable than such a peace as this.

Unhappily, the peace proved only of short duration, and Cavalier's anticipations of unity and brotherly love were not destined to be fulfilled. Whether Roland was jealous of the popularity achieved by Cavalier, or suspected treachery on the part of the Royalists, or whether he still believed in the ability of his followers to conquer religious liberty and compel the re-establishment of the ancient edicts by the sword, does not clearly appear. At all events, he refused to be committed in any way by what Cavalier had done; and when the treaty entered into with Villars was submitted to Roland for approval, he refused to sign it. A quarrel had almost occurred between the chiefs, and hot words passed between them. But Cavalier controlled himself, and still hoped to persuade Roland to adopt a practicable course, and bring the unhappy war to a conclusion.

It was at length agreed between them that a further effort should be made to induce Villars to grant more liberal terms, particularly with respect to the rebuilding of the Protestant temples; and Cavalier consented that Salomon should accompany him to an interview with the marshal, and endeavour to obtain such a modification of the treaty as should meet Roland's views. Accordingly, another meeting shortly after took place in the Garden of the Récollets at Nismes, Cavalier leaving it to Salomon to be the spokesman on the occasion.

But Salomon proved as uncompromising as his chief. He stated his *ultimatum* bluntly and firmly—re-establishment of the Edict of Nantes, and complete liberty of conscience. On no other terms, he said, would the Camisards lay down their arms. Villars was courtly and polite as usual, but he was as firm as Salomon. He would adhere to the terms that had been agreed to, but could not comply with the conditions proposed. The discussion lasted for two hours, and at length became stormy and threatening on the part of Salomon, on which the marshal turned on his heel and left the apartment.

Cavalier's followers had not yet been informed of the conditions of the treaty into which he had entered with Villars, but they had been led to believe that the Edict was to be re-established and liberty of worship restored. Their suspicions had already been roused by the hints thrown out by Ravanel, who was as obdurate as Roland in his refusal to lay down his arms until the Edict had been re-established.

While Cavalier was still at Nismes, on his second mission to Villars, accompanied by Salomon, Ravanel, who had been left in charge of the troop at Calvisson, assembled the men, and told them he feared they were being betrayed—that they were to be refused the free exercise of their religion in temples of their own, but were to be required to embark as King's soldiers on shipboard, perhaps to perish at sea. "Brethren," said he, "let us cling by our own native land, and live and die for the Eternal." The men enthusiastically applauded the stern resolve of Ravanel, and awaited with increasing impatience the return of the negotiating chief.

On Cavalier's return to his men, he found, to his dismay, that instead of being welcomed back with the usual cordiality, they were drawn up in arms under Ravanel, and received him in silence, with angry and scowling looks. He upbraided Ravanel for such a reception, on which the storm immediately burst. "What is the treaty, then," cried Ravanel, "that thou hast made with this marshal?"

Cavalier, embarrassed, evaded the inquiry; but Ravanel, encouraged by his men, proceeded to press for the information. "Well," said Cavalier, "it is arranged that we shall go to serve in Portugal." There was at once a violent outburst from the ranks. "Traitor! coward! then thou hast sold us! But we shall have no peace—no peace without our temples."

At sound of the loud commotion and shouting, Vincel, the King's commissioner, who remained at Calvisson pending the negotiations, came running up, and the men in their rage would have torn him to pieces, but Cavalier threw himself in their way, exclaiming, "Back, men! Do him no harm, kill me instead." His voice, his gesture, arrested the Camisards, and Vincel turned and fled for his life.

Ravanel then ordered the *générale* to be beaten. The men drew up in their ranks, and putting himself at their head, Ravanel marched them out of Calvisson by the northern gate. Cavalier, humiliated and downcast, followed the troop—their leader no more. He could not part with them thus—the men he had so often led to victory, and who had followed him so devotedly—but hung upon their rear, hoping they would yet relent and return to him as their chief.

Catinat, his general of horse, observing Cavalier following the men, turned upon him. "Whither wouldst thou go, traitor?" cried Catinat. What! Catinat, of all others, to prove unfaithful? Yet it was so! Catinat even presented his pistol at his former chief, but he did not fire.

Cavalier would not yet turn back. He hung upon the skirts of the column, entreating, supplicating, adjuring the men, by all their former love for him, to turn and follow him. But they sternly marched on, scarcely even deigning to answer him. Ravanel endeavoured to drive him back by reproaches, which at length so irritated Cavalier, that he drew his sword, and they were about to rush at each other, when one of the prophets ran between them and prevented bloodshed.

Cavalier did not desist from following them for several miles, until at length, on reaching St. Estève, the men were appealed to as to whom they would follow, and they declared themselves for Ravanel. Cavalier made a last appeal to their allegiance, and called out, "Let those who love me, follow me!" About forty of his old adherents detatched themselves from the ranks, and followed Cavalier in the direction of Nismes. But the principal body remained with Ravanel, who, waving his sabre in the air, and shouting, "Vive l'Epée de l'Eternel!" turned his men's faces northward and marched on to rejoin Roland in the Upper Cevennes.

Cavalier was completely prostrated by the desertion of his followers. He did not know where next to turn. He could not rejoin the Camisard camp nor enter the villages of the Cevennes, and he was ashamed to approach Villars, lest he should be charged with deceiving him. But he sent a letter to the marshal, informing him of the failure of his negotiations, the continued revolt of the Camisards, and their rejection of him as their chief. Villars, however, was gentle and generous; he was persuaded that Cavalier had acted loyally and in good faith throughout, and he sent a message by the Baron d'Aigalliers, urgently inviting him to return to Nismes and arrange as to the future. Cavalier accordingly set out forthwith, accompanied by his brother and the prophet Daniel, and escorted by the ten horsemen and thirty foot who still remained faithful to his person.

It is not necessary further to pursue the history of

Cavalier. Suffice it to say that, at the request of Marshal Villars, he proceeded to Paris, where he had an unsatisfactory interview with Louis XIV.; that fearing an intention on the part of the Roman Catholic party to make him a prisoner, he fled across the frontier into Switzerland; that he eventually reached England, and entered the English army, with the rank of Colonel; that he raised a regiment of refugee Frenchmen, consisting principally of his Camisard followers, at the head of whom he fought most valiantly at the battle of Almanza; that he was afterwards appointed governor of Jersey, and died a major-general in the British service in the year 1740, greatly respected by all who knew him.

Although Cavalier failed in carrying the treaty into effect, so far as he was concerned, his secession at this juncture proved a deathblow to the insurrection. The remaining Camisard leaders endeavoured in vain to incite that enthusiasm amongst their followers which had so often before led them to victory. The men felt that they were fighting without hope, and as it were with halters round their necks. Many of them began to think that Cavalier had been justified in seeking to secure the best terms practicable; and they dropped off, by tens and fifties, to join their former leader, whose head-quarters for some time continued to be at Vallabergue, an island in the Rhone a little above Beaucaire.

The insurgents were also in a great measure disarmed by Marshal Villars, who continued to pursue a policy of clemency, and at the same time of severity. He offered a free pardon to all who surrendered themselves, but threatened death to all who continued to resist the royal troops. In sign of his clemency, he ordered the gibbets which had for some years stood *en permanence* in all the villages of the Cevennes, to be removed; and he went from town to town, urging all well-disposed people, of both religions, to co-operate with him in putting an end to the dreadful civil war that had so long desolated the province.

Moved by the marshal's eloquent appeals, the principal towns along the Gardon and the Vidourle appointed deputies to proceed in a body to the camp of Roland, and induce him if possible to accept the profferred amnesty. They waited upon him accordingly at his camp of St. Felix and told him their errand. But his answer was to order them at once to leave the place on pain of death.

Villars himself sent messengers to Roland—amongst others the Baron d'Aigalliers—offering to guarantee that no one should be molested on account of his religion, provided he and his men would lay down their arms; but Roland remained inflexible—nothing short of complete religious liberty would induce him to surrender.

Roland and Joany were still at the head of about a thousand men in the Upper Cevennes. Pont-de-Montvert was at the time occupied by a body of Miguelets, whom they determined if possible to destroy. Dividing their army into three bodies, they proceeded to assail simultaneously the three quarters of which the village is composed. But the commander of the Miguelets, informed of Roland's intention, was prepared to receive him. One of the Camisard wings was attacked at the same time in front and rear, thrown into confusion and defeated; and the other wings were driven back with heavy loss.

This was Roland's last battle. About a month later—in August, 1704—while a body of Camisards occupied the Chateau of Castelnau, not far from Ners, the place was suddenly surounded at night by a body of royalist dragoons. The alarm was raised, and Roland, half-dressed, threw himself on horseback and fled. He was pursued, overtaken, and brought to a stand in a wood, where, setting his back to a tree he defended himself bravely for a time against overpowering numbers, but was at last shot through the heart by a dragoon, and the Camisard chief lay dead upon the ground.

The insurrection did not long survive the death of Roland. The other chiefs wandered about from place to place with their followers, but they had lost heart and hope, and avoided further encounters with the royal forces. One after another of them surrendered. Castanet and Catinat both laid down their arms, and were allowed to leave France for Switzerland, accompanied by twenty-two of their men. Joany also surrendered with forty-six of his followers.

One by one the other chiefs laid down their arms—all excepting Abraham and Ravanel, who preferred liberty and misery at home to peace and exile abroad. They continued for some time to wander about in the Upper Cevennes, hiding in the woods by day and sleeping in caves by night—hunted, deserted, and miserable. And thus at last was Languedoc pacified ; and at the beginning of January, 1705, Marshal Villars returned to Versailles to receive the congratulations and honours of the King.

Several futile attempts were afterwards made by the banished leaders to rekindle the insurrection from its embers. Catinat and Castanet, wearied of their inaction at Geneva, stole back across the frontiner and rejoined Ravanel in the Cevennes; but their rashness cost them their lives. They were all captured and condemned to death. Castanet and Salomon were broken alive on the wheel on the Peyrou at Montpellier, and Catinat, Ravanel, with several others, were burnt alive on the Place de la Beaucaire at Nismes.

The last to perish were Abraham and Joany. The one was shot while holding the royal troops at bay, firing upon them from the roof of a cottage at Mas-de-Couteau; the other was captured in the mountains near the source of the Tarn. He was on his way to prison, tied behind a trooper, like Rob Roy in Scott's novel, when, suddenly freeing himself from his bonds while crossing the bridge of Pont-de-Montvert, he slid from the horse, and leapt over the parapet into the Tarn. The soldiers at once opened fire upon the fugitive, and he fell, pierced with many balls, and was carried away in the torrent. And thus Pont-de-Montvert, which had seen the beginning, also saw the end of the insurrection.

CHAPTER IX.

GALLEY-SLAVES FOR THE FAITH.

AFTER the death of the last of the Camisard leaders, there was no further effort at revolt. The Huguenots seemed to be entirely put down, and Protestantism completely destroyed. There was no longer any resistance nor protest. If there were any Huguenots who had not become Catholics, they remained mute. Force had at last succeeded in stifling them.

A profound quiet reigned for a time throughout France. The country had become a circle, closely watched by armed men—by dragoons, infantry, archers, and coastguards—beyond which the Huguenots could not escape without running the risk of the prison, the galley, or the gibbet.

The intendants throughout the kingdom flattered Louis XIV., and Louis XIV. flattered himself, that the Huguenots had either been converted, extirpated, or expelled the kingdom. The King had medals struck, announcing the "*extinction of heresy.*" A proclamation to this effect was also published by the King, dated the 8th of March, 1715, declaring the entire conversion of the French Huguenots, and sentencing those who, after that date, relapsed from Catholicsm to Protestantism, to all the penalties of heresy.

What, then, had become of the Huguenots? They were for the moment prostrate, but their life had not gone out of them. Many were no doubt "converted." They had not strength to resist the pains and penalties threatened by the State if they refused. They accordingly attended Mass, and assisted in ceremonies which at heart they detested. Though they blushed at their apostasy, they were too much broken down and weary of oppression and suffering to attempt to be free.

But though many Huguenots pretended to be "converted," the greater number silently refrained. They held their peace and bided their time. Meanwhile, however, they were subject to all the annoyances of persecution. Persecution had seized them from the day of their birth, and never relaxed its hold until the day of their death. Every new-born child must be taken to the priest to be baptized. When the children had grown into boys and girls, they must go to school and be educated, also by the priest. If their parents refused to send them, the children were forcibly seized, taken away, and brought up in the Jesuit schools and nunneries. And lastly, when grown up into young men and women, they must be married by the priest, or their offspring be declared illegitimate.

The Huguenots refused to conform to all this. Nevertheless, it was by no means easy to continue to refuse obeying the priest. The priest was well served with spies, though the principal spy in every parish was himself. There were also numerous other professional spies—besides idlers, mischief-makers, and "good-natured friends." In time of peace, also, soldiers were usually employed in performing the disgraceful duty of acting as spies upon the Huguenots.

The Huguenot was ordered to attend Mass under the

penalty of fine and imprisonment. Supposing he refused, because he did not believe that the priest had the miraculous power of converting bread and wine into something the very opposite. The priest insisted that he did possess this power, and that he was supported by the State in demanding that the Huguenot *must* come and worship his transubstantiation of bread into flesh and wine into blood." "I do not believe it," said the Huguenot. "But I *order* you to come, for Louis XIV. has proclaimed you to be a converted Catholic, and if you refuse you will be at once subject to all the penalties of heresy." It was certainly very difficult to argue with a priest who had the hangman at his back, or with the King who had his hundred thousand dragoons. And so, perhaps, the threatened Huguenot went to Mass, and pretended to believe all that the priest had said about his miraculous powers.

But many resolutely continued to refuse, willing to incur the last and heaviest penalties. Then it came to be seen that Protestantism, although declared defunct by the King's edict, had not in fact expired, but was merely reposing for a time in order to make a fresh start forward. The Huguenots who still remained in France, whether as "new converts" or as "obstinate heretics," at length began to emerge from their obscurity. They met together in caves and solitary places—in deep and rocky gorges—in valleys among the mountains—where they prayed together, sang together their songs of David, and took counsel one with another.

At length, from private meetings for prayer, religious assemblies began to be held in the Desert, and preachers made their appearance. The spies spread about the country informed the intendants. The meetings were often surprised by the military. Sometimes the soldiers would come upon them suddenly, and fire into the crowd of men, women, and children. On some occasions a hundred persons or more would be killed upon the spot. Of those taken prisoners, the preachers were hanged or broken on the wheel, the women were sent to prison, and the children to nunneries, while the men were sent to be galley-slaves for life.*

The persecutions to which Huguenot women and children were exposed caused a sudden enlargement of all the prisons and nunneries in France. Many of the old castles were fitted up as gaols, and even their dungeons were used for the incorrigible heretics. One of the worst of these was the Tour de Constance in the town of Aiguemortes, which is to this day remembered with horror as the principal dungeon of the Huguenot women.

The town of Aiguemortes is situated in the department of Gard, close to the Mediterranean, whose waters wash into the salt marshes and lagunes by which it is surrounded. It was erected in the thirteenth century for Philip the Bold, and is still interesting as an example of the ancient feudal fortress. The fosse has since been filled up, on account of the malaria produced by the stagnant water which it contained.

* In the Viverais and elsewhere they sang the song of the persecuted Church :—

"Nos filles dans les monastères,
  Nos prisonniers dans les cachots,
Nos martyrs dont le sang se répand à grands flots,
  Nos confesseurs sur les galères,
  Nos malades persécutés,
Nos mourants exposés à plus d'une furie,
  Nos morts traînés à la voierie,
  Te disent (ô Dieu !) nos calamités."

The place is approached by a long causeway raised above the marsh, and the entrance to the tower is spanned by an ancient gatehouse. In advance of the tower, to the north, in an angle of the wall, is a single, large round tower, which served as a citadel. It is sixty-six feet in diameter and ninety feet high, surmounted by a lighthouse turret of thirty-four feet. It consists of two large vaulted apartments, the staircase from the one to the other being built within the wall itself, which is about eighteen feet thick. The upper chamber is dimly lighted by narrow chinks through the walls. The lowest of the apartments is the dungeon, which is almost without light and air. In the centre of the floor is a hole connected with a reservoir of water below.

This Tour de Constance continued to be the principal prison for Huguenot women in France for a period of about a hundred years. It was always horribly unhealthy; and to be condemned to this dungeon was considered almost as certain though a slower death than to be condemned to the gallows. Sixteen Huguenot women confined there in 1686 died within five months. Most of them were the wives of merchants of Nismes, or of men of property in the district. When the prisoners died off, the dungeon was at once filled up again with more victims, and it was rarely, if ever, empty, down to a period within only a few years before the outbreak of the French Revolution.

The punishment of the men found attending religious meetings, and taken prisoners by the soldiers, was to be sentenced to the galleys, mostly for life. They were usually collected in large numbers, and sent to the seaports attached together by chains. They were sent openly, sometimes through the entire length of the kingdom, by way of a show. The object was to teach the horrible delinquency of professing Protestantism; for it could not be to show the greater beautifulness and mercifulness of Catholicism.

The punishment of the Chain varied in degree. Sometimes it was more cruel than at other times. This depended upon the drivers of the prisoners. Marteilhe describes the punishment during his conveyance from Havre to Marseilles in the winter of 1712.* The Chain to which he belonged did not reach Marseilles until the 17th January, 1713. The season was bitterly cold; but that made no difference in the treatment of Huguenot prisoners.

The Chain consisted of a file of prisoners, chained one to another in various ways. On this occasion, each pair was fastened by the neck with a thick chain three feet long, in the middle of which was a round ring. After being thus chained, the pairs were placed in file, couple behind couple, when another long thick chain was passed through the rings, thus running along the centre of the gang, and the whole were thus doubly chained together. There were no less than four hundred prisoners in the chain described by Marteilhe. The number had, however, greatly fallen off through deaths by barbarous treatment before it reached Marseilles.

It must, however, be added, that the whole gang did not consist of Huguenots, but only a part of it—the Huguenots being distinguished by their red jackets. The rest consisted of murderers, thieves, deserters, and criminals of various sorts.

* "Autobiography of a French Protestant condemned to the Galleys because of his Religion." Rotterdam, 1757. (Since reprinted by the Religious Tract Society.)

The difficulty which the prisoners had in marching along the roads was very great; the weight of chain which each member had to carry being no less than one hundred and fifty pounds. The lodging they had at night was of the worst description. While at Paris, the galley-slaves were quartered in the Château de la Tournelle, which was under the spiritual direction of the Jesuits. The gaol consisted of a large cellar or dungeon, fitted with huge beams of oak fixed close to the floor. Thick iron collars were attached by iron chains to the beams. The collar being placed round the prisoner's neck, it was closed and riveted upon an anvil with heavy blows of a hammer.

Twenty men in pairs were thus chained to each beam. The dungeon was so large that five hundred men could thus be fastened up. They could not sleep lying at full length, nor could they sleep sitting or standing up straight; the beam to which they were chained being too high in the one case and too low in the other. The torture which they endured, therefore, is scarcely to be described. The prisoners were kept there until a sufficient number could be collected to set out in a great chain for Marseilles.

When they arrived at the first stage out of Paris, at Charenton, after a heavy day's fatigue, their lodging was no better than before. A stable was found in which they were chained up in such a way that they could with difficulty sit down, and then only on a dung-heap. After they had lain there for a few hours, the prisoners' chains were taken off, and they were turned out into the spacious courtyard of the inn, where they were ordered to strip off their clothes, put them down at their feet, and march over to the other side of the courtyard.

The object of this proceeding was to search the pockets of the prisoners, examine their clothes, and find whether they contained any knives, files, or other tools which might be used for cutting the chains. All money and other valuables or necessaries that the clothes contained were at the same time taken away.

The night was cold and frosty, with a keen north wind blowing; and after the prisoners had been exposed to it for about half an hour, their bodies became so benumbed that they could scarcely move across the yard to where their clothes were lying. Next morning it was found that eighteen of the unfortunates were happily released by death.

It is not necessary to describe the tortures endured by the galley-slaves to the end of their journey. One little circumstance may, however, be mentioned. While marching towards the coast, the exhausted Huguenots, weary and worn out by the heaviness of their chains, were accustomed to stretch out their little wooden cups for a drop of water to the inhabitants of the villages through which they passed. The women, whom they mostly addressed, answered their entreaties with the bitterest spite. "Away, away!" they cried, "you are going where you will have *water enough!*"

When the gang or chain reached the port at which the prisoners were to be confined, they were drafted on board the different galleys. These were for the most part stationed at Toulon, but there were also other galleys in which Huguenots were imprisoned — at Marseilles, Dunkirk, Brest, St. Malo, and Bordeaux. Let us briefly describe the galley of those days.

The royal galley was about a hundred and fifty feet long and forty feet broad, and was capable of containing about five hundred men. It had fifty benches for rowers, twenty-five on each side. Between these two rows of benches was the raised middle gallery, commonly called the waist of the ship, four feet high and about three or four feet broad. The oars were fifty feet long, of which thirty-seven feet were outside the ship and thirteen within. Six men worked at each oar, all chained to the same bench. They had to row in unison, otherwise they would be heavily struck by the return rowers both before and behind them. They were under the constant command of the *comite* or galley-slave-driver, who struck all about him with his long whip in urging them to work. To enable his strokes to *tell*, the men sat naked while they rowed.* Their dress was always insufficient, summer and winter—the lower part of their bodies being covered with a short red jacket and a sort of apron, for their manacles prevented them wearing any other dress.

The chain which bound each rower to his bench was fastened to his leg, and was of such a length as to enable his feet to come and go whilst rowing. At night, the galley-slave slept where he sat—on the bench on which he had been rowing all day. There was no room for him to lie down. He never quitted his bench except for the hospital or the grave; yet some of the Huguenot rowers contrived to live upon their benches for thirty or forty years!

During all these years they toiled in their chains in a hell of foul and disgusting utterance, for they were

---

* Le comite ou chef de chiourme, aidé de deux *sous-comites*, allait et venait sans cesse sur le coursier, frappant les forçats à coup de nerfs de bœuf, comme un cocher ses chevaux. Pour rendre les coups plus sensible et pour économiser les vêtements, *les galériens étaient nus* quand ils ramaient.—ATHANASE COQUEREL FILS. *Le Forçats pour la Foi*, 64.

mixed up with thieves and the worst of criminals. They ate the bread and drank the waters of bitterness. They seemed to be forsaken by the world. They had no one to love them, for most had left their families behind them at home, or perhaps in convents or prisons. They lived under the constant threats of their keepers, who lashed them to make them row harder, who lashed them to make them sit up, or lashed them to make them lie down. The Chevalier Langeron, captain of *La Palme*, of which Marteilhe was at first a rower, used to call the *comite* to him and say, "Go and refresh the backs of these Huguenots with a salad of strokes of the whip." For the captain, it seems, "held the most Jesuitical sentiments," and hated his Huguenot prisoners far worse than his thieves or his murderers. *

And yet, at any moment, a word spoken would have made these Huguenots free. The Catholic priests frequently visited the galleys and entreated them to become converted. If "converted," and the Huguenots would only declare that they believed in the miraculous powers of the clergy, their chains would fall away from their limbs at once; and they would have been restored to the world, to their families, and to liberty! And who would not have declared themselves "converted," rather than endure these horrible punishments? Yet by far the greater number of the Huguenots did not. They could not be hypocrites. They would not lie to God. Rather than do this, they had the heroism—some will call it the obstinacy—to remain galley-slaves for life!

Many of the galley-slaves did not survive their torture long. Men of all ages and conditions, accustomed to indoor life, could not bear the exposure to the sun,

* "The Autobiography of a French Protestant, "68.

rain, and snow, which the punishment of the galley-slave involved. The old men and the young soon succumbed and died. Middle-aged men survived the longest. But there was always a change going on. When the numbers of a galley became thinned by death, there were other Huguenots ready to be sent on board—perhaps waiting in some inland prison until another " Great Chain " could be made up for the seaports, to go on board the galley-ships, to be manacled, tortured, and killed off as before.

Such was the treatment of the galley-slaves in time of peace. But the galleys were also war-ships. They carried large numbers of armed men on board. Sometimes they scoured the Mediterranean, and protected French merchant-ships against the Sallee rovers. At other times they were engaged in the English channel, attacking Dutch and English ships, sometimes picking up a prize, at other times in actual sea-fight.

When the service required, they were compelled to row incessantly night and day, without rest, save in the last extremity; and they were treated as if, on the first opportunity, in sight of the enemy, they would revolt and betray the ship; hence they were constantly watched by the soldiers on board, and if any commotion appeared amongst them, they were shot down without ceremony, and their bodies thrown into the sea. Loaded cannons were also placed at the end of the benches of rowers, so as to shoot them down in case of necessity.

Whenever an enemy's ship came up, the galley-slaves were covered over with a linen screen, so as to prevent them giving signals to the enemy. When an action occurred, they were particularly exposed to danger, for the rowers and their oars were the first to be shot at— just as the boiler or screw of a war-steamer would be shot at now—in order to disable the ship. The galley-slaves thus suffered much more from the enemy's shot than the other armed men of the ship. The rowers' benches were often filled with dead, before the soldiers and mariners on board had been touched.

Marteilhe, while a galley-slave on board *La Palme*, was engaged in an adventure which had nearly cost him his life. Four French galleys, after cruising along the English coast from Dover to the Downs, got sight of a fleet of thirty-five merchant vessels on their way from the Texel to the Thames, under the protection of one small English frigate. The commanders of the galleys, taking counsel together, determined to attack the frigate (which they thought themselves easily able to master), and so capture the entire English fleet.

The captain of the frigate, when he saw the galleys approach him, ordered the merchantmen to crowd sail and make for the Thames, the mouth of which they had nearly reached. He then sailed down upon the galleys, determined to sacrifice his ship if necessary for the safety of his charge. The galleys fired into him, but he returned never a shot. The captain of the galley in which Marteilhe was, said, "Oh, he is coming to surrender!" The frigate was so near that the French musqueteers were already firing full upon her. All of a sudden the frigate tacked and veered round as if about to fly from the galleys. The Frenchmen called out that the English were cowards in thus trying to avoid the battle. If they did not surrender at once, they would sink the frigate!

The English captain took no notice. The frigate then turned her stern towards the galley, as if to give the Frenchmen an opportunity of boarding her. The French commander ordered the galley at once to run at the enemy's stern, and the crew to board the frigate. The rush was made; the galley-slaves, urged by blows of the whip, rowing with great force. The galley was suddenly nearing the stern of the frigate, when by a clever stroke of the helm the ship moved to one side, and the galley, missing it, rushed past. All the oars on that side were suddenly broken off, and the galley was placed immediately under the broadside of the enemy.

Then began the English part of the game. The French galley was seized with grappling irons and hooked on to the English broadside. The men on board the galley were as exposed as if they had been upon a raft or a bridge. The frigate's guns, which were charged with grapeshot, were discharged full upon them, and a frightful carnage ensued. The English also threw hand grenades, which went down amongst the rowers and killed many. They next boarded the galley, and cut to pieces all the armed men they could lay hold of, only sparing the convicts, who could make no attempt at defence.

The English captain then threw off the galley, which he had broadsided and disarmed, in order to look after the merchantmen, which some of the other galleys had gone to intercept on their way to the mouth of the Thames. Some of the ships had already been captured; but the commanders of the galleys, seeing their fellow-commodores flying signals of distress, let go their prey, and concentrated their attack upon the frigate. This they surrounded, and after a very hard struggle the frigate was captured, but not until the English captain had ascertained that all the fleet of which he had been in charge had entered the Thames and were safe.

In the above encounter with the English frigate Marteilhe had nearly lost his life. The bench on which he was seated, with five other slaves, was opposite one of the loaded guns of the frigate. He saw that it must be discharged directly upon them. His fellows tried to lie down flat, while Marteilhe himself stood up. He saw the gunner with his lighted match approach the touchhole; then he lifted up his heart to God; the next moment he was lying stunned and prostrate in the centre of the galley, as far as the chain would allow him to reach. He was lying across the body of the lieutenant, who was killed. A long time passed, during which the fight was still going on, and then Marteilhe came to himself, towards dark. Most of his fellow-slaves were killed. He himself was bleeding from a large open wound on his shoulder, another on his knee, and a third in his stomach. Of the eighteen men around him he was the only one that escaped, with his three wounds.

The dead were all thrown into the sea. The men were about to throw Marteilhe after them, but while attempting to release him from his chain, they touched the wound upon his knee, and he groaned heavily. They let him remain where he lay. Shortly after, he was taken down to the bottom of the hold with the other men, where he long lay amongst the wounded and dying. At length he recovered from his wounds, and was again returned to his bench, to re-enter the horrible life of a galley-slave.

There was another mean and unmanly cruelty, connected with this galley-slave service, which was practised only upon the Huguenots. If an assassin or other criminal received a wound in the service of the state while engaged in battle, he was at once restored to his liberty; but if a Huguenot was wounded, he was never released. He was returned to his bench and chained as before; the wounds he had received being only so many additional tortures to be borne by him in the course of his punishment.

Marteilhe, as we have already stated, was disembarked when he had sufficiently recovered, and marched through the entire length of France, enchained with other malefactors. On his arrival at Marseilles, he was placed on board the galley *Grand Réale*, where he remained until peace was declared between England and France by the Treaty of Utrecht.*

Queen Anne of England, at the instigation of the Marquis de Rochegade, then made an effort to obtain the liberation of Protestants serving at the galleys; and at length, out of seven hundred and forty-two Huguenots who were then enslaved, a hundred and thirty-six were liberated, of whom Marteilhe was one. He was thus enabled to get rid of his inhuman countrymen, and to spend the remainder of his life in Holland and England, where Protestants were free.

* "Autobiography of a French Protestant," 112—21.

CHAPTER X.

ANTOINE COURT

ALMOST at the very time that Louis XIV. was lying on his death-bed at Versailles, a young man conceived the idea of re-establishing Protestantism in France! Louis XIV. had tried to enter heaven by superstition and cruelty. On his death-bed he began to doubt whether he "had not carried his authority too far."* But the Jesuits tried to make death easy for him, covering his body with relics of the true cross.

Very different was the position of the young man who tried to undo all that Louis XIV., under the influence of his mistress De Maintenon, and his Jesuit confessor, Père la Chase,† had been trying all his life to accomplish. He was an intelligent youth, the son of

---

* Saint-Simon and Dangeau.

† Amongst the many satires and epigrams with which Louis XIV. was pursued to the grave, the following epitaph may be given:—

"Ci gist le mari de Thérèse
De la Montespan le Mignon,
L'esclave de la Maintenon,
Le valet du père La Chaise."

At the death of Louis XIV., Voltaire, an *élève* of the Jesuits, was appropriately coming into notice. At the age of about twenty he was thrown into the Bastille for having written a satire on Louis XIV., of which the following is an extract:—

Huguenot parents in Viverais, of comparatively poor and humble condition. He was, however, full of energy, activity, and a zealous disposition for work. Observing the tendency which Protestantism had, while bereft of its pastors, to run into gloomy forms of fanaticism, Antoine Court conceived the idea of reviving the pastorate, and restoring the proscribed Protestant Church of France. It was a bold idea, but the result proved that Antoine Court was justified in entertaining it.

Louis XIV. died in August, 1715. During that very month, Court summoned together a small number of Huguenots to consider his suggestions. The meeting was held at daybreak, in an empty quarry near Nismes, which has already been mentioned in the course of this history. But it may here be necessary to inform the reader of the early life of this enthusiastic young man.

Antoine Court was born at Villeneuve de Berg, in Viverais, in the year 1696. Religious persecution was then at its height; assemblies were vigorously put down; and all pastors taken prisoners were hanged on the Peyrou at Montpellier. Court was only four years old when his father died, and his mother resolved, if the boy lived, to train him up so that he might consecrate himself to the service of God. He was still very

> "J'ai vu sous l'habit d'une femme
> Un démon nous donner la loi;
> Elle sacrifia son Dieu, sa foi, son âme,
> Pour séduire l'esprit d'un trop crédule roi.
>
> * * * * *
>
> J'ai vu l'hypocrite honoré :
> J'ai vu, c'est dire tout, le jésuite adoré :
> J'ai vu ces maux sous le règne funeste
> D'un prince que jadis la colère céleste
> Accorda, par vengeance, à nos désirs ardens;
> J'ai vu ces maux, et je n'ai pas vingt ans."

Voltaire denied having written this satire.

young while the Camisard war was in progress, but he heard a great deal about it, and vividly remembered all that he heard.

Antoine Court, like many Protestant children, was compelled to attend a Jesuit school in his neighbourhood. Though but a boy he abhorred the Mass. With Protestants the Mass was then the symbol of persecution; it was identified with the Revocation of the Edict—the dragonnades, the galleys, the prisons, the nunneries, the monkeries, and the Jesuits. The Mass was not a matter of knowledge, but of fear, of terror, and of hereditary hatred.

At school, the other boys were most bitter against Court, because he was the son of a Huguenot. Every sort of mischief was practised upon him, for little boys are generally among the greatest of persecutors. Court was stoned, worried, railed at, laughed at, spit at. When leaving school, the boys called after him "He, he! the eldest son of Calvin!" They sometimes pursued him with clamour and volleys of stones to the door of his house, collecting in their riotous procession all the other Catholic boys of the place. Sometimes they forced him into church whilst the Mass was being celebrated. In fact, the boy's hatred of the Mass and of Catholicism grew daily more and more vehement.

All these persecutions, together with reading some of the books which came under his notice at home, confirmed his aversion to the Jesuitical school to which he had been sent. At the same time he became desirous of attending the secret assemblies, which he knew were being held in the neighbourhood. One day, when his mother set out to attend one of them, the boy set out to follow her. She discovered him, and demanded whither he was going. "I follow you, mother," said he, "and I wish you to permit me to go where you go. I know that you go to pray to God, and will you refuse me the favour of going to do so with you?"

She shed tears at his words, told him of the danger of attending the assembly, and strongly exhorted him to secrecy; but she allowed him to accompany her. He was at that time too little and weak to walk the whole way to the meeting; but other worshippers coming up, they took the boy on their shoulders and carried him along with them.

At the age of seventeen, Court began to read the Bible at the assemblies. One day, in a moment of sudden excitement, common enough at secret meetings, he undertook to address the assembly. What he said was received with much approval, and he was encouraged to go on preaching. He soon became famous among the mountaineers, and was regarded as a young man capable of accomplishing great things.

As he grew older, he at length determined to devote his life to preaching and ministering to the forsaken and afflicted Protestants. It was a noble, self-denying work, the only earthly reward for which was labour, difficulty, and danger. His mother was in great trouble, for Antoine was her only remaining son. She did not, however, press him to change his resolution. Court quoted to her the text, "Whoever loves father and mother more than me, is not worthy of me." After this, she only saw in her son a victim consecrated, like another Abraham, to the Divine service.

After arriving at his decision, Court proceeded to visit the Huguenots in Low Languedoc, passing by Uzes to Nismes, and preaching wherever he could draw assemblies of the people together. His success during this rapid excursion induced him to visit Dauphiny. There he met Brunel, another preacher, with knapsack on his back, running from place to place in order to avoid spies, priests, and soldiers. The two were equally full of ardour, and they went together preaching in many places, and duly encouraging each other.

From Dauphiny, Court directed his steps to Marseilles, where the royal galleys stationed there contained about three hundred Huguenot galley-slaves. He penetrated these horrible floating prisons, without being detected, and even contrived to organize amongst them a regular system of secret worship. Then he returned to Nismes, and from thence went through the Cevennes and the Viverais, preaching to people who had never met for Protestant worship since the termination of the wars of the Camisards. To elude the spies, who began to make hot search for him, because of the enthusiasm which he excited, Court contrived to be always on the move, and to appear daily in some fresh locality.

The constant fatigue which he underwent undermined his health, and he was compelled to remain for a time inactive at the mineral waters of Euzet. This retirement proved useful. He began to think over what might be done to revivify the Protestant religion in France. Remember that he was at that time only nineteen years of age! It might be thought presumptuous in a youth, comparatively uninstructed, even to dream of such a subject. The instruments of earthly power—King, Pope, bishops, priests, soldiers, and spies —were all arrayed against him. He had nothing to oppose to them but truth, uprightness, conscience, and indefatigable zeal for labour.

When Court had last met the few Protestant preachers

who survived in Languedoc, they were very undecided about taking up his scheme. They had met at Nismes to take the sacrament in the house of a friend. There were Bombonnoux (an old Camisard), Crotte, Corteiz, Brunel, and Court. Without coming to any decision, they separated, some going to Switzerland, and others to the South and West of France. It now rested with Court, during his sickness, to study and endeavour to arrange the method of reorganization of the Church.

The Huguenots who remained in France were then divided into three classes—the "new converts," who professed Catholicism while hating it; the lovers of the ancient Protestant faith, who still clung to it; and, lastly, the more ignorant, who still clung to prophesying and inspiration. These last had done the Protestant Church much injury, for the intelligent classes generally regarded them as but mere fanatics.

Court found it would be requisite to keep the latter within the leading-strings of spiritual instruction, and to encourage the "new converts" to return to the church of their fathers by the re-establishment of some efficient pastoral service. He therefore urged that religious assemblies must be continued, and that discipline must be established by the appointment of elders, presbyteries, and synods, and also by the training up of a body of young pastors to preach amongst the people, and discipline them according to the rules of the Protestant Church. Nearly thirty years had passed since it had been disorganized by the Revocation of the Edict of Nantes, so that synods, presbyteries, and the training of preachers had become almost forgotten.

The first synod was convened by Court, and held in the abandoned quarry near Nismes, above referred to, in the very same month in which Louis XIV. breathed his last. It was a very small beginning. Two or three laymen and a few preachers* were present, the whole meeting numbering only nine persons. The place in which the meeting was held had often before been used as a secret place of worship by the Huguenots. Religious meetings held there had often been dispersed by the dragoons, and there was scarcely a stone in it that had not been splashed by Huguenot blood. And now, after Protestantism had been "finally suppressed," Antoine Court assembled his first synod to re-establish the proscribed religion!

The first meeting took place on the 21st of August, 1715, at daybreak. After prayer, Court, as moderator, explained his method of reorganization, which was approved. The first elders were appointed from amongst those present. A series of rules and regulations was resolved upon and ordered to be spread over the entire province. The preachers were then charged to go forth, to stir up the people and endeavour to bring back the "new converts."

They lost no time in carrying out their mission. The first districts in which they were appointed to work were those of Mende, Alais, Viviers, Uzes, Nismes, and Montpellier, in Languedoc—districts which, fifteen years before, had been the scenes of the Camisard war. There, in unknown valleys, on hillsides, on the mountains, in the midst of hostile towns and villages, the missionaries sought out the huts, the farms, and the dwellings of the scattered, concealed, and half-frightened Huguenots. Amidst the open threats of the magistrates and others in office, and the fear of the still more hateful priests and spies, they went from house to house, and

* Edmund Hughes says the preachers were probably Rouviere (or Crotte), Jean Huc, Jean Vesson, Etienne Arnaud, and Durand.

prayed, preached, advised, and endeavoured to awaken the zeal of their old allies of the " Religion."

The preachers were for the most part poor, and some of them were labouring men. They were mostly natives of Languedoc. Jean Vesson, a cooper by trade, had in his youth been "inspired," and prophesied in his ecstasy. Mazelet, now an elderly man, had formerly been celebrated among the Camisards, and preached with great success before the soldiers of Roland. At forty he was not able to read or write; but having been forced to fly into Switzerland, he picked up some education at Geneva, and had studied divinity under a fellow-exile.

Bombonnoux had been a brigadier in the troop of Cavalier. After his chief's defection he resolved to continue the war to the end, by preaching, if not by fighting. He had been taken prisoner and imprisoned at Montpellier, in 1705. Two of his Camisard friends were first put upon the rack, and then, while still living, thrown upon a pile and burnt to death before his eyes. But the horrible character of the punishment did not terrify him. He contrived to escape from prison at Montpellier, and then went about convoking assemblies and preaching to the people as before.

Besides these, there were Huc, Corteiz, Durand, Arnaud, Brunel, and Rouviere or Crotte, who all went about from place to place, convoking assemblies and preaching. There were also some local preachers, as they might be called—old men who could not move far from home—who worked at their looms or trades, sometimes tilling the ground by day, and preaching at night. Amongst these were Monteil, Guillot, and Bonnard, all more than sixty years of age.

Court, because of his youth and energy, seems to have been among the most active of the preachers. One day, near St. Hypolite, a chief centre of the Huguenot population, he convoked an assembly on a mountain side, the largest that had taken place for many years. The priests of the parish gave information to the authorities; and the governor of Alais offered a reward of fifty pistoles to anyone who would apprehend and deliver up to him the young preacher. Troops were sent into the district; upon which Court descended from the mountains towards the towns of Low Languedoc, and shortly after he arrived at Nismes.

At Nismes, Court first met Jacques Roger, who afterwards proved of great assistance to him in his work. Roger had long been an exile in Wurtemburg. He was originally a native of Boissieres, in Languedoc, and when a young man was compelled to quit France with his parents, who were Huguenots. His heart, however, continued to draw him towards his native country, although it had treated himself and his family so cruelly.

As Roger grew older, he determined to return to France, with the object of helping his friends of the "Religion." A plan had occurred to him, like that which Antoine Court was now endeavouring to carry into effect. The joy with which Roger encountered Court at Nismes, and learnt his plans, may therefore be conceived. The result was, that Roger undertook to "awaken" the Protestants of Dauphiny, and to endeavour to accomplish there what Court was already gradually effecting in Languedoc. Roger held his first synod in Dauphiny in August, 1716, at which seven preachers and several elders or *anciens* assisted.

In the meantime Antoine Court again set out to visit

the churches which had been reconstructed along the banks of the Gardon. He had been suffering from intermittent fever, and started on his journey before he was sufficiently recovered. Having no horse, he walked on foot, mostly by night, along the least known by-paths, stopping here and there upon his way. At length he became so enfeebled and ill as to be unable to walk further. He then induced two men to carry him. By crossing their hands over each other, they took him up between them, and carried him along on this improvised chair.

Court found a temporary lodging with a friend. But no sooner had he laid himself down to sleep, than the alarm was raised that he must get up and fly. A spy had been observed watching the house. Court rose, put on his clothes, and though suffering great pain, started afresh. The night was dark and rainy. By turns shivering with cold and in an access of fever, he wandered alone for hours across the country, towards the house of another friend, where he at last found shelter. Such were the common experiences of these wandering, devoted, proscribed, and heroic ministers of the Gospel.

Their labours were not carried on without encountering other and greater dangers. Now that the Protestants were becoming organized, it was not so necessary to incite them to public worship. They even required to be restrained, so that they might not too suddenly awaken the suspicion or excite the opposition of the authorities. Thus, at the beginning of 1717, the preacher Vesson held an open assembly near Anduze. It was surprised by the troops; and seventy-two persons made prisoners, of whom the men were sent to the galleys for life, and the women imprisoned in the Tour de Constance. Vesson was on this occasion reprimanded by the synod, for having exposed his brethren to unnecessary danger.

While there was the danger of loss of liberty to the people, there was the danger of loss of life to the pastors who were bold enough to minister to their religious necessities. Etienne Arnaud having preached to an assembly near Alais, was taken prisoner by the soldiers. They took him to Montpellier, where he was judged, condemned, and sent back to Alais to be hanged. This brave young man gave up his life with great courage and resignation. His death caused much sorrow amongst the Protestants, but it had no effect in dissuading the preachers and pastors from the work they had taken in hand. There were many to take the place of Arnaud. Young Bètrine offered himself to the synod, and was accepted.

Scripture readers were also appointed, to read the Bible at meetings which preachers were not able to attend. There was, however, a great want of Bibles amongst the Protestants. One of the first things done by the young King Louis XV.—the "Well-beloved" of the Jesuits—on his ascending the throne, was to issue a proclamation ordering the seizure of Bibles, Testaments, Psalm-books, and other religious works used by the Protestants. And though so many books had already been seized and burnt in the reign of Louis XIV., immense piles were again collected and given to the flames by the executioners.

"Our need of books is very great," wrote Court to a friend abroad; and the same statement was repeated in many of his letters. His principal need was of Bibles and Testaments; for every Huguenot knew the greater part of the Psalms by heart. When a Testament was obtained, it was lent about, and for the most part learnt off. The labour was divided in this way. One person, sometimes a boy or girl, of good memory, would undertake to learn one or more chapters in the Gospels, another a certain number in the Epistles, until at last a large portion of the book was committed to memory, and could be recited at the meetings of the assemblies. And thus also it happened, that the conversation of the people, as well as the sermons of their preachers, gradually assumed a strongly biblical form.

Strong appeals were made to foreign Protestants to supply the people with books. The refugees who had settled in Switzerland, Holland, and England sent the Huguenots remaining in France considerable help in this way. They sent many Testaments and Psalm-books, together with catechisms for the young, and many devotional works written by French divines residing in Holland and England—by Drelincourt, Saurin, Claude and others. These were sent safely across the frontier in bales, put into the hands of colporteurs, and circulated amongst the Protestants all over the South of France. The printing press of Geneva was also put in requisition; and Court had many of his sermons printed there and distributed amongst the people.

Until this time, Court had merely acted as a preacher; and it was now determined to ordain and consecrate him as a pastor. The ceremony, though comparatively unceremonious, was very touching. A large number of Protestants in the Vaunage assembled on the night of the 21st November, 1718, and, after prayer, Court rose and spoke for some time of the responsible duties of the ministry, and of the necessity and advantages of preaching. He thanked God for having raised up ministers to serve the Church when so many of her enemies were seeking for her ruin. He finally asked the whole assembly to pray for grace to enable him to fulfil with renewed zeal the duties to which he was about to be called, together with all the virtues needed for success. At these touching words the assembled hearers shed tears. Then Corteiz, the old pastor, drew near to Court, now upon his knees, and placing a Bible upon his head, in the name of Jesus Christ, and with the authority of the synod, gave him power to exercise all the functions of the ministry. Cries of joy were heard on all sides. Then, after further prayer, the assembly broke up in the darkness of the night.

The plague which broke out in 1720 helped the progress of the new Church. The Protestants thought the plague had been sent as a punishment for their backsliding. Piety increased, and assemblies in the Desert were more largely attended than before. The intendants ceased to interfere with them, and the soldiers were kept strictly within their cantonments. More preachers were licensed, and more elders were elected. Many new churches were set up throughout Languedoc; and the department of the Lozere, in the Cevennes, became again almost entirely Protestant. Roger and Villeveyre were almost equally successful in Dauphiny; and Saintonge, Normandy, and Poitou were also beginning to maintain a connection with the Protestant churches of Languedoc.

CHAPTER XI.

REORGANIZATION OF THE CHURCH IN THE DESERT.

THE organization of the Church in the Desert is one of the most curious things in history. Secret meetings of the Huguenots had long been held in France. They were began several years before the Act of Revocation was proclaimed, when the dragonnades were on foot, and while the Protestant temples were being demolished by the Government. The Huguenots then arranged to meet and hold their worship in retired places.

As the meetings were at first held, for the most part, in Languedoc, and as much of that province, especially in the district of the Cevennes, is really waste and desert land, the meetings were at first called "Assemblies in the Desert," and for nearly a hundred years they retained that name.

When Court began to reorganize the Protestant Church in France, shortly after the Camisard war, meetings in the Desert had become almost unknown. There were occasional prayer-meetings, at which chapters of the Bible were read or recited by those who remembered them, and psalms were sung; but there were few or no meetings at which pastors presded. Court, however, resolved not only to revive the meetings of the Church in the Desert, but to reconstitute the congregations, and restore the system of governing them according to the methods of the Huguenot Church.

The first thing done in reconstituting a congregation, was to appoint certain well-known religious men, as *anciens* or elders. These were very important officers. They formed the church in the first instance; for where there were no elders, there was no church. They were members of the *consistoire* or presbytery. They looked after the flock, visited them in their families, made collections, named the pastors, and maintained peace, order, and discipline amongst the people. Though first nominated by the pastors, they were elected by the congregation; and the reason for their election was their known ability, zeal, and piety.

The elder was always present at the assemblies, though the minister was absent. He prevented the members from succumbing to temptation and falling away; he censured scandal; he kept up the flame of religious zeal, and encouraged the failing and helpless; he distributed amongst the poorest the collections made and intrusted to him by the Church.

We have said that part of the duty of the elders was to censure scandal amongst the members. If their conduct was not considered becoming the Christian life, they were not visited by the pastors and were not allowed to attend the assemblies, until they had declared their determination to lead a better life. What a punishment for infraction of discipline! to be debarred attending an assembly, for being present at which, the pastor, if detected, might be hanged, and the penitent member sent to the galleys for life!*

The elders summoned the assemblies. They gave

* C. Coquerel, "Eglise du Désert," i. 105.

the word to a few friends, and these spread the notice about amongst the rest. The news soon became known, and in the course of a day or two, the members of the congregation, though living perhaps in distant villages, would be duly informed of the time and place of the intended meeting. It was usually held at night, —in some secret place—in a cave, a hollow in the woods, a ravine, or an abandoned farmstead.

Men, women, and even children were taken thither, after one, two, or sometimes three leagues' walking. The meetings were always full of danger, for spies were lurking about. Catholic priests were constant informers; and soldiers were never far distant. But besides the difficulties of spies and soldiers, the meetings were often dispersed by the rain in summer, or by the snow in winter.

After the Camisard war, and before the appearance of Court, these meetings rarely numbered more than a hundred persons. But Court and his fellow-pastors often held meetings at which more than two thousand people were present. On one occasion, not less than four thousand persons attended an assembly in Lower Languedoc.

When the meetings were held by day, they were carefully guarded and watched by sentinels on the look-out, especially in those places near which garrisons were stationed. The fleetest of the young men were chosen for this purpose. They watched the garrison exits, and when the soldiers made a sortie, the sentinels communicated by signal from hill to hill, thus giving warning to the meeting to disperse. But the assemblies were mostly held at night; and even then the sentinels were carefully posted about, but not at so great a distance.

The chief of the whole organization was the pastor. First, there were the members entitled to church privileges; next the *anciens;* and lastly the pastors. As in Presbyterianism, so in Huguenot Calvinism, its form of government was republican. The organization was based upon the people who elected their elders; then upon the elders who selected and recommended the pastors; and lastly upon the whole congregation of members, elders, and pastors (represented in synods), who maintained the entire organization of the Church.

There were three grades of service in the rank of pastor—first students, next preachers, and lastly pastors. Wonderful that there should have been students of a profession, to follow which was almost equal to a sentence of death! But there were plenty of young enthusiasts ready to brave martyrdom in the service of the proscribed Church. Sometimes it was even necessary to restrain them in their applications.

Court once wrote to Pierre Durand, at a time when the latter was restoring order and organization in Viverais: "Sound and examine well the persons offering themselves for your approval, before permitting them to enter on this glorious employment. Secure good, virtuous men, full of zeal for the cause of truth. It is piety only that inspires nobility and greatness of soul. Piety sustains us under the most extreme dangers, and triumphs over the severest obstacles. The good conscience always marches forward with its head erect."

When the character of the young applicants was approved, their studies then proceeded, like everything else connected with the proscribed religion, in secret. The students followed the professor and pastor in his wanderings over the country, passing long nights in marching, sometimes hiding in caves by day, or sleeping under the stars by night, passing from meeting to meeting, always with death looming before them.

"I have often pitched my professor's chair," said Court, "in a torrent underneath a rock. The sky was our roof, and the leafy branches thrown out from the crevices in the rock overhead, were our canopy. There I and my students would remain for about eight days; it was our hall, our lecture-room, and our study. To make the most of our time, and to practise the students properly, I gave them a text of Scripture to discuss before me—say the first eleven verses of the fifth chapter of Luke. I would afterwards propose to them some point of doctrine, some passage of Scripture, some moral precept, or sometimes I gave them some difficult passages to reconcile. After the whole had stated their views upon the question under discussion, I asked the youngest if he had anything to state against the arguments advanced; then the others were asked in turn; and after they had finished, I stated the views which I considered most just and correct. When the more advanced students were required to preach, they mounted a particular place, where a pole had been set across some rocks in the ravine, and which for the time served for a pulpit. And when they had delivered themselves, the others were requested by turns to express themselves freely upon the subject of the sermon which they had heard."

When the *proposant* or probationer was considered sufficiently able to preach, he was sent on a mission to visit the churches. Sometimes he preached the approved sermons of other pastors; sometimes he preached his own sermons, after they had been examined by persons appointed by the synod. After a time, if approved by the moderator and a committee of the synod, the *proposant* was licensed to preach. His work then resembled that of a pastor; but he could not yet administer the sacrament. It was only when he had passed the synod, and been appointed by the laying on of hands, that he could exercise the higher pastoral functions.

Then, with respect to the maintenance of the pastors and preachers, Court recounts, not without pride, that for the ten years between 1713 and 1723 (excepting the years which he spent at Geneva), he served the Huguenot churches without receiving a farthing. His family and friends saw to the supply of his private wants. With respect to the others, they were supported by collections made at the assemblies; and, as the people were nearly all poor, the amount collected was very small. On one occasion, three assemblies produced a halfpenny and six half-farthings.

But a regular system of collecting moneys was framed by the synods (consisting of a meeting of pastors and elders), and out of the common fund so raised, emoluments were assigned, first to those preachers who were married, and afterwards to those who were single. In either case the pay was very small, scarcely sufficient to keep the wolf from the door.

The students for the ministry were at first educated by Court and trained to preach, while he was on his dangerous journeys from one assembly in the Desert to another. Nor was the supply of preachers sufficient to visit the congregations already organized. Court had long determined, so soon as the opportunity offered, of starting a school for the special education of preachers and pastors, so that the work he was engaged in might be more efficiently carried on. He at first corresponded with influential French refugees in England and Holland with reference to the subject. He wrote to Basnage and Saurin, but they received his propositions coolly. He wrote to William Wake, then Archbishop of Canterbury, who promised his assistance. At last Court resolved to proceed into Switzerland, to stir up the French refugees disposed to help him in his labours.

Arrived at Geneva, Court sought out M. Pictet, to whom he explained the state of affairs in France. It had been rumoured amongst the foreign Protestants that fanaticism and "inspiration" were now in the ascendant among the Protestants of France. Court showed that this was entirely a mistake, and that all which the proscribed Huguenots in France wanted, was a supply of properly educated pastors. The friends of true religion, and the enemies of fanaticism, ought therefore to come to their help and supply them with that of which they stood most in need. If they would find teachers, Court would undertake to supply them with congregations. And Huguenot congregations were rapidly increasing, not only in Languedoc and Dauphiny, but in Normandy, Picardy, Poitou, Saintonge, Bearn, and the other provinces.

At length the subject became matured. It was not found desirable to establish the proposed school at Geneva, that city being closely watched by France, and frequently under the censure of its government for giving shelter to refugee Frenchmen. It was eventually determined that the college for the education of preachers should begin at Lausanne. It was accordingly commenced in the year 1726, and established under the superintendence of M. Duplan.

A committee of refugees called the "Society of Help

REORGANIZATION OF THE CHURCH. 225

for the Afflicted Faithful," was formed at Lausanne to collect subscriptions for the maintenance of the preachers, the pastors, and the seminary. These were in the first place received from Huguenots settled in Switzerland, afterwards increased by subscriptions obtained from refugees settled in Holland, Germany, and England. The King of England subscribed five hundred guineas yearly. Duplan was an indefatigable agent. In fourteen years he collected fourteen thousand pounds. By these efforts the number of students was gradually increased. They came from all parts of France, but chiefly from Languedoc. Between 1726 (the year in which it was started) and 1753, ninety students had passed through the seminary.

When the students had passed the range of study appointed by the professors, they returned from Switzerland to France to enter upon the work of their lives. They had passed the school for martyrdom, and were ready to preach to the assemblies—they had paved their way to the scaffold!

The preachers always went abroad with their lives in their hands. They travelled mostly by night, shunning the open highways, and selecting abandoned routes, often sheep-paths across the hills, to reach the scene of their next meeting. The trace of their steps is still marked upon the soil of the Cevennes, the people of the country still speaking of the solitary routes taken by their instructors when passing from parish to parish, to preach to their fathers.

They were dressed, for disguise, in various ways; sometimes as peasants, as workmen, or as shepherds. On one occasion, Court and Duplan travelled the country disguised as officers! The police heard of it, and ordered their immediate arrest, pointing out the town and the very house where they were to be taken. But the preachers escaped, and assumed a new dress.

When living near Nismes, Court was one day seated under a tree composing a sermon, when a party of soldiers, hearing that he was in the neighbourhood, came within sight. Court climbed up into the tree, where he remained concealed among the branches, and thus contrived to escape their search.

On another occasion, he was staying with a friend, in whose house he had slept during the previous night. A detachment of troops suddenly surrounded the house, and the officer knocked loudly at the door. Court made his friend go at once to bed pretending to be ill, while he himself cowered down in the narrow space between the bed and the wall. His wife slowly answered the door, which the soldiers were threatening to blow open. They entered, rummaged the house, opened all the chests and closets, sounded the walls, examined the sick man's room, and found nothing!

Court himself, as well as the other pastors, worked very hard. On one occasion, Court made a round of visits in Lower Languedoc and in the Cevennes, at first alone, and afterwards accompanied by a young preacher. In the space of two months and a few days he visited thirty-one churches, holding assemblies, preaching, and administering the sacrament, during which he travelled over three hundred miles. The weather did not matter to the pastors—rain nor snow, wind nor storm, never hindered them. They took the road and braved all. Even sickness often failed to stay them. Sickness might weaken but did not overthrow them.

The spies and police so abounded throughout the country, and were so active, that they knew all the houses in which the preachers might take refuge. A list of these was prepared and placed in the hands of the intendant of the province.* If preachers were found in them, both the shelterers and the sheltered knew what they had to expect. The whole property and goods of the former were confiscated and they were sent to the galleys for life; and the latter were first tortured by the rack, and then hanged. The houses in which preachers were found were almost invariably burnt down.

Notwithstanding the great secrecy with which the whole organization proceeded, preachers were frequently apprehended, assemblies were often surprised, and many persons were imprisoned and sent to the galleys for life. Each village had its chief spy—the priest; and beneath the priest there were a number of other spies—spies for money, spies for cruelty, spies for revenge.

Was an assembly of Huguenots about to be held? A spy, perhaps a traitor, would make it known. The priest's order was sufficient for the captain of the nearest troop of soldiers to proceed to disperse it. They marched and surrounded the assembly. A sound of volley-firing was heard. The soldiers shot down, hanged, or made prisoners of the unlawful worshippers. Punishments were sudden, and inquiry was never made into them, however brutal. There was the fire for Bibles, Testaments, and psalm-books; galleys for men; prisons and convents for women; and gibbets for preachers.

* It has since been published in the "Bulletin de la Société du Protestantisme Française."

In 1720 a large number of prisoners were captured in the famous old quarry near Nismes, long the seat of secret Protestant worship. But the troops surrounded the meeting suddenly, and the whole were taken. The women were sent for life to the Tour de Constance, and the men, chained in gangs, were sent all through France to La Rochelle, to be imprisoned in the galleys there. The ambassador of England made intercession for the prisoners, and their sentence was commuted into one of perpetual banishment from France. They were accordingly transported to New Orleans on the Mississippi, to populate the rising French colony in that quarter of North America.

Thus crimes abounded, and cruelty when practised upon Huguenots was never investigated. The seizure and violation of women was common. Fathers knew the probable consequence when their daughters were seized. The daughter of a Huguenot was seized at Uzes, in 1733, when the father immediately died of grief. Two sisters were seized at the same place to be "converted," and their immediate relations were thrown into gaol in the meantime. This was a common proceeding. The Tour de Constance was always filling, and kept full.

The dying were tortured. If they refused the viaticum they were treated as "damned persons." When Jean de Molènes of Cahors died, making a profession of Protestantism, his body was denounced as damned, and it was abandoned without sepulture. A woman who addressed some words of consolation to Joseph Martin when dying was condemned to pay a fine of six thousand livres, and be imprisoned in the castle of Beauregard; and as for Martin, his memory was declared to be damned for ever. Many such outrages to the living and dead were constantly occurring.* Gaolers were accustomed to earn money by exhibiting the corpses of Huguenot women at fairs, inviting those who paid for admission, to walk up and " see the corpse of a damned person." †

Notwithstanding all these cruelties, Protestantism was making considerable progress, both in Languedoc and Dauphiny. In reorganizing the Church, the whole country had been divided into districts, and preachers and pastors endeavoured to visit the whole of their members with as much regularity as possible. Thus Languedoc was divided into seven districts, and to each of those a *proposant* or probationary preacher was appointed. The presbyteries and synods met regularly and secretly in a cave, or the hollow bed of a river, or among the mountains. They cheered each other up, though their progress was usually over the bodies of their dead friends.

For any pastor or preacher to be apprehended, was, of course, certain death. Thus, out of thirteen Huguenots who were found worshipping in a private apartment at Montpellier, in 1723, Vesson, the pastor, and Bonicel and Antoine Comte, his assistants, were at once condemned and hanged on the Peyrou, the other ten persons being imprisoned or sent to the galleys for life.

Shortly after, Huc, the aged pastor, was taken prisoner in the Cevennes, brought to Montpellier, and hanged in the same place. A reward of a thousand livres was offered by Bernage, the intendant, for the heads of the remaining preachers, the fatal list com-

* Edmund Hughes, "Histoire de la Restauration du Protestantisme en France," ii. 94.
† Bénoît, "Edit de Nantes," v. 987.

prising the names of Court, Cortez, Durand, Rouvierè, Bombonnoux, and others. The names of these "others" were not mentioned, not being yet thought worthy of the gibbet.

And yet it was at this time that the Bishop of Alais made an appeal to the government against the toleration shown to the Huguenots! In 1723, he sent a long memorial to Paris, alleging that Catholicism was suffering a serious injury; that not only had the "new converts" withdrawn themselves from the Catholic Church, but that the old Catholics themselves were resorting to the Huguenot assemblies; that sometimes their meetings numbered from three to four thousand persons; that their psalms were sometimes overheard in the surrounding villages; that the churches were becoming deserted, the curés in some parishes not being able to find a single Catholic to serve at Mass; that the Protestants had ceased to send their children to school, and were baptized and married without the intervention of the Church.

In consequence of these representations, the then Regent, the Duke of Bourbon, sent down an urgent order to the authorities to carry out the law—to prevent meetings, under penalty of death to preachers, and imprisonment at the galleys to all who attended them, ordering that the people should be *forced* to go to church and the children to school, and reviving generally the severe laws against Protestantism issued by Louis XIV. The result was that many of the assemblies were shortly after attacked and dispersed, many persons were made prisoners and sent to the galleys, and many more preachers were apprehended, racked, and hanged.

Repeated attempts were made to apprehend Antoine

REORGANIZATION OF THE CHURCH.

Court, as being the soul of the renewed Protestant organization. A heavy reward was offered for his head. The spies and police hunted after him in all directions. Houses where he was supposed to be concealed were surrounded by soldiers at night, and every hole and corner in them ransacked. Three houses were searched in one night. Court sometimes escaped with great difficulty. On one occasion he remained concealed for more than twenty hours under a heap of manure. His friends endeavoured to persuade him to leave the country until the activity of the search for him had passed.

Since the year 1722, Court had undertaken new responsibilities. He had become married, and was now the father of three children. He had married a young Huguenot woman of Uzes. He first met her in her father's house, while he was in hiding from the spies. While he was engaged in his pastoral work his wife and family continued to live at Uzes. Court was never seen in her company, but could only visit his family secretly. The woman was known to be of estimable character, but it gave rise to suspicions that she had three children without a known father. The spies were endeavouring to unravel the secret, tempted by the heavy reward offered for Court's head.

One day the new commandant of the town, passing before the door of the house where Court's wife lived, stopped, and, pointing to the house, put some questions to the neighbours. Court was informed of this, and immediately supposed that his house had become known, that his wife and family had been discovered and would be apprehended. He at once made arrangements for having them removed to Geneva. They reached that city in safety, in the month of April, 1729.

Shortly after, Court, still wandering and preaching about Languedoc, became seriously ill. He feared for his wife, he feared for his family, and conceived the design of joining them in Switzerland. A few months later, exhausted by his labours and continued illness, he left Languedoc and journeyed by slow stages to Geneva. He was still a young man, only thirty-three; but he had worked excessively hard during the last dozen years. Since the age of fourteen, in fact, he had evangelized Languedoc.

Shortly before Court left France for Switzerland, the preacher, Alexandre Roussel, was, in the year 1728, added to the number of martyrs. He was only twenty-six years of age. The occasion on which he was made prisoner was while attending an assembly near Vigan. The whole of the people had departed, and Roussel was the last to leave the meeting. He was taken to Montpellier, and imprisoned in the citadel, which had before held so many Huguenot pastors. He was asked to abjure, and offered a handsome bribe if he would become a Catholic. He refused to deny his faith, and was sentenced to die. When Antoine Court went to offer consolation to his mother, she replied, "If my son had given way I should have been greatly distressed; but as he died with constancy, I thank God for strengthening him to perform this last work in his service."

Court did not leave his brethren in France without the expostulations of his friends. They alleged that his affection for his wife and family had cooled his zeal for God's service. Duplan and Cortez expostulated with him; and the churches of Languedoc, which he himself had established, called upon him to return to his duties amongst them.

But Court did not attend to their request. His

REORGANIZATION OF THE CHURCH. 233

determination was for the present unshaken. He had a long arrears of work to do in quiet. He had money to raise for the support of the suffering Church of France, and for the proper maintenance of the college for students, preachers, and pastors. He had to help the refugees, who still continued to leave France for Switzerland, and to write letters and rouse the Protestant kingdoms of the north, as Brousson had done before him some thirty years ago.

The city of Berne was very generous in its treatment of Court and the Huguenots generally. The Bernish Government allotted Court a pension of five hundred livres a-year—for he was without the means of supporting his family—all his own and his wife's property having been seized and sequestrated in France. Court preached with great success in the principal towns of Switzerland, more particularly at Berne, and afterwards at Lausanne, where he spent the rest of his days.

Though he worked there more peacefully, he laboured as continuously as ever in the service of the Huguenot churches. He composed addresses to them; he educated preachers and pastors for them; and one of his principal works, while at Lausanne, was to compose a history of the Huguenots in France subsequent to the Revocation of the Edict of Nantes.

What he had done for the reorganization of the Huguenot Church in France may be thus briefly stated. Court had begun his work in 1715, at which time there was no settled congregation in the South of France. The Huguenots were only ministered to by occasional wandering pastors. In 1729, the year in which Court finally left France, there were in Lower Languedoc 29 organized, though secretly governed, churches; in

Upper Languedoc, 11; in the Cevennes, 18; in the Lozère 12; and in Viverais, 42 churches. There were now over 200,000 recognised Protestants in Languedoc alone. The ancient discipline had been restored; 120 churches had been organized; a seminary for the education of preachers and pastors had been established; and Protestantism was extending in Dauphiny, Bearn, Saintonge,* and other quarters.

Such were, in a great measure, the results of the labours of Antoine Court and his assistants during the previous fifteen years.

* In 1726, a deputation from Guyenne, Royergue, and Poitou, appeared before the Languedoc synod, requesting preachers and pastors to be sent to them. The synod agreed to send Maroger as preacher. Bétrine (the first of the Lausanne students) and Grail were afterwards sent to join him. Protestantism was also re-awakening in Saintonge and Picardy, and pastors from Languedoc journeyed there to administer the sacrament. Preachers were afterwards sent to join them, to awaken the people, and reorganize the congregations.

CHAPTER XII.

THE CHURCH IN THE DESERT, 1730-62—
PAUL RABAUT.

THE persecutions of the Huguenots increased at one time and relaxed at another. When France was at war, and the soldiers were fighting in Flanders or on the Rhine, the bishops became furious, and complained bitterly to the government of the toleration shown to the Protestants. The reason was that there were no regiments at liberty to pursue the Huguenots and disperse their meetings in the Desert. When the soldiers returned from the wars, persecution began again.

It usually began with the seizing and burning of books. The book-burning days were considered amongst the great days of fête.

One day in June, 1730, the Intendant of Languedoc visited Nismes, escorted by four battalions of troops. On arriving, the principal Catholics were selected, and placed as commissaries to watch the houses of the suspected Huguenots. At night, while the inhabitants slept, the troops turned out, and the commissaries pointed out the Huguenot houses to be searched. The inmates were knocked up, the soldiers entered, the houses were rummaged, and all the books that could be found were taken to the Hôtel de Ville.

A few days after a great *auto-da-fé* was held. The entire Catholic population turned out. There were the four battalions of troops, the gendarmes, the Catholic priests, and the chief dignitaries; and in their presence all the Huguenot books were destroyed. They were thrown into a pile on the usual place of execution, and the hangman set fire to this great mass of Bibles, psalm-books, catechisms, and sermons.* The officers laughed, the priests sneered, the multitude cheered. These bonfires were of frequent occurrence in all the towns of Languedoc.

But if the priests hated the printed word, still more did they hate the spoken word. They did not like the Bible, but they hated the preachers. Fines, *auto-da-fés*, condemnation to the galleys, seizures of women and girls, and profanation of the dead, were tolerable punishments, but there was nothing like hanging a preacher. "Nothing," said Saint-Florentin to the commandant of La Devese, "can produce more impression than hanging a preacher; and it is very desirable that you should immediately take steps to arrest one of them."

The commandant obeyed orders, and apprehended Pierre Durand. He was on his way to baptize the child of one of his congregation, who lived on a farm in Viverais. An apparent peasant, who seemed to be waiting his approach, offered to conduct him to the farm. Durand followed him. The peasant proved to be a soldier in disguise. He led Durand directly into the midst of his troop. There he was bound and carried off to Montpellier.

Durand was executed at the old place—the Peyrou—

---

* E. Hughes, "Histoire de la Restauration du Protestantisme en France," ii. 96.

the soldiers beating their drums to stifle his voice while he prayed. His corpse was laid beside that of Alexandre Roussel, under the rampart of the fortress of Montpellier. Durand was the last of the preachers in France who had attended the synod of 1715. They had all been executed, excepting only Antoine Court, who was safe in Switzerland.

The priests were not so successful with Claris, the preacher, who contrived to escape their clutches. Claris had just reached France on his return from the seminary at Lausanne. He had taken shelter for the night with a Protestant friend at Foissac, near Uzes. Scarcely had he fallen asleep, when the soldiers, informed by the spies, entered his chamber, bound him, and marched him off on foot by night, to Alais. He was thrown into gaol, and was afterwards judged and condemned to death. His friends in Alais, however, secretly contrived to get an iron chisel passed to him in prison. He raised the stone of a chamber which communicated with his dungeon, descended to the ground, and silently leapt the wall. He was saved.

Pastors and preachers continued to be tracked and hunted with renewed ardour in Saintonge, Poitou, Gascony, and Dauphiny. "The Chase," as it was called, was better organized than it had been for twenty years previously. The Catholic clergy, however, continued to complain. The chase, they said, was not productive enough! The hangings of pastors were too few. The curates of the Cevennes thus addressed the intendants: "You do not perform your duty: you are neither active enough nor pitiless enough;"* and they requested the government to adopt more vigorous measures.

* E. Hughes, ii. 99. Coquerel, "L'Eglise dans le Desert," i. 258.

The intendants, who were thus accused, insisted that they *had* done their duty. They had hanged all the Huguenot preachers that the priests and their spies had discovered and brought to them. They had also offered increased rewards for the preachers' heads. If Protestantism counted so large a number of adherents, *they* were surely not to blame for that! Had the priests themselves done *their* duty? Thus the intendants and the curés reproached each other by turns.

And yet the pastors and preachers had not been spared. They had been hanged without mercy. They knew they were in the peril of constant death. "I have slept fifteen days in a meadow," wrote Cortez, the pastor, "and I write this under a tree." Morel, the preacher, when attending an assembly, was fired at by the soldiers and died of his wounds. Pierre Dortial was also taken prisoner when holding an assembly. The host with whom he lived was condemned to the galleys for life; the arrondissement in which the assembly had been held was compelled to pay a fine of three thousand livres; and Dortial himself was sentenced to be hanged. When the aged preacher was informed of his sentence he exclaimed: "What an honour for me, oh my God! to have been chosen from so many others to suffer death because of my constancy to the truth." He was executed at Nismes, and died with courage.

In 1742 France was at war, and the Huguenots enjoyed a certain amount of liberty. The edicts against them were by no means revoked; their execution was merely suspended. The provinces were stripped of troops, and the clergy could no longer call upon them to scatter the meetings in the Desert. Hence the assemblies increased. The people began to think that the commandants of the provinces had received orders to shut their eyes, and see nothing of the proceedings of the Huguenots.

At a meeting held in a valley between Calvisson and Langlade, in Languedoc, no fewer than ten thousand persons openly met for worship. No troops appeared. There was no alarm nor surprise. Everything passed in perfect quiet. In many other places, public worship was celebrated, the sacrament was administered, children were baptized, and marriages were celebrated in the open day.*

The Catholics again urgently complained to the government of the increasing number of Huguenot meetings. The Bishop of Poitiers complained that in certain parishes of his diocese there was not now a single Catholic. Low Poitou contained thirty Protestant churches, divided into twelve arrondissements, and each arrondissement contained about seven thousand members. The Procureur-General of Normandy said, "All this country is full of Huguenots." But the government had at present no troops to spare, and the Catholic bishops and clergy must necessarily wait until the war with the English and the Austrians had come to an end.

Antoine Court paid a short visit to Languedoc in 1744, to reconcile a difference which had arisen in the Church through the irregular conduct of Pastor Boyer. Court was received with great enthusiasm, and when Boyer was re-established in his position as pastor, after making his submission to the synod, a convocation of

* Although marriages by the pastors had long been declared illegal, they nevertheless married and baptized in the Desert. After 1730, the number of Protestant marriages greatly multiplied, though it was known that the issue of such marriages were declared by the laws of France to be illegal. Many of the Protestants of Dauphiny went across the frontier into Switzerland, principally to Geneva, and were there married.

Huguenots was held near Sauzet, at which thousands of people were present. Court remained for about a month in France, preaching almost daily to immense audiences. At Nismes, he preached at the famous place for Huguenot meetings—in the old quarry, about three miles from the town. There were about twenty thousand persons present, ranged, as in an amphitheatre, along the sides of the quarry. It was a most impressive sight. Peasants and gentlemen mixed together. Even the "beau monde" of Nismes was present. Everybody thought that there was now an end of the persecution.*

In the meantime the clergy continued to show signs of increasing irritation. They complained, denounced, and threatened. Various calumnies were invented respecting the Huguenots. The priests of Dauphiny gave out that Roger, the pastor, had read an edict purporting to be signed by Louis XV. granting complete toleration to the Huguenots! The report was entirely without foundation, and Roger indignantly denied that he had read any such edict. But the report reached the ears of the King, then before Ypres with his army; on which he issued a proclamation announcing that the rumour publicly circulated that it was his intention to tolerate the Huguenots was absolutely false.

No sooner had the war terminated, and the army returned to France, than the persecutions recommenced as hotly as ever. The citizens of Nismes,

---

* Of the preachers about this time (1740-4) the best known were Morel, Foriel, Mauvillon, Voulaud, Corteiz, Peyrot, Roux, Gauch, Coste, Dugnière, Blachon, Gabriac, Déjours, Rabaut, Gibert, Mignault Desubas, Dubesset, Pradel, Morin, Defferre, Loire, Pradon,— with many more. Defferre restored Protestantism in Berne. Loire (a native of St. Omer, and formerly a Catholic), Viala, Préneuf, and Prudon, were the apostles of Normandy, Rouergue, Guyenne, and Poitou.

for having recently encouraged the Huguenots and attended Court's great meeting, were heavily fined. All the existing laws for the repression and destruction of Protestantism were enforced. Suspected persons were apprehended and imprisoned without trial. A new "hunt" was set on foot for preachers. There were now plenty of soldiers at liberty to suppress the meetings in the Desert, and they were ordered into the infested quarters. In a word, persecution was let loose all over France. Nor was it without the usual results. It was very hot in Dauphiny. There a detachment of horse police, accompanied by regular troops and a hangman, ran through the province early in 1745, spreading terror everywhere. One of their exploits was to seize a sick old Huguenot, drag him from his bed, and force him towards prison. He died upon the road.

In February, it was ascertained that the Huguenots met for worship in a certain cavern. The owner of the estate on which the cavern was situated, though unaware of the meetings, was fined a thousand crowns, and imprisoned for a year in the Castle of Cret.

Next month, Louis Ranc, a pastor, was seized at Livron while baptizing an infant, taken to Diè, and hanged. He had scarcely breathed his last, when the hangman cut the cord, hewed off the head, and made a young Protestant draw the corpse along the streets of Diè.

In the month of April, 1745, Jacques Roger, the old friend and coadjutor of Court—the apostle of Dauphiny as Court had been of Languedoc—was taken prisoner and conducted to Grenoble. Roger was then eighty years old, worn out with privation and hard work. He was condemned to death. He professed his joy at being still able to seal with his blood the truths he had so often proclaimed. On his way to the scaffold, he sang aloud the fifty-first Psalm. He was executed in the Place du Breuil. After he had hung for twenty-four hours, his body was taken down, dragged along the streets of Grenoble, and thrown into the Isere.

At Grenoble also, in the same year, seven persons were condemned to the galleys. A young woman was publicly whipped at the same place for attending a Huguenot meeting. Seven students and pastors who could not be found, were hanged in effigy. Four houses were demolished for having served as asylums for preachers. Fines were levied on all sides, and punishments of various kinds were awarded to many hundred persons. Thus persecution ran riot in Dauphiny in the years 1745 and 1746.

In Languedoc it was the same. The prisons and the galleys were always kept full. Dragoons were quartered in the Huguenot villages, and by this means the inhabitants were soon ruined. The soldiers pillaged the houses, destroyed the furniture, tore up the linen, drank all the wine, and, when they were in good humour, followed the cattle, swine, and fowl, and killed them off sword in hand. Montauban, an old Huguenot town, was thus ruined in the course of a very few months.

One day, in a Languedoc village, a soldier seized a young girl with a foul intention. She cried aloud, and the villagers came to her rescue. The dragoons turned out in a body, and fired upon the people. An old man was shot dead, a number of the villagers were taken prisoners, and, with their hands tied to the horses' tails, were conducted for punishment to Montauban.

All the towns and villages in Upper Languedoc were treated with the same cruelty. Nismes was fined over and over again. Viverais was treated with the usual severity. M. Désubas, the pastor, was taken prisoner there, and conducted to Vernoux. As the soldiers led him through the country to prison, the villagers came out in crowds to see him pass. Many followed the pastor, thinking they might be able to induce the magistrates of Vernoux to liberate him. The villagers were no sooner cooped up in a mass in the chief street of the town, than they were suddenly fired upon by the soldiers. Thirty persons were killed on the spot, more than two hundred were wounded, and many afterwards died of their wounds.

Désubas, the pastor, was conducted to Nismes, and from Nismes to Montpellier. While on his way to death at Montpellier, some of his peasant friends, who lived along the road, determined to rescue him. But when Paul Rabaut heard of the proposed attempt, he ran to the place where the people had assembled and held them back. He was opposed to all resistance to the governing power, and thought it possible, by patience and righteousness, to live down all this horrible persecution.

Désubas was judged, and, as usual, condemned to death. Though it was winter time, he was led to his punishment almost naked; his legs uncovered, and only a thin linen vest over his body. Arrived at the gallows, his books and papers were burnt before his eyes, and he was then delivered over to the executioner. A Jesuit presented a crucifix for him to kiss, but he turned his head to one side, raised his eyes upwards, and was then hanged.

The same persecution prevailed over the greater part

of France. In Saintonge, Elie Vivien, the preacher, was taken prisoner, and hanged at La Rochelle. His body remained for twenty-four hours on the gallows. It was then placed upon a forked gibbet, where it hung until the bones were picked clean by the crows and bleached by the wind and the sun.*

The same series of persecutions went on from one year to another. It was a miserable monotony of cruelty. There was hanging for the pastors; the galleys for men attending meetings in the Desert; the prisons and convents for women and children. Wherever it was found that persons had been married by the Huguenot pastors, they were haled before the magistrate, fined and imprisoned, and told that they had been merely living in concubinage, and that their children were illegitimate.

Sometimes it was thought that the persecutors would relent. France was again engaged in a disastrous war with England and Austria; and it was feared that England would endeavour to stir up a rebellion amongst the Huguenots. But the pastors met in a general synod, and passed resolutions assuring the government of their loyalty to the King, † and of their devotion to the laws of France !

Their "loyalty" proved of no use. The towns of Languedoc were as heavily fined as before, for attending meetings in the Desert.‡ Children were, as usual, taken

---

* E. Hughes, "Histoire de la Restauration," &c.,'ii. 202.

† On the 1st of November, 1746, the ministers of Languedoc met in haste, and wrote to the Intendant, Le Nain: "Monseigneur, nous n'avons aucune connaissance de ces gens qu'on appelle émissaires, et qu'on dit être envoyés des pays étrangers pour solliciter les Protestants à la révolte. Nous avons exhorté, et nous nous proposons d'exhorter encore dans toutes les occasions, nos troupeaux à la soumission au souverain et à la patience dans les afflictions, et de nous écarter jamais de la pratique de ce précepte: Craignez Dieu et honorez le roi."

‡ Près de Saint-Ambroix (Cevennes) se tint un jour une assemblée.

away from their parents and placed in Jesuit convents. Le Nain apprehended Jean Desjours, and had him hanged at Montpellier, on the ground that he had accompanied the peasants who, as above recited, went into Vernoux after the martyr Désubas.

The Catholics would not even allow Protestant corpses to be buried in peace. At Levaur a well-known Huguenot died. Two of his friends went to dig a grave for him by night; they were observed by spies and informed against. By dint of money and entreaties, however, the friends succeeded in getting the dead man buried. The populace, stirred up by the White Penitents (monks), opened the grave, took out the corpse, sawed the head from the body, and prepared to commit further outrages, when the police interfered, and buried the body again, in consideration of the large sum that had been paid to the authorities for its interment.

The populace were always wild for an exhibition of cruelty. In Provence, a Protestant named Montague died, and was secretly interred. The Catholics having discovered the place where he was buried determined to disinter him. The grave was opened, and the corpse taken out. A cord was attached to the neck, and the body was hauled through the village to the music of a tambourine and flageolet. At every step it was kicked or mauled by the crowd who accompanied it. Under the kicks the corpse burst. The furious brutes then took out the entrails and attached them to poles, going through the village crying, "Who wants preachings? Who wants preachings?"*

To such a pitch of brutality had the kings of France

Survint un détachement. Les femmes et les filles furent dépouillées, insultées, violées, et quelques hommes furent blessés.—E. HUGHES, *Histoire de la Restauration, &c.*, ii. 212.

* Antoine Court, "Memoire Historique," 140.

and their instigators, the Jesuits—who, since the Revocation of the Edict, had nearly the whole education of the country in their hands—reduced the people; from whom they were themselves, however, to suffer almost an equal amount of indignity.

In the midst of these hangings and cruelties, the bishops again complained bitterly of the tolerance granted to the Huguenots. M. de Montclus, Bishop of Alais, urged "that the true cause of all the evils that afflict the country was the relaxation of the laws against heresy by the magistrates, that they gave themselves no trouble to persecute the Protestants, and that their further emigration from the kingdom was no more to be feared than formerly." It was, they alleged, a great danger to the country that there should be in it two millions of men allowed to live without church and outside the law.*

The afflicted Church at this time had many misfortunes to contend with. In 1748, the noble, self-denying, indefatigable Claris died—one of the few Protestant pastors who died in his bed. In 1750, the eloquent young preacher, Francois Benezet,† was taken and hanged at Montpellier. Meetings in the Desert were more vigorously attacked and dispersed, and when surrounded by the soldiers, most persons were shot; the others were taken prisoners.

The Huguenot pastors repeatedly addressed Louis XV. and his ministers, appealing to them for protection as loyal subjects. In 1750 they addressed the King in a new memorial, respectfully representing that their meetings for public worship, sacraments, baptisms,

---

* See "Memorial of General Assembly of Clergy to the King," in *Collection des procès-verbaux*, 345.

† The King granted 480 livres of reward to the spy who detected Benezet and procured his apprehension by the soldiers.

and marriages, were matters of conscience. They added: "Your troops pursue us in the deserts as if we were wild beasts; our property is confiscated; our children are torn from us; we are condemned to the galleys; and although our ministers continually exhort us to discharge our duty as good citizens and faithful subjects, a price is set upon their heads, and when they are taken, they are cruelly executed." But Louis XV. and his ministers gave no greater heed to this petition than they had done to those which had preceded it.

After occasional relays the Catholic persecutions again broke out. In 1752 there was a considerable emigration in consequence of a new intendant having been appointed to Languedoc. The Catholics called upon him to put in force the powers of the law. New brooms sweep clean. The Intendant proceeded to carry out the law with such ferocity as to excite great terror throughout the province. Meetings were surrounded; prisoners taken and sent to the galleys; and all the gaols and convents were filled with women and children.

The emigration began again. Many hundred persons went to Holland; and a still larger number went to settle with their compatriots as silk and poplin weavers in Dublin. The Intendant of Languedoc tried to stop their flight. The roads were again watched as before. All the outlets from the kingdom were closed by the royalist troops. Many of the intending emigrants were made prisoners. They were spoiled of everything, robbed of their money, and thrown into gaol. Nevertheless, another large troop started, passed through Switzerland, and reached Ireland at the end of the year.

At the same time, emigration was going on from

Normandy and Poitou, where persecution was compelling the people to fly from their own shores and take refuge in England. This religious emigration of 1752 was, however, almost the last which took place from France. Though the persecutions were drawing to an end, they had not yet come to a close.

In 1754, the young pastor Tessier (called Lafage), had just returned from Lausanne, where he had been pursuing his studies for three years. He had been tracked by a spy to a certain house, where he had spent the night. Next morning the house was surrounded by soldiers. Tessier tried to escape by getting out of a top window and running along the roofs of the adjoining houses. A soldier saw him escaping and shot at him. He was severely wounded in the arm. He was captured, taken before the Intendant of Languedoc, condemned, and hanged in the course of the same day.

Religious meetings also continued to be surrounded, and were treated in the usual brutal manner. For instance, an assembly was held in Lower Languedoc on the 8th of August, 1756, for the purpose of ordaining to the ministry three young men who had arrived from Lausanne, where they had been educated. A number of pastors were present, and as many as from ten to twelve thousand men, women, and children were there from the surrounding country. The congregation was singing a psalm, when a detachment of soldiers approached. The people saw them; the singing ceased; the pastors urging patience and submission. The soldiers fired; every shot told; and the crowd fled in all directions. The meeting was thus dispersed, leaving the murderers —in other words, the gallant soldiers—masters of the field; a long track of blood remaining to mark the site on which the prayer-meeting had been held.

THE CHURCH IN THE DESERT. 249

It is not necessary to recount further cruelties and tortures. Assemblies surrounded and people shot; preachers seized and hanged; men sent to the galleys; women sent to the Tour de Constance; children carried off to the convents—such was the horrible ministry of torture in France. When Court heard of the re-inflictions of some old form of torture—"Alas," said he, "there is nothing new under the sun. In all times, the storm of persecution has cleansed the threshing-floor of the Lord."

And yet, notwithstanding all the bitterness of the persecution, the number of Protestants increased. It is difficult to determine their numbers. Their apologists said they amounted to three millions;[*] their detractors that they did not amount to four hundred thousand. The number of itinerant pastors, however, steadily grew. In 1756 there were 48 pastors at work, with 22 probationary preachers and students. In 1763 there were 62 pastors, 35 preachers, and 15 students.

Then followed the death of Antoine Court himself in Switzerland—after watching over the education and training of preachers at the Lausanne Seminary. Feeling his powers begining to fail, he had left Lausanne, and resided at Timonex. There, assisted by his son Court de Gébelin, Professor of Logic at the College, he conducted an immense correspondence with French Protestants at home and abroad.

Court's wife died in 1755, to his irreparable loss. His "Rachel," during his many years of peril, had been his constant friend and consoler. Unable, after

[*] Ripert de Monclar, procureur-général, writing in 1755, says: "According to the jurisprudence of this kingdom, there are no French Protestants, and yet, according to the truth of facts, there are three millions. These imaginary beings fill the towns, provinces, and rural districts, and the capital alone contains sixty thousand of them."

her death, to live at Timonex, so full of cruel recollections, Court returned to Lausanne. He did not long survive his wife's death. While engaged in writing the history of the Reformed Church of France, he was taken ill. His history of the Camisards was sent to press, and he lived to revise the first proof-sheets. But he did not survive to see the book published. He died on the 15th June, 1760, in the sixty-fourth year of his age.

From the time of Court's death—indeed from the time that Court left France to settle at Lausanne—Paul Rabaut continued to be looked upon as the leader and director of the proscribed Huguenot Church. Rabaut originally belonged to Bedarieux in Languedoc. He was a great friend of Pradel's. Rabaut served the Church at Nismes, and Pradel at Uzes. Both spent two years at Lausanne in 1744-5. Court entertained the highest affection for Rabaut, and regarded him as his successor. And indeed he nobly continued the work which Court had begun.

Besides being zealous, studious, and pious, Rabaut was firm, active, shrewd, and gentle. He stood strongly upon moral force. Once, when the Huguenots had become more than usually provoked by the persecutions practised on them, they determined to appear armed at the assemblies. Rabaut peremptorily forbade it. If they persevered, he would forsake their meetings. He prevailed, and they came armed only with their Bibles.

The directness of Rabaut's character, the nobility of his sentiments, the austerity of his life, and his heroic courage, evidently destined him as the head of the work which Court had begun. Antoine Court! Paul Rabaut! The one restored Protestantism in France, the other rooted and established it.

THE CHURCH IN THE DESERT. 251

Rabaut's enthusiasm may be gathered from the following extract of a letter which he wrote to a friend at Geneva: "When I fix my attention upon the divine fire with which, I will not say Jesus Christ and the Apostles, but the Reformed and their immediate successors, burned for the salvation of souls, it seems to me that, in comparison with them, we are ice. Their immense works astound me, and at the same time cover me with confusion. What would I not give to resemble them in everything laudable!"

Rabaut had the same privations, perils, and difficulties to undergo as the rest of the pastors in the Desert. He had to assume all sorts of names and disguises while he travelled through the country, in order to preach at the appointed places. He went by the names of M. Paul, M. Denis, M. Pastourel, and M. Theophile; and he travelled under the disguises of a common labourer, a trader, a journeyman, and a baker.

He was condemned to death, as a pastor who preached in defiance of the law; but his disguises were so well prepared, and the people for whom he ministered were so faithful to him, that the priests and other spies never succeeded in apprehending him. Singularly enough, he was in all other respects in favour of the recognition of legal authority, and strongly urged his brethren never to adopt any means whatever of forcibly resisting the King's orders.

Many of the military commanders were becoming disgusted with the despicable and cowardly business which the priests called upon them to do. Thus, on one occasion, a number of Protestants had assembled at the house of Paul Rabaut at Nismes, and, while they were on their knees, the door was suddenly burst open, when a man, muffled up, presented himself, and throwing open his cloak, discovered the military commandant of the town. "My friends," he said, "you have Paul Rabaut with you; in a quarter of an hour I shall be here with my soldiers, accompanied by Father ———, who has just laid the information against you." When the soldiers arrived, headed by the commandant and the father, of course no Paul Rabaut was to be found.

"For more than thirty years," says one of Paul Rabaut's biographers, "caverns and huts, whence he was unearthed like a wild animal, were his only habitation. For a long time he dwelt in a safe hiding-place that one of his faithful guides had provided for him, under a pile of stones and thorn-bushes. It was discovered at length by a shepherd, and such was the wretchedness of his condition, that, when he was forced to abandon the place, he still regretted this retreat, which was more fit for savage beasts than men."

Yet this hut of piled stones was for some time the centre of Protestant affairs in France. All the faithful instinctively turned to Rabaut when assailed by fresh difficulties and persecutions, and acted on his advice. He obtained the respect even of the Catholics themselves, because it was known that he was a friend of peace, and opposed to all risings and rebellions amongst his people.

Once he had the courage to present a petition to the Marquis de Paulmy, Minister of War, when changing horses at a post-house between Nismes and Montpellier. Rabaut introduced himself by name, and the Marquis knew that it was the proscribed pastor who stood before him. He might have arrested and hanged Rabaut on the spot; but, impressed by the noble bearing of the pastor, he accepted the petition, and promised to lay it before the king.

CHAPTER XIII

END OF THE PERSECUTIONS—THE FRENCH REVOLUTION.

IN the year 1762, the execution of an unknown Protestant at Toulouse made an extraordinary noise in Europe. Protestant pastors had so often been executed, that the punishment had ceased to be a novelty. Sometimes they were simply hanged; at other times they were racked, and then hanged; and lastly, they were racked, had their larger bones broken, and were then hanged. Yet none of the various tortures practised on the Protestant pastors had up to that time excited any particular sensation in France itself, and still less in Europe.

Cruelty against French Huguenots was so common a thing in those days, that few persons who were of any other religion, or of no religion at all, cared anything about it. The Protestants were altogether outside the law. When a Protestant meeting was discovered and surrounded, and men, women, and children were at once shot down, no one could call the murderers in question, because the meetings were illegal. The persons taken prisoners at the meetings were brought before the magistrates and sentenced to punishments even worse than death. They might be sent to the galleys, to spend the remainder of their lives amongst thieves, murderers, and assassins. Women and children found at such meetings might also be sentenced to be imprisoned in the Tour de Constance. There were even cases of boys of twelve years old having been sent to the galleys for life, because of having accompanied their parents to "the Preaching."*

The same cruelties were at that time practised upon the common people generally, whether they were Huguenots or not. The poor creatures, whose only pleasure consisted in sometimes hunting a Protestant, were so badly off in some districts of France that they even fed upon grass. The most distressed districts in France were those in which the bishops and clergy were the principal owners of land. They were the last to abandon slavery, which continued upon their estates until after the Revolution.

All these abominations had grown up in France, because the people had begun to lose the sense of individual liberty. Louis XIV. had in his time prohibited the people from being of any religion different from his own. "His Majesty," said his Prime Minister Louvois, "will not suffer any person to remain in his kingdom who shall not be of his religion." And Louis XV. continued the delusion. The whole of the tyrannical edicts and ordinances of Louis XIV. continued to be maintained.

It was not that Louis XIV. and Louis XV. were kings of any virtue or religion. Both were men of exceedingly immoral habits. We have elsewhere described Louis XIV., but Louis XV., the Well-beloved, was perhaps the greatest profligate of the two. Madame de Pompadour, when she ceased to be his mistress, became

* Athanase Coquerel, "Les Forcats pour la Foi," 91.

his procuress. This infamous woman had the command of the state purse, and she contrived to build for the sovereign a harem, called the Parc-aux-Cerfs, in the park of Versailles, which cost the country at least a hundred millions of francs.* The number of young girls taken from Paris to this place excited great public discontent; and though morals generally were not very high at that time, the debauchery and intemperance of the King (for he was almost constantly drunk) † contributed to alienate the nation, and to foster those feelings of hatred which broke forth without restraint in the ensuing reign.

In the midst of all this public disregard for virtue, a spirit of ribaldry and disregard for the sanctions of religion had long been making its appearance in the literature of the time. The highest speculations which can occupy the attention of man were touched with a recklessness and power, a brilliancy of touch and a bitterness of satire, which forced the sceptical productions of the day upon the notice of all who studied, read, or delighted in literature;—for those were the

---

* "Madame de Pompadour découvrit que Louis XV. pourrait lui-même s'amuser à faire l'éducation de ces jeunes malheureuses. De petites filles de neuf à douze ans, lorsqu'elles avaient attiré les regards de la police par leur beauté, étaient enlevées à leurs mères par plusieurs artifices, conduites à Versailles, et retenues dans les parties les plus élevées et les plus inaccessibles des petits appartements du roi. . . . Le nombre des malheureuses qui passèrent successivement à Parc-aux-Cerfs est immense; à leur sortie elles étaient mariées à des hommes vils ou crédules auxquels elles apportaient une bonne dot. Quelques unes conservaient un traitement fort considerable."
" Les dépenses du Parc-aux-Cerfs, dit Lacratelle, se payaient avec des acquits du comptant. Il est difficile de les évaluer; mais il ne peut y avoir aucune exagération à affirmer qu'elles coûtèrent plus de 100 millions à l'Etat. Dans quelques libelles on les porté jusqu'à un milliard."—SISMONDI, *Histoire de Française*, Brussels, 1844, xx. 153-4. The account given by Sismondi of the debauches of this persecutor of the Huguenots is very full. It is *not* given in the "Old Court Life of France," recently written by a lady.

† Sismondi, xx. 157.

days of Voltaire, Rousseau, Condorcet, and the great men of "The Encyclopædia."

While the King indulged in his vicious pleasures, and went reeking from his debaucheries to obtain absolution from his confessors, the persecution of the Protestants went on as before. Nor was it until public opinion (such as it was) was brought to bear upon the hideous incongruity that religious persecutions were at once brought summarily to an end.

The last executions of Huguenots in France because of their Protestantism occurred in 1762. Francis Rochette, a young pastor, twenty-six years old, was laid up by sickness at Montauban. He recovered sufficiently to proceed to the waters of St. Antonin for the recovery of his health, when he was seized, together with his two guides or bearers, by the burgess guard of the town of Caussade. The three brothers Grenier endeavoured to intercede for them; but the mayor of Caussade, proud of his capture, sent the whole of the prisoners to gaol.

They were tried by the judges of Toulouse on the 18th of February. Rochette was condemned to be hung in his shirt, his head and feet uncovered, with a paper pinned on his shirt before and behind, with the words written thereon—"*Ministre de la religion prétendue réformée.*" The three brothers Grenier, who interfered on behalf of Rochette, were ordered to have their heads taken off for resisting the secular power; and the two guides, who were bearing the sick Rochette to St. Antonin for the benefit of the waters, were sent to the galleys for life.

Barbarous punishments such as these were so common when Protestants were the offenders, that the decision of the judges did not excite any particular sensation.

END OF THE PERSECUTIONS.

It was only when Jean Calas was shortly after executed at Toulouse that an extraordinary sensation was produced—and that not because Calas was a Protestant, but because his punishment came under the notice of Voltaire, who exposed the inhuman cruelty to France, Europe, and the world at large.

The reason why Protestant executions terminated with the death of Calas was as follows:—The family of Jean Calas resided at Toulouse, then one of the most bigoted cities in France. Toulouse swarmed with priests and monks, more Spanish than French in their leanings. They were great in relics, processions, and confraternities. While "mealy-mouthed" Catholics in other quarters were becoming somewhat ashamed of the murders perpetrated during the Massacre of St. Bartholomew, and were even disposed to deny them, the more outspoken Catholics of Toulouse were even proud of the feat, and publicly celebrated the great southern Massacre of St. Bartholomew which took place in 1562. The procession then held was one of the finest church commemorations in the south; it was followed by bishops, clergy, and the people of the neighbourhood, in immense numbers.

Calas was an old man of sixty-four, and reduced to great weakness by a paralytic complaint. He and his family were all Protestants excepting one son, who had become a Catholic. Another of the sons, however, a man of ill-regulated life, dissolute, and involved in pecuniary difficulties, committed suicide by hanging himself in an outhouse.

On this, the brotherhood of White Penitents stirred up a great fury against the Protestant family in the minds of the populace. The monks alleged that Jean

Calas had murdered his son because he wished to become a Catholic. They gave out that it was a practice of the Protestants to keep an executioner to murder their children who wished to abjure the reformed faith, and that one of the objects of the meetings which they held in the Desert, was to elect this executioner. The White Penitents celebrated mass for the suicide's soul; they exhibited his figure with a palm branch in his hand, and treated him as a martyr.

The public mind became inflamed. A fanatical judge, called David, took up the case, and ordered Calas and his whole family to be sent to prison. Calas was tried by the court of Toulouse. They tortured the whole family to compel them to confess the murder;* but they did not confess. The court wished to burn the mother, but they ended by condemning the paralytic father to be broken alive on the wheel.† The parliament of Toulouse confirmed the atrocious sentence, and the old man perished in torments, declaring to the last his entire innocence. The rest of the family were discharged, although if there had been any truth in the charge for which Jean Calas was racked to death,

---

* Sismondi, xx. 328.

† To be broken alive on the wheel was one of the most horrible of tortures, a bequest from ages of violence and barbarism. It was preserved in France mainly for the punishment of Protestants. The prisoner was extended on a St. Andrew's cross, with eight notches cut on it —one below each arm between the elbow and wrist, another between each elbow and the shoulders, one under each thigh, and one under each leg. The executioner, armed with a heavy triangular bar of iron, gave a heavy blow on each of these eight places, and broke the bone. Another blow was given in the pit of the stomach. The mangled victim was lifted from the cross and stretched on a small wheel placed vertically at one of the ends of the cross, his back on the upper part of the wheel, his head and feet hanging down. There the tortured creature hung until he died. Some lingered five or six hours, others much longer. This horrible method of torture was only abolished at the French Revolution in 1790.

END OF THE PERSECUTIONS.

they must necessarily have been his accomplices, and equally liable to punishment.

The ruined family left Toulouse and made for Geneva, then the head-quarters of Protestants from the South of France. And here it was that the murder of Jean Calas and the misfortunes of the Calas family came under the notice of Voltaire, then living at Ferney, near Geneva.

In the midst of the persecutions of the Protestants a great many changes had been going on in France. Although the clergy had for more than a century the sole control of the religious education of the people, the people had not become religious. They had become very ignorant and very fanatical. The upper classes were anything but religious; they were given up for the most part to frivolity and libertinage. The examples of their kings had been freely followed. Though ready to do honour to the court religion, the higher classes did not believe in it. The press was very free for the publication of licentious and immoral books, but not for Protestant Bibles. A great work was, however, in course of publication, under the editorship of D'Alembert and Diderot, to which Voltaire, Rousseau, and others contributed, entitled "The Encyclopædia." It was a description of the entire circle of human knowledge; but the dominant idea which pervaded it was the utter subversion of religion.

The abuses of the Church, its tyranny and cruelty, the ignorance and helplessness in which it kept the people, the frivolity and unbelief of the clergy themselves, had already condemned it in the minds of the nation. The writers in "The Encyclopædia" merely gave expression to their views, and the publication of its successive numbers was received with rapture. In the midst of the free publication of obscene books, there had also appeared, before the execution of Calas, the Marquis de Mirabeau's "Ami de Hommes," Rousseau's "Emile," the "Contrat Sociale," with other works, denying religion of all kinds, and pointing to the general downfall, which was now fast approaching.

When the Calas family took refuge in Geneva, Voltaire soon heard of their story. It was communicated to him by M. de Végobre, a French refugee. After he had related it, Voltaire said, "This is a horrible story. What has become of the family?" "They arrived in Geneva only three days ago." "In Geneva!" said Voltaire; "then let me see them at once." Madame Calas soon arrived, told him the whole facts of the case, and convinced Voltaire of the entire innocence of the family.

Voltaire was no friend of the Huguenots. He believed the Huguenot spirit to be a republican spirit. In his "Siècle de Louis XIV.," when treating of the Revocation of the Edict of Nantes, he affirmed that the Reformed were the enemies of the State; and though he depicted feelingly the cruelties they had suffered, he also stated clearly that he thought they had deserved them. Voltaire probably owed his hatred of the Protestants to the Jesuits, by whom he was educated. He was brought up at the Jesuit College of Louis le Grand, the chief persecutor of the Huguenots. Voltaire also owed much of the looseness of his principles to his godfather, the Abbé Chateauneuf, grand-prior of Vendôme, the Abbé de Chalieu, and others, who educated him in an utter contempt for the doctrines they were appointed and paid to teach. It was when but a mere youth that Father Lejay, one of Voltaire's

END OF THE PERSECUTIONS.

instructors, predicted that he would yet be the Coryphæus of Deism in France.

Nor was Voltaire better pleased with the Swiss Calvinists. He encountered some of the most pedantic of them while residing at Lausanne and Geneva.* At the latter place, he covered with sarcasm the "twenty-four periwigs"—the Protestant council of the city. They would not allow him to set up a theatre in Geneva, so he determined to set up one himself at La Chatelaine, about a mile off, but beyond the Genevese frontier. His object, he professed, was " to corrupt the pedantic city." The theatre is still standing, though it is now used only as a hayloft. The box is preserved from which Voltaire cheered the performance of his own and other plays.

But though Voltaire hated Protestantism like every other religion, he also hated injustice. It was because of this that he took up the case of the Calas family, so soon as he had become satisfied of their innocence. But what a difficulty he had to encounter in endeavouring to upset the decision of the judges, and the condemnation of Calas by the parliament of Toulouse. Moreover, he had to reverse their decision against a dead man, and that man a detested Huguenot.

Nevertheless Voltaire took up the case. He wrote letters to his friends in all parts of France. He wrote to the sovereigns of Europe. He published letters in the newspapers. He addressed the Duke de Choiseul, the King's Secretary of State. He appealed to philo-

---

* While Voltaire lived at Lausanne, one of the baillies (the chief magistrates of the city) said to him: "Monsieur de Voltaire, they say that you have written against the good God: it is very wrong, but I hope He will pardon you. . . . . But, Monsieur de Voltaire, take very good care not to write against their excellencies of Berne, our sovereign lords, for be assured that they will *never* forgive you."

sophers, to men of letters, to ladies of the court, and even to priests and bishops, denouncing the sentence pronounced against Calas,—the most iniquitous, he said, that any court professing to act in the name of justice had ever pronounced. Ferney was visited by many foreigners, from Germany, America, England, and Russia; as well as by numerous persons of influence in France. To all these he spoke vehemently of Calas and his sentence. He gave himself no rest until he had inflamed the minds of all men against the horrible injustice.

At length, the case of Calas became known all over France, and in fact all over Europe. The press of Paris rang with it. In the boudoirs and salons, Calas was the subject of conversation. In the streets, men meeting each other would ask, "Have you heard of Calas?" The dead man had already become a hero and a martyr!

An important point was next reached. It was decided that the case of Calas should be remitted to a special court of judges appointed to consider the whole matter. Voltaire himself proceeded to get up the case. He prepared and revised the memorials, he revised all the pleadings of the advocates, transforming them into brief, conclusive arguments, sparkling with wit, reason, and eloquence. The revision of the process commenced. The people held their breaths while it proceeded.

At length, in the spring of 1766—four years after Calas had been broken to death on the wheel—four years after Voltaire had undertaken to have the unjust decision of the Toulouse magistrates and parliament reversed, the court of judges, after going completely over the evidence, pronounced the judgment to have been entirely unfounded!

The decree was accordingly reversed. Jean Calas was declared to have been innocent. The man was, however, dead. But in order to compensate his family, the ministry granted 36,000 francs to Calas's widow, on the express recommendation of the court which reversed the abominable sentence.*

The French people never forgot Voltaire's efforts in this cause. Notwithstanding all his offences against morals and religion, Voltaire on this occasion acted on his best impulses. Many years after, in 1778, he visited Paris, where he was received with immense enthusiasm. He was followed in the streets wherever he went. One day when passing along the Pont Royal, some person asked, "Who is that man the crowd is following?" "Ne savez vous pas," answered a common woman, "que c'est le sauveur de Calas!" Voltaire was more touched with this simple tribute to his fame than with all the adoration of the Parisians.

It was soon found, however, that there were many persons still suffering in France from the cruelty of priests and judges; and one of these occurred shortly after the death of Calas. One of the ordinary practices of the Catholics was to seize the children of Protestants and carry them off to some nunnery to be educated at the expense of their parents. The priests of Toulouse had obtained a *lettre de cachet* to take away the daughter of a Protestant named Sirven, to compel her to change her religion. She was accordingly seized and carried off to a nunnery. She manifested such reluctance to embrace Catholicism, and she was treated with such cruelty, that she fled from the convent in the night, and fell into a well, where she was found drowned.

* It may be added that, after the reversal of the sentence, David, the judge who had first condemned Calas, went insane, and died in a madhouse.

The prejudices of the Catholic bigots being very much excited about this time by the case of Calas, blamed the family of Sirven (in the same manner as they had done that of Calas) with murdering their daughter. Foreseeing that they would be apprehended if they remained, the whole family left the city, and set out for Geneva. After they left, Sirven was in fact sentenced to death *par contumace*. It was about the middle of winter when they set out, and Sirven's wife died of cold on the way, amidst the snows of the Jura.

On his arrival at Geneva, Sirven stated his case to Voltaire, who took it up as he had done that of Calas. He exerted himself as before. Advocates of the highest rank offered to conduct Sirven's case; for public opinion had already made considerable progress. Sirven was advised to return to Toulouse, and offer himself as a prisoner. He did so. The case was tried with the same results as before; the advocates, acting under Voltaire's instructions and with his help, succeeded in obtaining the judges' unanimous decision that Sirven was innocent of the crime for which he had already been sentenced to death.

After this, there were no further executions of Protestants in France. But what became of the Huguenots at the galleys, who still continued to endure a punishment from day to day, even worse than death itself? *

---

* The Huguenots sometimes owed their release from the galleys to money payments made by Protestants (but this was done secretly), the price of a galley-slave being about a thousand crowns; sometimes they owed it to the influence of Protestant princes; but never to the voluntary mercy of the Catholics. In 1742, while France was at war with England, and Prussia was quietly looking on, Antoine Court made an appeal to Frederick the Great, and at his intervention with Louis XV. thirty galley-slaves were liberated. The Margrave of Bayreuth, Culmbach and his wife, the sister of the Great Frederick, afterwards visited the galleys at Toulon, and succeeded in obtaining the liberation of several galley-slaves.

Although they were often cut off by fever, starvation, and exposure, many of them contrived to live on to a considerable age. After the trials of Calas and Sirven, the punishment of the galleys was evidently drawing to an end. Only two persons were sent to the galleys during the year in which Pastor Rochette was hanged. But a circumstance came to light respecting one of the galley-slaves who had been liberated in that very year (1762), which had the effect of eventually putting an end to the cruelty.

The punishment was not, however, abolished by Christian feeling, or by greater humanity on the part of the Catholics; nor was it abolished through the ministers of justice, and still less by the order of the King. It was put an end to by the Stage! As Voltaire, the Deist, terminated the hanging of Protestants, so did Fenouillot, the player, put an end to their serving as galley-slaves. The termination of this latter punishment has a curious history attached to it.

It happened that a Huguenot meeting for worship was held in the neighbourhood of Nismes, on the first day of January, 1756. The place of meeting was called the Lecque,* situated immediately north of the Tour Magne, from which the greater part of the city has been built. It was a favourable place for holding meetings; but it was not so favourable for those who wished to escape. The assembly had scarcely been constituted by prayer, when the alarm was given that the soldiers were upon them! The people fled on all sides. The youngest and most agile made their escape by climbing the surrounding rocks.

Amongst these, Jean Fabre, a young silk merchant

* This secret meeting-place of the Huguenots is well known from the engraved picture of Boze.

of Nismes, was already beyond reach of danger, when he heard that his father had been made a prisoner. The old man, who was seventy-eight, could not climb as the others had done, and the soldiers had taken him and were leading him away. The son, who knew that his father would be sentenced to the galleys for life, immediately determined, if possible, to rescue him from this horrible fate. He returned to the group of soldiers who had his father in charge, and asked them to take him prisoner in his place. On their refusal, he seized his father and drew him from their grasp, insisting upon them taking himself instead. The sergeant in command at first refused to adopt this strange substitution; but, conquered at last by the tears and prayers of the son, he liberated the aged man and accepted Jean Fabre as his prisoner.

Jean Fabre was first imprisoned at Nismes, where he was prevented seeing any of his friends, including a certain young lady to whom he was about shortly to be married. He was then transferred to Montpellier to be judged; where, of course, he was condemned, as he expected, to be sent to the galleys for life. With this dreadful prospect before him, of separation from all that he loved—from his father, for whom he was about to suffer so much; from his betrothed, who gave up all hope of ever seeing him again—and having no prospect of being relieved from his horrible destiny, his spirits failed, and he became seriously ill. But his youth and Christian resignation came to his aid, and he finally recovered.

The Protestants of Nismes, and indeed of all Languedoc, were greatly moved by the fate of Jean Fabre. The heroism of his devotion to his parent soon became known, and the name of the volunteer convict was in every mouth. The Duc de Mirepoix, then governor of the province, endeavoured to turn the popular feeling to some account. He offered pardon to Fabre and Turgis (who had been taken prisoner with him) provided Paul Rabaut, the chief pastor of the Desert, a hard-working and indefatigable man, would leave France and reside abroad. But neither Fabre, nor Rabaut, nor the Huguenots generally, had any confidence in the mercy of the Catholics, and the proposal was coldly declined.

Fabre was next sent to Toulon under a strong escort of cavalry. He was there registered in the class of convicts; his hair was cut close; he was clothed in the ignominious dress of the galley-slave, and placed in a galley among murderers and criminals, where he was chained to one of the worst. The dinner consisted of a porridge of cooked beans and black bread. At first he could not touch it, and preferred to suffer hunger. A friend of Fabre, who was informed of his starvation, sent him some food more savoury and digestible; but his stomach was in such a state that he could not eat even that. At length he became accustomed to the situation, though the place was a sort of hell, in which he was surrounded by criminals in rags, dirt, and vermin, and, worst of all, distinguished for their abominable vileness of speech. He was shortly after seized with a serious illness, when he was sent to the hospital, where he found many Huguenot convicts imprisoned, like himself, because of their religion.*

Repeated applications were made to Saint-Florentin, the Secretary of State, by Fabre's relatives, friends,

* Letter of Jean Fabre, in Athanase Cocquerel's "Forçats pour la Foi," 201-3.

and fellow Protestants for his liberation, but without result. After he had been imprisoned for some years, a circumstance happened which more than anything else exasperated his sufferings. The young lady to whom he was engaged had an offer of marriage made to her by a desirable person, which her friends were anxious that she should accept. Her father had been struck by paralysis, and was poor and unable to maintain himself as well as his daughter. He urged that she should give up Fabre, now hopelessly imprisoned for life, and accept her new lover.

Fabre himself was consulted on the subject; his conscience was appealed to, and how did he decide? It was only after the bitterest struggle, that he determined on liberating his betrothed. He saw no prospect of his release, and why should he sacrifice her? Let her no longer be bound up with his fearful fate, but be happy with another if she could.

The young lady yielded, though not without great misgivings. The day for her marriage with her new lover was fixed; but, at the last moment, she relented. Her faithfulness and love for the heroic galley-slave had never been shaken, and she resolved to remain constant to him, to remain unmarried if need be, or to wait for his liberation until death!

It is probable that her noble decision determined Fabre and Fabre's friends to make a renewed effort for his liberation. At last, after having been more than six years a galley-slave, he bethought him of a method of obtaining at least a temporary liberty. He proposed —without appealing to Saint-Florentin, who was the bitter enemy of the Protestants—to get his case made known to the Duc de Choiseul, Minister of Marine. This nobleman was a just man, and it had been in a

END OF THE PERSECUTIONS.

great measure through his influence that the judgment of Calas had been reconsidered and reversed.

Fabre, while on the rowers' bench, had often met with a M. Johannot, a French Protestant, settled at Frankfort-on-Maine, to whom he stated his case. It may be mentioned that Huguenot refugees, on their visits to France, often visited the Protestant prisoners at the galleys, relieved their wants, and made intercession for them with the outside world. It may also be incidentally mentioned that this M. Johannot was the ancestor of two well-known painters and designers, Alfred and Tony, who have been the illustrators of some of our finest artistic works.

Johannot made the case of Fabre known to some French officers whom he met at Frankfort, interested them greatly in his noble character and self-sacrifice, and the result was that before long Fabre obtained, directly from the Duc de Choiseul, leave of absence from the position of galley-slave. The annoyance of Saint-Florentin, Minister of State, was so well-known, that Fabre, on his liberation, was induced to conceal himself. Nor could he yet marry his promised wife, as he had not been discharged, but was only on leave of absence; and Saint-Florentin obstinately refused to reverse the sentence that had been pronounced against him.

In the meantime, Fabre's name was becoming celebrated. He had no idea, while privately settled at Ganges as a silk stocking maker, that great people in France were interesting themselves about his fate. The Duchesse de Grammont, sister of the Duc de Choiseul, had heard about him from her brother; and the Prince de Beauvau, governor of Languedoc, the Duchesse de Villeroy, and many other distinguished personages, were celebrating his heroism.

Inquiry was made of the sergeant who had originally apprehended Fabre, upon his offering himself in exchange for his father (long since dead), and the sergeant confirmed the truth of the noble and generous act. At the same time, M. Alison, first consul at Nismes, confirmed the statement by three witnesses, in presence of the secretary of the Prince de Beauvau. The result was, that Jean Fabre was completely exonerated from the charge on account of which he had been sent to the galleys. He was now a free man, and at last married the young lady who had loved him so long and so devotedly.

One day, to his extreme surprise, Fabre received from the Duc de Choiseul a packet containing a drama, in which he found his own history related in verse, by Fenouillot de Falbaire. It was entitled "The Honest Criminal." Fabre had never been a criminal, except in worshipping God according to his conscience, though that had for nearly a hundred years been pronounced a crime by the law of France.

The piece, which was of no great merit as a tragedy, was at first played before the Duchesse de Villeroy and her friends, with great applause, Mdlle. Clairon playing the principal female part. Saint-Florentin prohibited the playing of the piece in public, protesting to the last against the work and the author. Voltaire played it at Ferney, and Queen Marie Antoinette had it played in her presence at Versailles. It was not until 1789 that the piece was played in the theatres of Paris, when it had a considerable success.

We do not find that any Protestants were sent to be galley-slaves after 1762, the year that Calas was executed. A reaction against this barbarous method of treating men for differences of opinion seems to have set in; or, perhaps, it was because most men were ceasing to believe in the miraculous powers of the priests, for which the Protestants had so long been hanged and made galley-slaves.

After the liberation of Fabre in 1762, other galley-slaves were liberated from time to time. Thus, in the same year, Jean Albiges and Jean Barran were liberated after eight years of convict life. They had been condemned for assisting at Protestant assemblies. Next year, Maurice was liberated; he had been condemned for life for the same reason.

While Voltaire had been engaged in the case of Calas he asked the Duc de Choiseul for the liberation of a galley-slave. The man for whom he interceded, had been a convict twenty years for attending a Protestant meeting. Of course, Voltaire cared nothing for his religion, believing Catholicism and Protestantism to be only two forms of the same superstition. The name of this galley-slave was Claude Chaumont. Like nearly all the other convicts he was a working man—a little dark-faced shoemaker. Some Protestant friends he had at Geneva interceded with Voltaire for his liberation.

On Chaumont's release in 1764, he waited upon his deliverer to thank him. "What!" said Voltaire, on first seeing him, "my poor little bit of a man, have they put *you* in the galleys? What could they have done with you? The idea of sending a little creature to the galley-chain, for no other crime than that of praying to God in bad French!"* Voltaire ended by handing the impoverished fellow a sum of money to set him up in the world again, when he left the house the happiest of men.

We may briefly mention a few of the last of the

* "Voltaire et les Genevois," par J. Gaberel, 74-5.

galley-slaves. Daniel Bic and Jean Cabdié, liberated in 1764, for attending religious meetings. Both were condemned for life, and had been at the galley-chain for ten years.

Jean Pierre Espinas, an attorney, of St. Felix de Châteauneuf, in Viverais, who had been condemned for life for having given shelter to a pastor, was released in 1765, at the age of sixty-seven, after being chained at the galleys for twenty-five years.

Jean Raymond, of Fangères, the father of six children, who had been a galley-slave for thirteen years, was liberated in 1767. Alexandre Chambon, a labourer, more than eighty years old, condemned for life in 1741, for attending a religious meeting, was released in 1769, on the entreaty of Voltaire, after being a galley-slave for twenty-eight years. His friends had forgotten him, and on his release he was utterly destitute and miserable.*

In 1772, three galley-slaves were liberated from their chains. André Guisard, a labourer, aged eighty-two, Jean Roque, and Louis Tregon, of the same class, all condemned for life for attending religious meetings. They had all been confined at the chain for twenty years.

The two last galley-slaves were liberated in 1775, during the first year of the reign of Louis XVI., and close upon the outbreak of the French Revolution. They had been quite forgotten, until Court de Gébelin, son of Antoine Court, discovered them. When he applied for their release to M. de Boyne, Minister of Marine, he answered that there were no more Protestant convicts at the galleys; at least, he believed so.

* "Lettres inédites des Voltaire," publiées par Athanase Coquerel fils, 247.

END OF THE PERSECUTIONS.

Shortly after, Turgot succeeded Boyne, and application was made to him. He answered that there was no need to recommend such objects to him for liberation, as they were liberated already.

On the two old men being told they were released, they burst into tears; but were almost afraid of returning to the world which no longer knew them. One of them was Antoine Rialle, a tailor of Aoste, in Dauphiny, who had been condemned by the parliament of Grenoble to the galleys for life " for contravening the edicts of the King concerning religion." He was seventy-eight years old, and had been a galley-slave for thirty years.

The other, Paul Achard, had been a shoemaker of Châtillon, also in Dauphiny. He was condemned to be a galley-slave for life by the parliament of Grenoble, for having given shelter to a pastor. Achard had also been confined at the galleys for thirty years.

It is not known when the last Huguenot women were liberated from the Tour de Constance, at Aiguesmorts. It would probably be about the time when the last Huguenots were liberated from the galleys. An affecting picture has been left by an officer who visited the prison at the release of the last prisoners. " I accompanied," he says, " the Prince de Beauveau (the intendant of Languedoc under Louis XVI.) in a survey which he made of the coast. Arriving at Aiguesmorts, at the gate of the Tour de Constance, we found at the entrance the principal keeper, who conducted us by dark steps through a great gate, which opened with an ominous noise, and over which was inscribed a motto from Dante—' Lasciate ogni speranza voi che'ntrate.'

" Words fail me to describe the horror with which we regarded a scene to which we were so unaccustomed—

a frightful and affecting picture, in which the interest was heightened by disgust. We beheld a large circular apartment, deprived of air and of light, in which fourteen females still languished in misery. It was with difficulty that the Prince smothered his emotion; and doubtless it was the first time that these unfortunate creatures had there witnessed compassion depicted upon a human countenance; I still seem to behold the affecting apparition. They fell at our feet, bathed in tears, and speechless, until, emboldened by our expressions of sympathy, they recounted to us their sufferings. Alas! all their crime consisted in having been attached to the same religion as Henry IV. The youngest of these martyrs was more than fifty years old. She was but *eight* when first imprisoned for having accompanied her mother to hear a religious service, and her punishment had continued until now!"[*]

After the liberation of the last of the galley-slaves there were no further apprehensions nor punishments of Protestants. The priests had lost their power; and the secular authority no longer obeyed their behests. The nation had ceased to believe in them; in some places they were laughed at; in others they were detested. They owed this partly to their cruelty and intolerance, partly to their luxury and self-indulgence amidst the poverty of the people, and partly to the sarcasms of the philosophers, who had become more powerful in France than themselves. "It is not enough," said Voltaire, "that we prove intolerance to be horrible; we must also prove to the French that it is ridiculous."

In looking back at the sufferings of the Huguenots remaining in France since the Revocation of the Edict

[*] Froissard, "Nismes et ses Environs," ii. 217.

END OF THE PERSECUTIONS.

of Nantes; at the purity, self-denial, honesty, and industry of their lives; at the devotion with which they adhered to religious duty and the worship of God; we cannot fail to regard them—labourers and peasants though they were—as amongst the truest, greatest, and worthiest heroes of their age. When society in France was falling to pieces; when its men and women were ceasing to believe in themselves and in each other; when the religion of the State had become a mass of abuse, consistent only in its cruelty; when the debauchery of its kings* had descended through the aristocracy to the people, until the whole mass was becoming thoroughly corrupt; these poor Huguenots seem to have been the only constant and true men, the only men holding to a great idea, for which they were willing to die—for they were always ready for martyrdom by the rack, the gibbet, or the galleys, rather than forsake the worship of God freely and according to conscience.

But their persecution was now in a great measure at

---

* Such was the dissoluteness of the manners of the court, that no less than 500,000,000 francs of the public debt, or £20,000,000 sterling, had been incurred for expenses too ignominious to bear the light, or even to be named in the public accounts. It appears from an authentic document, quoted in Soulavie's history, that in the sixteen months immediately preceding the death of Louis XV., Madame du Barry (originally a courtezan,) had drawn from the royal treasury no less than 2,450,000 francs, or equal to about £200,000 of our present money. ["Histoire de la Décadence de la Monarchie Française," par Soulavie l'Aîné, iii. 330.] "La corruption," says Lacretelle, "entrait dans les plus paisibles ménages, dans les familles les plus obscures. Elle [Madame du Barri] était savamment et longtemps combinée par ceux qui servaient les débauches de Louis. Des émissaires étaient employées à séduire des filles qui n'étaient point encore nubiles, à combattre dans de jeunes femmes des principes de pudeur et de fidélité. Amant de grade, il livrait à la prostitution publique celles de ses sujettes qu'il avait prématurement corrompues. Il souffrait que les enfans de ses infames plaisirs partageassent la destinée obscure et dangereuse de ceux qu'un père n'avoue point." LACRETELLE, *Histoire de France pendant le* xviii *Siècle*, iii. 171-173.

an end. It is true the Protestants were not recognised, but they nevertheless held their worship openly, and were not interfered with. When Louis XVI. succeeded to the throne in 1774, on the administration of the oath for the extermination of heretics denounced by the Church, the Archbishop of Toulouse said to him: "It is reserved for you to strike the final blow against Calvinism in your dominions. Command the dispersion of the schismatic assemblies of the Protestants, exclude the sectarians, without distinction, from all offices of the public administration, and you will insure among your subjects the unity of the true Christian religion."

No attention was paid to this and similar appeals for the restoration of intolerance. On the contrary, an Edict of Toleration was issued by Louis XVI. in 1787, which, though granting a legal existence to the Protestants, nevertheless set forth that "The Catholic, Apostolic, and Roman religion alone shall continue to enjoy the right of public worship in our realm."

Opinion, however, moved very fast in those days. The Declaration of Rights of 1789 overthrew the barriers which debarred the admission of Protestants to public offices. On the question of tolerance, Rabaut Saint-Etienne, son of Paul Rabaut, who sat in the National Assembly for Nismes, insisted on the freedom of the Protestants to worship God after their accustomed forms. He said he represented a constituency of 360,000, of whom 120,000 were Protestants. The penal laws against the worship of the Reformed, he said, had never been formally abolished. He claimed the rights of Frenchmen for two millions of useful citizens. It was not toleration he asked for, *it was liberty.*"

"Toleration!" he exclaimed; "sufferance! pardon! clemency! ideas supremely unjust towards the Protestants, so long as it is true that difference of religion, that difference of opinion, is not a crime! Toleration! I demand that toleration should be proscribed in its turn, and deemed an iniquitous word, dealing with us as citizens worthy of pity, as criminals to whom pardon is to be granted!"*

The motion before the House was adopted with a modification, and all Frenchmen, without distinction of religious opinions, were declared admissible to all offices and employments. Four months later, on the 15th March, 1790, Rabaut Saint-Etienne himself, son of the long proscribed pastor of the Desert, was nominated President of the Constituent Assembly, succeeding to the chair of the Abbé Montesquieu.

He did not, however, occupy the position long. In the struggles of the Convention he took part with the Girondists, and refused to vote for the death of Louis XVI. He maintained an obstinate struggle against the violence of the Mountain. His arrest was decreed; he was dragged before the revolutionary tribunal, and condemned to be executed within twenty-four hours.

The horrors of the French Revolution hide the doings of Protestantism and Catholicism alike for several years, until Buonaparte came into power. He recognised Catholicism as the established religion, and paid for the maintenance of the bishops and priests. He also protected Protestantism, the members of which were entitled to all the benefits secured to the other Chris-

---

* "History of the Protestants of France," by G. de Félice, book v. sect. i.

tian communions, "with the exception of pecuniary subvention."

The comparative liberty which the Protestants of France had enjoyed under the Republic and the Empire seemed to be in some peril at the restoration of the Bourbons. The more bigoted Roman Catholics of the South hailed their return as the precursors of renewed persecution : and they raised the cry of " Un Dieu, un Roi, une Foi."

The Protestant mayor of Nismes was publicly insulted, and compelled to resign his office. The mob assembled in the streets and sang ferocious songs, threatening to " make black puddings of the blood of the Calvinists' children."* Another St. Bartholomew was even threatened; the Protestants began to conceal themselves, and many fled for refuge to the Upper Cevennes. Houses were sacked, their inmates outraged, and in many cases murdered.

The same scenes occurred in most of the towns and villages of the department of Gard; and the authorities seemed to be powerless to prevent them. The Protestants at length began to take up arms for their defence; the peasantry of the Cevennes brought from their secret places the rusty arms which their fathers had wielded more than a century before; and another Camisard war seemed imminent.

In the meantime, the subject of the renewed Protestant persecutions in the South of France was, in May, 1816, brought under the notice of the British House of Commons by Sir Samuel Romilly—himself the descendant of a Languedoc Huguenot—in a powerful

* See the Rev. Mark Wilks's "History of the Persecutions endured by the Protestants of the South of France, 1814, 1815, 1816." Longmans, 1821.

END OF THE PERSECUTIONS.

speech; and although the motion was opposed by the Government, there can be little doubt that the discussion produced its due effect; for the Bourbon Government, itself becoming alarmed, shortly after adopted vigorous measures, and the persecution was brought to an end.

Since that time the Protestants of France have remained comparatively unmolested. Evidences have not been wanting to show that the persecuting spirit of the priest-party has not become extinct. While the author was in France in 1870, to visit the scenes of the wars of the Camisards, he observed from the papers that a French deputy had recently brought a case before the Assembly, in which a Catholic curé of Ville-d'Avray refused burial in the public cemetery to the corpse of a young English lady, because she was a Protestant, and remitted it to the place allotted for criminals and suicides. The body accordingly lay for eighteen days in the cabin of the gravedigger, until it could be transported to the cemetery of Sèvres, where it was finally interred.

But the people of France, as well as the government, have become too indifferent about religion generally, to persecute any one on its account. The nation is probably even now suffering for its indifference, and the spectacle is a sad one. It is only the old, old story. The sins of the fathers are being visited on the children. Louis XIV. and the French nation of his time sowed the wind, and their descendants at the Revolution reaped the whirlwind. And who knows how much of the sufferings of France during the last few years may have been due to the ferocious intolerance, the abandonment to vicious pleasures, the thirst for dominion, and the hunger for "glory," which above all others characterized the reign of that monarch who is in history miscalled "the Great?"

It will have been noted that the chief scenes of the revival of Protestantism described in the preceding pages occurred in Languedoc and the South of France, where the chief strength of the Huguenots always lay. The Camisard civil war which happened there, was not without its influence. The resolute spirit which it had evoked survived. The people were purified by suffering, and though they did not conquer civil liberty, they continued to live strong, hardy, virtuous lives. When Protestantism was at length able to lift up its head after so long a period of persecution, it was found that, during its long submergence, it had lost neither in numbers, in moral or intellectual vigour, nor in industrial power.

To this day the Protestants of Languedoc cherish the memory of their wanderings and worshippings in the Desert; and they still occasionally hold their meetings in the old frequented places. Not far from Nismes are several of these ancient meeting-places of the persecuted, to which we have above referred. One of them is about two miles from the city, in the bed of a mountain torrent. The worshippers arranged themselves along the slopes of the narrow valley, the pastor preaching to to them from the grassy level in the hollow, while sentinels posted on the adjoining heights gave warning of the approach of the enemy. Another favourite place of meeting was the hollow of an ancient quarry called the Echo, from which the Romans had excavated much of the stone used in the building of the city. The congregation seated themselves around the craggy sides, the preacher's pulpit being placed in the narrow pass leading into the quarry. Notwithstanding all the

END OF THE PERSECUTIONS.

vigilance of the sentinels, many persons of both sexes and various ages were often dragged from the Echo to imprisonment or death. Even after the persecutions had ceased, these meeting-places continued to be frequented by the Protestants of Nismes, and they were sometimes attended by five or six thousand persons, and on sacrament days by even double that number.

Although the Protestants of Languedoc for the most part belong to the National Reformed Church, the independent character of the people has led them to embrace Protestantism in other forms. Thus, the Evangelical Church is especially strong in the South, whilst the Evangelical Methodists number more congregations and worshippers in Languedoc than in all the rest of France. There are also in the Cevennes several congregations of Moravian Brethren. But perhaps one of the most curious and interesting issues of the Camisard war is the branch of the Society of Friends still existing in Languedoc—the only representatives of that body in France, or indeed on the European continent.

When the Protestant peasants of the Cevennes took up arms and determined to resist force by force, there were several influential men amongst them who kept back and refused to join them. They held that the Gospel they professed did not warrant them in taking up arms and fighting, even against the enemies who plundered and persecuted them. And when they saw the excesses into which the Camisards were led by the war of retaliation on which they had entered, they were the more confirmed in their view that the attitude which the rebels had assumed, was inconsistent with the Christian religion.

After the war had ceased, these people continued to associate together, maintaining a faithful testimony against war, refusing to take oaths, and recognising silent worship, without dependence on human acquirements. They were not aware of the existence of a similar body in England and America until the period of the French Revolution, when some intercourse began to take place between them.

In 1807, Stephen Grellet, an American Friend, of French origin, visited Languedoc, and held many religious meetings in the towns and villages of the Lower Cevennes, which were not only attended by the Friends of Congenies, St. Hypolite, Ganges, St. Gilles, Fontanés, Vauvert, Quissac, and other places in the neighbourhood of Nismes, but by the inhabitants at large, Roman Catholics as well as Protestants. At that time, as now, Congenies was regarded as the centre of the district principally inhabited by the Friends, and there they possess a large and commodious meeting-house, built for the purpose of worship.

At the time of Stephen Grellet's visit, he especially mentioned Louis Majolier as "a father and a pillar" amongst the little flock.* And it may not be unworthy to note that the daughter of the same Louis Majolier is at the present time one of the most acceptable female preachers of the Society of Friends in England.

It may also be mentioned, in passing, that there still exist amongst the Vosges mountains the remnants of an ancient sect—the Anabaptists of Munster—who hold views in many respects similar to those of the Friends. Amongst other things, they testify against war as unchristian, and refuse under any circumstances to carry arms. Rather than do so, they have at different times suffered imprisonment, persecution, and even death. The republic of 1793 respected their

* "Life of Stephen Grellet," third edition. London, 1870.

END OF THE PERSECUTIONS.

scruples, and did not require the Anabaptists to fight in the ranks, but employed them as pioneers and drivers, while Napoleon made them look after the wounded on the field of battle, and attend to the waggon train and ambulances.* And we understand that they continue to be similarly employed down to the present time.

It forms no part of our subject to discuss the present state of the French Protestant Church. It has lost no part of its activity during the recent political changes. Although its clergy had for some time been supported by the State, they had not met in public synod until June, 1872, after an interval of more than two hundred years. During that period many things had become changed. Rationalism had invaded Evangelicalism. Without a synod, or a settled faith, the Protestant churches were only so many separate congregations, often representing merely individual interests. In fact, the old Huguenot Church required reorganization; and great results are expected from the proceedings adopted at the recently held synod of the French Protestant Church.†

With respect to the French Catholic Church, its relative position to the Protestants remains the same as before. But it has no longer the power to persecute. The Gallican Church has been replaced by the Ultramontane Church, but its impulses are no kindlier, though it has become "Infallible."

The principal movement of the Catholic priests of late years has been to get up appearances of the Virgin.

---

* Michel, "Les Anabaptistes des Vosges." Paris, 1862.
† The best account of the proceedings at this synod is given in *Blackwood's Magazine* for January, 1873.

The Virgin appears, usually, to a child or two, and pilgrimages are immediately got up to the scene of her visit. By getting up religious movements of this kind, the priests and their followers believe that France will yet be helped towards the *Revanche,* which she is said to long for.

But pilgrimages will not make men; and if France wishes to be free, she will have to adopt some other methods. Bismarck will never be put down by pilgrimages. It was a sad saying of Father Hyacinthe at Geneva, that "France is bound to two influences—Superstition and Irreligion."

MEMOIRS OF DISTINGUISHED HUGUENOT REFUGEES.

I.
STORY OF SAMUEL DE PÉCHELS.

WHEN Louis XIV. revoked the Edict of Nantes, he issued a number of decrees or edicts for the purpose of stamping out Protestantism in France. Each decree had the effect of an Act of Parliament. Louis combined in himself the entire powers of the State. The King's word was law. "*L'état c'est Moi*" was his maxim.

The Decrees which Louis issued were tyrannical, brutal, and cowardly. Some were even ludicrous in their inhumanity. Thus Protestant grooms were forbidden to give riding-lessons; Protestant barbers were forbidden to cut hair; Protestant washerwomen were forbidden to wash clothes; Protestant servants were forbidden to serve either Roman Catholic or Protestant mistresses. They must all be "converted." A profession of the Roman Catholic faith was required from simple artisans—from shoemakers, tailors, masons, carpenters, and such-like—before they were permitted to labour at their respective callings.

The cruelty went further. Protestants were forbidden to be employed as librarians and printers. They could not even be employed as labourers upon the King's highway. They could not serve in any public office whatever. They were excluded from the collection of the taxes, and from all government departments. Protestant apothecaries must shut up their shops. Protestant advocates were forbidden to plead before the courts. Protestant doctors were forbidden to practise medicine and surgery. The *sages-femmes* must necessarily be of the Roman Catholic religion.

The cruelty was extended to the family. Protestant parents were forbidden to instruct their children in their own faith. They were enjoined, under a heavy penalty, to have their children baptized by the Roman Catholic priest, and brought up in the Roman Catholic religion. When the law was disobeyed, the priests were empowered to seize and carry off the children, and educate them, at the expense of the parents, in monasteries and nunneries.

Then, as regards the profession of the Protestant religion:—It was decreed by the King, that all the Protestant temples in France should be demolished, or converted to other uses. Protestant pastors were ordered to quit the country within fifteen days after the date of the Revocation of the Edict of Nantes. If found in the country after that period, they were condemned to death. A reward of five thousand five hundred livres was offered for the apprehension of any Protestant pastor. When apprehended he was hung. Protestant worship was altogether prohibited. If any Protestants were found singing psalms, or engaged in prayer, in their own houses, they were liable to have their entire property confiscated, and to be sent to the galleys for life.

These monstrous decrees were carried into effect—at a time when France reigned supreme in the domain of intellect, poetry, and the arts—in the days of Racine, Corneille, Molière—of Bossuet, Bourdaloue, and Fénélon. Louis XIV. had the soldier, the hangman, and the priest at his command; but they all failed him. They could imprison, they could torture, they could kill, they could make the Protestants galley-slaves; they could burn their Bibles, and deprive them of everything that they valued; but the impregnable rights of conscience defied them.

The only thing left for the Protestants was to fly from France in all directions. They took refuge in Switzerland, Germany, Holland, and England. The flight from France had begun before the Revocation of the Edict of Nantes, but after that act the flight rapidly increased. Not less than a million of persons are supposed to have escaped from France in consequence of the Revocation.

Steps were, however, taken by the King to stop the emigration. He issued a decree ordering that the property and goods of all those Protestants who had already escaped should be confiscated to the Crown, unless they returned within three months from the date of the Revocation. Then, with respect to the Protestants who remained in France, he decreed that all Frenchmen found attempting to escape were to be sent to the galleys for life; and that all Frenchwomen found attempting to escape were to be imprisoned for life. The spies who denounced the fugitive Protestants were rewarded by the apportionment of half their goods.

This decree was not, however, considered sufficiently severe, and it was shortly after followed by another, proclaiming that any captured fugitives, as well as any person found acting as their guide, should be condemned to death. Another royal decree was issued respecting those fugitives who attempted to escape by sea. It was to the effect, that before any ship was allowed to set sail for a foreign port, the hold should be fumigated with a deadly gas, so that any hidden

Huguenot who could not otherwise be detected, might be suffocated to death.

These measures, however, did not seem to have the effect of "converting" the French Protestants. The Dragonnades were next resorted to. Louis XIV. was pleased to call the dragoons his Booted Missionaries, *ses missionnaires bottés*. The dragonnades are said to have been the invention of Michel de Marillac, whose name will doubtless descend to infamous notoriety, like those of Catherine de Médicis, the Guises, and the authors of the Massacre of St. Bartholomew.

Yet there was not much genius displayed in the invention of the Dragonnades. It merely consisted in this: whenever it was found that a town abounded with Huguenots, the dragoons, hussars, and troops of various kinds were poured into it, and quartered on the inhabitants. Twenty, thirty, or forty were quartered together, according to the size of the house. They occupied every room; they beat their drums and blew their trumpets; they smoked, drank, and swore, without any regard to the infirm, the sick, or the dying, until the inmates were "converted."

The whole army of France was let loose upon the Huguenots. They had been beaten out of Holland by the Dutch Calvinists; and they could now fearlessly take their revenge out of their unarmed Huguenot fellow-countrymen. Whenever they quartered themselves in a dwelling, it was, for the time being, their own. They rummaged the cellars, drank the wines, ordered the best of everything, pillaged the house, and treated everybody who belonged to it as a slave. The Huguenots were not only compelled to provide for the entertainment of their guests, but to pay them their wages. The superior officers were paid fifteen francs a day, the lieutenants nine francs, and the common soldiers three francs. If the money was not paid, the household furniture, the horses and cows, and all the other articles that could be seized, were publicly sold.

No wonder that so many Huguenots were "converted" by the dragoons. Forty thousand persons were converted in Poitou. The regiment of Asfeld was the instrument of their conversion. A company and a half of dragoons occupied the house of a single lady at Poitiers until she was converted to the Roman Catholic faith. What bravery!

The Huguenots of Languedoc were amongst the most obstinate of all. They refused to be converted by the priests; and then Louis XIV. determined to dragonnade them. About sixty thousand troops were concentrated on the province. Noailles, the governor, shortly after wrote to the King that he had converted the city of Nismes in twenty-four hours. Twenty thousand converts had been made in Montauban; and he promised that by the end of the month there would be no more Huguenots left in Languedoc.

Many persons were doubtless converted by force, or by the fear of being dragonnaded; but there were also many more who were ready to run all risks rather than abjure their faith. Of those who abjured, the greater number took the first opportunity of flying from France, by land or by sea, and taking refuge in Switzerland, Germany, Holland, or England. Many instances might be given of the heroic fortitude with which the Huguenots bore the brutality of their enemies; but, for the present, it may be sufficient to mention the case of the De Péchels of Montauban.

The citizens of Montauban had been terribly treated before and after the Revocation of the Edict of Nantes. The town had been one of the principal Huguenot places of refuge in France. Hence its population was principally Protestant. Its university had been shut up. Its churches had been levelled to the ground. Its professors and pastors had been banished from France. And now it was to be dragonnaded.

The town was filled with troops, who were quartered on the Protestants. One of the burgesses called upon the Intendant, threw himself at his feet, and prayed to be delivered from the dragoons. "On one condition only!" replied Dubois, "that you become a Catholic." "I cannot," said the townsman, "because, if the Sultan quartered twenty janissaries on me, I might, for the same reason, be forced to become a Turk."

Although many of the townsmen pretended to be converted, the Protestant chiefs held firm to their convictions, and resisted all persuasions, promises, and threats, to induce them to abjure their religion. Amongst them were Samuel de Péchels de la Boissonade and the Marquise de Sabonnières, his wife, who, in the midst of many trials and sorrows, preferred to do their duty to every other consideration.

The family of De Péchels had long been settled at Montauban. Being regarded as among the heads of the Protestant party in Montauban, they were marked out by the King's ministers for the most vigorous treatment. When the troops entered the town on the 20th of August, 1685, they treated the inhabitants as if the town had been taken by assault. The officers and soldiers vied with each other in committing acts of violence. They were sanctioned by the magistrate, who authorised their excesses, in conformity with the King's will. Tumult and disorder prevailed everywhere. Houses were broken into. Persons of the reformed religion, without regard to age, sex, or condition, were treated with indignity. They were sworn at, threatened, and beaten. Their families were turned out of doors. Every room in the house was entered and ransacked of its plate, silk, linen, and clothes. When the furniture was too heavy to be carried away, it was demolished. The mirrors were slashed with swords, or shot at with pistols. In short, so far as regarded their household possessions, the greater number of the Protestants were completely ruined.

Samuel de Péchels de la Boissonade had no fewer than thirty-eight dragoons and fusiliers quartered upon him. It was intended at first to quarter these troopers on Roupeiroux, the King's adjutant; but having promptly changed his religion to avoid the horrors of the dragonnade, they were removed to the house of De Péchels, and he was ordered by Chevalier Duc, their commander, to pay down the money which he had failed to get from Roupeiroux, during the days that the troopers should have occupied his house. De Péchels has himself told the story of his sufferings, and we proceed to quote his own words:—

"Soon after," he says, "my house was filled with officers, troopers, and their horses, who took possession of every room with such unfeeling harshness that I could not reserve a single one for the use of my family; nor could I make these unfeeling wretches listen to my declaration that I was ready to give up all that I possessed without resistance. Doors were broken open, boxes and cupboards forced. They liked better to carry off what belonged to me in this violent manner than to take the keys which my wife and I, standing on either side, continued to offer. The granaries served for the reception of their horses among the grain and meal, which the wretches, with the greatest barbarity, made them trample underfoot. The very bread destined for my little children, like the rest, was contemptuously trodden down by the horses.

"Nothing could stop the brutality of these madmen. I was thrust out into the street with my wife, now very near her confinement, and four very young children, taking nothing with me but a little cradle and a small supply of linen, for the babe whose birth was almost momentarily expected. The street being full of people, diverted at seeing us thus exposed, we were delayed some moments near the door, during which we were pitilessly drenched by the troopers, who amused themselves at the windows with emptying upon our heads pitchers of water, to add to their enjoyment of our sad condition.

"From this moment I gave up both house and goods to be plundered, without having in view any place of refuge but the street, ill suited, it must be owned, for such a purpose, and especially so to a woman expecting her confinement hourly, and to little children of too tender an age to make their own way —some of them, indeed, being unable to walk or speak—and having no hope but in the mercy of God and His gracious protection."

De Péchels proceeded to the house of Marshal Boufflers, commander of the district, thinking it probable that a man of honour, such as he was supposed to be, would discourage such barbarities, and place the dragoons under some sort of military control. But no! The Marshal could not be found. He carefully kept out of the way of all Protestant complainants. De Péchels, however, met Chevalier Duc, who commanded the soldiers that had turned him out of his house. In answer to the expostulations of De Péchels, the Chevalier gave him to understand that the same treatment would be continued unless he "changed his religion." "Then," answered De Péchels, "by God's help I never will."

At length, when De Péchels' house had been thoroughly stripped, and the dragoons had decamped elsewhere, he received an order to return, in order to entertain another detachment of soldiers. The criminal judge, who had possession of the keys, entered the house, and found it in extreme disorder. "I was obliged to remain in it," says De Péchels, "amidst dirt and vermin, in obedience to the Intendant's orders, reiterated in the strictest manner by the criminal judge, that I should await the arrival of a fresh party of lodgers, who accordingly came on the day following."

The new party consisted of six soldiers of the regiment of fusiliers, who called themselves simply "missionaries," as distinct from the "booted missionaries" who had just left. They were savage at not finding anything to plunder, their predecessors having removed everything in the shape of booty. The fusiliers were shortly followed by six soldiers of Dampier's regiment, who were still more ferocious. They gave De Péchels and his wife no peace day or night; they kept the house in a constant uproar; swore and sang obscene songs, and carried their insolence to the utmost pitch. At length De Péchels was forced to quit the house, on account of his wife, who was near the time of her confinement. These are his own words:—

"For a long time we were wandering through the streets, no one daring to offer us an asylum, as the ordinance of the Intendant imposed a fine of four or five hundred livres* upon any one who should receive Protestants into their houses. My mother's house had long been filled with soldiers, as well as that of my sister De Darassus; and not knowing where to go, I suffered great agony of mind for fear my poor wife

---

* The French livre was worth three francs, or about two shillings and sixpence English money.

should give birth to her infant in the street. In this lamentable plight, the good providence of God led us to the house of Mdlle. de Guarrison, my wife's sister, from whence, most fortunately, a large number of soldiers, with their officers, were issuing. They had occupied it for some time, and had allowed the family no rest. Now they were changing their quarters, to continue their lawless mission in some country town. The stillness of the house after their departure induced us to enter it at once, and hardly had my wife accepted the bed Mdlle. de Guarrison offered her, than she was happily delivered of a daughter, blessed be God, who never leaves Himself without a witness to those who fear His name.

"That same evening a great number of soldiers arrived, and took up their quarters in M. de Guarrison's house, and two days after, this burden was augmented by the addition of a colonel, a captain, and two lieutenants, with a large company of soldiers and several servants, all of whom conducted themselves with a degree of violence scarcely to be described. They had no regard for the owners of the house, but robbed them with impunity. They had no pity for my poor wife, weak and ill as she was; nor for the helpless children, who suffered much under these miserable conditions.

"Officers, soldiers, and servants pillaged the house with odious rivalry, took possession of all the rooms, drove out the owners, and obliged the poor sick woman (by their continual threats and abominable conduct) to get up and try to retire to some other place. She crept into the courtyard, where, with her infant, she was detained in the cold for a long time by the soldiers, who would not allow her to quit the premises. At length, however, my poor wife got into the street, still, however, guarded by soldiers, who would not allow her to go out of their sight, or to speak with any one. She complained to the Intendant of their cruel ways, but instead of procuring her any relief, he aggravated her affliction, ordering the soldiers to keep strict watch over her, never to leave her, and to inform him with what persons she found a refuge, that he might make them pay the penalty."

De Péchels' wife was thus under the necessity of sleeping, with her babe and her children, in the street. After all was quiet, they sought for a door-step, and lay down for the night under the stars.

Madame de Péchels at length found temporary shelter. Mademoiselle de Delada, a friend of the Intendant, touched by the poor woman's sad condition, implored the magistrate's permission to give her refuge; and being a well-known Roman Catholic, she was at length permitted to take Madame de Péchels and her babe into her house, but on condition that four soldiers should still keep her in view. She remained there for a short time, until she was able to leave her bed, when she was privily removed to a country house belonging to Mademoiselle de Delada, not far from the town of Montauban.

To return to Samuel de Péchels. His house was still overflowing with soldiers. They proceeded to wreck what was left of his household effects; they carried off and sold his papers and his library, which was considerable. Some of the soldiers of Dampier's regiment carried off in a sack a pair of brass chimney dogs, the shovel and tongs, a grate, and some iron spits, the wretched remains of his household furniture. They proceeded to lay waste his farms and carry off his cattle, selling the latter by public auction in the square. They next pulled down his house, and sold the materials. After this, ten soldiers were quartered in a neighbouring tavern, at De Péchels' expense. Not being able to pay the expenses, the Intendant sent some archers to him to say that he would be carried off to prison unless he changed his religion. To that proposal he answered, as before, that "by the help of God he would never make that change, and that he was quite prepared to go to any place to which his merciful Saviour might lead him."

He was accordingly taken into custody, and placed, for a time, in the Royal Château. On the same day, his sister De Darassus was committed to prison. Still holding steadfast by his faith, De Péchels was, after a month's imprisonment at Montauban, removed to the prison of Cahors, where he was put into the lowest dungeon. "By the grace of my Saviour," said he, "I strengthened myself more in my determination to die rather than renounce the truth."

After lying for more than three months in the dampest mould of the lowest dungeon in the prison of Cahors, and being still found immovable in his faith, De Péchels was ordered to be taken to the citadel of Montpellier, to wait there until he could be transported to America. His wife, the Marquise de Sabonnières, having heard of his condemnation (though he was never tried), determined to see him before he left France for ever. The road from Cahors to Montpellier did not pass through Montauban, but a few miles to the east of it. Having spent the night in prayer to God, that He might endow her with firmness to sustain the trials of a scene, which was as heroic in her as it was touching to those who witnessed it, she went forth in the morning to wait along the roadside for the arrival of the illustrious body of prisoners, who were on their way, some to the galleys, some to banishment, some to imprisonment, and some to death.

At length the glorious band arrived. They were chained two and two. They were for the most part ladies and gentlemen who had refused to abjure their religion. Among them were M. Desparvés, a gentleman from the neighbourhood of Laitoure, old and blind, led by his wife; M. de la Rességuerie, of Montauban, and many more. Madame de Péchels implored leave of the guard who conducted the prisoners to have an interview with her husband. It was granted. She had been supplied with the fortitude for which she had so ardently and piously prayed to God during the whole of the past night. It seemed as if some supernatural power had prompted the discourse with her husband, which softened the hearts of those who, up to that time, had appeared inaccessible to the sentiments of humanity. The superintendent allowed the noble couple to pray together; after which they were separated without the least weakness betraying itself on the part of Madame de Péchels, who remained unmoved, whilst all the bystanders were melted into tears. The procession of guards and prisoners then went on its way.

The trials of Madame de Péchels were not yet ended. Though she had parted with her husband, who was now on his way to banishment, she had still the children with her; and, cruellest torture of all! these were now to be torn from her. One evening a devoted friend came to inform her that a body of men were to arrive next morning and take her children, even the baby from her breast, and immure them in a convent. She was also informed that she herself was to be seized and imprisoned.

The intelligence fell like a thunderbolt upon the tender mother. What was she to do? Was she to abjure her religion? She prayed for help from God. Part of the night was thus spent before she could make up her mind to part from her innocent children, who were to be brought up in a religion at variance with her own. In any case, a separation was necessary. Could she not fly, like so many other Protestant women, and live in hopes of better days to come? It was better to fly from France than encounter the horrors of a French prison. Before she parted with her children she embraced them while they slept; she withdrew a few steps to tear herself from them, and again she came back to bid them a last farewell!

At length, urged by the person who was about to give her a refuge in his house, she consented to follow him. The man was a weaver by trade, and all day long he carried on his work in the only room which he possessed. Madame de Péchels passed the day in a recess, concealed by the bed of her entertainers, and in the evening she came out, and the good people supplied her with what was necessary. She passed six months in this retreat, without any one knowing what had become of her. It was thought that she had taken refuge in some foreign country.

Numbers of ladies had already been able to make their escape. The frontier was strictly guarded by troops, police, and armed peasantry. The high-roads as well as the byways were patrolled day and night, and all the bridges were strongly guarded. But the fugitives avoided the frequented routes. They travelled at night, and hid themselves during the day. There were Protestant guides who knew every pathway leading out of France, through forests, wastes, or mountain paths, where no patrols were on the watch; and they thus succeeded in leading thousands of refugee Protestants across the frontier. And thus it was that Madame de Péchels was at length enabled, with the help of a guide, to reach Geneva, one of the great refuges of the Huguenots.

On arrival there she felt the loss of her children

more than ever. She offered to the guide who had conducted her all the money that she possessed to bring her one or other of her children. The eldest girl, then nine or ten years old, was communicated with, but having already tasted the pleasure of being her own mistress, she refused the proposal to fly into Switzerland to join her mother. Her son Jacob was next communicated with. He was seven years old. He was greatly moved at the name of his mother, and he earnestly entreated to be taken to where she was. The guide at once proceeded to fulfil his engagement. The boy fled with him from France, passing for his son. The way was long—some five hundred miles. The journey occupied them about three weeks. They rested during the day, and travelled at night. They avoided every danger, and at length the faithful guide was able to place the loving son in the arms of his noble and affectionate mother.

Samuel de Péchels was condemned to banishment without the shadow of a trial. He could not be dragooned into denying his faith, and he was therefore imprisoned, preparatory to his expulsion from France. "I was told," he said, "by the Sieur Raoul, Roqueton (or chief archer) to the Intendant of Montauban, that if I would not change my religion, he had orders from the King and the Intendant to convey me to the citadel of Montpellier, from thence to be immediately shipped for America. My reply was, that I was ready to go forthwith whithersoever it was God's pleasure to lead me, and that assuredly, by God's help, I would make no change in my religion."

After five months' imprisonment at Cahors, he was taken out and marched, as already related, to the citadel of Montpellier. The citadel adjoins the Peyrou, a lofty platform of rock, which commands a splendid panoramic view of the surrounding country. It is now laid out as a pleasure-ground, though it was then the principal hanging-place of the Languedoc Protestants. Brousson, and many other faithful pastors of the "Church in the Desert," laid down their lives there. Half-a-dozen decaying corpses might sometimes be seen swinging from the gibbets on which the ministers had been hung.

A more bitter fate was, however, reserved for De Péchels. After about a month's imprisonment in the citadel, he was removed to Aiguemortes, under the charge of several mounted archers and foot soldiers. He was accompanied by fourteen Protestant ladies and gentlemen, on their way to perpetual imprisonment, to the galleys, or to banishment. Aiguemortes was the principal fortified dungeon in the south of France, used for the imprisonment of Huguenots who refused to be converted. It is situated close to the Mediterranean, and is surrounded by lagunes and salt marshes. It is a most unhealthy place; and imprisonment at Aiguemortes was considered a slower but not a less certain death than hanging. Sixteen Huguenot women were confined there in 1686, and the whole of them died within five months. When the prisoners died off, the place was at once filled again. The castle of Aiguemortes was thus used as a prison for nearly a hundred years.

De Péchels gives the following account of his journey from Montpellier to Aiguemortes:—"Mounted on asses, harnessed in the meanest manner, without stirrups, and with wretched ropes for halters, we entered Aiguemortes, and were there locked up in the Tower of Constance, with thirty other male prisoners and twenty women and girls, who had also been brought hither, tied two and two. The men were placed in an upper apartment of the tower, and the women and girls below, so that we could hear each other pray to God and sing His praises with a loud voice."

De Péchels did not long remain a prisoner at Aiguemortes. He was shortly after put on board a king's ship bound for Marseilles. He was very ill during the voyage, suffering from sea-sickness and continual fainting fits. On reaching Marseilles he was confined in the hospital prison used for common felons and galley-slaves. It was called the Chamber of Darkness, because of its want of light. The single apartment contained two hundred and thirty prisoners. Some of them were chained together, two and two; others, three and three. The miserable palliasses on which they slept had been much worn by the galley-slaves, who had used them during their illnesses. The women were separated from the men by a linen cloth attached to the ceiling, which was drawn across every evening, and formed the only partition between them.

As may easily be supposed, the condition of the prisoners was frightful. The swearing of the common felons was mixed with the prayers of the Huguenots. The guards walked about all night to keep watch and ward over them. They fell upon any who assembled and knelt together, separating them and swearing at them, and mercilessly ill-treating them, men and women alike. "But all their strictness and rage," says De Péchels, "could not prevent one from seeing always, in different parts of the dungeon, little groups upon their knees, imploring the mercy of God and singing His praises, whilst others kept near the guards so as to hinder them from interfering with the little bands of worshippers."

At length the time arrived for the embarkation of the Huguenots for America. On the 18th of September, 1687, De Péchels, with fifty-eight men and twenty-one women, was put on board a *flûte* called the *Mary*—the French *flûte* consisting of a heavy narrow-sterned vessel, called in England a "pink." De Péchels was carefully separated from all with whom he had formed habits of intimacy, and whose presence near him would doubtless have helped him to bear the bitterness of his fate. On the same day, ninety prisoners of both sexes were embarked in another ship, named the *Concord*, bound for the same destination. The two vessels set sail in the first place for Toulon, in order to obtain an escort of two ships-of-war.

The voyage was very disastrous. Three hours after the squadron had left Toulon, the *Mary* was nearly dashed against a rock, owing to the roughness of the weather. Three days after, a frightful storm arose, and dashed the prisoners against each other. All were sick; indeed, De Péchels' malady lasted during the entire voyage. The squadron first cast anchor amongst the Formentera Islands, off the coast of Spain, where they took in water. On the next day they anchored in the Straits of Gibraltar for the same purpose. They next sailed for Cadiz, but a strong west wind having set in, the ship was forced back to the road of Gibraltar. After waiting there for three days they again started, under the shelter of a Dutch fleet of eighteen sail, "which," says De Péchels, "providentially saved us from falling into the hands of the Algerine corsairs, some of whom had appeared in sight, and from whose hands God, in His great mercy, delivered us." As if the Algerine corsairs would have treated the Huguenots worse than their own king was now treating them. The Algerine corsairs would have sold them into slavery; whilst the French king was transporting them to America for the same purpose.

At length the squadron reached Cadiz roads. Many ships were there—English as well as Dutch. When the foreigners heard of the state and misfortunes of the Huguenots on board the French ships, they came to visit them in their anchoring ground, and were profuse in their charity to the prisoners for conscience' sake confined in the two French vessels. "God, who never leaves Himself without witness, brought us consolation and relief from this town, where superstition and bigotry reign in their fullest force." As it was in De Péchels' day, so it is now.

At length the French squadron set sail for America. The voyage was tedious and miserable. There were about a hundred and thirty prisoners on board. Seventy of them were sick felons, chained with heavy irons. Being useless for the French galleys, they were now being transported to America, to be sold as slaves. The imprisoned Huguenots—men and women—were fifty-nine in number. They were crammed into a part of the ship that could scarcely hold them. They could not stand upright; nor could they lie down. They had to lie upon each other. The den was moreover very dark, the only light that entered it being through the narrow hatchway; and even this was often closed. The wonder is that they were not suffocated outright.

The burning heat of the sun shining on the deck above them, the never-ceasing fire of the kitchen, which was situated alongside their place of confinement, created such a stifling heat, that the prisoners had to take off their shirts to relieve their agony. The horrid stench arising from so many persons being crowded together, and the entire want of the means of cleanliness, caused the inmates to become covered with vermin. They were also tormented by the intolerable thirst which no means were taken to allay. Their feeding was horrible; for they must be kept alive in some way, in order that the intentions of their gracious sovereign might be carried into effect. One day they had stinking salt beef; the next, cod fish half boiled; then peas as hard as when they were put into the pot; and at other times, dried cod fish, or rank cheese. These things, together with the violent motion of the sea, occasioned severe sickness, from which many of the sufferers were relieved by death. This deplorable voyage extended over five months. Here is De Péchels' account of the sufferings of the prisoners, written in his own words:—

"The intense and suffocating heat, the horrible odour, the maddening swarm of vermin that devoured us, the incessant thirst and wretched fare, sufficed not to satisfy our overseers. They sometimes struck us rudely, and very often threw down sea-water upon us, when they saw us engaged in prayer and praise to God. The common talk of these enemies of the truth was how they would hang, when they came to America, every man who would not go to mass, and how they would deliver the women to the natives. But far from being frightened at these threats, or even moved by all the barbarities of which we were the victims, many of us felt a secret joy that we were chosen to suffer for the holy name of Jesus, who strengthened us with a willingness to die for His sake. For myself, these menaces had been so often repeated during my imprisonments, that they had become familiar; insomuch that, far from being shaken by them any more than by the sufferings to which it had pleased my Saviour to call me, I considered them as transient things, not worthy to be weighed against the glory to come, and such as would procure me a weight of glory supremely excellent.

"'Blessed are they who are persecuted for righteousness' sake, for theirs is the kingdom of heaven.'"

On the 2nd of January, 1688, the island of San Domingo came in sight. It was for the most part inhabited by savages. The French had a settlement on the west coast of the island, and the Spaniards occupied the eastern part. Dense forests separated the two settlements. The *Mary* coasted along the island, and afterwards made sail for Guadaloupe, another colony belonging to the French. The ship seemed as yet to have had no proper destination, for, four days later, the *Mary* weighed her anchor, and sailed to St. Christopher, another island partly belonging to the French. "It was well situated," says De Péchels, "as may readily be believed, when I add that it possessed a colony of Jesuits—an order which never selects a bad situation. The Jesuits here are very rich and in high repute. Two of the fraternity, having come on board, were received by the crew with every demonstration of respect; and on their retirement, three guns were fired as a mark of honour to the distinguished visitors."

The Huguenots were still under hatches,—weary, longing, wretched, and miserable. They were most anxious to be put on shore—anywhere, even among savages. But the *Mary* had not yet arrived at her destination. She again set sail, and passed St. Kitts, St. Eustace, St. Croix, Porto Rico, and at length again reached San Domingo. The ship dropped anchor before Port au Prince, the residence of the governor. The galley-slaves were disembarked and sold. Some of the Huguenots were also sold for slaves, though De Péchels was not among them. The rest were transferred to the *Maria*, a king's ship, commanded by M. de Beauguay, who treated the prisoners with much humanity. The ship then set sail for Léogane, another part of the colony, where the remaining Huguenots were disembarked. They were quartered on the inhabitants at the pleasure of the governor.

De Péchels says that he passed his time at this place in tranquillity, waiting till it might please God to afford him an opportunity of escaping from his troubles. He visited the inhabitants, especially those of his own religious persuasion—a circumstance which gave much umbrage to the Dominican monks. They ordered some of the bigots among their parishioners to lodge a complaint against him with the governor, to the effect that he was hindering his fellow-prisoners from becoming Roman Catholics, and preventing those who had become so from going to mass. He accordingly received a verbal command from M. Dumas, the King's lieutenant, to repair immediately to Avache (probably La Vache), an island about a hundred leagues distant from Léogane. He was accordingly despatched by ship to Avache, which he reached on the 8th of June. He was put in charge of Captain Laurans, a renowned freebooter, and was specially lodged under his roof. The captain was ordered never to lose sight of his prisoner.

De Péchels suffered much at this place in consequence of the intense heat, and the insects, mosquitoes, and horrible flies by which he was surrounded. "And yet," he says, "God in His great mercy willed that in this very place I should find the means of escaping from my exile, and making my way to the English island of Jamaica. On the 13th of August a little shallop of that generous nation, in its course from the island of St. Thomas to Jamaica, stopped at Avache to water and take provisions. Two months already had I watched for such an opportunity, and now that God had presented me with this, I thought it should not be neglected. So fully was I persuaded of this, that without reflecting upon the smallness of the shallop, I put myself on board with victuals for four days, although assured that the passage would only occupy three. But instead of performing the passage in three days, as we had thought, it was ten days before we made the island, during the whole of which time I was constantly unwell from bad weather and consequent sea-sickness. During the last three days I suffered also from hunger, my provisions being spent, with the exception of some little wretched food, salt and smoky, which the sailors eat to keep themselves from starving. God, in His great compassion, preserved me from all dangers, and brought me happily to Jamaica, where, however, I thought to leave my bones."

The voyage was followed by a serious illness. De Péchels was obliged to take to his bed, where he lay for fifteen days prostrated by fever, accompanied by incessant pains in his head. After the fever had left him, he could neither walk nor stand. By slow degrees his strength returned. He was at length able to walk; and he then began to make arrangements for setting out for England. On the 1st of October he embarked on board an English vessel bound for London. During his voyage north he suffered from cold, as much as he had before suffered from heat. At length the coast of England was sighted. Two days after, the ship reached the Downs; and on the 22nd of December it was borne up the Thames by the tide, to within about seven miles from London Bridge. There the ship stopped to discharge part of her cargo; and De Péchels, having taken his place on board a small sloop for the great city, arrived there at ten o'clock the same night.

On arrival in London, De Péchels proceeded to make inquiry amongst his Huguenot friends—who had by that time reached England in great numbers—for his wife, his children, his mother, and his sisters. Alas! what disappointment! He found no wife, no child, nor any relation ready to welcome him. His wife, however, was living at Geneva, with their only son; for the youngest had died at Montauban during De Péchels' exile. His daughters were still at Montauban —the eldest in a convent. His mother and youngest sister were both in prison—the one at Moissac, the other at Auvillard. A message was, however, sent to Madame de Péchels, that her husband was now in England, and longing to meet her.

It was long before the message reached Madame de Péchels; and still longer before she could join her husband in London. While at Geneva, she had maintained herself and her son by the work of her hands. On receiving the message she immediately set out, but her voyage could not fail to be one of hardship to a person in her reduced circumstances. We are not informed how she and her son contrived to travel the long distance of eight hundred miles (by way of the Rhine and Holland) from Geneva to London; but at length she reached the English capital, when she had the mortification to find that her husband was not there, but had left London for Ireland only four days before. During the absence of her husband, Madame de Péchels, whose courage never abandoned her, chose rather to stoop to the most toilsome labours than to have recourse to the charity of the government, of which many, less self-helping, or perhaps more necessitous, did not scruple to take advantage.

We must now revert to the circumstances under which De Péchels left London for Ireland. At the time when he arrived in England, the country was in the throes of a Revolution. Only a month before, William of Orange had landed at Torbay, with a large body of troops, a considerable proportion of which consisted of Huguenot officers and soldiers. There were three strong regiments of Huguenot infantry, and a complete squadron of Huguenot cavalry. Marshal Schomberg, next in command to William of Orange, was a banished Huguenot; and many of his principal officers were French.

James II. had so distinctly shown his disposition to carry back the nation to the Roman Catholic religion, that the Prince of Orange, on his landing at Torbay, was hailed as the deliverer of England. His troops advanced direct upon London. He was daily joined by fresh adherents; by the gentry, officers, and soldiers. There was scarcely a show of resistance; and when he entered London, James was getting on board a smack in the Thames, and slinking ignominiously out of his kingdom. Towards the end of June, 1689, William and Mary were proclaimed King and Queen of Great Britain; and they were solemnly crowned at Westminster about three months after.

But James II. had not yet been got rid of. In the spring of 1689 he landed at Kinsale, in Ireland, with substantial help obtained from the French king. Before many weeks had elapsed, forty thousand Irish stood in arms to support his cause. It was clear that William III. must fight for his throne, and that Ireland was to be the battle-field. He accordingly called his forces together again—for the greater part had been disbanded—when he prepared to take the field in person. Four Huguenot regiments were at once raised, three infantry regiments, and one cavalry regiment. The cavalry regiment was raised by Marshal Schomberg, its colonel. It was composed of French gentlemen, privates as well as officers. De Péchels was offered a commission in the regiment, which he cheerfully accepted. He assumed the name of his barony, La

Boissonade, as was common in those days; and he acted as lieutenant in the company of La Fontain.

The regiment, when completed, was at once despatched to the north of Ireland to join the little army of about ten thousand Protestants, who had already laid siege to and taken the fortified town of Carrickfergus. Schomberg's regiment embarked from Chester, on Monday, the 25th of August, 1689; and on the following Saturday the squadron arrived in Belfast Lough. The troopers were landed a little to the west of Carrickfergus, and marched along the road towards Belfast, which is still known as "Troopers' Lane." Next day the Duke moved on in pursuit of the enemy. The regiment passed through Belfast, which was then a very small place. It consisted of a few streets of thatched cottages, grouped around what is now known as the High Street of Belfast. Schomberg's regiment joined the infantry and the Enniskilleners, who were encamped in a wood on the west of the town.

Next morning the little army started in pursuit of the enemy, who, though in much greater numbers, fled before them, laying waste the country. At night Schomberg's troops encamped at Lisburn; on the following day at Dromore; on the third at Brickclay (this must be Loughbrickland); and then on to Newry. All the villages they passed were either burnt or burning. At length they heard that James's Irish army was at Newry, and that the Duke of Berwick (James's natural son) was in possession of the town with a strong body of horse. But before Schomberg could reach the place the Duke of Berwick had evacuated it, leaving the town in flames. The Duke had fled with such haste that he had left some of his baggage behind him, and thrown his cannon into the river. Schomberg ordered his cavalry to advance rapidly upon Dundalk,

IN CAMP AT DUNDALK.

in order to prevent the town from sharing the same fate as Newry. This forced march took the enemy by surprise. They suddenly abandoned Dundalk, without burning it, and never paused until they had reached the entrenched camp of King James.

The weather had now become cold, dreary, and rainy. Provisions were scarcely to be had. The people of Dundalk were themselves starving. Strong bodies of cavalry foraged the country, but were able to find next to nothing in the shape of food for themselves, or corn for their horses. The ships from England, laden with provisions which ought to have arrived at Belfast, were forced back by contrary winds. Thus the army was becoming rapidly famished. Disease soon made its appearance, and carried off the men by hundreds. Schomberg's camp, outside Dundalk, was situated by the side of a marsh—a most unwholesome position; but the marsh protected him from the enemy, who were not far off. The rain and snow continued; the men and the horses were perpetually drenched; and scouring winds blew across the camp. Ague, dysentery, and fever everywhere prevailed. Dalrymple has recorded that of fifteen thousand men who belonged to Schomberg's army, not less than eight thousand perished. Under these circumstances, the greatly reduced force broke up from their cantonments and went into winter quarters. Schomberg's cavalry regiment was stationed at Lurgan, then a small village, which happily had not been burnt. De Péchels was one of those who had been sick in camp, and was disabled from pursuing the campaign further. After remaining for some weeks at Lurgan, he obtained leave from the Duke of Schomberg to return to London. And there, after the lapse of four years, he found and embraced his beloved and noble wife.

De Péchels continued invalided, and was unable to rejoin the army of King William. "After some stay in London," he says, in the memoir from which the above extracts are made, "it was the King's pleasure to exempt from further service certain officers specified by name, and to assign them a pension. Through a kind Providence I was included in the number. When I had lived in London on the pension which it had pleased the king to allow those officers who were no longer in a position to serve him, until the 1st of August, 1692, I then left that city, in company with my wife and son, to remove into Ireland, whither my pension was transferred."

De Péchels accordingly arrived in Dublin, where he spent the rest of his days in peace and quiet. He lived to experience the truth of the promise "that every one that hath forsaken houses, or brethren, or sisters, or father, or mother, or wife, or children, or lands for my name's sake, shall receive an hundredfold, and shall inherit everlasting life." De Péchels died in 1732, at a ripe old age, in his eighty-seventh year, and was interred in the Huguenot cemetery in the neighbourhood of Dublin.

And what of the children left by De Péchels at Montauban? The two daughters who were torn from their mother's care, and immured in a convent, were brought up in the Roman Catholic faith. The little boy, who was also taken from her, died shortly after. The daughters accordingly secured the possession of the family estates. The eldest married M. de Cahuzac, and the youngest, who was taken as a babe from her mother's breast, married M. de St. Sardos; and the descendants of the latter still possess La Boissonade, which exists as an old château near Montauban.

It was left for Jacob de Péchels, the only son of

HIS DESCENDANTS.

Samuel de Péchels and his wife, the Marquise de Sabonnières, to build up the family fortunes in England. Following the military instincts of the French, he entered the English army at an early age. His name was entered "Pechell" in his War Office commission. Probably this change of name originated in the disposition of the naturalised Huguenots to adopt names of an English sound rather than to retain their French names. Numerous instances of this have already been given.* Jacob Pechell was a gallant officer. He rose in the army, step by step. He fought through the wars in the Low Countries, under Marlborough and Ligonier, the latter being a Huguenot like himself. He rose through the various grades of ensign, lieutenant, captain, and major, until he attained the rank of colonel of the 16th regiment. Colonel Pechell married an Irish heiress, Jane Elizabeth Boyd, descended from the Earls of Kilmarnock. By her he had three sons and a daughter. Samuel, the eldest, studied law, and became a Master in Chancery. George and Paul, obedient to their military instincts, entered the army, and became distinguished officers. George was killed at Carthagena, and it was left for Paul to maintain the fortunes of the family.

In those days the exiled Huguenots and their descendants lived very much together. They married into each other's families. The richer helped the poorer. There were distinguished French social circles, where, though their country was forbidden them, they delighted to speak in their own language. Like many others, the Pechells intermarried with Huguenot families. Thus Samuel Pechell married the daughter of François Gaultier, Esq., and his sister Mary married Brigadier-General Cailland, of Aston Rowant.

* In "The Huguenots in England and Ireland," 319, 323, last edition.

Among the distinguished French nobles in London was the Marquis de Montandre, descended from the De la Rochefoucaulds, one of the greatest families in France. De Montandre was a field-marshal in the English army, having rendered important services in the Spanish war. His wife was daughter of Baron de Spanheim, Ambassador Extraordinary for the King of Prussia, and descended from another Protestant refugee. The field-marshal left his fortune to his wife, and when she died, she left Samuel Pechell, Master in Chancery, her sole executor and residuary legatee. The sum of money to which he became entitled on her decease amounted to upwards of £40,000. But Mr. Pechell, from a highly sensitive conscience—such as is rarely equalled—did not feel himself perfectly justified in acquiring so large a fortune until he knew that there were no relations of the testatrix in existence, whose claim to inherit the property might be greater than his own. He therefore collected all her effects, and put them into Chancery, in order that those who could make good their claims by kindred to the Marchioness might do so before the Chancellor. Accordingly, one family from Berlin and another from Geneva appeared, and claimed, and obtained the inheritance. These relations, in acknowledgment of the kindness and honesty of Mr. Pechell, resolved on presenting him with a set of Sèvres china, which was at that time beyond all price in value. It could only be had as a great favour from the manufactory at Sèvres, and was only purchased by, or presented to, crowned heads.*

Paul Pechell, who had entered the army, became a distinguished officer, and rose to the rank of general. In 1797 he was created a baronet, and married Mary,

---

* This china is now at Castle Goring, and, with the whole of the family documents, is in the possession of the Dowager Lady Burrell.

the only daughter and heiress of Thomas Brooke, Esq., of Pagglesham, Essex. His eldest son, Sir Thomas, was a major-general in the army, and was for some time M.P. for Downton. The second son, Augustus, was appointed Receiver-General of the Post Office in 1785, and of the Customs in 1790. Many of his descendants still survive, and the baronetcy reverted to his second son. He was succeeded by his two sons, one of whom became rear-admiral, and the other vice-admiral. The latter, Sir George Richard Brooke Pechell, entered the Royal Navy in 1803, and served with distinction in several engagements. After the peace, he represented the important borough of Brighton in Parliament for twenty-four years. He married the daughter and coheir of Cecil, Lord Zouche, and added Castle Goring to part of the ancient possessions of the Bisshopp family, which she inherited at her father's death.

William Cecil Pechell, the only son of Sir George, again following the military instincts of his race, entered the army, and became captain of the 77th regiment, with which he served during the Crimean war. He fell leading on his men to repel an attack made by the Russians on the advanced trenches before Sebastopol, on the 3rd of September, 1855. He was beloved and deeply lamented by all who knew him; and sorrow at his loss was expressed by the Queen, by the Commander-in-Chief, by the whole of the light division, and by the mayor and principal inhabitants of Brighton. A statue of Captain Pechell, by Noble, was erected by public subscription, and now stands in the Pavilion at Brighton.

II.

CAPTAIN RAPIN,

AUTHOR OF THE "HISTORY OF ENGLAND."

WHEN Louis XIV. revoked the Edict of Nantes, he expelled from France nearly all his subjects who would not conform to the Roman Catholic religion. He drove out the manufacturers, who were for the most part Protestants, and thus destroyed the manufacturing supremacy of France. He expelled Protestants of every class—advocates, judges, doctors, artists, scientists, teachers, and professors. And, last of all, he expelled the Protestant soldiers and sailors.

According to Vauban, 12,000 tried soldiers, 9,000 sailors, and 600 officers left France, and entered into foreign service. Some went to England, some to Holland, and some to Prussia. Those who took refuge in Holland entered the service of William, Prince of Orange. Most of them accompanied him to Torbay in 1688. They fought against the armies of Louis XIV. at the Boyne, at Athlone, and at Aughrim, and finally drove the French out of Ireland.

The sailors also did good service under the flags of England and Holland. They distinguished themselves at the sea-fight off La Hogue, where the English and

Dutch fleets annihilated the expedition prepared by Louis XIV. for a descent upon England.

The expatriated French soldiers occasionally revisited the country of their birth, not as friends, but as enemies. They encountered the armies of Louis XIV. in all the battles of the Low Countries. They fought at Ramilies, Blenheim, and Malplacquet. A Huguenot engineer directed the operations at the siege of Namur, which ended in the capture of the fortress. Another Huguenot engineer conducted the operations at Lisle, which was also taken by the allied forces. While there, a flying party, consisting chiefly of French Huguenots, penetrated as far as the neighbourhood of Paris, when they nearly succeeded in carrying off the Dauphin.

The Huguenot officers who took refuge in Prussia entered the service of Frederick William, Elector of Brandenburg. Some were raised to the highest offices in his army. Marshal Schomberg was one of the number. But when he found that William of Orange was assembling a large force in Holland for the purpose of making a descent upon England, he requested leave to join him; and his friend Prince Frederick William, though with great regret, at length granted him permission to leave the Prussian service.

The subject of the following narrative was a French refugee, who entered the service of William of Orange. To find the beginning of his ancestry, we must reach far back into history. The Rapins were supposed to have been driven from the Campagna of Rome during the persecutions of Nero. They took refuge in one of the wildest and most picturesque valleys of the Alps. In 1250 we find the Rapins established near Saint-Jean de la Maurienne, in Savoy, close upon the French frontier. Saint-Jean de la Maurienne was so called because of the supposed relic of the bones of St. John the Baptist, which had been deposited there by a female pilgrim, Sainte Thècle, who was, it is supposed, a Rapin by birth. The fief of Chaudane en Valloires was the patrimony of the Rapins, which they long continued to hold. In 1692 the descendants of the family endeavoured to prove, from the numerous titles which they possessed, that they had been nobles for eight or nine hundred years.

The home of the Rapins was situated in the country of the Vaudois. In 1375 the Vaudois descended from their mountains and preached the gospel in the valleys of Savoy. The Pope appealed to the King of France, who sent an army into the district. The Vaudois were crushed. Those who remained fled back to the mountains. Nevertheless the Reformed religion spread in the district. An Italian priest, Raphaël Bordeille, even preached the gospel in the cathedral of Saint-Jean de Maurienne. But he was suddenly arrested. He was seized, tried for the crime of heresy, and burnt in front of the cathedral on Holy Thursday, in Passion Week, 1550.

Though the Rapin family held many high offices in Church and State, several of them attached themselves to the Reformed religion. Three brothers at length left their home in Savoy, and established themselves in France during the reign of Francis I. Without entering into their history during the long-continued religious wars which devastated the south of France, it may be sufficient to state that two of the brothers took an active part under Condé. Antoine de Rapin held important commands at Toulouse, at Montauban, at Castres and Montpellier. Philibert de Rapin, his younger brother, was one of the most reliant and trusted officers of the Reformed party. He was selected by the Prince of Condé to carry into Languedoc the treaty of peace signed at Longjumeaux on the 20th March, 1568.

Feeling safe under the royal commission, he presented to the Parliament at Toulouse the edict with which he was intrusted. He then retired to his country house at Grenade, on the outskirts of Toulouse. He was there seized like a criminal, brought before the judges, and sentenced to be beheaded in three days. The treaty was thus annulled. War went on as before. Two years after, the army of Coligny appeared before Toulouse. The houses and châteaux of the councillors of Parliament were burnt, and on their smoking ruins were affixed the significant words, "*Vengeance de Rapin.*"

Philibert de Rapin's son Pierre embraced the career of arms almost from his boyhood. He served under the Prince of Navarre. He was almost as poor as the Prince. One day he asked him for some pistoles to replace a horse which had been killed under him in action. The Prince replied, "I should like to give you them, but do you see I have only three shirts!" Pierre at length became Seigneur and Baron of Manvers, though his château was destroyed and burnt during his absence with the army. Destructions of the same kind were constantly taking place throughout the whole of France. But, to the honour of humanity, it must be told that when his château was last destroyed, the Catholic gentlemen of the neighbourhood brought their labourers to the place, and tilled and sowed his abandoned fields. When Rapin arrived eight months later, he was surprised and gratified to find his estate in perfect order. This was a touching proof of the esteem with which this Protestant gentleman was held by his Catholic neighbours.

Pierre de Rapin died in 1647 at the age of eighty-nine. He left twenty-two children by his second wife. His eldest son Jean succeeded to the estate of Manvers and to the title of baron. Like his father, he was a soldier. He first served under the Prince of Orange, who was then a French prince, head of the principality of Orange. He served under the King of France in the war with Spain. He was a frank and loyal soldier, yet firmly attached to the faith of his fathers. He belonged to the old Huguenot phalanx, who, as the Duke de Mayenne said, "were always ready for death, from father to son." After the wars were over, he gave up the sword for the plough. His château was in ruins, and he had to live in a very humble way until his fortunes were restored. He used to say that his riches consisted in his four sons, who were all worthy of the name they bore.

Jacques de Rapin, Seigneur de Thoyras, was the second son of Pierre de Rapin. Thoyras was a little hamlet near Grenade, adjacent to the baronial estate of Manvers. Jacques studied the law. He became an advocate, and practised with success, for about fifty years, at Castres and other cities and towns in the south of France. When the Edict of Nantes was revoked, the Protestants were no longer permitted to practise the law, and he was compelled to resign his profession. He died shortly after, but the authorities would not even allow his corpse to be buried in the family vault. They demolished his place of interment, and threw his body into a ditch by the side of the road.

In the meantime Paul de Rapin, son of Jean, Baron

de Manvers, had married the eldest daughter of Jacques, Seigneur de Thoyras. Paul, like many of his ancestors, entered the army. He served with distinction under the Duke of Luxembourg in Holland, Flanders, and Italy, yet he never rose above the rank of captain. On his death in 1685, his widow and two daughters (being Protestants) were apprehended in their château at Manvers, and incarcerated in convents at Montpellier and Toulouse. Her sons were also taken away, and placed in other convents. They were only liberated after five years' confinement.

Madame de Rapin then resolved to quit France entirely. She contrived to reach Holland, and established her family at Utrecht. Her brother-in-law, Daniel de Rapin, had already escaped from France, and achieved the position of colonel in the Dutch service.

Raoul de Cazenove, the author of "Rapin-Thoyras, sa Famille, sa Vie, et ses Œuvres," says, "The women of the house of Rapin distinguished themselves more than once by like courage. Strengthened and fortified by persecutions, the Reformed were willing to die in exile, far from their beloved children who had been violently snatched from them, but leaving with them a holy heritage of example and of firmness in their faith. The pious lessons of their mothers, profoundly engraved on the hearts of their daughters, sufficed more than once to save them from apostacy, which was rendered all the more easy by the feebleness of their youth and the perfidious suggestions by which they were surrounded."

We return to Paul de Rapin-Thoyras, second son of Madame de Rapin. He was born at Castres in 1661. He received his first lessons at home. He learnt the

Latin rudiments, but his progress was not such as to please his father. He was then sent to the academy at Puylaurens, where the Protestant noblesse of the south of France were still permitted to send their sons. The celebrated Bayle was educated there. But in 1685 the academy of Puylaurens was suppressed, as that of Montauban had been a few years before; and then young Rapin was sent to Saumur, one of the few remaining schools in France where Protestants were allowed to be educated.

Rapin finished his studies and returned home. He wished to enter the army, but his father was so much opposed to it, that he at length acceded to his desires and commenced the study of the law. He was already prepared for being received to the office of advocate, when the royal edict was passed which prevented Protestants from practising before the courts; and, indeed, prevented them from following any profession whatever. Immediately after the death of his father, Paul de Rapin, accompanied by his younger brother Solomon, emigrated from France and proceeded into England.

It was not without a profound feeling of sadness that Rapin-Thoyras left his native country. He left his widowed mother in profound grief, arising from the recent death of her husband. She was now exposed to persecutions which were bitterer by far than the perils of exile. It was at her express wish that Rapin left his native country and emigrated to England. And yet it was for France that his fathers had shed their blood and laid down their lives. But France now repelled the descendants of her noblest sons from her bosom.

Shortly after his arrival in London, Rapin made the acquaintance of the Abbé of Denbeck, nephew of the

Bishop of Tournay. The Abbé was an intimate friend of Rapin's uncle, Pélisson, a man notorious in those times for buying up consciences with money. Louis XIV. consecrated to this traffic one-third of the benifices which fell to the Crown during their vacancy. They were left vacant for the purpose of paying for the abjurations of the heretics. Pélisson had the administration of the fund. He had been born a Protestant, but he abjured his religion, and from a convert he became a converter. Voltaire says of him, in his "Siècle de Louis XIV.," "Much more a courtier than a philosopher, Pélisson changed his religion and made a fortune."

Pélisson wrote to his friend the Abbé of Denbeck, then in London at the court of James II., to look after his nephew Rapin-Thoyras, and endeavour to bring him over to the true faith. It is even said that Pélisson offered Rapin the priory of Saint-Orens d'Auch if he would change his religion. The Abbé did his best. He introduced Rapin to M. de Barillon, then ambassador at the English court. James II. was then the pensioner of France, and accordingly had many intimate transactions with the French ambassador. M. de Barillon received the young refugee with great kindness, and, at the recommendation of the Abbé and Pélisson, offered to present him to the King. Their object was to get Rapin appointed to some public office, and thereby help his conversion.

But Rapin fled from the temptation. Though no great theologian, he felt it to be wrong to be thus entrapped into a faith which was not his own; and without much reasoning about his belief, but merely acting from a sense of duty, he left London at once and embarked for Holland.

At Utrecht he joined his uncle, Daniel de Rapin, who was in command of a company of cadets wholly composed of Huguenot gentlemen and nobles. Daniel had left the service of France on the 25th of October, 1685, three days after the Revocation of the Edict of Nantes. He was then captain of a French regiment in Picardy, but he could no longer, without denying his God, serve his country and his King. In fact, he was compelled, like all other Protestant officers, to leave France unless he would at once conform to the King's faith.

Rapin was admitted to the company of refugee cadets commanded by his uncle. He was now twenty-seven years old. His first instincts had been military, and now he was about to pursue the profession of arms in his adopted country. His first prospects were not brilliant. He was put under a course of discipline, his pay amounting to only sixpence a day. Indeed, the States-General of Holland were at first unwilling to take so large a number of refugee Frenchmen into their service; but on the Prince of Orange publicly declaring that he would himself pay the expenses of maintaining the military refugees, they hesitated no longer, but voted money enough to enrol them in their service.

The Prince of Orange had now a large body of troops at his command. No one knew for what purpose they were enrolled. Some thought they were intended for an attack upon France in revenge for Louis' devastation of Holland a few years before. James II. never dreamt that they were intended for a descent upon the coasts of England. Yet he was rapidly alienating the loyalty of his subjects by hypocrisy, by infidelity to the laws of England, and by unmitigated persecution of those who differed from him in religious belief. In this state of affairs England looked to the Prince of Orange for help.

William III. was doubly related to the royal family of England. He was nephew of Charles I. and son-in-law of James II. His wife was the heiress-presumptive to the British throne. Above all, he was a Protestant, while James II. was a Roman Catholic. "Here," said the Archbishop of Rheims of the latter, "is a good sort of man who has lost his three kingdoms for a mass!"

William was at length ready with his troops. Louis XIV. suddenly withdrew his army from Flanders and poured them into Germany. William seized the opportunity. A fleet of more than six hundred vessels, including fifty men-of-war, assembled at Helvoetsluys, near the mouth of the Maas. The troops were embarked with great celerity. William hoisted his flag with the words emblazoned on it, "The Protestant Religion and Liberties of England," and underneath the motto of the House of Nassau, *Je maintiendra*— "I will maintain."

The fleet set sail on the 19th October, the English Admiral Herbert leading the van, the Prince of Orange commanding the main body of the fleet, and the Dutch Vice-Admiral Evertzen bringing up the rear.

The wind was fair. It was the "Protestant wind" that the people of England had so long been looking for. In a few hours the strong eastern breeze had driven the fleet half across the sea that divides the Dutch and English coasts. Then the wind changed. It began to blow from the west. The wind increased until it blew a violent tempest. The fleet seemed to be in the midst of a cyclone. The ships were blown hither and thither, so that in less than two hours the fleet was completely dispersed. At daybreak next morning scarce two ships could be seen together.

The several ships returned to their rendezvous at Goeree, in the Maas. They returned in a miserable condition — some with their sails blown away, some without their bulwarks, some without their masts. Many ships were still missing. The horses had suffered severely. They had been stowed away in the holds and driven against each other during the storm. Many had been suffocated, others had their legs broken, and had to be killed when the vessels reached the shore. The banks at Goeree were covered with dead horses taken from the ships. Four hundred had been lost.

Rapin de Thoyras and M. de Chavernay, commanding two companies of French Huguenots, were on board one of the missing ships. The frightful tempest had separated them from the fleet. They had been driven before the wind as far as the coast of Norway. They thought that each moment might be their last. But the sailors were brave, and the ship was manageable. After enduring a week's storm the wind at last abated. The ship was tacked, and winged its way towards the south. At length, after about eight days' absence, they rejoined the fleet, which had again assembled in the Maas. There were now only two vessels missing, containing four companies of the Holstein regiment, and about sixty French Huguenot officers.

In the meantime the Prince of Orange had caused all the damages in the combined fleet to be repaired. New horses were embarked, new men were added to the army, and new ships were hired for the purpose of accommodating them. The men-of-war were also increased. After eleven days the fleet was prepared to put to sea again.

On the 1st of November, 1688, the armament started on its second voyage for the English coast. The fleet at first steered northward, and it was thought to be the Prince's intention to land at the mouth of the Humber. But a violent east wind having begun to blow during the night, the fleet steered towards the south-eastern coast of England; after which the ships shortened sail for fear of accidents.

The same wind that blew the English and Dutch fleet towards the Channel, had the effect of keeping King James's fleet in the Thames, where they remained anchored at Gunfleet, sixty-one men-of-war, under command of Admiral Lord Dartmouth.

On the 3rd of November, the fleet under the Prince of Orange entered the English Channel, and lay between Calais and Dover to wait for the ships that were behind. "It is easy," says Rapin Thoyras, " to imagine what a glorious show the fleet made. Five or six hundred ships in so narrow a channel, and both the English and French shores covered with numberless spectators, are no common sight. For my part, who was then on board the fleet, I own it struck me extremely."

Sunday, the 4th of November, was the Prince's birthday, and it was dedicated to devotion. The fleet was then off the Isle of Wight. Sail was slackened during the performance of divine service. The fleet then sped on its way down-channel, in order that the troops might be landed at Dartmouth or Torbay; but during the night the wind freshened, and the fleet was carried beyond the desired ports. Soon after, however, the wind changed to the south, when the fleet tacked in splendid order, and made for the shore in Torbay. The landing was effected with such diligence and tranquillity that the whole army was on shore before night.

There was no opposition to the landing. King James's army greatly outnumbered that of the Prince of Orange. It amounted to about forty thousand troops, exclusive of the militia. But the King's forces had been sent northward to resist the anticipated landing of the delivering army at the mouth of the Humber, so that the south-west of England was nearly stripped of troops.

Nor could the King depend upon his forces. The King had already outraged and insulted the gallant noblemen and gentlemen who had heretofore been the bulwark of his throne. He had imprisoned the bishops, dismissed Protestant clergymen from their livings, refused to summon a Parliament, and caused terror and dismay throughout England and Scotland. He had created discontent throughout the army by his dismissal of Protestant officers, and the King now began to fear that the common soldiers themselves would fail to serve him in his time of need.

His fears proved prophetic. When the army of the Prince of Orange advanced from Brixton (where it had landed) to Exeter, and afterwards to Salisbury and London, it was joined by noblemen, gentlemen, officers, and soldiers. Lord Churchill, afterwards Duke of Marlborough, Lord Cornbury, with four regiments of dragoons, passed over to the Prince of Orange. The Prince of Denmark, the King's son-in-law, deserted him. His councillors abandoned him. His mistresses left him. The country was up against him. At length the King saw no remedy before him but a precipitate flight.

The account given by Rapin of James's departure

from England is somewhat ludicrous. The Queen went first. On the night between the 9th and 10th of December she crossed the Thames in disguise. She waited under the walls of a church at Lambeth until a coach could be got ready for her at the nearest inn. She went from thence to Gravesend, where she embarked with the Prince of Wales on a small vessel, which conveyed them safely to France. The King set out on the following night. He entered a small boat at Whitehall, dressed in a plain suit and a bob wig, accompanied by a few friends. He threw the Great Seal into the water, from whence it was afterwards dragged up by a fisherman's net. Before he left, he gave the Earl of Feversham orders to disband the army without pay, in order, probably, to create anarchy after his flight.

James reached the south shore of the Thames. He travelled, with relays of horses, to Emley Ferry, near the Island of Sheppey. He went on board the little vessel that was to convey him to a French frigate lying in the mouth of the Thames ready to transport him to France. The wind blew strong, and the vessel was unable to sail.

The fishermen of the neighbourhood boarded the vessel in which the King was. They took him for the chaplain of Sir Edward Hales, one of his attendants. They searched the King, and found upon him four hundred guineas and several valuable seals and jewels, which they seized. A constable was present who knew the King, and he ordered restitution of the valuables which had been taken from him. The King wished to be gone, but the people by a sort of violence conducted him to a public inn in the town of Feversham. He then sent for the Earl of Winchelsea, Lord-

Lieutenant of the county, who prevailed upon him not to leave the kingdom, but to return to London.

And to London he went. The Prince of Orange was by this time at Windsor. On the King's arrival in London he was received with acclamations, as if he had returned from victory. He resumed possession of his palace. He published a proclamation, announcing that having been given to understand that divers outrages had been committed in various parts of the kingdom, by burning, pulling down, and defacing of houses, he commanded all lord-lieutenants, &c., to prevent such outrages for the future, and suppress all riotous assemblies.

This was his last public act. He was without an army. He had few friends. The Dutch Guards arrived in London, and took possession of St. James's and Whitehall. The Prince of Orange sent three lords to the King to desire his Majesty's departure for Ham—a house belonging to the Duchess of Lauderdale; but the King desired them to tell the Prince that he wished rather to go to Rochester. The Prince gave his consent.

Next morning the King entered his barge, accompanied by four earls, six of the Yeomen of his Guard, and about a hundred of the Dutch Guard, commanded by a colonel of the regiment. They arrived at Gravesend, where the King entered his coach, and proceeded across the country to Rochester.

In the meantime, Barillon, the French ambassador, was requested to leave England. St. Ledger, a French refugee, was requested to attend him and see him embark. While they were on the road St. Ledger could not forbear saying to the ambassador, "Sir, had any one told you a year ago that a French refugee should be commissioned to see you out of England, would you have believed it?" To which the ambassador answered, "Sir, cross over with me to Calais, and I will give you an answer."

Shortly after, James embarked in a small French ship, which landed him safely at Ambleteuse, a few miles north of Boulogne; while the army of William marched into London amidst loud congratulations, and William himself took possession of the Palace of St. James's, which the recreant King had left for his occupation.

James II. fled from England at the end of December, 1688. Louis XIV. received him courteously, and entertained him and his family at St. Germain and Versailles. But he could scarcely entertain much regard for the abdicated monarch. James had left his kingdom in an ignominious manner. Though he was at the head of a great fleet and army, he had not struck a single blow in defence of his kingly rights. And now he had come to the court of Louis XIV. to beg for the assistance of a French fleet and army to recover his throne.

Though England had rejected James, Ireland was still in his favour. The Lord-Deputy Tyrconnel was devoted to him; and the Irish people, excepting those of the north, were ready to fight for him. About a hundred thousand Irishmen were in arms. Half were soldiers; the rest were undrilled Rapparees. James was urged by messengers from Ireland to take advantage of this state of affairs. He accordingly begged Louis XIV. to send a French army with him into Ireland to help him to recover his kingdom.

But the French monarch, who saw before him the prospect of a continental war, was unwilling to send a large body of troops out of his kingdom. But he did what he could.

He ordered the Brest fleet to be ready. He put on board arms and ammunition for ten thousand men. He selected four hundred French officers for the purpose of disciplining the Irish levies. Count Rosen, a veteran warrior, was placed in command. Over a hundred thousand pounds of money was also put on board. When the fleet was ready to sail, James took leave of his patron, Louis XIV. "The best thing that I can wish you," said the French king, "is that I may never see you again in this world."

The fleet sailed from Brest on the 7th of March, 1689, and reached Kinsale, in the south of Ireland, four days later. James II. was received with the greatest rejoicing. Next day he went on to Cork; he was received by the Earl of Tyrconnel, who caused one of the magistrates to be executed because he had declared for the Prince of Orange.

The news went abroad that the King had landed. He entered Dublin on the 24th of March, and was received in a triumphant manner. All Roman Catholic Ireland was at his feet. The Protestants in the south were disarmed. There was some show of resistance in the north; but no doubt was entertained that Enniskillen and Derry, where the Protestants had taken refuge, would soon be captured and Protestantism crushed.

The Prince of Orange, who had now been proclaimed King at Westminster, found that he must fight for his throne, and that Ireland was to be the battle-field. Londonderry was crowded with Protestants, who held out for William III. James believed that the place would fall without a blow. Count Rosen was of the same opinion. The Irish army proceeded northwards without resistance. The country, as far as the walls of Derry, was found abandoned by the population. Everything valuable had been destroyed by bands of Rapparees. There was great want of food for the army.

Nevertheless, James proceeded as far as Derry. Confident of success, he approached within a hundred yards of the southern gate, when he was received with a shout of "No surrender!" The cannon were fired from the nearest bastion. One of James's officers was killed by his side. Then he fled. A few days later he was on his way to Dublin, accompanied by Count Rosen.

Londonderry, after an heroic contest, was at length relieved. A fleet from England, laden with food, broke the boom which had been thrown by the Irish army across the entrance to the harbour. The ships reached the quay at ten o'clock at night. The whole population were there to receive them. The food was unloaded, and the famished people were at length fed. Three days after, the Irish army burnt their huts, and left the long-beleaguered city. They retreated along the left bank of the Boyne to Strabane.

While the Irish forces were lying there, the news of another disaster reached them. The Duke of Berwick lay with a strong detachment of Irish troops before Enniskillen. He had already gained some advantage over the Protestant colonists, and the command reached him from Dublin that he was immediately to attack them. The Irish were five thousand in number; the Enniskilleners under three thousand.

An engagement took place at Newton Butler. The Enniskillen horse swept the Irish troops before them.

Fifteen hundred were put to the sword, and four hundred prisoners were taken. Seven pieces of cannon, fourteen barrels of powder, and all the drums and colours were left in the hands of the victors. The Irish army were then at Strabane, on their retreat from Londonderry. They at once struck their tents, threw their military stores into the river, and set out in full retreat for the south.

In the meantime a French fleet had landed at Bantry Bay, with three thousand men on board, and a large convoy of ammunition and provisions. William III., on his part, determined, with the consent of the English Parliament, to send a force into Ireland to encounter the French and Irish forces under King James.

William's troops consisted of English, Scotch, Dutch, and Danes, with a large admixture of French Huguenots. There were a regiment of Huguenot horse, of eight companies, commanded by the Duke of Schomberg, and three regiments of Huguenot foot, commanded by La Mellonière, Du Cambon, and La Caillemotte. Schomberg, the old Huguenot chief, was put in command of the entire force.

Rapin accompanied the expedition as a cadet. The army assembled at Highlake, about sixteen miles from Chester. About ninety vessels of all sorts were assembled near the mouth of the Dee. Part of the army was embarked on the 12th of August, and set sail for Ireland. About ten thousand men, horse and foot, were landed at Bangor, near the southern entrance to Belfast Lough. Parties were sent out to scour the adjacent country, and to feel for the enemy. This done, the army set out for Belfast.

James's forces had abandoned the place, and retired

to Carrickfergus, some ten miles from Belfast, on the north coast of the Lough. Carrickfergus was a fortified town. The castle occupies a strong position on a rock overlooking the Lough. The place formed a depôt for James's troops, and Schomberg therefore determined to besiege the fortress.

Rapin has written an account of William's campaigns in England and Ireland; but with becoming modesty he says nothing about his own achievements. We must therefore supply the deficiency. Before the siege of Carrickfergus, he had been appointed ensign in Lord Kingston's regiment. He was helped to this office by his uncle Daniel, who accompanied the expedition. Several regiments of Schomberg's army were detached from Belfast to Carrickfergus, to commence the siege. Among these was Lord Kingston's regiment.

On their approach, the enemy beat a parley. They desired to march out with arms and baggage. Schomberg refused, and the siege began. The trenches were opened, the batteries were raised, and the cannon thundered against the walls of the old town. Several breaches were made. The attacks were pursued with great vigour for four days, when a general assault was made. The besieged hoisted the white flag. After a parley, it was arranged that the Irish should surrender the place, and march out with their arms, and as much baggage as they could carry on their backs.

Carrickfergus was not taken without considerable loss to the besiegers. Lieutenant Briset, of the Flemish Guards, was killed by the first shot fired from the castle. The Marquis de Venours was also killed while leading the Huguenot regiments to the breach. Rapin distinguished himself so much during the siege that he was promoted to the rank of lieutenant. He was at the same time transferred to another regiment, and served under Lieutenant-General Douglas during the rest of the campaign.

More troops having arrived from England, Schomberg marched with his augmented army to Lisburn, Drummore, and Loughbrickland. Here the Enniskillen Horse joined them, and offered to be the advanced guard of the army. The Enniskilleners were a body of irregular horsemen, of singularly wild and uncouth appearance. They rode together in a confused body, each man being attended by a mounted servant, bearing his baggage. The horsemen were each mounted and accoutred after their own fashion, without any regular dress, or arms, or mode of attack. They only assumed a hasty and confused line when about to rush into action. They fell on pell-mell. Yet they were the bravest of the brave, and were never deterred from attacking by inequality of numbers. They were attended by their favourite preachers, who urged them on to deeds of valour, and encouraged them "to purge the land of idolatry."

Thus reinforced, Schomberg pushed on to Newry. The Irish were in force there, under command of the Duke of Berwick. But although it was a very strong place, the Irish abandoned the town, first setting fire to it. This news having been brought to Schomberg, he sent a trumpet to the Duke of Berwick, acquainting him that if they went on to burn towns in that barbarous manner, he would give no quarter. This notice seems to have had a good effect, for on quitting Dundalk the retreating army did no harm to the town. Schomberg encamped about a mile north of Dundalk, in a low, moist ground, where he entrenched his army.

Count Rosen was then at Drogheda with about twenty thousand men, far outnumbering the forces under Schomberg.

About the end of September, King James's army approached the lines of Dundalk. They drew up in order of battle. The English officers were for attacking the enemy, but Schomberg advised them to refrain. A large party of horse appeared within cannon shot, but they made no further attempt. In a day or two after James drew off his army to Ardee, Count Rosen indignantly exclaiming, "If your Majesty had ten kingdoms, you would lose them all." In the meantime, Schomberg remained entrenched in his camp. The Enniskilleners nevertheless made various excursions, and routed a body of James's troops marching towards Sligo.

Great distress fell upon Schomberg's army. The marshy land on which they were encamped, the wet and drizzly weather, the scarcity and badness of the food, caused a raging sickness to break out. Great numbers were swept away by disease. Among the officers who died were Sir Edward Deering, of Kent; Colonel Wharton, son of Lord Wharton; Sir Thomas Gower and Colonel Hungerford, two young gentlemen of distinguished merit. Two thousand soldiers died in the camp. Many afterwards perished from cold and hunger. Schomberg at length left the camp at Dundalk, and the remains of his army went into winter quarters.

Rapin shared all the suffering of the campaign. When the army retreated northward, Rapin was sent with a party of soldiers to occupy a fortified place between Stranorlar and Donegal. It commanded the Pass of Barnes Gap. This is perhaps the most magnificent defile in Ireland. It is about four miles long. Huge mountains rise on either side. The fortalice occupied by Rapin is now in ruins. It stands on a height overlooking the northern end of the pass. It is now called Barrack Hill. The Rapparees who lived at the lower end of the Gap were accustomed to come down upon the farming population of the lowland country on the banks of the rivers Finn and Mourne, and carry off all the cattle that they could seize; Rapin was accordingly sent with a body of troops to defend the lowland farmers from the Rapparees. Besides, it was found necessary to defend the pass against the forces of King James, who then occupied Sligo and the neighbouring towns, under the command of General Sarsfield.

Schomberg was very much blamed by the English Parliament for having effected nothing decisive in Ireland. But what could he do? He had to oppose an army more than three times stronger in numbers than his own. King William, Rapin says, wrote twice to him, "pressing him to put somewhat to the venture." But his army was wasted by disease, and had he volunteered an encounter and been defeated, his whole army, and consequently all Ireland, would have been lost, for he could not have made a regular retreat. "His sure way," says Rapin, "was to preserve his army, and that would save Ulster and keep matters entire for another year. And therefore, though this conduct of his was blamed by some, yet better judges thought that the managing of this campaign as he did was one of the greatest parts of his life."

Winter passed. Nothing decisive had been accomplished on either side. Part of Ulster was in the hands of William; the remainder of Ireland was in the hands of James. Schomberg's army was wasted by famine and disease. James made no use of his opportunity to convert his athletic peasants into good soldiers. On the contrary, Schomberg recruited his old regiments, drilled them constantly, and was ready to take the field at the approach of spring.

His first achievement was the capture of Charlemont, midway between Armagh and Dungannon. It was one of the strongest forts in the north of Ireland. It overlooked the Blackwater, and commanded an important pass. It was surrounded by a morass, and approachable only by two narrow causeways. When Teague O'Regan, who commanded the fort, was summoned to surrender, he replied, "Schomberg is an old rogue, and shall not have this castle!" But Caillemotte, with his Huguenot regiments, sat down before the fortress, and starved the garrison into submission. Captain Francis Rapin, cousin of our hero, was killed during the siege.

The armies on both sides were now receiving reinforcements. Louis XIV. sent seven thousand two hundred and ninety men of all ranks to the help of James, under the command of Count Lauzun. They landed at Cork in March, 1689, and marched at once to Dublin. Lauzun described the country as a chaos such as he had read of in the Book of Genesis. On his arrival at Dublin, Lauzun was appointed Commander-in-Chief of the Irish army, and took up his residence in the castle.

On the other hand, Schomberg's forces were recruited by seven thousand Danes, under a treaty which William III. had entered into with the King of Denmark. New detachments of English and Scotch, of Huguenots, Dutch, Flemings, and Brandenburgers, were also added to the allied army.

William landed at Carrickfergus on the 14th of June. He passed on to Belfast, where he met Schomberg, the Prince of Wurtemberg, Major-General Kirk, and other general officers. He then pushed on to Lisburn, the head-quarters of his army. He there declared that he would not let the grass grow under his feet, but would pursue the war with the utmost vigour. He ordered the whole army to assemble at Loughbrickland. He found them to consist of sixty-two squadrons of cavalry and fifty-two battalions of infantry—in all, thirty-six thousand English, Dutch, French, Danes, and Germans, well appointed in every respect. Lieutenant-General Douglas commanded the advance-guard—to which Rapin belonged—and William III., Schomberg, and St. Gravenmore commanded the main body.

William III. had no hesitation in entering at once on the campaign. He had been kept too long in London by parliamentary turmoil, by intrigues between Whigs and Tories, and sometimes by treachery on both sides. But now that he was in the field his spirits returned, and he determined to lose not a day in measuring swords with his enemy. He had very little time to spare. He must lose or win his crown; though his determination was to win. Accordingly he marched southward without delay.

William had been in Ireland six days before James knew of his arrival. The passes between Newry and Dundalk had been left unguarded—passes where a small body of well-disciplined troops might easily have checked the advance of William's army. Dundalk was abandoned. Ardee was abandoned. The Irish army were drawn up in a strong position on the south of the Boyne to arrest the progress of the invading army. James had all the advantages that nature could give him. He had a deep river in front, a morass on his left, and the narrow bridge of Slane on his right. Behind was a rising ground stretching along the whole of the field. In the rear lay the church and village of Donore, and the Pass of Duleek. Drogheda lay towards the mouth of the river, where the green and white flags of Ireland and France were flying, emblazoned with the harp and the lilies.

William never halted until he reached the summit of a rising ground overlooking the beautiful valley of the Boyne. It is about the most fertile ground in Ireland. As he looked from east to west, William said to one of his staff, "Behold a land worth fighting for!" Rapin was there, and has told the story of the crossing of the Boyne. He says that the forces of King James, lying on the other side of the river, amounted to about the same number as those under King William. They included more than seven thousand veteran French soldiers. There was a splendid body of Irish horse, and about twenty thousand Irish foot.

James's officers were opposed to a battle; they wished to wait for the large fleet and the additional forces promised by Louis XIV. But James resolved to maintain his position, and thought that he might have one fair battle for his crown. "But," says Rapin, "notwithstanding all his advantages—the deep river in front, the morass on his right, and the rising ground behind him—he ordered a ship to be prepared for him at Waterford, that in case of a defeat he might secure his retreat to France."

On the morning of the 30th of June, William ordered his whole army to move by break of day by three lines towards the river, about three miles distant. The King marched in front. By nine o'clock they were within two miles of Drogheda. Observing a hill east of the enemy, the King rode up to view the enemy's camp. He found it to lie all along the river in two lines. Here he had a long consultation with his leading officers. He then rode to the pass at Old Bridge, within musket-shot of the ford; next he rode westward, so as to take a full view of the enemy's camp. He fixed the place where his batteries were to be planted, and decided upon the spot where his army was to cross the river on the following day.

The Irish on the other side of the river had not been unobservant of the King's movements. They could see him riding up and down the banks, for they were not sixty yards apart. The Duke of Berwick, the Viceroy Tyrconnel, General Sarsfield, and other officers were carefully watching his movements. While the army was marching up the river-side, William dismounted and sat down upon a rising ground to partake of some refreshments, for he had been on horseback since early dawn. During this time a party of Irish horse on the other side brought forward two field-pieces through a ploughed field, and planted them behind a hedge. They took their sight and fired. The first shot killed a man and two horses close by the King. William immediately mounted his horse. The second gun was not so well aimed. The shot struck the water, but rising *en ricochet*, it slanted on the King's right shoulder, took a piece out of his coat, and tore the skin and the flesh. William rode away stooping in his saddle. The Earl of Coningsby put a handkerchief over the wound, but William said "there was no necessity, the bullet should have come nearer."

The enemy, seeing the discomfiture of the King's party, and that he rode away wounded, spread abroad the news that he was killed. "They immediately," says Rapin, "set up a shout all over their camp, and drew down several squadrons of their horse upon a plain towards the river, as if they meant to pass and pursue the English army. Nay, the report of the King's death flew presently to Dublin, and from thence spread as far as Paris, where the people were encouraged to express their joy by bonfires and illuminations." In the meantime William returned to his tent, where he had his wound dressed, and again mounted and showed himself to the whole army, in order to dissipate their apprehensions. He remained on horseback until nine at night, though he had been up since one o'clock in the morning.

William then called a council of war, and declared his resolution of forcing the river next day. Schomberg opposed this, but finding the King determined, he urged that a strong body of horse and foot should be sent to Slane bridge that night, so as to be able to cross the bridge and get between the enemy and the Pass of Duleek, which lay behind King James's army. This advice, if followed, might perhaps have ended the war in one campaign. Such is Rapin's opinion. The proposal was, however, rejected; and it was determined to cross the river in force on the following morning. William inspected the troops at midnight. He rode along the whole army by torchlight, and after giving out the password "Westminster," he returned to his tent for a few hours' sleep.

The shades of night lay still over that sleeping host.

The stars looked down in peace on these sixty thousand brethren of the same human family, ready to rise with the sun and imbrue their hands in each other's blood. Tyrannical factions and warring creeds had set them at enmity with each other, and turned the sweetness and joy of their nature into gall and bitterness. The night was quiet. The murmur of the river fell faintly on the ear. A few trembling lights gleamed through the dark from the distant watch-towers of Drogheda. The only sounds that rose from the vast host that lay encamped in the valley of the Boyne were the challenges of the sentinels to each other as they paced their midnight rounds.

The sun rose clear and beautiful. It was the first day of July—a day for ever memorable in the history of Ireland as well as England. The *générale* was beat in the camp of William before daybreak, and as soon as the sun was up the battle began. Lieutenant-General Douglas marched towards the right with six battalions of foot, accompanied by Count Schomberg (son of the Marshal) with twenty-four squadrons of horse. They crossed the river below the bridge of Slane, and though opposed by the Irish, they drove them back and pressed them on towards Duleek.

When it was supposed that the left wing had crossed the Boyne, the Dutch Blue Guards, beating a march till they reached the river's edge, went in eight or ten abreast, the water reaching above their girdles. When they had gained the centre of the stream they were saluted with a tremendous fire from the Irish foot, protected by the breastworks, lanes, and hedges on the farther side of the river. Nevertheless they pushed on, formed in two lines, and drove the Irish before them. Several Irish battalions were brought to bear upon them, but without effect. Then a body of Irish cavalry assailed them, but still they held their ground.

William, seeing his troops hardly pressed, sent across two Huguenot regiments and one English regiment to their assistance. But a regiment of Irish dragoons, at the moment of their reaching the shore, fell upon their flank, broke their ranks, and put many of them to the sword. Colonel Caillemotte, leader of the Huguenots, received a mortal wound. He was laid on a litter and carried to the rear. As he met his men coming up to the help of their comrades, he called out, "A la gloire, mes enfants! à la gloire!" A squadron of Danish horse forded the river, but the Irish dragoons, in one of their dashing charges, broke and defeated them, and drove them across the river in great confusion.

Duke Schomberg, who was in command of the centre, seeing that the day was going against King William, and that the French Huguenots were fighting without their leader, crossed the river and put himself at their head. Pointing to the Frenchmen in James's ranks, he cried out to his men, "Allons, messieurs, voilà vos persécuteurs!" The words were scarcely out of his mouth when a troop of James's guards, returning full speed to their main body, fell furiously upon the Duke and inflicted two sword cuts upon his head. The regiment of Cambon began at once to fire upon the enemy, but by a miss shot they hit the Duke. "They shot the Duke," says Rapin, "through the neck, of which he instantly died, and M. Foubert, alighting to receive him, was shot in the arm."

The critical moment had arrived. The centre of William's army was in confusion. Their leaders, Schomberg and Caillemotte, were killed. The men were waiting for orders. They were exposed to the galling fire of the Irish infantry and cavalry. King James was in the rear on the hill of Dunmore surrounded by his French body-guard. He was looking down upon the field of battle, viewing now here, now there. It is even said that when he saw the Irish dragoons routing the cavalry and riding down the broken infantry of William, he exclaimed, "Spare! oh, spare my English subjects!"

The firing had now lasted uninterruptedly for more than an hour, when William seized the opportunity of turning the tide of battle against his spiritless adversary. Putting himself at the head of the left wing, he crossed the Boyne by a dangerous and difficult ford a little lower down the river; his cavalry for the most part swimming across the tide. The ford had been left unguarded, and the whole soon reached the opposite bank in safety. But even there the horse which William rode sank in a bog, and he was forced to alight until the horse was got out. He was helped to remount, for the wound in his shoulder was very painful. So soon as the troops were got into sufficient order, William drew his sword, though his wound made it uneasy for him to wield it. He then marched on towards the enemy.

When the Irish saw themselves menaced by William's left wing, they halted, and retired towards Dunmore. But gaining courage, they faced about and fell upon the English horse. They gave way. The King then rode up to the Enniskilleners, and asked, "What they would do for him?" Not knowing him, the men were about to shoot him, thinking him to be one of the enemy. But when their chief officer told them that it was the King who wanted their help, they at once declared their intention of following him. They marched forward and received the enemy's fire. The Dutch troops came up, at the head of whom William placed himself. "In this place," says Rapin, "Duke Schomberg's regiment of horse, composed of French Protestants, and strengthened by an unusual number of officers, behaved with undaunted resolution, like men who fought for a nation amongst whom themselves and their friends had found shelter against the persecution of France."

Ginckel's troops now arrived on the scene; but they were overpowered by the Irish horse, and forced to give way. Sir Albert Cunningham's and Colonel Levison's dragoons then came up, and enabled Ginckel's troops to rally; and the Irish were driven up the hill, after an hour's hard fighting. James's lieutenant-general, Hamilton, was taken prisoner and brought before the King. He was asked "Whether the Irish would fight any more?" "Yes," he answered; "upon my honour I believe they will." The Irish slowly gave way, their dragoons charging again and again, to cover the retreat of the foot. At Dunmore they made a gallant stand, driving back the troops of William several times. The farmstead of Sheephouse was taken and retaken again and again.

At last the Irish troops slowly retreated up the hill. The French troops had scarcely been engaged. Sarsfield implored James to put himself at their head, and make a last fight for his crown. Six thousand fresh men coming into action, when the army of William was exhausted by fatigue, might have changed the fortune of the day. But James would not face the enemy. He put himself at the head of the French troops and Sarsfield's regiment—the first occasion on which he had led during the day—and set out for

Dublin, leaving the rest of his army to shift for themselves.

The Irish army now poured through the Pass of Duleek. They were pursued by Count Schomberg at the head of the left wing of William's army. The pursuit lasted several miles beyond the village of Duleek, when the Count was recalled by express orders of the King. The Irish army retreated in good order, and they reached Dublin in safety. James was the first to carry thither the news of his defeat. On reaching Dublin Castle, he was received by Lady Tyrconnel, the wife of the Viceroy. "Madam," said he, "your countrymen can run well." "Not quite so well as your Majesty," was her retort, "for I see that you have won the race."

The opinion of the Irish soldiers may be understood from their saying, after their defeat, "Change generals, and we will fight the battle over again." "James had no royal quality about him," says an able Catholic historian; "nature had made him a coward, a monk, and a gourmand; and, in spite of the freak of fortune that had placed him on a throne, and seemed inclined to keep him there, she vindicated her authority, and dropped him ultimately in the niche that suited him—

'The meanest slave of France's despot lord.'

William halted on the field that James had occupied in the morning. The troops remained under arms all night. The loss of life was not so great as was expected. On William's side not more than four hundred men were killed; but amongst them were Duke Schomberg, Colonel Caillemotte, and Dr. George Walker, the defender of Derry. "King James's whole loss in this battle," says Rapin, "was generally computed at fifteen hundred men, amongst whom were the Lord Dungan, the Lord Carlingford, Sir Neil O'Neil, Colonel Fitzgerald, the Marquis d'Hocquincourt, and several prisoners, the chief of whom was Lieutenant-General Hamilton, who, to do him justice, behaved with great courage, and kept the victory doubtful, until he was taken prisoner.

On the following day Drogheda surrendered without resistance. The garrison laid down their arms, and departed for Athlone. James stayed at Dublin for a night, and on the following morning he started for Waterford, causing the bridges to be broken down behind him, for fear of being pursued by the allied forces. He then embarked on a ship-of-war, and was again conveyed to France.

William's army proceeded slowly to Dublin. The Duke of Ormond entered the city two days after the battle of the Boyne, at the head of nine troops of horse. On the next day the King, with his whole army, marched to Finglas, in the neighbourhood of Dublin; and on the 6th of July he entered the city, and proceeded to St. Patrick's Church, to return thanks for his victory.

The whole of the Irish army proceeded towards Athlone and Limerick, intending to carry on the war behind the Shannon. William sent a body of his troops, under Lieutenant-General Douglas, to Athlone, while he himself proceeded to reduce and occupy the towns of the South. Rapin followed his leader, and hence his next appearance at the siege of Athlone.

Rapin conducted himself throughout the Irish campaign as a true soldier. He was attentive, accurate, skilful, and brave. He did the work he had to do without any fuss; but he *did* it. Lieutenant-

General Douglas, under whom he served, soon ascertained his merits, saw through his character, and became much attached to him. He promoted him to the rank of aide-de-camp, so that he might have this able Frenchman continually about his person.

Douglas proceeded westward, with six regiments of horse and ten of foot, to reduce Athlone. But the place was by far too strong for so small a force to besiege, and still less to take it. Athlone had always been a stronghold. For centuries the bridge and castle had formed the great highway into Connaught. The Irish town is defended on the eastern side by the Shannon, a deep and wide river, almost impossible to pass in the face of a hostile army.

Douglas summoned the Irish garrison to surrender. Colonel Richard Grace, the gallant old governor, returned a passionate defiance. "These are my terms," he said, discharging a pistol at the messenger: "when my provisions are consumed, I will defend my trust until I have eaten my boots."

Abandoning as indefensible the English part of the town, situated on the east side of the Shannon, Grace set fire to it, and retired with all his forces to the western side, blowing up an arch of the bridge behind him. The English then brought up the few cannon they had with them, and commenced battering the walls. The Irish had more cannon, and defended themselves with vigour. The besiegers made a breach in the castle, but it was too high and too small for an assault. "Notwithstanding this," says Rapin, "the firing continued very brisk on both sides; but the besiegers having lost Mr. Neilson, their best gunner, and the cavalry suffering very much for want of forage; and at the same time it being reported that Sarsfield was advancing with fifteen thousand men to relieve the place, Douglas held a council of war, wherein it was thought fit to raise the siege, which he accordingly did on the 25th, having lost near four hundred men before the town, the greatest part of whom died of sickness."

Thus, after a week's ineffectual siege, Douglas left Athlone, and made all haste to rejoin the army of William, which had already reduced the most important towns in the south of Ireland. On the 7th of August he rejoined William at Cahirconlish, a few miles west of Limerick. The flower of the Irish army was assembled at Limerick. The Duke of Berwick and General Sarsfield occupied the city with their forces. The French general, Boileau, commanded the garrison. The besieged were almost as numerous as the besiegers. William, by garrisoning the towns of which he took possession, had reduced his forces to about twenty thousand men.

Limerick was fortified by walls, batteries, and ramparts. It was also defended by a castle and citadel. It had always been a place of great strength. The chivalry of the Anglo-Norman monarch, the Ironsides of Cromwell, had been defeated under its walls; and now the victorious army of William III. was destined to meet with a similar repulse.

Limerick is situated in an extensive plain, watered by the noble Shannon. The river surrounds the town on three sides. Like Athlone, the city is divided into the English and Irish towns, connected together by a bridge. The English town was much the strongest. It was built upon an island, surrounded by morasses, which could at any time be flooded on the approach of an enemy. The town was well supplied with **provi-**

sions—all Clare and Galway being open to it, from whence it could draw supplies.

Notwithstanding the strength of the fortress, William resolved to besiege it. He was ill supplied with cannon, having left his heavy artillery at Dublin. He had only a field train with him, which was quite insufficient for his purpose. William's advance-guards drove the Irish outposts before them; the pioneers cutting down the hedges and filling up the ditches, until they came to a narrow pass between two bogs, where a considerable body of Irish horse and foot were assembled to dispute the pass.

Two field-pieces were brought up, which played with such effect upon the Irish horse that they soon quitted their post. At the same time Colonel Earle, at the head of the English foot, attacked the Irish who were firing through the hedges, so that they also retired after two hours' fighting. The Irish were driven to the town walls, and William's forces took possession of two important positions, Cromwell's fort and the old Chapel. The Danes also occupied an old Danish fort, built by their ancestors, of which they were not a little proud.

The army being thus posted, a trumpeter was sent, on the 9th of August, to summon the garrison to surrender. General Boileau answered, that he intended to make a vigorous defence of the town with which his Majesty had intrusted him. In the meantime, William had ordered up his train of artillery from Dublin. They were on their way to join him, when a spy from William's camp went over to the enemy, and informed them of the route, the motions, and the strength of the convoy. Sarsfield at once set out with a strong body of horse. He passed the Shannon in the

ASSAULT OF LIMERICK.   353

night, nine miles above Limerick, lurked all day in the mountains near Ballyneety, and waited for the approach of the convoy.

The men of William's artillery, seeing no enemy, turned out their horses to graze, and went to sleep in the full sense of security. Sarsfield's body of horse came down upon them, slew or dispersed the convoy, and took possession of the cannon. Sarsfield could not, however, take the prizes into Limerick. He therefore endeavoured to destroy them. Cramming the guns with powder up to their muzzles, and burying their mouths deep in the earth, then piling the stores, waggons, carriages, and baggage over them, he laid a train and fired it, just as Sir John Lanier, with a body of cavalry, was arriving to rescue the convoy. The explosion was tremendous, and was heard at the camp of William, more than seven miles off. Sarsfield's troops returned to Limerick in triumph.

Notwithstanding these grievous discouragements, William resolved to persevere. He recovered two of the guns, which remained uninjured. He obtained others from Waterford. The trenches were opened on the 17th of August. A battery was raised below the fort to the right of the trenches. Firing went on on both sides. Several redoubts were taken. By the 25th, the trenches were advanced to within thirty paces of the ditch near St. John's Gate, and a breach was made in the walls about twelve yards wide.

The assault was ordered to take place on the 27th. The English grenadiers took the lead, supported by a hundred French officers and volunteers. The enemy were dislodged from the covered way and the two forts which guarded the breach on each side. The assailants entered the breach, but they were not sufficiently supported. The Irish rallied. They returned to the charge, helped by the women, who pelted the besiegers with stones, broken bottles, and such other missiles as came readily to hand. A Brandenburg regiment having assailed and taken the Black Battery, it was blown up by an explosion, which killed many of the men. In fine, the assault was vigorously repulsed; and William's troops retreated to the main body, with a loss of six hundred men killed on the spot and as many mortally wounded.

Rapin was severely wounded. A musket shot hit him in the shoulder, and completely disabled him. His brother Solomon was also wounded. His younger brother fell dead by his side. They belonged to the "forlorn hope," and were volunteers in the assault on the breach. Rapin was raised to the rank of captain.

The siege of Limerick was at once raised. The heavy baggage and cannon were sent away on the 30th of August, and the next day the army decamped and marched towards Clonmel. The King intrusted the command of his army to Lieutenant-General Ginckel, and set sail for England from Duncannon Fort, near Waterford, on the 5th of September.

The campaign was not yet over. The Earl of Marlborough landed near Cork with four thousand men. Reinforced by four thousand Danes and French Huguenots, he shortly succeeded in taking the fortified towns of Cork and Kinsale. After garrisoning these places the Earl returned to England.

General Ginckel went into winter quarters at Mullingar, in Westmeath. The French troops, under command of Count Lauzun, went into Galway. Lauzun shortly after returned to France, and St. Ruth was sent over to take command of the French and Irish army.

SIEGE OF ATHLONE.

But they hung about Galway doing nothing. In the meantime Ginckel was carefully preparing for the renewal of the campaign. He was reinforced by an excellent body of troops from Scotland, commanded by General Mackay. He was also well supplied, through the vigilance of William, with all the necessaries of war.

Rapin's friend, Colonel Lord Douglas, pressed him to accompany him to Flanders as his aide-de camp; but the wound in his shoulder still caused him great pain, and he was forced to decline the appointment. Strange to say, his uncle Pélisson—the converter, or rather the buyer, of so many Romish converts in France—sent him a present of fifty pistoles through his cousin M. de la Bastide, which consoled him greatly during his recovery.

General Ginckel broke up his camp at Mullingar at the beginning of June, and marched towards Athlone. The Irish had assembled a considerable army at Ballymore, about midway between Mullingar and Athlone. They had also built a fort there, and intended to dispute the passage of Ginckel's army. A sharp engagement took place when his forces came up. The Irish were defeated, with the loss of over a thousand prisoners and all their baggage.

Ginckel then appeared before Athlone, but the second resistance of the besieged was much less successful than the first. St. Ruth, the French general, treated the Irish officers and soldiers under his command with supercilious contempt. He admitted none of their officers into his councils. He was as ignorant of the army which he commanded as of the country which he occupied. Nor was he a great general. He had been principally occupied in France in hunting and hanging the poor Protestants of Dauphiny and the Cevennes. He had never fought a pitched battle;

and his incapacity led to the defeat of the Irish army at Athlone, and afterwards at Aughrim.

St. Ruth treated his English adversaries with as much contempt as he did his Irish followers. When he heard that the English were about to cross the Shannon, he said "it was impossible for them to take the town, and he so near with an army to succour it." He added that he would give a thousand louis if they *durst* attempt it. To which Sarsfield retorted, "Spare your money and mind your business; for I know that no enterprise is too difficult for British courage to attempt."

Ginckel took possession of the English town after some resistance, when the Irish army retreated to the other side of the Shannon. Batteries were planted, pontoons were brought up, and the siege began with vigour. Ginckel attempted to get possession of the bridge. One of the arches was broken down, on the Connaught side of the river. Under cover of a heavy fire, a party of Ginckel's men succeeded in raising a plank-work for the purpose of spanning the broken arch. The work was nearly completed, when a sergeant and ten bold Scots belonging to Maxwell's Brigade on the Irish side, pushed on to the bridge; but they were all slain. A second brave party was more successful than the first. They succeeded in throwing all the planks and beams into the river, only two men escaping with their lives.

Ginckel then attempted to repair the broken arch by carrying a close gallery on the bridge, in order to fill up the gap with heavy planks. All was ready, and an assault was ordered for next day. It was resolved to cross the Shannon in three places—one body to cross by the narrow ford below the bridge, another by the pontoons above it, while the main body was to force the bridge itself. On the morning of the intended crossing, the Irish sent a volley of grenades among the wooden work of the bridge, when some of the fascines took fire, and the whole fabric was soon in a blaze. The smoke blew into the faces of the English, and it was found impossible to cross the river that day.

A council of war was held, to debate whether it was advisable to renew the attack or to raise the siege and retreat. The cannonade had now continued for eight days, and nothing had been gained. Some of the officers were for withdrawing, but the majority were in favour of making a general assault on the following day —seeing more danger in retreating than in advancing. The Duke of Wurtemberg, Major-Generals Mackay, Talmash, Ruvigny, Tetleau, and Colonel Cambon urged "that no brave action could be performed without hazard; and that the attempt was like to be attended with success." Moreover, they proffered themselves to be the first to pass the river and attack the enemy.

The assault was therefore agreed upon. The river was then at the lowest state at which it had been for years. Next morning, at six o'clock—the usual hour for relieving guards—the detachments were led down to the river. Captain Sands led the first party of sixty grenadiers. They were supported by another strong detachment of grenadiers and six battalions of foot. They went into the water twenty abreast, clad in armour, and pushed across the ford a little below the bridge. The stream was very rapid, and the passage difficult, by reason of the great stones which lay at the bottom of the river. The guns played over them from the batteries and covered their passage. The grenadiers reached the other side amidst the fire and smoke of their enemies. They held their ground and made for the bridge. Some of them laid planks over the broken arch, and others helped at preparing the pontoons. Thus the whole of the English army were able to cross to the Irish side of the river. In less than half an hour they were masters of the town. The Irish were entirely surprised. They fled in all directions, and lost many men. The besiegers did not lose above fifty.

St. Ruth, the Irish commander-in-chief, seemed completely idle during the assault. It is true he ordered several detachments to drive the English from the town after it had been taken; but, remembering that the fortifications of Athlone, nearest to his camp, had not been razed, and that they were now in possession of the enemy, he recalled his troops, and decamped from before Athlone that very night. In a few days Ginckel followed him, and inflicted on his army a terrible defeat at the battle of Aughrim. With that, however, we have nothing to do at present, but proceed to follow the fortunes of Rapin.

Rapin entered Athlone with his regiment, and conducted himself with his usual valour. Ginckel remained only a few days in the place, in order to repair the fortifications. That done, he set out in pursuit of the enemy. He left two regiments in the castle, one of which was that to which Rapin belonged. The soldiers, who belonged to different nationalities, had many contentions with each other. The officers stood upon their order of precedence. The men were disposed to quarrel. Aided by a friend, a captain like himself, Rapin endeavoured to pacify the men, and to bring the officers to reason. By his kind, gentle, and conciliatory manner, he soon succeeded in restoring quiet and mutual confidence; and during his stay at Athlone no further disturbance occurred among the garrison.

Rapin was ordered to Kilkenny, where he had a similar opportunity of displaying his qualities of conciliation. A quarrel had sprung up between the chief magistrate of the town and the officers of the garrison. Rapin interceded, and by his firmness and moderation he reconciled all differences; and, at the same time, he gained the respect and admiration of both the disputing parties.

By this time the second siege of Limerick had occurred. Ginckel surrounded the city, and battered the walls and fortresses for six weeks. The French and Irish armies at length surrendered. Fourteen thousand Irish marched out with the honours of war. A large proportion of them joined the army of Louis XIV., and were long after known as "The Irish Brigade." Although they fought valiantly and honourably in many well-known battles, they were first employed in Louis' persecution of the Protestants in the Vaudois and Cevennes mountains. Their first encounter was with the Camisards, under Cavalier, their peasant leader. They gained no glory in that campaign, but a good deal of discredit.

In the meantime Ireland had been restored to peace. After the surrender of Limerick no further resistance was offered to the arms of William III. A considerable body of English troops remained in Ireland to garrison the fortresses. Rapin's regiment was stationed at Kinsale, and there he rejoined it in 1693. He made the intimate friendship of Sir James Waller, the governor of the town. Sir James was a man of much intelligence, a keen observer, and an ardent student. By his knowledge of political history, he inspired Rapin with a like taste, and determined him at a later period in his life to undertake what was a real want at the time, an intelligent and readable history of England.

Rapin was suddenly recalled to England. He was required to leave his regiment and report himself to King William. No reason was given; but with his usual obedience to orders he at once set out. He did not leave Ireland without regret. He was attached to his numerous Huguenot comrades, and he hoped yet to rise to higher grades in the King's service. By special favour he was allowed to hand over his company to his brother Solomon, who had been wounded at the first siege of Limerick. His brother received the promotion which he himself had deserved, and afterwards became lieutenant-colonel of dragoons. Rapin's fortune led him in quite another direction.

It turned out that, by the recommendation of the Earl of Galway (formerly the Marquis de Ruvigny, another French Huguenot), he had been recalled to London for the purpose of being appointed governor and tutor to Lord Woodstock, son of Bentinck, Earl of Portland, one of King William's most devoted servants. Lord Galway was consulted by the King as to the best tutor for the son of his friend. He knew of Rapin's valour and courage during his campaigns in Ireland; he also knew of his discretion, his firmness, and his conciliatory manners, in reconciling the men under his charge at Athlone and Kilkenny; and he was also satisfied about his thoughtfulness, his delicacy of spirit, his grace and his nobleness—for he had been bred a noble, though he had first served as a common soldier in the army of William.

The King immediately approved the recommendation of Lord Galway. He knew of Rapin's courage at the battle of the Boyne; and he remembered—as every true captain does remember—the serious wound he had received while accompanying the forlorn hope at the first siege of Limerick. Hence the sudden recall of Rapin from Ireland. On his arrival in London he was presented to the King, and immediately after he entered upon his new function of conducting the education of the future Duke of Portland.

Henry, Lord Woodstock, was then about fifteen. Being of delicate health, he had hitherto been the object of his father's tender care, and it was not without considerable regret that Lord Portland yielded to the request of the King and handed over his son to the government of M. Rapin. Though of considerable intelligence, the powers of his heart were greater than those of his head. Thus Rapin had no difficulty in acquiring the esteem and affection of his pupil.

Portland House was then the resort of the most eminent men of the Whig party, through whose patriotic assistance the constitution of England was placed in the position which it now occupies. Rapin was introduced by Lord Woodstock to his friends. Having already mastered the English language, he had no difficulty in understanding the conflicting opinions of the times. He saw history developing itself before his eyes. He heard with his ears the discussions which eventuated in Acts of Parliament, confirming the liberties of the English people, the liberty of speech, the liberty of writing, the liberty of doing, within the limits of the common law.

All this was of great importance to Rapin. It prepared him for writing his afterwards famous works, his "History of England," and his Dissertation on the Whigs and Tories. Rapin was not only a man of great accomplishments, but he had a remarkable aptitude for languages. He knew French and English, as well as Italian, Spanish, and German. He had an extraordinary memory, and a continuous application and perseverance, which enabled him to suck the contents of many volumes, and to bring out the facts in future years during the preparation of his works. His memory seems to have been of the same order as that of Lord Macaulay, who afterwards made use of his works, and complimented his predecessor as to their value.

According to the custom of those days, the time arrived when Rapin was required to make "the grand tour" with his pupil and friend, Lord Woodstock. This was considered the complement of English education amongst the highest classes. It was thought necessary that young noblemen should come in contact with foreigners, and observe the manners and customs of other countries besides their own; and that thus they might acquire a sort of cosmopolitan education. Archbishop Leighton even considered a journey of this sort as a condition of moral perfection. He quoted the words of the Latin poet: "Homo sum, et nihil hominem à me alienum puto."

No one could be better fitted than Rapin to accompany the young lord on his foreign travels. They went to Holland, Germany, France, Spain, and Italy. Rapin diligently improved himself, while instructing his friend. He taught him the languages of the countries through which they passed; he rendered him familiar with Greek and Latin; he rendered him familiar with the principles of mathematics. He also studied with him the destinies of peoples and of kings, and pointed out to him the Divine will accomplishing itself amidst the destruction of empires. Withal he sought to penetrate the young soul of the friend committed to his charge with that firmness of belief and piety of sentiment which pervaded his own.

It was while in Italy that the Earl of Portland, at the instigation of Rapin, requested copies to be made for him of the rarest and most precious medals in point of historic interest; and also to purchase for him objects of ancient workmanship. Hence Rapin was able to secure for him the *Portland Vase,* now in the British Museum, one of the most exquisite products of Roman and Etruscan ceramic art.

In 1699, the Earl of Portland was sent by William III. as ambassador to the court of Louis XIV., in connection with the negotiations as to the Spanish succession. Lord Woodstock attended the embassy, and Rapin accompanied him. They were entertained at Versailles. Persecution was still going on in France, although about eight hundred thousand persons had already left the country. Rapin at one time thought of leaving Lord Woodstock for a few days, and making a rapid journey south to visit his friends near Toulouse. But the thought of being made a prisoner and sent to the galleys for life stayed him, and he remained at Versailles until the return of the embassy.

Rapin remained with Lord Woodstock for thirteen years. In the meantime he had married, at the Hague, Marie Anne Testart, a refugee from Saint-Quentin. Jean Rou describes her as a true helpmeet for him, young, beautiful, rich, and withal virtuous, and of the most pleasing and gentle temper in the world. Her riches, however, were not great. She had merely, like Rapin, rescued some portion of her heritage from the devouring claws of her persecutors. Rapin accumulated very little capital during his tutorship of Lord Woodstock; but to compensate him, the King granted him a pension of £100 a year, payable by the States of Holland, until he could secure some better income.

Rapin lived for some time at the Hague. While there he joined a society of learned French refugees. Among them were Rotolf de la Denèse, Basnage de Beauval, and Jean Rou, secretary to the States-General. One of the objects of the little academy was to translate the Psalms anew into French verse; but before the version was completed, Rapin was under the necessity of leaving the Hague. William III., his patron, died in 1701, when his pension was stopped. He was promised some remunerative employment, but he was forgotten amidst the press of applicants.

At length he removed to the little town of Wesel, on the Lower Rhine, in the beginning of May, 1707. He had a wife and four children to maintain, and living was much more reasonable at Wesel than at the Hague. His wife's modest fortune enabled him to live there to the end of his days. Wesel was also a resort of the French refugees—persons of learning and taste, though of small means. It was at his modest retreat at Wesel that Rapin began to arrange the immense mass of documents which he had been accumulating during so many years, relating to the history of England. The first work which he published was "A Dissertation on the Origin and Nature of the English Constitution." It met with great success, and went through many editions, besides being translated into nearly all the continental languages.

He next proceeded with his great work, "The History of England." During his residence in Ireland and England, he had read with great interest all books relating to the early history of the Government of England. He began with the history of England after the Norman Conquest; but he found that he must begin at the beginning. He studied the history of the Anglo-Saxons, but found it "like a vast forest, where the traveller, with great difficulty, finds a few narrow paths to guide his wandering steps. It was this, however, that inspired him with the design of clearing this part of the English history, by removing the rubbish, and carrying on the thread so as to give, at least, a general knowledge of the earlier history." Then he went back to Julius Cæsar's account of his invasion of Britain, for the purpose of showing how the Saxons came to send troops into this country, and how the conquest which had cost them so much was at last abandoned by the Romans. He then proceeded, during his residence in England, with his work of reading and writing; but when he came to the reign of Henry II. he was about to relinquish his undertaking, when an unexpected assistance not only induced him to continue it, but to project a much larger history of England than he had at first intended.

This unexpected assistance was the publication of Rymer's "Fœdera," at the expense of the British Government. The volumes as they came out were sent to Rapin by Le Clerc (another refugee), a friend of Lord Halifax, who was one of the principal promoters of the publication. This book was of infinite value to Rapin in enabling him to proceed with his history. He prepared abstracts of seventeen volumes (now in the Cottonian collection), to show the relation of the acts narrated in Rymer's "Fœdera" to the history of England. He was also able to compare the facts stated by English historians with those of the neighbouring states, whether they were written in Latin, French, Italian, or Spanish.

The work was accomplished with great labour. It occupied seventeen years of Rapin's life. The work was published at intervals. The first two volumes appeared in November, 1723. During the following year six more volumes were published. The ninth and tenth volumes were left in manuscript ready for the press. They ended with the coronation of William and Mary at Westminster. Besides, he left a large number of MSS., which were made use of by the editor of the continuation of Rapin's history.

Rapin died at Wesel in 1725, at the age of sixty-four. His work, the cause of his fatal illness, was almost his only pleasure. He was worn out by hard study and sedentary confinement, and at last death came to his rescue. He had struggled all his life against persecution; against the difficulties of exile; against the enemy; and though he did not die on the field of battle, he died on the breach pen in hand, in work and duty, striving to commemorate the independence through which a noble people had worked their way to ultimate freedom and liberty. The following epitaph was inscribed over his grave:—

> "Ici le casque et la science,
> L'esprit vif, la solidité,
> La politesse et la sincérité
> Ont fait une heureuse alliance,
> Dont le public a profité."

The first edition of Rapin's history, consisting of ten volumes, was published at the Hague by Rogessart. The Rev. David Durand added two more volumes to the second edition, principally compiled from the memoranda left by Rapin at his death. The twelfth volume concluded the reign of William III.

The fourth edition appeared in 1733. Being originally composed and published in French, the work was translated into English by Mr. N. Tindal, who added numerous notes. Two editions were published simultaneously in London, and a third translation was published some sixty years later. The book was attacked by the Jacobite authors, who defended the Stuart party against the statements of the author. In those fanatical times impartiality was nothing to them. A man must be emphatically for the Stuarts, or against them. Yet the work of Rapin held its ground, and it long continued to be regarded as the best history that had up to that time been written.

The Rapin family are now scattered over the world. Some remain in Holland, some have settled in Switzerland, some have returned to France, but the greater number are Prussian subjects. James, the only son of Rapin, studied at Cleves, then at Antwerp, and at thirty-one he was appointed to the important office of Director of the French Colonies at Stettin and Stargardt. Charles, Rapin's eldest brother, was a captain of infantry in the service of Prussia. Two sons of Louis de Rapin were killed in the battles of Smolensko and Leipsic.

Many of the Rapins attained high positions in the military service of Prussia. Colonel Philip de Rapin-Thoyras was the head of the family in Prussia. He was with the Allied Army in their war of deliverance against France in the years 1813, 1814, and 1815. He was consequently decorated with the Cross and the Military Medal for his long and valued services to the country of his adoption.

The handsome volume by Raoul de Cazenove, entitled "Rapin-Thoyras, sa Famille, sa Vie, et ses Œuvres," to which we are indebted for much of the above information, is dedicated to this distinguished military chief.

III.

CAPTAIN RIOU, R.N.

———◆———

> "Brave hearts! to Britain's pride
> Once so faithful and so true,
> On the deck of fame that died,
> With the gallant good Riou:
> Soft sigh the winds of heaven o'er their grave!"
> CAMPBELL'S *Battle of the Baltic.*

THE words in which Campbell describes Captain Riou in his noble ode are nearly identical with those used by Lord Nelson himself when alluding to his death in the famous despatch relative to the battle of Copenhagen. These few but pregnant words, "the gallant and the good," constitute nearly all the record that exists of the character of this distinguished officer, though it is no slight glory to have them embalmed in the poetry of Campbell and the despatches of Nelson.

Having had the good fortune, in the course of recent inquiries as to the descendants of illustrious Huguenots in England, to become acquainted with the principal events in Captain Riou's life, drawn from family papers, I now propose to supplement Lord Nelson's brief epitome of his character by the following memoir of this distinguished seaman.

Captain Riou was descended from the ancient Riou family of Vernoux, in Languedoc, of whom early mention is made in French history, several members of it having specially distinguished themselves as generals in the wars in Spain. Like many other noble families of Languedoc in the seventeenth century, the Rious were staunch Huguenots; and when, in 1685, Louis XIV. determined to stamp out Protestantism in France, and revoked the Edict of Nantes, the principal members of the family, refusing to conform, left the country, and their estates were confiscated by the Crown.

Estienne Riou, heir to the estate at Vernoux, was born after the death of his father, who was a man of eminent repute in his neighbourhood; and he did not leave France until his eleventh year, when he fled with his paternal uncle, Matthew Labrune, across the frontier, and took refuge with him at Berne, in Switzerland. There the uncle engaged in business as a merchant, while the nephew, when of sufficient age, desirous of following the usual career of his family, went into Piedmont to join the little Huguenot army from England, then engaged in assisting the Duke of Savoy against the armies of the French king. Estienne was admitted a cadet in Lord Galway's regiment, then engaged in the siege of Casale; and he remained with it for two years, when, on the army returning to England, he received an honourable discharge, and went back to reside for a time with his bachelor uncle at Berne.

In 1698 both uncle and nephew left Switzerland to settle in London as merchants, bringing with them a considerable capital. They exported English manufactured goods to the East Indies, Holland, Germany, and Italy; and imported large quantities of raw silk, principally from Spain and Italy, carrying on their business with uniform probity and credit. In course of time Estienne married Magdalen Baudoin, the daughter of a refugee gentleman from Touraine,—the members of refugee families usually intermarrying for several generations after their settlement in England. The issue of this marriage was an only son, Stephen Riou, who, like his ancestors, embraced the profession of arms, rising to be captain in the Horse Grenadier Guards. He afterwards attended the Confederate forces in Flanders as an engineer, and on the conclusion of peace, he travelled for nearly four years through the principal countries of Europe, accompanying Sir P. Ker Porter on his embassy to Constantinople. He afterwards settled, married, and had two sons,—Philip, the elder, who entered the Royal Artillery, and died senior colonel at Woolwich in 1817; and Edward, the second son, who entered the navy—the subject of the present memoir.

Edward Riou was born at Mount Ephraim, near Faversham, on the 20th November, 1762. The family afterwards removed to London, where Edward received his education, partly at the Marylebone Grammar School and partly at home, where his father superintended his instruction in fortification and navigation. Though of peculiarly sweet and amiable disposition, young Riou displayed remarkable firmness and even fearlessness as a boy. He rejoiced at all deeds of noble daring, and it was perhaps his love of adventure that early determined his choice of a profession; for, even when a very little fellow, he was usually styled by the servants and by his playmates, " the noble captain."

Accordingly, when only twelve years old, he went to sea as midshipman on board Admiral Pye's ship, the *Harfleur;* from whence, in the following year, he was removed to the *Romney,* Captain Keith Elphinstone, on the Newfoundland station; and on the return of the ship to England in 1776, he had the good fortune to be appointed midshipman on board the *Discovery*, Captain Charles Clarke, which accompanied Captain Cook in the *Resolution* in his last voyage round the world. Nothing could have been more to the mind of our sailor-boy than this voyage of adventure and discovery, in company with the greatest navigator of the age.

The *Discovery* sailed from the Downs on the 18th of June, but had no sooner entered the Channel than a storm arose which did considerable damage to the ship, which was driven into Portland Roads. At Plymouth, the *Discovery* was joined by the *Resolution*; but as the former had to go into harbour for repairs, Captain Cook set sail for the Cape alone, leaving orders for Captain Clarke to follow him there. The *Discovery* at length put to sea, and after a stormy voyage joined Captain Cook in Table Bay on the 11th of August. Before setting sail on the longer voyage, Riou had the felicity of being transferred to the *Resolution*, under the command of Captain Cook himself.

It is not necessary that we should describe this celebrated voyage, with which every boy is familiar—its storms and hurricanes; the landings on islands where the white man's face had never been seen before; the visits to the simple natives of Huahine and Otaheite, then a little Eden; the perilous coasting along the North American seaboard to Behring's Straits, in search of the North-Western passage; and finally, the wintering of the ships at Owyhee, where Captain Cook met his cruel death, of which young Riou was a horror-struck spectator from the deck of the *Resolution*, on the morning of the 14th of February, 1779.

After about four years' absence on this voyage, so full of adventure and peril, Riou returned to England with the *Resolution*, and was shortly after appointed lieutenant of the sloop *Scourge*, Captain Knatchbull, Commander, which took part, under Lord Rodney, in the bombardment and capture of St. Eustatia. Here Riou was so severely wounded in the eye by a splinter that he lost his sight for many months. In March, 1782, he was removed to the *Mediator*, forty-four guns, commanded by Captain Luttrell, and shared in the glory which attached to the officers and crew of that ship through its almost unparalleled achievement of the 12th of December of that year.

It was at daybreak that the *Mediator* sighted five sail of the enemy, consisting of the *Ménagère*, thirty-six guns *en flûte*; the *Eugène*, thirty-six; and the *Dauphin Royal*, twenty-eight (French); in company with the *Alexander*, twenty-eight guns, and another brig, fourteen (American), formed in line of battle to receive the *Mediator*, which singly bore down upon them. The skilful seamanship and dashing gallantry of the English disconcerted the combinations of the enemy, and after several hours' fighting two of their vessels fell out of the line, and went away, badly crippled, to leeward. About an hour later the *Alexander* was cut off, the *Mediator* wearing between her and her consorts, and in ten minutes she struck. A chase then ensued after the larger vessels, and late in the evening the *Ménagère*, being raked within pistol shot, hailed for quarter. The rest of the squadron escaped, and the gallant *Mediator*, having taken possession of her two prizes, set sail with them for England, arriving in Cawsand Bay on the 17th of December.

In the year following, Captain Luttrell, having been appointed to the *Ganges*, took with him Mr. Riou as second lieutenant. He served in this ship until the following summer, when he retired for a time on half-pay, devoting himself to study and continental travel until March, 1786, when we find him serving under Admiral Elliot as second lieutenant of the *Salisbury*. It was about this time that he submitted to the Admiralty a plan, doubtless suggested by his voyage with Captain Cook, "for the discovery and preservation of a passage through the continent of North America, and for the increase of commerce to this kingdom." The plan was very favourably received, but as war seemed imminent, no steps were then taken to carry it into effect.

The young officer had, however, by this time recommended himself for promotion by his admirable conduct and his good service; and in the spring of 1789 he was appointed to the command of the *Guardian*, forty-four guns, armed *en flûte*, which was under orders to take out stores and convicts to New South Wales. In a chatty, affectionate letter written to his widowed mother, from on shipboard at the Cape while on the voyage out, he says,—"I have no expectation, after the promotion that took place before I left England, of finding myself master and commander on my return." After speculating as to what might happen in the meantime while he was so far from home, and expressing an anxiety which was but natural on the part of an enterprising young officer eager for advancement in his profession, he proceeded, —"Politics must take a great turn, I think, by the time of my return. War will likely be begun; in that case we may bring a prize in with us. But our foresight is short—and mine particularly so. I hardly ever look forward to beyond three months. 'Tis in vain to be otherwise, for Providence, which directs all things, is inscrutable." And he concluded his letter thus,—"Now for Port Jackson. I shall sail to-night if the wind is fair. God for ever bless you."

But neither Riou nor the ill-fated *Guardian* ever reached Port Jackson! A fortnight after setting sail from the Cape, while the ship was driving through a thick fog (in lat. 44·5, long. 41) a severe shock suddenly called Riou to the deck, where an appalling spectacle presented itself. The ship had struck upon an iceberg. A body of floating ice twice as high as the masthead was on the lee beam, and the ship appeared to be entering a sort of cavern in its side. In a few minutes the rudder was torn away, a severe leak was sprung, and all hands worked for bare life at the pumps. The ship became comparatively unmanageable, and masses of overhanging ice threatened every moment to overwhelm her. At length, by dint of incessant efforts, the ship was extricated from the ice, but the leak gained fearfully, and stores, cattle, guns, booms, everything that could be cut away, was thrown overboard.

It was all in vain. The ship seemed to be sinking; and despair sat on every countenance save that of the young commander. He continued to hope even against hope. At length, after forty-eight hours of incessant pumping, a cry arose for "the boats," as presenting the only chance of safety. Riou pleaded with the men to persevere, and they went on bravely again at the pumps. But the dawn of another day revealed so fearful a position of affairs that the inevitable foundering of the ship seemed to be a matter of minutes rather than of hours. The boats were hoisted out, discipline being preserved to the last. Riou's servant hastened to him to ask what boat he would select to go in, that he himself might take a place beside him. His answer was that "he would stay by the ship, save her if he could, and if needs be sink with her, but that the people were at liberty to consult their own safety." He then sat down and wrote the following letter to the Admiralty, giving it in charge to Mr. Clements, the master, whose boat was the only one that ever reached land:—

"Her Majesty's Ship *Guardian,*
"*December,* 1789.

"If any part of the officers or crew of the *Guardian* should ever survive to reach home, I have only to say that their conduct, after the fatal stroke against an island of ice, was admirable and wonderful in everything that relates to their duties, considered either as private men or in his Majesty's service. As there seems no possibility of my remaining many hours in this world, I beg leave to recommend to the consideration of the Admiralty a sister, to whom, if my conduct or services should be found deserving any memory, favour might be shown, together with a widowed mother.

"I am, sir, with great respect,
"Your ever obedient servant,
"EDWARD RIOU.

"PHILIP STEPHENS, ESQ.,
"Admiralty."

About half the crew remained with Riou, some because they determined to stand by their commander, and others because they could not get away in the boats, which, to avoid being overcrowded, had put off in haste, for the most part insufficiently stored and provided. The sea, still high, continued to make breaches over the ship, and many were drowned in their attempts to reach the boats. Those who remained were exhausted by fatigue; and, without the most distant hope of life, some were mad with despair. A party of these last contrived to break open the spirit-room, and found a temporary oblivion in intoxication. "It is hardly a time to be a disciplinarian," wrote Riou in his log, which continues a valued treasury in his family, "when only a few more hours of life seem to present themselves; but this behaviour greatly hurts me." This log gives a detailed account, day by day, of the eight weeks' heroic fortitude and scientific seamanship which preserved the *Guardian* afloat until she got into the track of ships, and was finally towed by Dutch whalers into Table Bay, Cape of Good Hope.

The master's boat, in which were also the purser and chaplain, had by a miracle been picked up, and those officers, on their return to England, reported to the Admiralty "the total loss of the *Guardian.*" They also at the same time spoke of Riou's noble conduct in terms of such enthusiasm as to awaken general admiration, and occasion the greatest regret at his loss. Accordingly, when the Admiralty received from his own hand the unexpected intelligence of his safety, his widowed mother and only sister had the affectionate sympathy of all England. Lord Hood himself, before unknown to the family, hastened to their house with the news, calling to the servants as he ran up the stairs to "throw off their mourning!" The following was Riou's brief letter to his mother, which he found time to scrawl and send off by a ship just leaving Table

Bay for England as the poor helpless *Guardian* was being towed in :—

"Cape of Good Hope,
"*February*, 22, 1790.

"DEAREST,—God has been merciful. I hope you have no fatal accounts of the *Guardian*. I am safe; I am well, notwithstanding you may hear otherwise. Join with me in prayer to that blessed Saviour who hath hung over my ship for two months, and kept thy dear son safe, to be, I hope, thankful for almost a miracle. I can say no more because I am hurried, and the ship sails for England this afternoon.

" Yours ever and ever,
" EDWARD RIOU."

Riou remained many months at the Cape trying to patch up the *Guardian*, and repair it so as to bring it back to port; but all his exertions were fruitless, and in October the Admiralty despatched the *Sphinx* ship-of-war to bring him and the survivors of his crew to England, where they landed shortly after. There was, of course, the usual court-martial held upon him for the loss of his ship, but it was merely a matter of form. At its conclusion he was complimented by the Court in the warmest terms; and " as a mark of the high consideration in which the magnanimity of his conduct was held, in remaining by his ship from an exalted sense of duty when all reasonable prospects of saving her were at an end," he received the special thanks of the Admiralty, was made commander, and at the same time promoted to the rank of post captain.

No record exists of the services of Captain Riou from the date of his promotion until 1794, when we find him in command of his Majesty's ship *Rose*, assisting in the reduction of Martinique. He was then transferred to the *Beaulieu*, and remained cruising in the West Indian seas till his health became so injured by the climate that he found himself compelled to solicit his recall, and he consequently returned to England in the *Theseus* in the following year. Shortly after, in recognition of his distinguished services, he was appointed to the command of the royal yacht, the *Princess Augusta*, in which he remained until the spring of 1790. So soon as his health was sufficiently re-established, he earnestly solicited active employment, and he was accordingly appointed to the command of the fine frigate, the *Amazon*, thirty-eight guns, whose name afterwards figured so prominently in Nelson's famous battle before Copenhagen.

After cruising about in her on various stations, and picking up a few prizes, the *Amazon*, early in 1801, was attached to Sir Hyde Parker's fleet, destined for the Baltic. The last letter which Riou wrote home to his mother was dated Sunday, the 29th March, "at the entrance to the Sound;" and in it he said:—"It yet remains in doubt whether we are to fight the Danes, or whether they will be our friends." Already, however, Nelson was arranging his plan of attack, and on the following day, the 30th, the Admiral and all the artillery officers were on board the *Amazon*, which proceeded to examine the northern channel outside Copenhagen Harbour. It was on this occasion that Riou first became known to Nelson, who was struck with admiration at the superior discipline and seamanship which were observable on board the frigate during the proceedings of that day.

Early in the evening of the 1st of April the signal to prepare for action was made; and Lord Nelson, with Riou and Foley, on board the *Elephant*—all the other officers having returned to their respective ships—arranged the order of battle on the following day. What remains to be told of Riou is matter of history. The science and skill in navigation which made Nelson intrust to him the last soundings, and place under his command the fire-ships which were to lead the way on the following morning,—the gallantry with which the captain of the *Amazon* threw himself, *impar congressus*, under the fearful fire of the Trekroner battery, to redeem the failure threatened by the grounding of the ships of the line,—have all been told with a skilful pen, and forms a picture of a great sailor's last hours, which is cherished with equal pride in the affections of his family and the annals of his country.

Sir Hyde Parker's signal to "leave off action," which Nelson, putting his telescope to his blind eye, refused to see, was seen by Riou and reluctantly obeyed. Indeed, nothing but that signal for retreat saved the *Amazon* from destruction, though it did not save its heroic commander. As he unwillingly drew off from the destructive fire of the battery he mournfully exclaimed, "What will Nelson think of us!" His clerk had been killed by his side. He himself had been wounded in the head by a splinter, but continued to sit on a gun encouraging his men, who were falling in numbers around him. "Come then, my boys," he cried, "let us all die together." Scarcely had he uttered the words, when a raking shot cut him in two. And thus, in an instant, perished the "gallant good Riou," at the early age of thirty-nine.

Riou was a man of the truest and tenderest feelings, yet the bravest of the brave. His private correspondence revealed the most endearing qualities of mind and heart, while the nobility of his actions was heightened by lofty Christian sentiment, and a firm reliance on the power and mercy of God. His chivalrous devotion to duty in the face of difficulty and danger heightened the affectionate admiration with which he was regarded, and his death before Copenhagen was mourned almost as a national bereavement. The monument erected to his memory in St. Paul's Cathedral represented, however inadequately, the widely felt sorrow which pervaded all classes at the early death of this heroic officer. "Except it had been Nelson himself," says Southey, "the British navy could not have suffered a severer loss."

Captain Riou's only sister married Colonel Lyde Browne, who closed his honourable career of twenty-three years' active service in Dublin, on July 23rd, 1803. Within two years of her bitter mourning for the death of her brother, she had also to mourn for the loss of her husband. He was colonel of the 21st Fusiliers. He was hastening to the assistance of Lord Kilwarden on the fatal night of Emmett's rebellion, when he was basely assassinated. He was buried in the churchyard of St. Paul's, Dublin, where his brother officers erected a marble tablet to his memory. He left an only daughter, who was married, in 1826, to M. G. Benson, Esq., of Lulwyche Hall, Salop. It is through this lady that we have been permitted to inspect the family papers relating to the life and death of Captain Riou.

A VISIT TO THE

COUNTRY OF THE VAUDOIS.

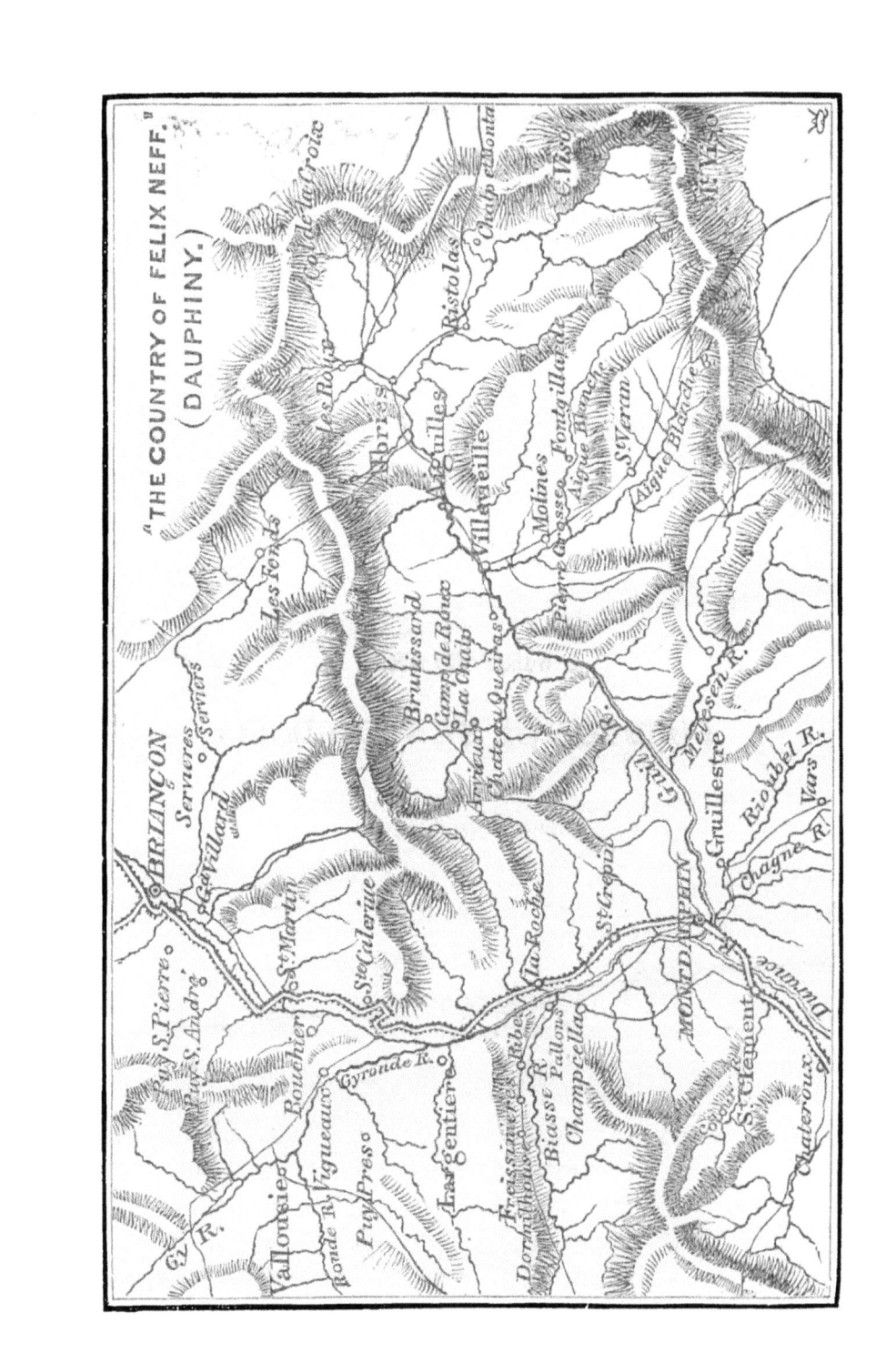

A VISIT TO THE COUNTRY OF THE VAUDOIS.

CHAPTER I.

INTRODUCTORY.

DAUPHINY is one of the least visited of all the provinces of France. It occupies a remote corner of the empire, lying completely out of the track of ordinary tourists. No great road passes through it into Italy, the Piedmontese frontier of which it adjoins; and the annual streams of English and American travellers accordingly enter that kingdom by other routes. Even to Frenchmen, who travel little in their own country and still less in others, Dauphiny is very little known; and M. Joanne, who has written an excellent Itinerary of the South of France, almost takes the credit of having discovered it.

Yet Dauphiny is a province full of interest. Its scenery almost vies with that of Switzerland in grandeur, beauty, and wildness. The great mountain masses of the Alps do not end in Savoy, but extend through the south-eastern parts of France, almost to the mouths of the Rhone. Packed closer together than in most parts of Switzerland, the mountains of Dauphiny are furrowed by deep valleys, each with its rapid stream or torrent at bottom, in some places overhung by precipitous rocks, in others hemmed in by green hills, over which are seen the distant snowy peaks and glaciers of the loftier mountain ranges. Of these, Mont Pelvoux—whose double pyramid can be seen from Lyons on a clear day, a hundred miles off—and the Aiguille du Midi, are among the larger masses, rising to a height little short of Mont Blanc itself.

From the ramparts of Grenoble the panoramic view is of wonderful beauty and grandeur, extending along the valleys of the Isère and the Drac, and across that of the Romanche. The massive heads of the Grand Chartreuse mountains bound the prospect to the north; and the summits of the snow-clad Dauphiny Alps on the south and east present a combination of bold valley and mountain scenery, the like of which is not to be seen in France, if in Europe.

But it is not the scenery, or the geology, or the flora of the province, however marvellous these may be, that constitutes the chief interest for the traveller through these Dauphiny valleys, so much as the human endurance, suffering, and faithfulness of the people who have lived in them in past times, and of which so many interesting remnants still survive. For Dauphiny forms a principal part of the country of the ancient Vaudois or Waldenses—literally, the people inhabiting the *Vaux*, or valleys—who for nearly seven hundred years bore the heavy brunt of Papal persecution, and are now, after all their sufferings, free to worship God according to the dictates of their conscience.

The country of the Vaudois is not confined, as is generally supposed, to the valleys of Piedmont, but extends over the greater part of Dauphiny and Provence. From the main ridge of the Cottian Alps, which divide France from Italy, great mountain spurs are thrown out, which run westward as well as eastward, and enclose narrow strips of pasturage, cultivable land, and green shelves on the mountain sides, where a poor, virtuous, and hard-working race have long contrived to earn a scanty subsistence, amidst trials and difficulties of no ordinary kind,—the greatest of which, strange to say, have arisen from the pure and simple character of the religion they professed.

The tradition which exists among them is, that the early Christian missionaries, when travelling from Italy into Gaul by the Roman road passing over Mont Genèvre, taught the Gospel in its primitive form to the people of the adjoining districts. It is even surmised that St. Paul journeyed from Rome into Spain by that route, and may himself have imparted to the people of the valleys their first Christian instruction. The Italian and Gallic provinces in that quarter were certainly Christianized in the second century at the latest, and it is known that the early missionaries were in the habit of making frequent journeys from the provinces to Rome. Wherefore it is reasonable to suppose that the people of the valleys would receive occasional visits from the wayfaring teachers who travelled by the mountain passes in the immediate neighbourhood of their dwellings.

As years rolled on, and the Church at Rome became rich and allied itself with the secular power, it gradually departed more and more from its primitive condition,*

* The ancient Vaudois had a saying, known in other countries—

until at length it was scarcely to be recognised from the Paganism which it had superseded. The heathen gods were replaced by canonised mortals; Venus and Cupid by the Virgin and Child; Lares and Penates by images and crucifixes; while incense, flowers, tapers, and showy dresses came to be regarded as essential parts of the ceremonial of the new religion as they had been of the old. Madonnas winked and bled again, as the statues of Juno and Pompey had done before; and stones and relics worked miracles as in the time of the Augurs.

Attempts were made by some of the early bishops to stem this tide of innovation. Thus, in the fourth century, Ambrose, Bishop of Milan, and Philastrius, Bishop of Brescia, acknowledging no authority on earth as superior to that of the Bible, protested against the introduction of images in churches, which they held to be a return to Paganism. Four centuries later, Claude, Bishop of Turin, advanced like views, and opposed with energy the worship of images, which he regarded as absolute idolatry. In the meanwhile, the simple Vaudois, shut up in their almost inaccessible valleys, and knowing nothing of these innovations, continued to adhere to their original primitive form of worship; and it clearly appears, from a passage in the writings of St. Ambrose, that, in his time, the superstitions which prevailed elsewhere had not at all extended into the mountainous regions of his diocese.

The Vaudois Church was never, in the ordinary sense of the word, a "Reformed" Church, simply because it had not become corrupted, and did not stand

---

"Religion brought forth wealth, and the daughter devoured the mother;" and another of like meaning, but less known—"When the bishops' croziers became golden, the bishops themselves became wooden."

in need of "reformation." It was not the Vaudois who left the Church, but the Roman Church that left them in search of idols. Adhering to their primitive faith, they never recognised the paramount authority of the Pope; they never worshipped images, nor used incense, nor observed Mass; and when, in the course of time, these corruptions became known to them, and they found that the Western Church had ceased to be Catholic, and become merely Roman, they openly separated from it, as being no longer in conformity with the principles of the Gospel as inculcated in the Bible and delivered to them by their fathers. Their ancient manuscripts, still extant, attest to the purity of their doctrines. They are written, like the Nobla Leyçon, in the Romance or Provençal—the earliest of the modern classical languages, the language of the troubadours—though now only spoken as a *patois* in Dauphiny, Piedmont, Sardinia, the north of Spain, and the Balearic Isles.*

If the age counts for anything, the Vaudois are justified in their claim to be considered one of the oldest churches in Europe. Long before the conquest of England by the Normans, before the time of Wallace and Bruce in Scotland, before England had planted its foot in Ireland, the Vaudois Church existed. Their remoteness, their poverty, and their comparative unimportance as a people, for a long time protected them from interference; and for centuries they remained unnoticed by Rome. But as the Western Church extended its power, it became insatiable for uniformity. It would not tolerate the independence which characterized the early churches, but aimed at subjecting them to the exclusive authority of Rome.

* Sismondi, "Littérature du Midi de l'Europe," i. 159.

The Vaudois, however, persisted in repudiating the doctrines and formularies of the Pope. When argument failed, the Church called the secular arm to its aid, and then began a series of persecutions, extending over several centuries, which, for brutality and ferocity, are probably unexampled in history. To crush this unoffending but faithful people, Rome employed her most irrefragable arguments—the curses of Lucius and the horrible cruelties of Innocent—and the "Vicar of Christ" bathed the banner of the Cross in a carnage from which the wolves of Romulus and the eagles of Cæsar would have turned with loathing.

Long before the period of the Reformation, the Vaudois valleys were ravaged by fire and sword because of the alleged heresy of the people. Luther was not born until 1483; whereas nearly four centuries before, the Vaudois were stigmatized as heretics by Rome. As early as 1096, we find Pope Urban II. describing Val Louise, one of the Dauphiny valleys — then called Vallis Gyrontana, from the torrent of Gyr, which flows through it—as "infested with heresy." In 1179, hot persecution raged all over Dauphiny, extending to the Albigeois of the South of France, as far as Lyons and Toulouse; one of the first martyrs being Pierre Waldo, or Waldensis,* of Lyons, who was executed for heresy by the Archbishop of Lyons in 1180.

Of one of the early persecutions, an ancient writer says: "In the year 1243, Pope Innocent II. ordered the Bishop of Metz rigorously to prosecute the Vaudois, especially because they read the sacred books in the

---

* It has been surmised by some writers that the Waldenses derived their name from this martyr; but being known as "heretics" long before his time, it is more probable that they gave the name to him than that he did to them.

vulgar tongue."* From time to time, new persecutions were ordered, and conducted with ever-increasing ferocity—the scourge, the brand, and the sword being employed by turns. In 1486, while Luther was still in his cradle, Pope Innocent VIII. issued a bull of extermination against the Vaudois, summoning all true Catholics to the holy crusade, promising free pardon to all manner of criminals who should take part in it, and concluding with the promise of the remission of sins to every one who should slay a heretic.† The consequence was, the assemblage of an immense horde of brigands, who were let loose on the valleys of Dauphiny and Piedmont, which they ravaged and pillaged, in company with eighteen thousand regular troops, jointly furnished by the French king and the Duke of Savoy.

Sometimes the valleys were under the authority of the kings of France, sometimes under that of the dukes of Savoy, whose armies alternately overran them; but change of masters and change of popes made little difference to the Vaudois. It sometimes, however, happened, that the persecution waxed hotter on one side of the Cottian Alps, while it temporarily relaxed on the other; and on such occasions the French and Italian Vaudois were accustomed to cross the mountain passes, and take refuge in each others' valleys. But when, as in the above case, the kings, soldiers, and brigands, on both sides, simultaneously plied the brand and the sword, the times were very troublous indeed for these poor hunted people. They had then no alternative but to climb up the mountains into the

* Jean Leger, "Histoire Générale des Eglises Evangéliques des Vallées de Piedmont, ou Vaudoises." Leyde, 1669. Part ii. 330.
† Leger, ii. 8-20.

least accessible places, or hide themselves away in dens and caverns with their families, until their enemies had departed. But they were often tracked to their hiding-places by their persecutors, and suffocated, strangled, or shot—men, women, and children. Hence there is scarcely a hiding-place along the mountain-sides of Dauphiny but has some tradition connected with it relating to these dreadful times. In one, so many women and children were suffocated; in another, so many perished of cold and hunger; in a third, so many were ruthlessly put to the sword. If these caves of Dauphiny had voices, what deeds of horror they could tell!

What is known as the Easter massacre of 1655 made an unusual sensation in Europe, but especially in England, principally through the attitude which Oliver Cromwell assumed in the matter. Persecution had followed persecution for nearly four hundred years, and still the Vaudois were neither converted nor extirpated. The dukes of Savoy during all that time pursued a uniform course of treachery and cruelty towards this portion of their subjects. Sometimes the Vaudois, pressed by their persecutors, turned upon them, and drove them ignominiously out of their valleys. Then the reigning dukes would refrain for a time; and, probably needing their help in one or other of the wars in which they were constantly engaged, would promise them protection and privileges. But such promises were invariably broken; and at some moment when the Vaudois were thrown off their guard by his pretended graciousness, the duke for the time being would suddenly pounce upon them and carry fire and sword through their valleys.

Indeed, the dukes of Savoy seem to have been about

the most wrong-headed line of despots that ever cursed a people by their rule. Their mania was soldiering, though they were oftener beaten than victorious. They were thrashed out of Dauphiny by France, thrashed out of Geneva by the citizens, thrashed out of the valleys by their own peasantry; and still they went on raising armies, making war, and massacring their Vaudois subjects. Being devoted servants of the Pope, in 1655 they concurred with him in the establishment of a branch of the society *De Propaganda Fide* at Turin, which extended over the whole of Piedmont, for the avowed purpose of extirpating the heretics. On Palm Sunday, the beginning of Holy Week, the society commenced active proceedings. The army of Savoy advanced suddenly upon La Tour, and were let loose upon the people. A general massacre began, accompanied with shocking brutalities, and continued for more than a week. In many hamlets not a cottage was left standing, and such of the people as had not been able to fly into the upper valleys were indiscriminately put to the sword. And thus was Easter celebrated.

The noise of this dreadful deed rang through Europe, and excited a general feeling of horror, especially in England. Cromwell, then at the height of his power, offered the fugitive Vaudois an asylum in Ireland; but the distance which lay between was too great, and the Vaudois asked him to help them in some other way. Forthwith, he addressed letters, written by his secretary, John Milton,[*] to the principal European powers, calling upon them to join him in putting a stop to these

[*] It was at this time that Milton wrote his noble sonnet, beginning—
"Avenge, O Lord, Thy slaughter'd saints, whose bones
Lie scattered on the Alpine mountains cold," &c.

horrid barbarities committed upon an unoffending people. Cromwell did more. He sent the exiles £2,000 out of his own purse; appointed a day of humiliation and a general collection all over England, by which some £38,000 were raised; and dispatched Sir Samuel Morland as his plenipotentiary to expostulate in person with the Duke of Savoy. Moreover, a treaty was on the eve of being signed with France; and Cromwell refused to complete it until Cardinal Mazarin had undertaken to assist him in getting right done to the people of the valleys.

These energetic measures had their effect. The Vaudois who survived the massacre were permitted to return to their devastated homes, under the terms of the treaty known as the "Patents of Grace," which was only observed, however, so long as Cromwell lived. At the Restoration, Charles II. seized the public fund collected for the relief of the Vaudois, and refused to remit the annuity arising from the interest thereon which Cromwell had assigned to them, declaring that he would not pay the debts of a usurper!

After that time, the interest felt in the Vaudois was very much of a traditional character. Little was known as to their actual condition, or whether the descendants of the primitive Vaudois Church continued to exist or not. Though English travellers—amongst others, Addison, Smollett, and Sterne—passed through the country in the course of last century, they took no note of the people of the valleys. And this state of general ignorance as to the district continued down to within about the last fifty years, when quite a new interest was imparted to the subject through the labours and researches of the late Dr. Gilly, Prebendary of Durham.

It happened that that gentleman was present at a meeting of the Society for Promoting Christian Knowledge, in the year 1820, when a very touching letter was read to the board, signed "Frederick Peyrani, minister of Pramol," requesting the assistance of the society in supplying books to the Vaudois churches of Piedmont, who were described as maintaining a very hard struggle with poverty and oppression. Dr. Gilly was greatly interested by the reading of this letter. Indeed, the subject of it so strongly arrested his attention, that he says it "took complete possession of him." He proceeded to make search for information about the Vaudois, but could find very little that was definite or satisfactory respecting them. Then it was that he formed the determination of visiting the valleys and ascertaining the actual condition of the people in person.

His visit was made in 1823, and in the course of the following year Dr. Gilly published the result in his "Narrative of an Excursion to the Mountains of Piedmont." The book excited much interest, not only in England, but in other countries; and a movement was shortly after set on foot for the relief and assistance of the Vaudois. A committee was formed, and a fund was raised—to which the Emperor of Russia and the Kings of Prussia and Holland contributed—with the object, in the first place, of erecting a hospital for the sick and infirm Vaudois at La Tour, in .the valley of Luzern. It turned out that the money raised was not only sufficient for this purpose, but also to provide schools and a college for the education of pastors, which were shortly after erected at the same place.

In 1829, Dr. Gilly made a second visit to the Piedmontese valleys, partly in order to ascertain how far the aid thus rendered to the poor Vaudois had proved effectual, and also to judge in what way certain further sums placed at his disposal might best be employed for their benefit.* It was in the course of his second visit that Dr. Gilly became aware of the fact that the Vaudois were not confined to the valleys of Piedmont, but that numerous traces of them were also to be found on the French side of the Alps, in Dauphiny and Provence. He accordingly extended his journey across the Col de la Croix into France, and cursorily visited the old Vaudois district of Val Fressinière and Val Queyras, of which an account will be given in the following chapters. It was while on this journey that Dr. Gilly became acquainted with the self-denying labours of the good Felix Neff among those poor outlying Christians, with whose life and character he was so fascinated that he afterwards wrote and published the memoir of Neff, so well known to English readers.

Since that time occasional efforts have been made in aid of the French Vaudois, though those on the Italian side have heretofore commanded by far the larger share of interest. There have been several reasons for this. In the first place, the French valleys are much less accessible; the roads through some of the most interesting valleys are so bad that they can only be travelled on foot, being scarcely practicable even for mules. There is no good hotel accommodation in the district, only *auberges*, and these of an indifferent character. The people are also more scattered, and even poorer than they are on the Italian side of the Alps. Then the climate is much more severe, from the greater eleva-

---

* Dr. Gilly's narrative of his second visit to the valleys was published in 1831, under the title of "Waldensian Researches."

tion of the sites of most of the Vaudois villages; so that when pastors were induced to settle there, the cold, and sterility, and want of domestic accommodation, soon drove them away. It was to the rigour of the climate that Felix Neff was eventually compelled to succumb.

Yet much has been done of late years for the amelioration of the French Vaudois; and among the most zealous workers in their behalf have been the Rev. Mr. Freemantle, rector of Claydon, Bucks, and Mr. Edward Milsom, the well-known merchant of Lyons. It was in the year 1851 that the Rev. Mr. Freemantle first visited the Vaudois of Dauphiny. His attention was drawn to the subject while editing the memoir of a young English clergyman, the Rev. Spencer Thornton, who had taken Felix Neff for his model; and he was thereby induced to visit the scene of Neff's labours, and to institute a movement on behalf of the people of the French valleys, which has issued in the erection of schools, churches, and pastors' dwellings in several of the most destitute places.

It is curious and interesting to trace the influence of personal example on human life and action. As the example of Oberlin in the Ban de la Roche inspired Felix Neff to action, so the life of Felix Neff inspired that of Spencer Thornton, and eventually led Mr. Freemantle to enter upon the work of extending evangelization among the Vaudois. In like manner, a young French pastor, M. Bost, also influenced by the life and labours of Neff, visited the valleys some years since, and wrote a book on the subject, the perusal of which induced Mr. Milsom to lend a hand to the work which the young Genevese missionary had begun. And thus good example goes on ever propagating itself; and though the tombstone may record "Hic jacet" over the crumbling dust of the departed, his spirit still lives and works through other minds—stimulates them to action, and inspires them with hope—"allures to brighter worlds, and leads the way."

A few words as to the origin of these fragmentary papers. In chalking out a summer holiday trip, one likes to get quite away from the ordinary round of daily life and business. Half the benefits of such a trip consists in getting out of the old ruts, and breathing fresh air amidst new surroundings. But this is very difficult if you follow the ordinary tourist's track. London goes with you and elbows you on your way, accompanied by swarms of commissionaires, guides, and beggars. You encounter London people on the Righi, on the Wengern Alp, and especially at Chamouni. Think of being asked, as I once was on entering the Pavilion at Montanvert, after crossing the Mer de Glace from the Mauvais Pas, "Pray, can you tell me what was the price of Brighton stock when you left town?"

There is no risk of such rencontres in Dauphiny, whose valleys remain in almost as primitive a state as they were hundreds of years ago. Accordingly, when my friend Mr. Milsom, above mentioned, invited me to accompany him in one of his periodical visits to the country of the Vaudois, I embraced the opportunity with pleasure. I was cautioned beforehand as to the inferior accommodation provided for travellers through the district. Tourists being unknown there, the route is not padded and cushioned as it is on all the beaten continental rounds. English is not spoken; Bass's pale ale has not yet penetrated into Dauphiny; nor do you encounter London tourists carrying their tin baths about with them as you do in Switzerland. Only an occasional negotiant comes up from Gap or Grenoble, seeking orders in the villages, for whom the ordinary auberges suffice.

Where the roads are practicable, an old-fashioned diligence may occasionally be seen plodding along, freighted with villagers bound for some local market; but the roads are, for the most part, as silent as the desert.

Such being the case, the traveller in the valleys must be prepared to "rough it" a little. I was directed to bring with me only a light knapsack, a pair of stout hob-nailed shoes, a large stock of patience, and a small parcel of insect powder. The knapsack and the shoes I found exceedingly useful, indeed indispensable; but I had very little occasion to draw upon either my stock of patience or insect powder. The French are a tidy people, and though their beds, stuffed with maize chaff, may be hard, they are tolerably clean. The food provided in the auberges is doubtless very different from what one is accustomed to at home; but with the help of cheerfulness and a good digestion that difficulty too may be got over.

Indeed, among the things that most strikes a traveller through France, as characteristic of the people, is the skill with which persons of even the poorest classes prepare and serve up food. The French women are careful economists and excellent cooks. Nothing is wasted. The *pot au feu* is always kept simmering on the hob, and, with the help of a hunch of bread, a good meal may at any time be made from it. Even in the humblest auberge, in the least frequented district, the dinner served up is of a quality such as can very rarely be had in any English public-house, or even in most of our country inns. Cooking seems to be one of the lost arts of England, if indeed it ever possessed it; and our people are in the habit, through want of knowledge, of probably *wasting* more food than would sustain many another nation. But in the great system of National Education that is to be, no one dreams of including as a branch of it skill in the preparation and economy in the use of human food.

There is another thing that the traveller through France may always depend upon, and that is civility. The politeness of even the French poor to each other is charming. They respect themselves, and they respect each other. I have seen in France what I have not yet seen in England—young working men walking out their aged mothers arm in arm in the evening, to hear the band play in the "Place," or to take a turn on the public promenade. But the French are equally polite to strangers. A stranger lady may travel all through the rural districts of France, and never encounter a rude look; a stranger gentleman, and never receive a rude word. That the French are a self-respecting people is also evinced by the fact that they are a sober people. Drunkenness is scarcely known in France; and one may travel all through it and never witness the degrading sight of a drunken man.

The French are also honest and thrifty, and exceedingly hard-working. The industry of the people is unceasing. Indeed it is excessive; for they work Sunday and Saturday. Sunday has long ceased to be a Sabbath in France. There is no day of rest there. Before the Revolution, the saints' days which the Church ordered to be observed so encroached upon the hours required for labour, that in course of time Sunday became an ordinary working day. And when the Revolution abolished saints' days and Sabbath days alike, Sunday work became an established practice.

What the so-called friends of the working classes are aiming at in England, has already been effected in France. The public museums and picture-galleries are open on Sunday. But you look for the working people there in vain. They are at work in the factories, whose chimneys are smoking as usual; or building houses, or working in the fields, or they are engaged in the various departments of labour. The government works all go on as usual on Sundays. The railway trains run precisely as on week days. In short, the Sunday is secularised, or regarded but as a partial holiday.*

As you pass through the country on Sundays, as on week-days, you see the people toiling in the fields. And as dusk draws on, the dark figures may be seen

---

* I find the following under the signature of "An Operative Bricklayer," in the *Times* of the 30th July, 1867: "I found there were a great number of men in Paris that worked on the buildings who were not residents of the city. The bricklayers are called *limousins;* they come from the old province Le Limousin, where they keep their home, and many of them are landowners. They work in Paris in the summer time; they come up in large numbers, hire a place in Paris, and live together, and by so doing they live cheap. In the winter time, when they cannot work on the buildings, they go back home again and take their savings, and stop there until the spring, which is far better than it is in London; when the men cannot work they are hanging about the streets. It was with regret that I saw so many working on the Sunday desecrating the Sabbath. I inquired why they worked on Sunday; they told me it was to make up the time they lose through wet and other causes. I saw some working with only their trousers and shoes on, with a belt round their waist to keep their trousers up. Their naked back was exposed to the sun, and was as brown as if it had been dyed, and shone as if it had been varnished. I asked if they had any hard-working hearty old men. They answered me "No; the men were completely worn out by the time they reached forty years." That was a clear proof that they work against the laws of nature. I thought to myself—Glory be to you, O Englishmen, you know the Fourth Commandment; you know the value of the seventh day, the day of rest!"

moving about so long as there is light to see by. It is the peasants working the land, and it is *their own*. Such is the "magical influence of property," said Arthur Young, when he observed the same thing.

It is to be feared, however, that the French peasantry are afflicted with the disease which Sir Walter Scott called the "earth-hunger;" and there is danger of the gravel getting into their souls. Anyhow, their continuous devotion to bodily labour, without a seventh day's rest, cannot fail to exercise a deteriorating effect upon their physical as well as their moral condition; and this we believe it is which gives to the men, and especially to the women of the country, the look of a prematurely old and overworked race.

CHAPTER II.

THE VALLEY OF THE ROMANCHE—BRIANÇON.

THE route from Grenoble to the frontier fortress of Briançon lies for the most part up the valley of the Romanche, which presents a variety of wild and beautiful scenery. In summer the river is confined within comparatively narrow limits; but in autumn and spring it is often a furious torrent, flooding the low-lying lands, and forcing for itself new channels. The mountain heights which bound it, being composed for the most part of schist, mica slate, and talcose slate, large masses become detached in winter—split off by the freezing of the water behind them—when they descend, on the coming of thaw, in terrible avalanches of stone and mud. Sometimes the masses are such as to dam up the river and form temporary lakes, until the accumulation of force behind bursts the barrier, and a furious flood rushes down the valley. By one of such floods, which occurred a few centuries since, through the bursting of the lake of St. Laurent in the valley of the Romanche, a large part of Grenoble was swept away, and many of the inhabitants were drowned.

The valley of the Romanche is no sooner entered, a few miles above Grenoble, than the mountains begin to close, the scenery becomes wilder, and the fury of the torrent is evinced by the masses of débris strewed along its bed. Shortly after passing the picturesque defile called L'Etroit, where the river rushes through a deep cleft in the rocks, the valley opens out again, and we shortly come in sight of the ancient town of Vizille—the most prominent building in which is the chateau of the famous Duc de Lesdiguières, governor of the province in the reign of Henry IV., and Constable of France in that of Louis XIII.

Wherever you go in Dauphiny, you come upon the footmarks of this great soldier. At Grenoble there is the Constable's palace, now the Prefecture; and the beautiful grounds adjoining it, laid out by himself, are now the public gardens of the town. Between Grenoble and Vizille there is the old road constructed by him, still known as "Le chemin du Connétable." At St. Bonnet, in the valley of the Drac, formerly an almost exclusively Protestant town, known as "the Geneva of the High Alps," you are shown the house in which the Constable was born; and a little lower down the same valley, in the commune of Glaizil, on a hill overlooking the Drac, stand the ruins of the family castle, where the Constable was buried. The people of the commune were in the practice of carrying away the bones from the family vault, believing them to possess some virtue as relics, until the prefect of the High Alps ordered it to be walled up to prevent the entire removal of the skeletons.

In the early part of his career, Lesdiguières was one of the most trusted chiefs of Henry of Navarre, often leading his Huguenot soldiers to victory; capturing town after town, and eventually securing possession of the entire province of Dauphiny, of which Henry appointed him governor. In that capacity he carried out many important public works—made roads, built bridges, erected fourteen fortresses, and enlarged and beautified his palace at Grenoble and his chateau at Vizille. He enjoyed great popularity during his life, and was known throughout his province as "King of the Mountains." But he did not continue staunch either to his party or his faith. As in the case of many of the aristocratic leaders of those times, Lesdiguières' religion was only skin deep. It was but a party emblem—a flag to fight under, not a faith to live by. So, when ambition tempted him, and the Constable's baton dangled before his eyes, it cost the old soldier but little compunction to abandon the cause which he had so brilliantly served in his youth. To secure the prize which he so coveted, he made public abjuration of his faith in the church of St. Andrew's at Grenoble in 1622, in the presence of the Marquis de Crequi, the minister of Louis XIII., who, immediately after Lesdiguières' first mass, presented him with the Constable's baton.

But the Lesdiguières family has long since passed away, and left no traces. At the Revolution, the Constable's tomb was burst open, and his coffin torn up. His monument was afterwards removed to Gap, which, when a Huguenot, he had stormed and ravaged. His chateau at Vizille passed through different hands, until in 1775 it came into the possession of the Périer family, to which the celebrated Casimir Périer belonged. The great Gothic hall of the chateau has witnessed many strange scenes. In 1623, shortly after his investment as Constable, Lesdiguières entertained Louis XIII. and his court there, while on his journey into Italy, in the course of which he so grievously ravaged the Vaudois villages. In 1788, the Estates of Dauphiny met there, and prepared the first bold remonstrance against aristocratic privileges, and in favour of popular representation, which, in a measure, proved the commencement of the great Revolution. And there too, in 1822, Felix Neff preached to large congregations, who were so anxious and attentive that he always after spoke of the place as his "dear Vizille;" and now, to wind up the vicissitudes of the great hall, it is used as a place for the printing of Bandana handkerchiefs!

When Neff made his flying visits to Vizille, he was temporarily stationed at Mens, which was the scene of his first labours in Dauphiny. The place lies not far from Vizille, away among the mountains towards the south. During the wars of religion, and more especially after the Revocation of the Edict of Nantes, Mens became a place of refuge for the Protestants, who still form about one-half of its population. Although, during the long dark period of religious persecution which followed the Revocation, the Protestants of Mens and the neighbouring villages did not dare to show themselves, and worshipped, if at all, only in their dwellings, in secret, or in "the Desert," no sooner did the Revolution set them at liberty than they formed themselves again into churches, and appointed pastors; and it was to serve them temporarily in that capacity that Felix Neff first went amongst them, and laboured there and at Vizille with such good effect.

Not far from Mens is a place which has made much more noise in the world—no other than La Salette, the scene of the latest Roman "miracle." La Salette is one of the side-valleys of the large valley of the Drac, which joins the Romanche a few miles above Grenoble. There is no village of La Salette, but a commune, which is somewhat appropriately called La Salette-Fallavaux, the latter word being from *fallax vallis*, or "the lying valley."

About twenty-seven years ago, on the 19th of September, 1846, two children belonging to the hamlet of Abladens—the one a girl of fourteen, the other a boy of twelve years old—came down from the lofty pasturage of Mont Gargas, where they had been herding cattle, and told the following strange story. They had seen the Virgin Mary descend from heaven with a crucifix suspended from her neck by a gold chain, and a hammer and pincers suspended from the chain, but without any visible support. The figure sat down upon a large stone, and wept so piteously as shortly to fill a large pool with her tears.

When the story was noised abroad, people came from all quarters, and went up the mountain to see where the Virgin had sat. The stone was soon broken off in chips and carried away as relics, but the fountain filled with the tears is still there, tasting very much like ordinary spring water.

Two priests of Grenoble, disgusted at what they believed to be an imposition, accused a young person of the neighbourhood, one Mdlle. de Lamerlière, as being the real author of the pretended miracle, on which she commenced an action against them for defamation of character. She brought the celebrated advocate Jules Favre from Paris to plead her cause, but the verdict was given in favour of the two priests. The " miracle " was an imposture !

Notwithstanding this circumstance, the miracle came

to be generally believed in the neighbourhood. The number of persons who resorted to the place with money in their pockets steadily increased. The question was then taken up by the local priests, who vouched for the authenticity of the miracle seen by the two children. The miracle was next accepted by Rome.* A church was built on the spot by means of the contributions of the visitors—L'Eglise de la Salette—and thither pilgrims annually resort in great numbers, the more devout climbing the hill, from station to station, on their knees. As many as four thousand persons of both sexes, and of various ages, have been known to climb the hill in one day—on the anniversary of the appearance of the apparition—notwithstanding the extreme steepness and difficulties of the ascent.

As a pendant to this story, another may be given of an entirely different character, relating to the inhabitants of another commune in the same valley, about midway between La Salette and Grenoble. In 1860, while the discussion about the miracle at La Salette was still in progress, the inhabitants of Notre-Dame-de-

* An authorised account was prepared by Cardinal Wiseman for English readers, entitled "Manual of the Association of our Lady of Reconciliation of La Salette," and published as a tract by Burns, 17, Portman Street, in 1853. Since I passed through the country in 1869, the Germans have invaded France, the surrender has occurred at Sedan, the Commune has been defeated at Paris, but Our Lady of La Salette is greater than ever. A temple of enormous dimensions has risen in her honour; the pilgrims number over 100,000 yearly, and the sale of the water from the Holy Well, said to have sprung from the Virgin's tears, realises more than £12,000. Since the success of La Salette, the Virgin has been making repeated appearances in France. Her last appearance was in a part of Alsace which is strictly Catholic. The Virgin appeared, as usual, to a boy of the mature age of six, "dressed in black, floating in the air, her hands bound with chains,"—a pretty strong religio-political hint. When a party of the 5th Bavarian Cavalry was posted in Bettweiler, the Virgin ceased to make her appearance.

Comiers, dissatisfied with the conduct of their curé, invited M. Fermaud, pastor of the Protestant church at Grenoble, to come over and preach to them, as they were desirous of embracing Protestantism. The pastor, supposing that they were influenced by merely temporary irritation against their curé, cautioned the deputation that waited upon him as to the gravity of their decision in such a matter, and asked them to reflect further upon it.

For several years M. Fermaud continued to maintain the same attitude, until, in 1865, a formal petition was delivered to him by the mayor of the place, signed by forty-three heads of families, and by nine out of the ten members of the council of the commune, urging him to send them over a minister of the evangelical religion. Even then he hesitated, and recommended the memorialists to appeal to the bishop of the diocese for redress of the wrongs of which he knew they complained, but in vain, until at length, in the beginning of 1868, with the sanction of the consistory of Grenoble a minister was sent over to Comiers to perform the first acts of Protestant worship, including baptism and marriage; and it was not until October in the same year that Pastor Fermaud himself went thither to administer the sacrament to the new church.

The service was conducted in the public hall of the commune, and was attended by a large number of persons belonging to the town and neighbourhood. The local clergy tried in vain to check the movement. Quite recently, when the curé entered one of the schools to inscribe the names of the children who were to attend their first mass, out of fifteen of the proper age eleven answered to the interrogatory of the priest, "Monsieur, nous sommes Protestantes." The movement has also extended into the neighbouring communes, helped by the zeal of the new converts, one of whom is known in the neighbourhood as "Père la Bible," and it is possible that before long it may even extend to La Salette itself.

The route from Vizille up the valley of the Romanche continues hemmed in by rugged mountains, in some places almost overhanging the river. At Séchilienne it opens out sufficiently to afford space for a terraced garden, amidst which stands a handsome chateau, flanked by two massive towers, commanding a beautiful prospect down the valley. The abundant water which rushes down from the mountain behind is partly collected in a reservoir, and employed to feed a *jet d'eau* which rises in a lofty column under the castle windows. Further up, the valley again contracts, until the Gorge de Loiret is passed. The road then crosses to the left bank, and used to be continued along it, but the terrible torrent of 1868 washed it away for miles, and it has not yet been reconstructed. Temporary bridges enable the route to be pursued by the old road on the right bank, and after passing through several hamlets of little interest, we arrive at length at the cultivated plain hemmed in by lofty mountains, in the midst of which Bourg d'Oisans lies seated.

This little plain was formerly occupied by the lake of St. Laurent, formed by the barrier of rocks and débris which had tumbled down from the flank of the Petite Voudène, a precipitous mountain escarpment overhanging the river. At this place, the strata are laid completely bare, and may be read like a book. For some distance along the valley they exhibit the most extraordinary contortions and dislocations, impressing the mind with the enormous natural forces that must have been at work to occasion such tremendous upheavings and disruptions. Elie de Beaumont, the French geologist, who has carefully examined the district, says that at the Montagne d'Oisans he found the granite in some places resting upon the limestone, cutting through the Calcareous beds, rising like a wall and lapping over them.

On arriving at Bourg d'Oisans, we put up at the Hôtel de Milan close by the bridge; but though dignified with the name of hotel, it is only a common roadside inn. Still, it is tolerably clean, and in summer the want of carpets is not missed. The people were civil and attentive, their bread wholesome, their pottage and bouilli good—being such fare as the people of the locality contrive to live and thrive upon. The accommodation of the place is, indeed, quite equal to the demand; for very few travellers accustomed to a better style of living pass that way. When the landlady was asked if many tourists had passed this year, she replied, "Tourists! We rarely see such travellers here. You are the first this season, and perhaps you may be the last."

Yet these valleys are well worthy of a visit, and an influx of tourists would doubtless have the same effect that it has already had in Switzerland and elsewhere, of greatly improving the hotel accommodation throughout the district. There are many domestic arrangements, costing very little money, but greatly ministering to cleanliness and comfort, which might very readily be provided. But the people themselves are indifferent to them, and they need the requisite stimulus of "pressure from without." One of the most prominent defects—common to all the inns of Dauphiny—having been brought under the notice of the landlady, she replied, "C'est vrai, monsieur ; mais—il laisse quelque chose à desirer!" How neatly evaded! The very defect was itself an advantage! What would life be—what would hotels be—if there were not "something left to be desired!"

The view from the inn at the bridge is really charming. The little river which runs down the valley, and becomes lost in the distance, is finally fringed with trees —alder, birch, and chestnut. Ridge upon ridge of mountain rises up behind on the right hand and the left, the lower clothed with patches of green larch, and the upper with dark pine. Above all are ranges of jagged and grey rocks, shooting up in many places into lofty peaks. The setting sun, shining across the face of the mountain opposite, brings out the prominent masses in bold relief, while the valley beneath hovers between light and shadow, changing almost from one second to another as the sun goes down. In the cool of the evening, we walked through the fields across the plain, to see the torrent, visible from the village, which rushes from the rocky gorge on the mountain-side to join its waters to the Romanche. All along the valleys, water abounds—sometimes bounding from the heights, in jets, in rivulets, in masses, leaping from rock to rock, and reaching the ground only in white clouds of spray, or, as in the case of the little river which flows alongside the inn at the bridge, bursting directly from the ground in a continuous spring; these waterfalls, and streams, and springs being fed all the year through by the immense glaciers that fill the hollows of the mountains on either side the valley.

Though the scenery of Bourg d'Oisans is not, as its eulogists allege, equal to that of Switzerland, it will at least stand a comparison with that of Savoy. Its mountains are more precipitous and abrupt, its peaks more jagged, and its aspect more savage and wild. The scenery of Mont Pelvoux, which is best approached from Bourg d'Oisans, is especially grand and sublime, though of a wild and desolate character. The road from Bourg d'Oisans to Briançon also presents some magnificent scenery; and there is one part of it that is not perhaps surpassed even by the famous Via Mala leading up to the Splügen. It is about three miles above Bourg d'Oisans, from which we started early next morning. There the road leaves the plain and enters the wild gorge of Freney, climbing by a steep road up the Rampe des Commières. The view from the height when gained is really superb, commanding an extremely bold and picturesque valley, hemmed in by mountains. The ledges on the hill-sides spread out in some places so as to afford sufficient breadths for cultivation; occasional hamlets appear amidst the fields and pine-woods; and far up, between you and the sky, an occasional church spire peeps up, indicating still loftier settlements, though how the people contrive to climb up to those heights is a wonder to the spectator who views them from below.

The route follows the profile of the mountain, winding in and out along its rugged face, scarped and blasted so as to form the road. At one place it passes along a gallery about six hundred feet in length, cut through a precipitous rock overhanging the river, which dashes, roaring and foaming, more than a thousand feet below, through the rocky abyss of the Gorge de l'Infernet. Perhaps there is nothing to be seen in Switzerland finer of its kind than the succession of charming landscapes which meet the eye in descending this pass.

Beyond the village of Freney we enter another defile, so narrow that in places there is room only for the river and the road; and in winter the river sometimes plays sad havoc with the engineer's constructions. Above this gorge, the Romanche is joined by the Ferrand, an impetuous torrent which comes down from the glaciers of the Grand Rousses. Immediately over their point of confluence, seated on a lofty promontory, is the village of Mizoën—a place which, because of the outlook it commands, as well as because of its natural strength, was one of the places in which the Vaudois were accustomed to take refuge in the times of the persecutions. Further on, we pass through another gallery in the rock, then across the little green valley of Chambon to Le Dauphin, after which the scenery becomes wilder, the valley—here called the Combe de Malaval (the "Cursed Valley")—rocky and sterile, the only feature to enliven it being the Cascade de la Pisse, which falls from a height of over six hundred feet, first in one jet, then becomes split by a projecting rock into two, and finally reaches the ground in a shower of spray. Shortly after we pass another cascade, that of the Riftort, which also joins the Romanche, and marks the boundary between the department of the Isere and that of the Hautes Alpes, which we now enter.

More waterfalls—the Sau de la Pucelle, which falls from a height of some two hundred and fifty feet, resembling the Staubbach—besides rivulets without number, running down the mountain-sides like silver threads; until we arrive at La Grave, a village about five thousand feet above the sea-level, directly opposite the grand glaciers of Tabuchet, Pacave, and Vallon, which almost overhang the Romanche, descending from the steep slopes of the gigantic Aiguille du Midi, the highest mountain in the French Alps,—being over 13,200 feet above the level of the sea.

After resting some two hours at La Grave, we proceeded by the two tunnels under the hamlet of Ventelong—one of which is 650 and the other 1,800 feet long—to the village of Villard d'Arene, which, though some five thousand feet above the level of the sea, is so surrounded by lofty mountains that for months together the sun never shines on it. From thence a gradual ascent leads up to the summit of the Col de Lauteret, which divides the valley of the Romanche from that of the Guisanne. The pastures along the mountain-side are of the richest verdure; and so many rare and beautiful plants are found growing there that M. Rousillon has described it as a "very botanical Eden." Here Jean Jacques Rousseau delighted to herborize, and here the celebrated botanist Mathonnet, originally a customs officer, born at the haggard village of Villard d'Arene, which we have just passed, cultivated his taste for natural history, and laid the foundations of his European reputation. The variety of temperature which exists along the mountain-side, from the bottom to the summit, its exposure to the full rays of the sun in some places, and its sheltered aspect in others, facilitate the growth of an extraordinary variety of beautiful plants and wild flowers. In the low grounds meridianal plants flourish; on the middle slopes those of genial climates; while on the summit are found specimens of the flora of Lapland and Greenland. Thus almost every variety of flowers is represented in this brilliant natural garden—orchids, cruciferæ, leguminæ, rosaceæ, caryophyllæ, lilies of various kinds, saxifrages, anemones, ranunculuses, swertia, primula, and varieties of the sedum, some of which are peculiar to this mountain, and are elsewhere unknown.

After passing the Hospice near the summit of the Col, the valley of the Guisanne comes in sight, showing a line of bare and rugged mountains on the right hand and on the left, with a narrow strip of land in the bottom, in many parts strewn with stones carried down by the avalanches from the cliffs above. Shortly we come in sight of the distant ramparts of Briançon, apparently closing in the valley, the snow-clad peak of Monte Viso rising in the distance. Halfway between the Col and Briançon we pass through the village of Monestier, where, being a saint's day, the bulk of the population are in the street, holding festival. The place was originally a Roman station, and the people still give indications of their origin, being extremely swarthy, black-haired, and large-eyed, evidently much more Italian than French.

But though the villagers of Monestier were taking holiday, no one can reproach them with idleness. Never was there a more hard-working people than the peasantry of these valleys. Every little patch of ground that the plough or spade can be got into is turned to account. The piles of stone and rock collected by the sides of the fields testify to the industry of the people in clearing the soil for culture. And their farming is carried on in the face of difficulties and discouragements of no ordinary character, for sometimes the soil of many of the little farms will be swept away in a night by an avalanche of snow in winter or of stones in spring. The wrecks of fields are visible all along the valley, especially at its upper part. Lower down it widens, and affords greater room for culture; the sides of the mountains become better wooded; and, as we approach the fortress of Briançon, with its battlements seemingly piled one over the other up the mountain-sides, the landscape becomes exceedingly bold and picturesque.

When passing the village of Villeneuve la Salle, a few miles from Briançon, we were pointed to a spot on the opposite mountain-side, over the pathway leading to the Col de l'Echuada, where a cavern was discovered a few years since, which, upon examination, was found to contain a considerable quantity of human bones. It was one of the caves in which the hunted Vaudois were accustomed to take refuge during the persecutions; and it continued to be called by the peasantry "La Roche armée"—the name being thus perpetuated, though the circumstances in which it originated had been forgotten.

The fortress of Briançon, which we entered by a narrow winding roadway round the western rampart, is the frontier fortress which guards the pass from Italy into France by the road over Mont Genévre. It must always have been a strong place by nature, overlooking as it does the valley of the Durance on the one hand, and the mountain road from Italy on the other, while the river Clairée, running in a deep defile, cuts it off from the high ground to the south and east. The highest part of the town is the citadel, or Fort du Chateau, built upon a peak of rock on the site of the ancient castle. It was doubtless the nucleus round which the early town became clustered, until it filled the lower plateau to the verge of the walls and battlements. There being no room for the town to expand, the houses are closely packed together and squeezed up, as it were, so as to occupy the smallest possible space. The streets are narrow, dark, gloomy, and steep, being altogether impassable for carriages. The liveliest sight in the place is a stream of pure water, that rushes down an open conduit in the middle of the principal street, which is exceedingly steep and narrow. The town is sacrificed to the fortifications, which dominate everywhere. With the increasing range and power of cannon, they have been extended in all directions, until they occupy the flanks of the adjoining mountains and many of their summits, so that the original castle now forms but a comparatively insignificant part of the fortress. The most important part of the population is the soldiery—the red-trousered missionaries of "civilisation," according to the gospel of Louis Napoleon, published a short time before our visit.

Other missionaries, are, however, at work in the town and neighbourhood; and both at Briançon and Villeneuve Protestant stations have been recently established, under the auspices of the Protestant Society of Lyons. In former times, the population of Briançon included a large number of Protestants. In the year 1575, three years after the massacre of St. Bartholomew, they were so numerous and wealthy as to be able to build a handsome temple, almost alongside the cathedral, and it still stands there in the street called Rue du Temple, with the motto over the entrance, in old French, "Cerches et vos troveres." But at the Revocation of the Edict of Nantes, the temple was seized by the King and converted into a granary, and the Protestants of the place were either executed, banished, or forced to conform to the Papal religion. Since then the voice of Protestantism has been mute in Briançon until within the last few years, during which a mission has been in operation. Some of the leading persons in the town have embraced the Reform faith, amongst others the professor of literature in the public college;

but he had no sooner acknowledged to the authorities the fact of his conversion, than he was dismissed from his office, though he has since been appointed to a more important profession at Nice. The number of members is, however, as yet very small, and the mission has to contend with limited means, and to carry on its operations in the face of many obstructions and difficulties.

What are the prospects of the extension of Protestantism in France? Various answers have been given to the question. Some think that the prevailing dissensions among French Protestants interpose a serious barrier in the way of progress. Others, more hopeful, think, that these divisions are only the indications of renewed life and vigour, of the friction of mind with mind, which evinces earnestness, and cannot fail to lead to increased activity and effort. The observations of a young Protestant pastor on this point are worth repeating. "Protestantism," said he, "is based on individualism: it recognises the free action of the human mind; and so long as the mind acts freely there will be controversy. The end of controversy is death. True, there is much incredulity abroad; but the incredulity is occasioned by the incredibilities of Popery. Let the ground once be cleared by free inquiry, and our Church will rise up amidst the ruins of superstition and unbelief, for man *must* have religion; only it must be consistent with reason on the one hand, and with Divine revelation on the other. I for one do not fear the fullest and freest inquiry, having the most perfect confidence in the triumph of the truth."

It is alleged by others that the bald form in which Protestantism is for the most part presented abroad, is not conformable with the "genius" of the men of Celtic and Latin race. However this may be, it is too generally the case that where Frenchmen, like Italians and Spaniards, throw off Roman Catholicism, they do not stop at rejecting its superstitions, but reject religion itself. They find no intermediate standpoint in Protestantism, but fly off into the void of utter unbelief. The same tendency characterizes them in politics. They seem to oscillate between Cæsarism and Red Republicanism; aiming not at reform so much as revolution. They are averse to any *via media*. When they have tried constitutionalism, they have broken down. So it has been with Protestantism, the constitutionalism of Christianity. The Huguenots at one time constituted a great power in France; but despotism in politics and religion proved too strong for them, and they were persecuted, banished, and stamped for a time out of existence, or at least out of sight.

Protestantism was more successful in Germany. Was it because it was more conformable to the " genius " of its people? When the Germans "protested" against the prevailing corruptions in the Church, they did not seek to destroy it, but to reform it. They "stood upon the old ways," and sought to make them broader, straighter, and purer. They have pursued the same course in politics. Cooler and less impulsive than their Gallican neighbours, they have avoided revolutions, but are constantly seeking reforms. Of this course England itself furnishes a notable example.

It is certainly a remarkable fact, that the stronghold of Protestantism in France was recently to be found among the population of Germanic origin seated along the valley of the Rhine; whereas in the western districts Protestantism is split up by the two irreconcilable parties of Evangelicals and Rationalists.

At the same time it should be borne in mind that Alsace did not become part of France until the year 1715, and that the Lutherans of that province were never exposed to the ferocious persecutions to which the Evangelical Protestants of Old France were subjected, before as well as after the Revocation of the Edict of Nantes.

In Languedoc, in Dauphiny, and in the southern provinces generally, men and women who professed Protestantism were liable to be hanged or sent to the galleys, down to nearly the end of the last century. A Protestant pastor who exercised his vocation did so at the daily peril of his life. Nothing in the shape of a Protestant congregation was permitted to exist, and if Protestants worshipped together, it was in secret, in caves, in woods, among the hills, or in the "Desert." Yet Protestantism nevertheless contrived to exist through this long dark period of persecution, and even to increase. And when at length it became tolerated, towards the close of the last century, the numbers of its adherents appeared surprising to those who had imagined it to be altogether extinct.

Indeed, looking at the persistent efforts made by Louis XIV. to exterminate the Huguenots, and to the fact that many hundred thousand of the best of them emigrated into foreign countries, while an equal number are supposed to have perished in prison, on the scaffold, at the galleys, and in their attempts to escape, it may almost be regarded as matter of wonder that the Eglise Reformée—the Church of the old Huguenots—should at the present day number about a thousand congregations, besides the five hundred Lutheran congregations of Alsatia; and that the Protestants of France should amount, in the whole, to about two millions of souls.

CHAPTER III.

VAL LOUISE—HISTORY OF FELIX NEFF.

SOME eight miles south of Briançon, on the road to Fort Dauphin, a little river called the Gyronde comes down from the glaciers of Mont Pelvoux, and falls into the Durance nearly opposite the village of La Bessie. This river flows through Val Louise, the entrance into which can be discerned towards the northwest. Near the junction of the rivers, the ruins of an embattled wall, with entrenchments, are observed extending across the valley of the Durance, a little below the narrow pass called the "Pertuis-Rostan," evidently designed to close it against an army advancing from the south. The country people still call these ruins the "Walls of the Vaudois;"* and according to tradition a great Vaudois battle was fought there; but of any such battle history makes no mention.

Indeed, so far as can be ascertained, the Vaudois of Dauphiny rarely if ever fought battles. They were too few in number, too much scattered among the

---

* A gap in the mountain-wall to the left, nearly over La Bessie, is still known as "La Porte de Hannibal," through which, it is conjectured, that general led his army. But opinion, which is much divided as to the route he took, is more generally in favour of his marching up the Isére, and passing into Italy by the Little St. Bernard.

VAL LOUISE. 421

mountains, and too poor and ill-armed, to be able to contend against the masses of disciplined soldiery that were occasionally sent into the valleys. All that they did was to watch, from their mountain look-outs, their enemies' approach, and hide themselves in caves; or flee up to the foot of the glaciers till they had passed by. The attitude of the French Vaudois was thus for the most part passive; and they very rarely, like the Italian Vaudois, offered any determined or organized resistance to persecution. Hence they have no such heroic story to tell of battles and sieges and victories. Their heroism was displayed in patience, steadfastness, and long-suffering, rather than in resisting force by force; and they were usually ready to endure death in its most frightful forms rather than prove false to their faith.

The ancient people of these valleys formed part of the flock of the Archbishop of Embrun. But history exhibits him as a very cruel shepherd. Thus, in 1335, there appears this remarkable entry in the accounts current of the bailli of Embrun: "Item, for persecuting the Vaudois, eight sols and thirty deniers of gold," as if the persecution of the Vaudois had become a regular department of the public service. What was done with the Vaudois when they were seized and tried at Embrun further appears from the records of the diocese. In 1348, twelve of the inhabitants of Val Louise were strangled at Embrun by the public executioner; and in 1393, a hundred and fifty inhabitants of the same valley were burned alive at the same place by order of the Inquisitor Borelli. But the most fatal of all the events that befell the inhabitants of Val Louise was that which occurred about a century later, in 1488, when nearly the whole of the remaining population of the valley were destroyed in a cavern near the foot of Mont Pelvoux.

This dreadful massacre was perpetrated by a French army, under the direction of Albert Catanée, the papal legate. The army had been sent into Piedmont with the object of subjugating or destroying the Vaudois on the Italian side of the Alps, but had returned discomfited to Briançon, unable to effect their object. The legate then determined to take his revenge by an assault upon the helpless and unarmed French Vaudois, and suddenly directed his soldiers upon the valleys of Fressinières and Louise. The inhabitants of the latter valley, surprised, and unable to resist an army of some twenty thousand men, abandoned their dwellings, and made for the mountains with all haste, accompanied by their families, and driving their flocks before them. On the slope of Mont Pelvoux, about a third of the way up, there was formerly a great cavern, on the combe of Capescure, called La Balme-Chapelle—though now nearly worn away by the disintegration of the mountain-side—in which the poor hunted people contrived to find shelter. They built up the approaches to the cavern, filled the entrance with rocks, and considered themselves to be safe. But their confidence proved fatal to them. The Count La Palud, who was in command of the troops, seeing that it was impossible to force the entrance, sent his men up the mountain provided with ropes; and fixing them so that they should hang over the mouth of the cavern, a number of the soldiers slid down in full equipment, landing on the ledge right in front of the concealed Vaudois. Seized with a sudden panic, and being unarmed, many of them precipitated themselves over the rocks and were killed. The soldiers slaughtered all whom they could reach, after which they proceeded to heap up wood at the cavern mouth which they set on fire, and thus suffocated the remainder. Perrin says four hundred children were afterwards found in the cavern, stifled, in the arms of their dead mothers, and that not fewer than three thousand persons were thus ruthlessly destroyed. The little property of the slaughtered peasants was ordered by the Pope's legate to be divided amongst the vagabonds who had carried out his savage orders. The population having been thus exterminated, the district was settled anew some years later, in the reign of Louis XII., who gave his name to the valley; and a number of "good and true Catholics," including many goitres and idiots,* occupied the dwellings and possessed the lands of the slaughtered Vaudois. There is an old saying that "the blood of the martyrs is the seed of the Church," but assuredly it does not apply to Val Louise, where the primitive Christian Church has been completely extinguished.

There were other valleys in the same neighbourhood, whither we are now wending, where the persecution, though equally ferocious, proved less destructive; the inhabitants succeeding in making their escape into comparatively inaccessible places in the mountains before they could be put to the sword. For instance, in Val Fressinière—also opening into the valley of the Durance a little lower down than Val Louise—the Vaudois Church has never ceased to exist, and to this day the majority of the inhabitants belong to it. From the earliest times the people of the valley were distinguished for their "heresy;" and as early as the

* It has been noted that these unfortunates abound most in the villages occupied by the new settlers. Thus, of the population of the village of St. Crepin, in the valley of the Durance, not fewer than one-tenth are deaf and dumb, with a large proportion of idiots.

fourteenth century eighty persons of Fressinières and the neighbouring valley of Argentières,—willing to be martyrs rather than apostates,—were burnt at Embrun because of their religion. In the following century (1483) we find ninety-nine informations laid before John Lord Archbishop of Embrun against supposed heretics of Val Fressinières. The suspected were ordered to wear a cross upon their dress, before and behind, and not to appear at church without displaying such crosses. But it further appears from the records, that, instead of wearing the crosses, most of the persons so informed against fled into the mountains and hid themselves away in caves for the space of five years.

The next steps taken by the Archbishop are described in a Latin manuscript,* of which the following is a translation:—

"Also, that in consequence of the above, the monk Francis Splireti, of the order of Mendicants, Professor in Theology, was deputed in the quality of Inquisitor of the said valleys; and that in the year 1489, on the 1st of January, knowing that those of Freyssiniér had relapsed into infamous heresy, and had not obeyed their orders, nor carried the cross on their dress, but on the contrary had received their excommunicated and banished brethren without delivering them over to the Church, sent to them new citation, to which not having appeared, an adjournment of their condemnation as hardened heretics, when their goods would be confiscated, and themselves handed over to the secular power, was made to the 28th of June; but they remaining more obstinate than ever, so much so that no hope remains of bringing them back, all persons were forbidden to hold any communication whatsoever with them without permission of the Church, and it was ordered by the Procureur Fiscal that the aforesaid Inquisitor do proceed, without further notice, to the execution of his office."

What the execution of the Inquisitor's office meant, is, alas! but too well known. Bonds and imprisonment, scourgings and burnings at Embrun. The poor people appealed to the King of France for help against

* This was one of the MSS deposited by Samuel Morland (Oliver Cromwell's ambassador to Piedmont) at Cambridge in 1658, and is quoted by Jean Leger in his History of the Vaudois Churches.

their persecutors, but in vain. In 1498 the inhabitants of Fressinières appeared by a procurator at Paris, on the occasion of the new sovereign, Louis XII., ascending the throne. But as the King was then seeking the favour of a divorce from his wife, Anne of Brittany, from Pope Alexander VI., he turned a deaf ear to their petition for mercy. On the contrary, Louis confirmed all the decisions of the clergy, and in return for the divorce which he obtained, he granted to the Pope's son, the infamous Cæsar Borgia, that very part of Dauphiny inhabited by the Vaudois, together with the title of Duke of Valentinois. They had appealed, as it were, to the tiger for mercy, and they were referred to the vulture.

The persecution of the people of the valleys thus suffered no relaxation, and all that remained for them was flight into the mountains, to places where they were most likely to remain unmolested. Hence they fled up to the very edge of the glaciers, and formed their settlements at almost the farthest limits of vegetation. There the barrenness of the soil, the inhospitality of the climate, and the comparative inaccessibility of their villages, proved their security. Of them it might be truly said, that they "wandered about in sheep-skins and goat-skins; being destitute, afflicted, tormented (of whom the world was not worthy); they wandered in deserts and in mountains, and in dens and caves of the earth." Yet the character of these poor peasants was altogether irreproachable. Even Louis XII. said of them, "Would to God that I were as good a Christian as the worst of these people!" The wonder is that, in the face of their long-continued persecutions, extending over so many centuries, any remnant of the original population of the valleys should have been preserved. Long after the time of Louis XII. and Cæsar Borgia, the French historian, De Thou (writing in 1556), thus describes the people of Val Fressinières: "Notwithstanding their squalidness, it is surprising that they are very far from being uncultivated in their morals. They almost all understand Latin; and are able to write fairly enough. They understand also as much of French as will enable them to read the Bible and to sing psalms; nor would you easily find a boy among them who, if he were questioned as to the religious opinions which they hold in common with the Waldenses, would not be able to give from memory a reasonable account of them." *

After the promulgation of the Edict of Nantes, the Vaudois enjoyed a brief respite from their sufferings. They then erected temples, appointed ministers, and worshipped openly. This, however, only lasted for a short time, and when the Edict was revoked, and persecution began again, in the reign of Louis XIV., their worship was suppressed wherever practicable. But though the Vaudois temples were pulled down and their ministers banished, the Roman Catholics failed to obtain a footing in the valley. Some of the pastors continued to brave the fury of the persecutors, and wandered about from place to place among the scattered flocks, ministering to them at the peril of their lives. Rewards were offered for their apprehension, and a sort of "Hue and Cry" was issued by the police, describing their age, and height, and features, as if they had been veritable criminals. And when they were apprehended they were invariably hanged. As late as 1767 the parliament of Grenoble

* De Thou's History, book xxvii.

condemned their pastor Berenger to death for continuing to preach to congregations in the "Desert."

This religious destitution of the Vaudois continued to exist until a comparatively recent period. The people were without either pastors or teachers, and religion had become a tradition with them rather than an active living faith. Still, though poor and destitute, they held to their traditional belief, and refused to conform to the dominant religion. And so they continued until within the last forty years, when the fact of the existence of these remnants of the ancient Vaudois in the valleys of the High Alps came to the knowledge of Felix Neff, and he determined to go to their help and devote himself to their service.

One would scarcely expect to find the apostle of the High Alps in the person of a young Swiss soldier of artillery. Yet so it was. In his boyhood, Neff read Plutarch, which filled his mind with admiration of the deeds of the great men of old. While passing through the soldier phase of his career the "Memoirs of Oberlin" accidentally came under his notice, the perusal of which gave quite a new direction to his life. Becoming impressed by religion, his ambition now was to be a missionary. Leaving the army, in which he had reached the rank of sergeant at nineteen, he proceeded to prepare himself for the ministry, and after studying for a time, and passing his preliminary examinations, he was, in conformity with the custom of the Geneva Church, employed on probation as a lay helper in parochial work. In this capacity Neff first went to Mens, in the department of Isére, where he officiated in the absence of the regular pastor, as well as occasionally at Vizille, for a period of about two years.

It was while residing at Mens that the young missionary first heard of the existence of the scattered communities of primitive Christians on the High Alps, descendants of the ancient Vaudois; and his mind became inflamed with the desire of doing for them what Oberlin had done for the poor Protestants of the Ban de la Roche. "I am always dreaming of the High Alps," he wrote to a friend, "and I would rather be stationed there than under the beautiful sky of Languedoc."

But it was first necessary that he should receive ordination for the ministry; and accordingly in 1823, when in his twenty-fifth year, he left Mens with that object. He did not, however, seek ordination by the National Church of Geneva, which, in his opinion, had in a great measure ceased to hold Evangelical truth; but he came over to London, at the invitation of Mr. Cook and Mr. Wilks, two Congregational ministers, by whom he was duly ordained a minister in the Independent Chapel, Poultry.

Shortly after his return to France, Neff, much to his own satisfaction, was invited as pastor to the very district in which he so much desired to minister—the most destitute in the High Alps. Before setting out he wrote in his journal, "To-morrow, with the blessing of God, I mean to push for the Alps by the sombre and picturesque valley of L'Oisan." After a few days, the young pastor was in the scene of his future labours; and he proceeded to explore hamlet after hamlet in search of the widely-scattered flock committed to his charge, and to arrange his plans for the working of his extensive parish.

But it was more than a parish, for it embraced several of the most extensive, rugged, and mountainous arrondissements of the High Alps. Though the whole number of people in his charge did not amount to more than six or seven hundred, they lived at great distances from each other, the churches to which he ministered being in some cases as much as eighty miles apart, separated by gorges and mountain-passes, for the most part impassable in winter. Neff's district extended in one direction from Vars to Briançon, and in another from Champsaur in the valley of the Drac to San Veran on the slope of Monte Viso, close to the Italian frontier. His residence was fixed at La Chalp, above Queyras, but as he rarely slept more than three nights in one place, he very seldom enjoyed its seclusion.

The labour which Neff imposed upon himself was immense; and it was especially in the poorest and most destitute districts that he worked the hardest. He disregarded alike the summer's heat and the winter's cold. His first visit to Dormilhouse, in Val Fressinières, was made in January, when the mountain-paths were blocked with ice and snow; but, assembling the young men of the village, he went out with them armed with hatchets, and cut steps in the ice to enable the worshippers from the lower hamlets to climb up to service in the village church. The people who first came to hear him preach at Violens brought wisps of straw with them, which they lighted to guide them through the snow, while others, who had a greater distance to walk, brought pine torches.

Nothing daunted, the valiant soldier, furnished with a stout staff and shod with heavy-nailed shoes, covered with linen socks to prevent slipping on the snow, would set out with his wallet on his back across the Col d'Orcières in winter, in the track of the lynx and the chamois, with the snow and sleet beating against his face, to visit his people on the other side of the mountain. His patience, his perseverance, his sweetness of temper, were unfailing. "Ah!" said one unbelieving Thomas of Val Fressinières in his mountain patois, "you have come among us like a woman who attempts to kindle a fire with green wood; she exhausts her breath in blowing it to keep the little flame alive, but the moment she quits it, it is instantly extinguished."

Neff nevertheless laboured on with hope, and neither discouragement nor obstruction slackened his efforts. And such labours could not fail of their effect. He succeeded in inspiring the simple mountaineers with his own zeal, he evoked their love, and excited their enthusiastic admiration. When he returned to Dormilhouse after a brief absence, the whole village would turn out and come down the mountain to meet and embrace him. "The rocks, the cascades, nay, the very glaciers," he wrote to a friend, "all seemed animated, and presented a smiling aspect; the savage country became agreeable and dear to me from the moment its inhabitants were my brethren."

Unresting and indefatigable, Neff was always at work. He exhorted the people in hovels, held schools in barns in which he taught the children, and catechised them in stables. His hand was in every good work. He taught the people to sing, he taught them to read, he taught them to pray. To be able to speak to them familiarly, he learnt their native patois, and laboured at it like a schoolboy. He worked as a missionary among savages. The poor mountaineers had been so long destitute of instruction, that everything had as it were to be begun with them from the beginning. Sharing in their hovels and stables, with their squalor and smoke, he taught them how to improve them by adding chimneys and windows, and showed how warmth might be obtained more healthfully than by huddling together in winter-time with the cattle. He taught them manners, and especially greater respect for women, inculcating the lesson by his own gentleness and tender deference. Out of doors, he showed how they might till the ground to greater advantage, and introduced an improved culture of the potato, which more than doubled the production. Observing how the pastures of Dormilhouse were scorched by the summer sun, he urged the adoption of a system of irrigation. The villagers were at first most obstinate in their opposition to his plans; but he persevered, laid out a canal, and succeeded at last in enlisting a body of workmen, whom he led out, pickaxe in hand, himself taking a foremost part in the work; and at last the waters were let into the canal amidst joy and triumph. At Violens he helped to build and finish the chapel, himself doing mason-work, smith-work, and carpenter-work by turns. At Dormilhouse a school was needed, and he showed the villagers how to build one; preparing the design, and taking part in the erection, until it was finished and ready for use. In short, he turned his hand to everything—nothing was too high or too low for this noble citizen of two worlds. At length a serious accident almost entirely disabled him. While on one of his mountain journeys, he was making a detour amongst a mass of rocky débris, to avoid the dangers of an avalanche, when he had the misfortune to fall and severely sprain his knee. He became laid up for a time, and when able to move, he set out for his mother's home at Geneva, in the hope of recovering health and strength; for his digestive powers were also by this time seriously injured. When he went away, the people of the valleys felt as if they should never see him more; and their sorrow at his departure was heart-rending. After trying the baths of Plombiéres without effect, he proceeded onwards to Geneva, which he reached only to die; and thus this good and noble soldier—one of the bravest of earth's heroes—passed away to his eternal reward at the early age of thirty-one.

The valley of Fressinières—the principle scene of Neff's labours—joins the valley of the Durance nearly opposite the little hamlet of La Roche. There we leave the high road from Briançon to Fort Dauphin, and crossing the river by a timber bridge, ascend the steep mountain-side by a mule path, in order to reach the entrance to the valley of Fressinières, the level of which is high above that of the Durance. Not many years since, the higher valley could only be approached from this point by a very difficult mountain-path amidst rocks and stones, called the Ladder, or Pas de l'Echelle. It was dangerous at all times, and quite impassable in winter. The mule-path which has lately been made, though steep, is comparatively easy.

What the old path was, and what were the discomforts of travelling through this district in Neff's time, may be appreciated on a perusal of the narrative of the young pastor Bost, who in 1840 determined to make a sort of pilgrimage to the scenes of his friend's labours some seventeen years before. M. Bost, however, rather exaggerates the difficulties and discomforts of the valleys than otherwise. He saw no beauty nor grandeur in the scenery, only "horrible mountains in a state of dissolution" and constantly ready to fall upon the heads of passing travellers. He had no eyes for the picturesque though gloomy lake of La Roche, but saw only the miserable hamlet itself. He slept in the dismal little inn, as doubtless Neff had often done before, and was horrified by the multitudinous companions that shared his bed; and, tumbling out, he spent the rest of the night on the floor. The food was still worse —cold *café noir*, and bread eighteen months old, soaked in water before it could be eaten. His breakfast that morning made him ill for a week. Then his mounting up the Pas de l'Echelle, which he did not climb "without profound emotion," was a great trouble to him. Of all this we find not a word in the journals or letters of Neff, whose early life as a soldier had perhaps better inured him to "roughing it" than the more tender bringing-up of Pastor Bost.

As we rounded the shoulder of the hill, almost directly overlooking the ancient Roman town of Rama in the valley of the Durance underneath, we shortly came in sight of the little hamlet of Palons, a group of "peasants' nests," overhung by rocks, with the one good house in it, the comfortable parsonage of the Protestant pastor, situated at the very entrance to the valley. Although the peasants' houses which constitute the hamlet of Palons are still very poor and miserable, the place has been greatly improved since Neff's time, by the erection of the parsonage. It was found that the pastors who were successively appointed to minister to the poor congregations in the valley very soon became unfitted for their work by the hardships to which they were exposed; and being without any suitable domestic accommodation, one after another of them resigned their charge.

To remedy this defect, a movement was begun in

1852 by the Rev. Mr. Freemantle, rector of Claydon, Bucks, assisted by the Foreign Aid Society and a few private friends, with the object of providing pastors' dwellings, as well as chapels when required, in the more destitute places. The movement has already been attended with considerable success; and among its first results was the erection in 1857 of the comfortable parsonage of Palons, the large lower room of which also serves the purpose of a chapel. The present incumbent is M. Charpiot, of venerable and patriarchal aspect, whose white hairs are a crown of glory—a man beloved by his extensive flock, for his parish embraces the whole valley, about twelve miles in extent, including the four villages of Ribes, Violens, Minsals, and Dormilhouse; other pastors having been appointed of late years to the more distant stations included in the original widely-scattered charge of Felix Neff.

The situation of the parsonage and adjoining grounds at Palons is charmingly picturesque. It stands at the entrance to the defile which leads into Val Fressinières, having a background of bold rocks enclosing a mountain plateau known as the "Camp of Catinat," a notorious persecutor of the Vaudois. In front of the parsonage extends a green field planted with walnut and other trees, part of which is walled off as the burying-ground of the hamlet. Alongside, in a deep rocky gully, runs the torrent of the Biasse, leaping from rock to rock on its way to the valley of the Durance, far below. This fall, or cataract, is not inappropriately named the "Gouffouran," or roaring gulf; and its sullen roar is heard all through the night in the adjoining parsonage. The whole height of the fall, as it tumbles from rock to rock, is about four hundred and fifty feet; and about half-way down, the water shoots into a deep, dark cavern, where it becomes completely lost to sight.

The inhabitants of the hamlet are a poor hard-working people, pursuing their industry after very primitive methods. Part of the Biasse, as it issues from the defile, is turned aside here and there to drive little fulling-mills of the rudest construction, where the people "waulk" the cloth of their own making. In the adjoining narrow fields overhanging the Gouffouran, where the ploughs are at work, the oxen are yoked to them in the old Roman fashion, the pull being by a bar fixed across the animals' foreheads.

In the neighbourhood of Palons, as at various other places in the valley, there are numerous caverns which served by turns in early times as hiding-places and as churches, and which were not unfrequently consecrated by the Vaudois with their blood. One of these is still known as the "Glesia," or "Eglise." Its opening is on the crest of a frightful precipice, but its diameter has of late years been considerably reduced by the disintegration of the adjoining rock. Neff once took Captain Cotton up to see it, and chanted the *Te Deum* in the rude temple with great emotion.

Palons is, perhaps, the most genial and fertile spot in the valley; it looks like a little oasis in the desert. Indeed, Neff thought the soil of the place too rich for the growth of piety. "Palons," said he in his journal, "is more fertile than the rest of the valley, and even produces wine: the consequence is, that there is less piety here." Neff even entertained the theory that the poorer the people the greater was their humility and fervour, and the less their selfishness and spiritual pride. Thus, he considered "the fertility of the commune of Champsaur, and its proximity to the high road and to

Gap, great stumbling-blocks." The loftiest, coldest, and most barren spots—such as San Veran and Dormilhouse—were, in his opinion, by far the most promising. Of the former he said, "It is the highest, and consequently the most pious, village in the valley of Queyras;" and of the inhabitants of the latter he said, "From the first moment of my arrival I took them to my heart, and I ardently desired to be unto them even as another Oberlin."

CHAPTER IV.

THE VAUDOIS MOUNTAIN-REFUGE OF DORMILHOUSE.

THE valley of Fressinières could never have maintained a large population. Though about twelve miles in extent, it contains a very small proportion of arable land—only a narrow strip, of varying width, lying in the bottom, with occasional little patches of cultivated ground along the mountain-sides, where the soil has settled on the ledges, the fields seeming in many cases to hang over precipices. At the upper end of the valley, the mountains come down so close to the river Biasse that no space is left for cultivation, and the slopes are so rocky and abrupt as to be unavailable even for pasturage, excepting of goats.

Yet the valley seems never to have been without a population, more or less numerous according to the rigour of the religious persecutions which prevailed in the neighbourhood. Its comparative inaccessibility, its inhospitable climate, and its sterility, combined to render it one of the most secure refuges of the Vaudois in the Middle Ages. It could neither be easily entered by an armed force, nor permanently occupied by them. The scouts on the hills overlooking the Durance could always see their enemies approach, and the inhabitants were enabled to take refuge in caves in the mountain-sides, or flee to the upper parts of the valley, before the soldiers could clamber up the steep Pas de l'Echelle, and reach the barricaded defile through which the Biasse rushes down the rocky gorge of the Gouffouran. When the invaders succeeded in penetrating this barrier, they usually found the hamlets deserted and the people fled. They could then only wreak their vengeance on the fields, which they laid waste, and on the dwellings, which they burned; and when the " brigands " had at length done their worst and departed, the poor people crept back to their ruined homes to pray, amidst their ashes, for strength to enable them to bear the heavy afflictions which they were thus called upon to suffer for conscience' sake.

The villages in the lower part of the valley were thus repeatedly ravaged and destroyed. But far up, at its extremest point, a difficult footpath led, across the face almost of a precipice, which the persecutors never ventured to scale, to the hamlet of Dormilhouse, seated on a few ledges of rock on a lofty mountain-side, five thousand feet above the level of the sea; and this place, which was for centuries a mountain fastness of the persecuted, remains a Vaudois settlement to this day.

An excursion to this interesting mountain hamlet having been arranged, our little party of five persons set out for the place on the morning of the 1st of July, under the guidance of Pastor Charpiot. Though the morning was fine and warm, yet, as the place of our destination was situated well up amongst the clouds, we were warned to provide ourselves with umbrellas and waterproofs, nor did the provision prove in vain. We were also warned that there was an utter want of accommodation for visitors at Dormilhouse, for which we must be prepared. The words scratched on the window of the Norwegian inn might indeed apply to it: "Here the stranger may find very good entertainment—*provided he bring it with him!*" We accordingly carried our entertainment with us, in the form of a store of blankets, bread, chocolate, and other articles, which, with the traveller's knapsacks, were slung across the back of a donkey.

After entering the defile, an open part of the valley was passed, amidst which the little river, at present occupying very narrow limits, meandered; but it was obvious from the width of the channel and the débris widely strewn about, that in winter it is a roaring torrent. A little way up wé met an old man coming down driving a loaded donkey, with whom one of our party, recognising him as an old acquaintance, entered into conversation. In answer to an inquiry made as to the progress of the good cause in the valley, the old man replied very despondingly. "There was," he said, "a great lack of faith, of zeal, of earnestness, amongst the rising generation. They were too fond of pleasures, too apt to be led away by the fleeting vanities of this world." It was only the old story—the complaint of the aged against the young. When this old peasant was a boy, his elders doubtless thought and said the same of him. The generation growing old always think the generation still young in a state of degeneracy. So it was forty years since, when Felix Neff was amongst them, and so it will be forty years hence. One day Neff met an old man near Mens, who recounted to him the story of the persecutions which his parents and himself had endured, and he added: "In those times there was more zeal than there is now; my father and mother used to cross mountains and forests by night, in the worst weather, at the risk of their lives, to be present at divine service performed in secret; but now we are grown lazy: religious freedom is the death-blow to piety."

An hour's walking brought us to the principal hamlet of the commune, formerly called Fressinières, but now known as Les Ribes, occupying a wooded height on the left bank of the river. The population is partly Roman Catholic and partly Protestant. The Roman Catholics have a church here, the last in the valley, the two other places of worship higher up being Protestant. The principal person of Les Ribes is M. Baridon, son of the Joseph Baridon, receiver of the commune, so often mentioned with such affection in the journal of Neff. He is the only person in the valley whose position and education give him a claim to the title of "Monsieur;" and his house contains the only decent apartment in the Val Fressinières where pastors and visitors could be lodged previous to the erection, by Mr. Freemantle, of the pleasant little parsonage at Palons. This apartment in the Baridons' house Neff used to call the "Prophet's Chamber."

Half an hour higher up the valley we reached the hamlet of Violens, where all the inhabitants are Protestants. It was at this place that Neff helped to build and finish the church, for which he designed the seats and pulpit, and which he opened and dedicated on the 29th of August, 1824, the year before he finally left the neighbourhood. Violens is a poor hamlet situated at the bottom of a deep glen, or rocky abyss, called La Combe; the narrow valleys of Dauphiny, like those of Devon, being usually called combes, doubtless from the same original Celtic word *cwm*, signifying a hollow or dingle.

A little above Violens the valley contracts almost to

a ravine, until we reach the miserable hamlet of Minsals, so shut in by steep crags that for nine months of the year it never sees the sun, and during several months in winter it lies buried in snow. The hamlet consists for the most part of hovels of mud and stone, without windows or chimneys, being little better than stables; indeed, in winter time, for the sake of warmth, the poor people share them with their cattle. How they contrive to scrape a living out of the patches of soil rescued from the rocks, or hung upon the precipices on the mountain-side, is a wonder.

One of the horrors of this valley consists in the constant state of disintegration of the adjoining rocks, which, being of a slaty formation, frequently break away in large masses, and are hurled into the lower grounds. This, together with the fall of avalanches in winter, makes the valley a most perilous place to live in. A little above Minsals, only a few years since, a tremendous fall of rock and mud swept over nearly the whole of the cultivated ground, since which many of the peasantry have had to remove elsewhere. What before was a well-tilled meadow, is now only a desolate waste, covered with rocks and débris.

Another of the horrors of the place is its liability to floods, which come rushing down from the mountains, and often work sad havoc. Sometimes a fall of rocks from the cliffs above dams up the bed of the river, when a lake accumulates behind the barrier until it bursts, and the torrent swoops down the valley, washing away fields, and bridges, and mills, and hovels.

Even the stouter-built dwelling of M. Baridon at Les Ribes was nearly carried away by one of such inundations twelve years ago. It stands about a hundred yards from the mountain-stream which comes down from the Pic de la Séa. One day in summer a storm burst over the mountain, and the stream at once became swollen to a torrent. The inmates of the dwelling thought the house must eventually be washed away, and gave themselves up to prayer. The flood, bearing with it rolling rocks, came nearer and nearer, until it reached a few old walnut trees on a line with the torrent. A rock of some thirty feet square tumbled against one of the trees, which staggered and bent, but held fast and stopped the rock. The débris at once rolled upon it into a bank, the course of the torrent was turned, and the dwelling and its inmates were saved.

Another incident, illustrative of the perils of daily life in Val Fressinières, was related to me by Mr. Milsom while passing the scene of one of the mud and rock avalanches so common in the valley. Etienne Baridon, a member of the same Les Ribes family, an intelligent young man, disabled for ordinary work by lameness and deformity, occupied himself in teaching the children in the Protestant school at Violens, whither he walked daily, accompanied by the pupils from Les Ribes. One day, a heavy thunderstorm burst over the valley, and sent down an avalanche of mud, débris, and boulders, which rolled quite across the valley and extended to the river. The news of the circumstance reached Etienne when in school at Violens; the road to Les Ribes was closed; and he was accordingly urged to stay over the night with the children. But thinking of the anxiety of their parents, he determined to guide them back over the fall of rocks if possible. Arrived at the place, he found the mass still on the move, rolling slowly down in a ridge of from ten to twenty feet high, towards the river. Supported by a stout staff, the lame Baridon took first one child and then another upon his hump-back, and contrived to carry them across in safety; but while making his last journey with the last child, his foot slipped and his leg got badly crushed among the still-rolling stones. He was, however, able to extricate himself, and reached Les Ribes in safety with all the children. "This Etienne," concluded Mr. Milsom, "was really a noble fellow, and his poor deformed body covered the soul of a hero."

At length, after a journey of about ten miles up this valley of the shadow of death, along which the poor persecuted Vaudois were so often hunted, we reached an apparent *cul-de-sac* amongst the mountains, beyond which further progress seemed impracticable. Precipitous rocks, with their slopes of débris at foot, closed in the valley all round, excepting only the narrow gullet by which we had come; but, following the footpath, a way up the mountain-side gradually disclosed itself—a zigzag up the face of what seemed to be a sheer precipice—and this we were told was the road to Dormilhouse. The zigzag path is known as the Tourniquet. The ascent is long, steep, and fatiguing. As we passed up, we observed that the precipice contained many narrow ledges upon which soil has settled, or to which it has been carried. Some of these are very narrow, only a few yards in extent, but wherever there is room for a spade to turn, the little patches bear marks of cultivation; and these are the fields of the people of Dormilhouse!

Far up the mountain, the footpath crosses in front of a lofty cascade—La Pisse du Dormilhouse—which leaps from the summit of the precipice, and sometimes dashes over the roadway itself. Looking down into the valley from this point, we see the Biasse meandering like a thread in the hollow of the mountains, becoming lost to sight in the ravine near Minsals. We have now ascended to a great height, and the air feels cold and raw. When we left Palons, the sun was shining brightly, and its heat was almost oppressive, but now the temperature feels wintry. On our way up, rain began to fall; as we ascended the Tourniquet the rain became changed to sleet; and at length, on reaching the summit of the rising ground from which we first discerned the hamlet of Dormilhouse, on the first day of July, the snow was falling heavily, and all the neighbouring mountains were clothed in the garb of winter.

This, then, is the famous mountain fastness of the Vaudois—their last and loftiest and least accessible retreat when hunted from their settlements in the lower valleys hundreds of years ago. Driven from rock to rock, from Alp to Alp, they clambered up on to this lofty mountain-ledge, five thousand feet high, and made good their settlement, though at the daily peril of their lives. It was a place of refuge, a fortress and citadel of the faithful, where they continued to worship God according to conscience during the long dark ages of persecution and tyranny. The dangers and terrors of the situation are indeed so great, that it never could have been chosen even for a hiding-place, much less for a permanent abode, but from the direst necessity. What the poor people suffered while establishing themselves on these barren mountain heights no one can tell, but they contrived at length to make the place their home, and to become inured to their hard life, until it became almost a second nature to them.

The hamlet of Dormilhouse is said to have existed

for nearly six hundred years, during which the religion of its inhabitants has remained the same. It has been alleged that the people are the descendants of a colony of refugee Lombards; but M. Muston, and others well able to judge, after careful inquiry on the spot, have come to the conclusion that they bear all the marks of being genuine descendants of the ancient Vaudois. In features, dress, habits, names, language, and religious doctrine, they have an almost perfect identity with the Vaudois of Piedmont at the present day.

Dormilhouse consists of about forty cottages, inhabited by some two hundred persons. The cottages are perched "like eagles' nests," one tier ranging over another on the rocky ledges of a steep mountain-side. There is very little soil capable of cultivation in the neighbourhood, but the villagers seek out little patches in the valley below and on the mountain shelves, from which they contrive to grow a little grain for home use. The place is so elevated and so exposed, that in some seasons even rye will not ripen at Dormilhouse, while the pasturages are in many places inaccessible to cattle, and scarcely safe for sheep.

The principal food of the people is goats' milk and unsifted rye, which they bake into cakes in the autumn, and these cakes last them the whole year—the grain, if left unbaked, being apt to grow mouldy and spoil in so damp an atmosphere. Besides, fuel is so scarce that it is necessary to exercise the greatest economy in its use, every stick burnt in the village having to be brought from a distance of some twelve miles, on the backs of donkeys, by the steep mountain-path leading up to the hamlet. Hence, also, the unsavoury means which they are under the necessity of adopting to economize warmth in the winter, by stabling the cattle with themselves in the cottages. The huts are for the most part wretched constructions of stone and mud, from which fresh air, comfort, and cleanliness seem to be entirely excluded. Excepting that the people are for the most part comfortably dressed, in clothing of coarse wool, which they dress and weave themselves, their domestic accommodation and manner of living are centuries behind the age; and were a stranger suddenly to be set down in the village, he could with difficulty be made to believe that he was in the land of civilised Frenchmen.

The place is dreary, stern, and desolate-looking even in summer. Thus, we entered it with the snow falling on the 1st of July! Few of the balmy airs of the sweet South of France breathe here. In the hollow of the mountains the heat may be like that of an oven; but here, far up on the heights, though the air may be fresh and invigorating at times, when the wind blows it often rises to a hurricane. Here the summer comes late and departs early. While flowers are blooming in the valleys, not a bud or blade of corn is to be seen at Dormilhouse. At the season when vegetation is elsewhere at its richest, the dominant features of the landscape are barrenness and desolation. The very shapes of the mountains are rugged, harsh, and repulsive. Right over against the hamlet, separated from it by a deep gully, rises up the grim, bare Gramusac, as black as a wall, but along the ledges of which, the hunters of Dormilhouse, who are very daring and skilful, do not fear to stalk the chamois.

But if the place is thus stern and even appalling in summer, what must it be in winter? There is scarcely a habitation in the village that is not exposed to the danger of being carried away by avalanches or falling rocks. The approach to the mountain is closed by ice and snow, while the rocks are all tapestried with icicles. The *tourmente*, or snow whirlwind, occasionally swoops up the valley, tears the roofs from the huts, and scatters them in destruction.

Here is a passage from Neff's journal, vividly descriptive of winter life at Dormilhouse:—

"The weather has been rigorous in the extreme; the falls of snow are very frequent, and when it becomes a little milder, a general thaw takes place, and our hymns are often sung amid the roar of the avalanches, which, gliding along the smooth face of the glacier, hurl themselves from precipice to precipice, like vast cataracts of silver."

Writing in January, he says:—

"We have been buried in four feet of snow since of 1st of November. At this very moment a terrible blast is whirling the snow in thick blinding clouds. Travelling is exceedingly difficult and even dangerous among these valleys, particularly in the neighbourhood of Dormilhouse, by reason of the numerous avalanches falling everywhere. . . . . One Sunday evening our scholars and many of the Dormilhouse people, when returing home after the sermon at Violens, narrowly escaped an avalanche. It rolled through a narrow defile between two groups of persons: a few seconds sooner or later, and it would have plunged the flower of our youth into the depths of an unfathomable gorge. . . . . In fact, there are very few habitations in these parts which are not liable to be swept away, for there is not a spot in the narrow corner of the valley which can be considered absolutely safe. But terrible as their situation is, they owe to it their religion, and perhaps their physical existence. If their country had been more secure and more accessible, they would have been exterminated like the inhabitants of Val Louise."

Such is the interesting though desolate mountain hamlet to the service of whose hardy inhabitants the brave Felix Neff devoted himself during the greater part of his brief missionary career. It was characteristic of him to prefer to serve them because their destitution was greater than that which existed in any other quarter of his extensive parish; and he turned from the grand mountain scenery of Arvieux and his comfortable cottage at La Chalp, to spend his winters in the dismal hovels and amidst the barren wastes of Dormilhouse.

When Neff first went amongst them, the people were in a state of almost total spiritual destitution. They had not had any pastor stationed amongst them for nearly a hundred and fifty years. During all that time they had been without schools of any kind, and generation after generation had grown up and passed away in ignorance. Yet with all the inborn tenacity of their race, they had throughout refused to conform to the dominant religion. They belonged to the Vaudois Church, and repudiated Romanism.

There was probably a Protestant church existing at Dormilhouse previous to the Revocation, as is shown by the existence of an ancient Vaudois church-bell, which was hid away until of late years, when it was dug up and hung in the belfry of the present church. In 1745, the Roman Catholics endeavoured to effect a settlement in the place, and then erected the existing church, with a residence for the curé. But the people, though they were on the best of terms with the curé, refused to enter his church. During the twenty years that he ministered there, it is said the sole congregation consisted of his domestic servant, who assisted him at mass.

The story is still told of the curé bringing up from Les Ribes a large bag of apples—an impossible crop at Dormilhouse—by way of tempting the children to come to him and receive instruction. But they went only so long as the apples lasted, and when they were gone the children disappeared. The curé complained that during the whole time he had been in the place he had not been able to get a single person to cross himself. So, finding he was not likely to be of any use there, he petitioned his bishop to be allowed to leave; on which, his request being complied with, the church was closed.

This continued until the period of the French Revolution, when religious toleration became recognised. The Dormilhouse people then took possession of the church. They found in it several dusty images, the basin for the holy water, the altar candlesticks, and other furniture, just as the curé had left them many years before; and they are still preserved as curiosities. The new occupants of the church whitewashed the pictures, took down the crosses, dug up the old Vaudois bell and hung it up in the belfry, and rang the villagers together to celebrate the old worship again. But they were still in want of a regular minister until the period when Felix Neff settled amongst them. A zealous young preacher, Henry Laget, had before then paid them a few visits, and been warmly welcomed; and when, in his last address, he told them they would see his face no more, "it seemed," said a peasant who related the incident to Neff, "as if a gust of wind had extinguished the torch which was to light us in our passage by night across the precipice." And even Neff's ministry, as we have above seen, only lasted for the short space of about three years.

Some years after the death of Neff, another attempt was made by the Roman Catholics to establish a mission at Dormilhouse. A priest went up from Les Ribes accompanied by a sister of mercy from Gap—"the pearl of the diocese," she was called—who hired a room for the purpose of commencing a school. To give *éclat* to their enterprise, the Archbishop of Embrun himself went up, clothed in a purple dress, riding a white horse, and accompanied by a party of men bearing a great red cross, which he caused to be set up at the entrance to the village. But when the archbishop appeared, not a single inhabitant went out to meet him; they had all assembled in the church to hold a prayer-meeting, and it lasted during the whole period of his visit. All that he accomplished was to set up the great red cross, after which he went down the Tourniquet again; and shortly after, the priest and the sister of mercy, finding they could not obtain a footing, also left the village. Somehow or other, the red cross which had been set up mysteriously disappeared, but how it had been disposed of no one would ever reveal. It was lately proposed to commemorate the event of the archbishop's visit by the erection of an obelisk on the spot where he had set up the red cross; and a tablet, with a suitable inscription, was provided for it by the Rev. Mr. Freemantle, of Claydon. But when he was told that the site was exposed to the full force of the avalanches descending from the upper part of the mountain in winter, and would speedily be swept away, the project of the memorial pillar was abandoned, and the tablet was inserted, instead, in the front wall of the village church, where it reads as follows :—

À LA GLOIRE DE DIEU
DONT DE LES TEMPS ANCIENS
ET À TRAVERS LE MARTYR DE LEURS PÈRES
A MAINTENU
À DORMILHOUSE
LA FOI DONNE AUX SAINTS
ET LA CONNAISSANCE DE LA PAROLE
LES HABITANTS ONT ÉLEVÉ
CETTE PIERRE
MDCCCLXIV.

Having thus described the village and its history, a few words remain to be added as to the visit of our little party of travellers from Palons. On reaching the elevated point at which the archbishop had set up the red cross, the whole of the huts lay before us, and a little way down the mountain-side we discerned the village church, distinguished by its little belfry. Leaving on our right the Swiss-looking châlet with overhanging roof, in which Neff used to lodge with the Baridon-Verdure family while at Dormilhouse, and now known as "Felix Neff's house," we made our way down a steep and stony footpath towards the schoolhouse adjoining the church, in front of which we found the large ash trees, shading both church and school, which Neff himself had planted. Arrived at the schoolhouse, we there found shelter and accommodation for the night. The schoolroom, fitted with its forms and desks, was our parlour, and our bedrooms, furnished with the blankets we had brought with us, were in the little chambers adjoining.

At eight in the evening the church bell rang for service—the summoning bell. The people had been expecting the visit, and turned out in full force, so that at nine o'clock, when the last bell rang, the church was found filled to the door. Every seat was occupied —by men on one side, and by women on the other. The service was conducted by Mr. Milsom, the missionary visitor from Lyons, who opened with prayer, then gave out the twenty-third Psalm, which was sung to an accompaniment on the harmonium; then another prayer, followed by the reading of a chapter in the New Testament, was wound up by an address, in which the speaker urged the people to their continuance in well-doing. In the course of his remarks he said: "Be not discouraged because the results of your labours may appear but small. Work on and faint not, and God will give the spiritual increase. Pastors, teachers, and colporteurs are too often ready to despond, because the fruit does not seem to ripen while they are watching it. But the best fruit grows slowly. Think how the Apostles laboured. They were all poor men, but men of brave hearts; and they passed away to their rest long before the seed which they planted grew up and ripened to perfection. Work on then in patience and hope, and be assured that God will at length help you."

Mr. Milsom's address was followed by another from the pastor, and then by a final prayer and hymn, after which the service was concluded, and the villagers dispersed to their respective homes a little after ten o'clock. The snow had ceased falling, but the sky was still overcast, and the night felt cold and raw, like February rather than July.

The wonder is, that this community of Dormilhouse should cling to their mountain eyrie so long after the necessity for their living above the clouds has ceased; but it is their home, and they have come to love it, and are satisfied to live and die there. Rather than live elsewhere, they will walk, as some of them do, twelve miles in the early morning, to their work down in the valley of the Durance, and twelve miles home again, in the evenings, to their perch on the rocks at Dormilhouse.

They are even proud of their mountain home, and would not change it for the most smiling vineyard of the plains. They are like a little mountain clan—all Baridons, or Michels, or Orcieres, or Bertholons, or Arnouds—proud of their descent from the ancient Vaudois. It is their boast that a Roman Catholic does not live among them. Once, when a young shepherd came up from the valley to pasture his flock in the mountains, he fell in love with a maiden of the village, and proposed to marry her. "Yes," was the answer, with this condition, that he joined the Vaudois Church. And he assented, married the girl, and settled for life at Dormilhouse.*

The next morning broke clear and bright overhead. The sun shone along the rugged face of the Gramusac right over against the hamlet, bringing out its bolder prominences. Far below, the fleecy clouds were still rolling themselves up the mountain-sides, or gradually dispersing as the sun caught them on their emerging from the valley below. The view was bold and striking, displaying the grandeur of the scenery of Dormilhouse in one of its best aspects.

Setting out on the return journey to Palons, we descended the face of the mountain on which Dormilhouse stands, by a steep footpath right in front of it, down towards the falls of the Biasse. Looking back, the whole village appeared above us, cottage over cottage, and ledge over ledge, with its stern background of rocky mountain.

Immediately under the village, in a hollow between two shoulders of rock, the cascade of the Biasse leaps down into the valley. The highest leap falls in a jet of about a hundred feet, and the lower, divided into two by a projecting ledge, breaks into a shower of spray which falls about a hundred and fifty feet more into the abyss below. Even in Switzerland this fall would

---

* Since the date of our visit, we learn that a sad accident—strikingly illustrative of the perils of village life at Dormilhouse—has befallen this young shepherd, by name Jean Joseph Lagier. One day in October, 1869, while engaged in gathering wood near the brink of the precipice overhanging Minsals, he accidently fell over and was killed on the spot, leaving behind him a widow and a large family. He was a person of such excellent character and conduct, that he had been selected as colporteur for the neighbourhood.

be considered a fine object; but in this out-of-the-way place, it is rarely seen except by the villagers, who have water and cascades more than enough.

We were told on the spot, that some eighty years since an avalanche shot down the mountain immediately on to the plateau on which we stood, carrying with it nearly half the village of Dormilhouse; and every year the avalanches shoot down at the same place, which is strewn with the boulders and débris that extend far down into the valley.

At the bottom of the Tourniquet we joined M. Charpiot, accompanying the donkey laden with the blankets and knapsacks, and proceeded with him on our way down the valley towards his hospitable parsonage at Palons.

CHAPTER V.

GUILLESTRE AND THE VALLEY OF QUEYRAS.

WE left Palons on a sharp, bright morning in July, with the prospect of a fine day before us, though there had been a fall of snow in the night, which whitened the tops of the neighbouring hills. Following the road along the heights on the right bank of the Biasse, and passing the hamlet of Chancellas, another favourite station of Neff's, a rapid descent led us down into the valley of the Durance, which we crossed a little above the village of St. Crepin, with the strong fortress of Mont Dauphin before us a few miles lower down the valley.

This remote corner in the mountains was the scene of much fighting in early times between the Roman Catholics and the Huguenots, and afterwards between the French and the Piedmontese. It was in this neighbourhood that Lesdiguières first gave evidence of his skill and valour as a soldier. The massacre of St. Bartholomew at Paris in 1572 had been followed by like massacres in various parts of France, especially in the south. The Roman Catholics of Dauphiny, deeming the opportunity favourable for the extirpation of the heretical Vaudois, dispatched the military commandant of Embrun against the inhabitants of Val

Fressinières at the head of an army of twelve hundred men. Lesdiguières, then scarce twenty-four years old, being informed of their march, hastily assembled a Huguenot force in the valley of the Drac, and, crossing the Col d'Orcières from Champsaur into the valley of the Durance, he suddenly fell upon the enemy at St. Crepin, routed them, and drove them down the valley to Embrun. Twelve years later, during the wars of the League, Lesdiguières distinguished himself in the same neighbourhood, capturing Embrun, Guillestre, and Château Queyras, in the valley of the Guil, thereby securing the entire province for his royal master, Henry of Navarre.

The strong fortress of Mont Dauphin, at the junction of the Guil with the Durance, was not constructed until a century later. Victor-Amadeus II., when invading the province with a Piedmontese army, at sight of the plateau commanding the entrance of both valleys, exclaimed, "There is a pass to fortify." The hint was not neglected by the French general, Catinat, under whose directions the great engineer, Vauban, traced the plan of the present fortifications. It is a very strong place, completely commanding the valley of the Durance, while it is regarded as the key of the passage into Italy by the Guil and the Col de la Croix.

Guillestre is a small old-fashioned town, situated on the lowest slope of the pine-clad mountain, the Tête de Quigoulet, at the junction of the Rioubel and the Chagne, rivulets in summer but torrents in winter, which join the Guil a little below the town. Guillestre was in ancient times a strong place, and had for its lords the Archbishops of Embrun, the ancient persecutors of the Vaudois. The castle of the archbishop, flanked by six towers, occupied a commanding site immediately overlooking the town; but at the French Revolution of 1789, the first thing which the archbishop's flock did was to pull his castle in pieces, leaving not one stone upon another; and, strange to say, the only walled enclosure now within its precincts is the little burying-ground of the Guillestre Protestants. One memorable stone has, however, been preserved, the stone trough in which the peasants were required to measure the tribute of grain payable by them to their reverend seigneurs. It is still to be seen laid against a wall in an open space in front of the church.

It happened that the fair of Guillestre, which is held every two months, was afoot at the time of our visit. It is frequented by the people of the adjoining valleys, of which Guillestre is the centre, as well as by Piedmontese from beyond the Italian frontier. On the principal day of the fair we found the streets filled with peasants buying and selling beasts. They were apparently of many races. Amongst them were many well-grown men, some with rings in their ears—horse-dealers from Piedmont, we were told; but the greater number were little, dark, thin, and poorly-fed peasants. Some of them, dark-eyed and tawny-skinned, looked like Arabs, possibly descendants of the Saracens who once occupied the province. There were one or two groups of gipsies, differing from all else; but the district is too poor to be much frequented by people of that race.

The animals brought for sale showed the limited resources of the neighbourhood. One hill-woman came along dragging two goats in milk; another led a sheep and a goat; a third a donkey in foal; a fourth a cow in milk; and so on. The largest lot consisted of about forty lambs, of various sizes and breeds, which had been driven down from the cool air of the mountains, and, gasping with heat, were cooling their heads against the shady side of a stone wall. There were several lots of pigs, of a bad but probably hardy sort—mostly black, round-backed, long-legged, and long-eared. In selling the animals, there was the usual chaffering, in shrill patois, at the top of the voice—the seller of some poor scraggy beast extolling its merits, the intending buyer running it down as a "miserable bossu," &c., and disputing every point raised in its behalf, until the contest of words rose to such a height—men, women, and even children, on both sides, taking part in it—that the bystander would have thought it impossible they could separate without a fight. But matters always came to a peaceable conclusion, for the French are by no means a quarrelsome people.

There were also various other sorts of produce offered for sale—wool, undressed sheepskins, sticks for firewood, onions and vegetable produce, and considerable quantities of honeycomb; while the sellers of scythes, whetstones, caps, and articles of dress, seemed to meet with a ready sale for their wares, arranged on stalls in the open space in front of the church. Altogether, the queer collection of beasts and their drivers, who were to be seen drinking together greedily and promiscuously from the fountains in the market-place; the steep streets, crowded with lean goats and cows and pigs, and their buyers and sellers; the braying of donkeys and the shrieking of chafferers, with here and there a goitred dwarf of hideous aspect, presented a picture of an Alpine mountain fair, which, once seen, is not readily forgotten.

There is a similar fair held at the village of La Bessie, before mentioned, a little higher up the Durance, on the road to Briançon; but it is held only once a year, at the end of October, when the inhabitants of Dormilhouse come down in a body to lay in their stock of necessaries for the winter. "There then arrives," says M. Albert, "a caravan of about the most singular character that can be imagined. It consists of nearly the whole population of the mountain hamlet, who resort thither to supply themselves with the articles required for family use during the winter, such as leather, lint, salt, and oil. These poor mountaineers are provided with very little money, and, to procure the necessary commodities, they have recourse to barter, the most ancient and primitive method of conducting trade. Hence they bring with them rye, barley, pigs, lambs, chamois skins and horns, and the produce of their knitting during the past year, to exchange for the required articles, with which they set out homeward, laden as they had come."

The same circumstances which have concurred in making Guillestre the seat of the principal fair of the valleys, led Felix Neff to regard it as an important centre of missionary operations amongst the Vaudois. In nearly all the mountain villages in its neighbourhood descendants of the ancient Vaudois are to be found, sometimes in the most remote and inaccessible places, whither they had fled in the times of the persecutions. Thus at Vars, a mountain hamlet up the torrent Rioubel, about nine miles from Guillestre, there is a little Christian community, which, though under the necessity of long concealing their faith, never ceased to be Vaudois in spirit.* Then, up the valley of the Guil, and in the lateral valleys which join it, there are, in some places close to the mountain barrier which divides France from Italy, other villages and hamlets, such as Arvieux, San Veran, Fongilarde, &c., the inhabitants of which, though they concealed their faith subsequent to the Revocation of the Edict of Nantes, never conformed to Roman Catholicism, but took the earliest opportunity of declaring themselves openly so soon as the dark period of persecution had passed by.

The people of these scattered and distant hamlets were, however, too poor to supply themselves with religious instructors, and they long remained in a state of spiritual destitution. Felix Neff's labours were too short, and scattered over too extensive a field, to produce much permanent effect. Besides, they were principally confined to the village of Dormilhouse, which, as being the most destitute, had, he thought, the greatest claim upon his help; and at his death comparatively little had been done or attempted in the Guillestre district. But he left behind him what was worth more than any endowment of money, a noble example, which still lives, and inspires the labourers who have come after him.

* The well-known Alpine missionary, J. L. Rostan, of whom an interesting biography has recently been published by the Rev. A. J. French, for the Wesleyan Conference, was a native of Vars. He was one of the favourite pupils of Felix Neff, with whom he resided at Dormilhouse in 1825-7; Neff saying of him: "Among the best of my pupils, as-regards spiritual things and secular too, is Jean Rostan, of Vars: he is probably destined for the ministry; such at least is my hope." Neff bequeathed to him the charge of his parish during his temporary absence, but he never returned; and shortly after, Rostan left, to pursue his studies at Montauban. He joined the Methodist Church, settled and ministered for a time in La Vaunage and the Cévennes, afterwards labouring as a missionary in the High Alps, and eventually settled as minister of the church at Lisieux, Jersey, in charge of which he died, July, 1859.

It was not until within the last twenty years that a few Vaudois families of Guillestre began to meet together for religious purposes, which they did at first in the upper chamber of an inn. There the Rev. Mr. Freemantle found them when paying his first visit to the valleys in 1851. He was rejoiced to see the zeal of the people, holding to their faith in the face of considerable opposition and opprobrium; and he exerted himself to raise the requisite funds amongst his friends in England to provide the Guillestre Vaudois with a place of worship of their own. His efforts were attended with success; and in 1854 a comfortable parsonage, with a commodious room for public worship, was purchased for their use. A fund was also provided for the maintenance of a settled ministry; a pastor was appointed; and in 1857 a congregation of from forty to seventy persons attended worship every Sunday. Mr. Freemantle, in a communication with which he has favoured us, says: "Our object has not been to make an aggression upon the Roman Catholics, but to strengthen the hands and establish the faith of the Vaudois. And in so doing we have found, not unfrequently, that when an interest has been excited among the Roman Catholic population of the district, there has been some family or hereditary connection with ancestors who were independent of the see of Rome, and such have again joined themselves to the faith of their fathers."

The new movement was not, however, allowed to proceed without great opposition. The "Momiers," or mummers—the modern nickname of the Vaudois— were denounced by the curé of the place, and the people were cautioned, as they valued their souls' safety, against giving any countenance to their proceedings.

The curé was doubtless seriously impressed by the gravity of the situation; and to protect the parish against the assaults of the evil one, he had a large number of crosses erected upon the heights overlooking the town. On one occasion he had a bad dream, in which he beheld the valley filled with a vast assembly come to be judged; and on the site of the judgment-seat which he saw in his dream, he set up, on the summit of the Come Chauve, a large tin cross hearted with wood. We were standing in the garden in front of the parsonage at Guillestre late in the evening, when M. Schell, the pastor, pointing up to the height, said, "There you see it now; that is the curé's erection." The valley below lay in deep shadow, while the cross upon the summit brightly reflected the last rays of the setting sun.

The curé, finding that the "Momiers" did not cease to exist, next adopted the expedient of preaching them down. On the occasion of the Fête Napoleon, 1862, when the Rev. Mr. Freemantle visited Guillestre for the purpose of being present at the Vaudois services on Sunday, the 10th of August, the curé preached a special sermon to his congregation at early morning mass, telling them that an Englishman had come into the town with millions of francs to buy up the souls of Guillestre, and warning them to abstain from such men.

The people were immediately filled with curiosity to know what it was that this stranger had come all the way from England to do, backed by "millions of francs." Many of them did not as yet know that there was such a thing as a Vaudois church in Guillestre; but now that they did know, they were desirous of ascertaining something about the doctrines taught there. The consequence was, that a crowd of people—amongst whom were some of the highest authorities in the town, the registrar, the douaniers, the chief of a neighbouring commune, and persons of all classes—assembled at noon to hear M. de Faye, the Protestant pastor, who preached to them an excellent sermon under the trees of the parsonage orchard, while a still larger number attended in the afternoon.

When the curé heard of the conduct of his flock he was greatly annoyed. "What did you hear from the heretics?" he asked of one of the delinquents. "I heard *your* sermon in the morning, and a sermon *upon charity* in the afternoon," was the reply.

Great were the surprise and excitement in Guillestre when it became known that the principal sergeant of gendarmerie—the very embodiment of law and order in the place—had gone over and joined the "Momiers" with his wife and family. M. Laugier was quite a model gendarme. He was a man of excellent character, steady, sensible, and patient, a diligent self-improver, a reader of books, a botanist, and a bit of a geologist. He knew all the rare mountain plants, and had a collection of those that would bear transplantation, in his garden at the back of the town. No man was more respected in Guillestre than the sergeant. His long and faithful service entitled him to the *médaille militaire*, and it would have been awarded to him, but for the circumstance which came to light, and which he did not seek to conceal, that he had joined the Protestant connexion. Not only was the medal withheld, but influence was used to get him sent away from the place; and he was packed off to a station in the mountains at Château Queyras.

Though this banishment from Guillestre was intended as a punishment, it only served to bring out the sterling qualities of the sergeant, and to ensure his eventual reward. It so happened that the station at Château Queyras commanded the approaches into an extensive range of mountain pasturage. Although not required specially to attend to their safety, our sergeant had nevertheless carefully noted the flocks and herds as they went up the valleys in the spring. When winter approached, they were all brought down again from the mountains for safety.

The winter of that year set in early and severely. The sergeant, making his observations on the flocks as they passed down the valley, noted that one large flock of about three thousand sheep had not yet made its appearance. The mountains were now covered with snow, and he apprehended that the sheep and their shepherds had been storm-stayed. Summoning to his assistance a body of men, he set out at their head in search of the lost flock. After a long, laborious, and dangerous journey—for the snow by this time lay deep in the hollows of the hills—he succeeded in discovering the shepherds and the sheep, almost reduced to their last gasp—the sheep, for want of food, actually gnawing each other's tails. With great difficulty the whole were extricated from their perilous position, and brought down the mountains in safety.

No representation was made to head-quarters by the authorities of Guillestre of the conduct of the Protestant sergeant in the matter; but when the shepherds got down to Gap, they were so full of the sergeant's praises, and of his bravery in rescuing them and their flock from certain death, that a paragraph descriptive of the affair was inserted in the local papers, and was eventually copied into the Parisian journals. Then it was that an inquiry was made into his conduct, and the result was so satisfactory that the sergeant was at once decorated not only with the *médaille militaire*, but with the *médaille de sauvetage*—a still higher honour; and, shortly after, he was allowed to retire from the service on full pay. He then returned to his home and family at Guillestre, where he now officiates as *Regent* of the Vaudois church, reading the prayers and conducting the service in the absence of the stated minister.

We spent a Sunday in the comfortable parsonage at Guillestre. There was divine service in the temple at half-past ten A.M., conducted by the regular pastor, M. Schell, and instruction and catechizing of the children in the afternoon. The pastor's regular work consists of two services at Guillestre and Vars on alternate Sundays, with Sunday-school and singing lesson; and on week days he gives religious instruction in the Guillestre school. The missionary's wife is a true "helpmeet," and having been trained as a deaconess at Strasbourg, she regularly visits the poor, occasionally assisting them with medical advice.

Another important part of the work at Guillestre is the girls' school, for which suitable premises have been taken; and it is conducted by an excellent female teacher. Here not only the usual branches of education are taught, but domestic industry of different kinds. Through the instrumentality of Mr. Milsom, glove-sewing has been taught to the girls, and it is hoped that by this and similar efforts this branch of home manufacture may become introduced in the High Alps, and furnish profitable employment to many poor persons during their long and dreary winter.

By the aid of a special fund, a few girl boarders, belonging to scattered Protestant families who have no other means for the education of their children, are also received at the school. The girls seem to be extremely well taken care of, and the house, which we went over, is a very pattern of cleanliness and comfort.

The route from Guillestre into Italy lies up the valley of the Guil, through one of the wildest and deepest gorges, or rather chasms, to be found in Europe. Brockedon says it is "one of the finest in the Alps." M. Bost compares it to the Moutier-Grand-Val, in the canton of Berne, but says it is much wilder. He even calls it frightful, which it is not, except in rainy weather, when the rocks occasionally fall from overhead. At such times people avoid travelling through the gorge. M. Bost also likens it to the Via Mala, though here the road, at the narrowest and most precipitous parts, runs in the *bottom* of the gorge, in a ledge cut in the rock, there being room only for the river and the road. It is only of late years that the road has been completed, and it is often partly washed away in winter, or covered with rock and stones brought down by the torrent. When Neff travelled the gorge, it was passable only on foot, or on muleback. Yet light-footed armies have passed into Italy by this route. Lesdiguières clambered over the mountains and along the Guil to reach Château Queyras, which he assaulted and took. Louis XIII. once accompanied a French army about a league up the gorge, but he turned back, afraid to go farther; and the hamlet at which his progress was arrested is still called Maison du Roi. About three leagues higher up, after crossing the Guil from bank to bank several times, in order to make use of such ledges of the rock as are suitable for the road, the gorge opens into the Combe du Queyras, and very shortly the picturesque looking Castle of Queyras comes in sight, occupying the summit of a lofty conical rock in the middle of the valley.

As we approached Château Queyras the ruins of a building were pointed out by Mr. Milsom in the bottom of the valley, close by the river-side. "That," said he, "was once the Protestant temple of the place. It was burnt to the ground at the Revocation. You see that old elm-tree growing near it. That tree was at the same time burnt to a black stump. It became a saying in the valley that Protestantism was as dead as that stump, and that it would only reappear when that dead stump came to life! And, strange to say, since Felix Neff has been here, the stump *has* come to life—you see how green it is—and again Protestantism is like the elm-tree, sending out its vigorous offshoots in the valley."

Château Queyras stands in the centre of the valley of the Guil, which is joined near this point by two other valleys, the Combe of Arvieux joining it on the right bank, and that of San Veran on the left. The heads of the streams which traverse these valleys have their origin in the snowy range of the Cottian Alps, which form the boundary between France and Italy. As in the case of the descendants of the ancient Vaudois at Dormilhouse, they are here also found at the farthest limit of vegetation, penetrating almost to the edge of the glacier, where they were least likely to be molested. The inhabitants of Arvieux were formerly almost entirely Protestant, and had a temple there, which was pulled down at the Revocation. From that time down to the Revolution they worshipped only in secret, occasionally ministered to by Vaudois pastors, who made precarious visits to them from the Italian valleys at the risk of their lives.

Above Arvieux is the hamlet of La Chalp, containing a considerable number of Protestants, and where Neff had his home—a small, low cottage undistinguishable from the others save by its whitewashed front. Its situation is cheerful, facing the south, and commanding a pleasant mountain prospect, contrasting strongly with the barren outlook and dismal hovels of Dormilhouse. But Neff never could regard the place as his home. "The inhabitants," he observed in his journal, "have more traffic, and the mildness of the climate appears somehow or other not favourable to the growth of piety. They are zealous Protestants, and show me a thousand attentions, but they are at present absolutely impenetrable." The members of the congregation at Arvieux, indeed, complained of his spending so little of his time among them; but the comfort of his cottage at La Chalp, and the comparative mildness of the climate of Arvieux, were insufficient to attract him from the barren crags but warm hearts of Dormilhouse.

The village of San Veran, which lies up among the mountains some twelve miles to the east of Arvieux, on the opposite side of the Val Queyras, was another of the refuges of the ancient Vaudois. It is at the foot of the snowy ridge which divides France from Italy. Dr. Gilly says, "There is nothing fit for mortal to take refuge in between San Veran and the eternal snows which mantle the pinnacles of Monte Viso." The village is 6,692 feet above the level of the sea, and there is a provincial saying that San Veran is the highest spot in Europe where bread is eaten. Felix Neff said, "It is the highest, and consequently the most pious, in the valley of Queyras." Dr. Gilly was the second Englishman who had ever found his way to the place, and he was accompanied on the occasion by Mrs. Gilly.

"The sight of a female," he says, "dressed entirely in linen, was a phenomenon so new to those simple peasants, whose garments are never anything but woollen, that Pizarro and his mail-clad companions were not greater objects of curiosity to the Peruvians than we were to these mountaineers."

Not far distant from San Veran are the mountain hamlets of Pierre Grosse and Fon-gillarde, also ancient retreats of the persecuted Vaudois, and now for the most part inhabited by Protestants. The remoteness and comparative inaccessibility of these mountain hamlets may be inferred from the fact that in 1786, when the Protestants of France were for the first time since the Revocation of the Edict of Nantes permitted to worship in public without molestation, four years elapsed before the intelligence reached San Veran.

We have now reached almost the extreme limits of France; Italy lying on the other side of the snowy peaks which shut in the upper valleys of the Alps. In Neff's time the parish of which he had charge extended from San Veran, on the frontier, to Champsaur, in the valley of the Drac, a distance of nearly eighty miles. His charge consisted of the scattered population of many mountain hamlets, to visit which in succession involved his travelling a total distance of not less than one hundred and eighty miles. It was, of course, impossible that any single man, no matter how inspired by zeal and devotion, could do justice to a charge so extensive. The difficulties of passing through a country so wild and rugged were also very great, especially in winter. Neff records that on one occasion he took six hours to make the journey, in the midst of a snow-storm which completely hid the footpath, from his cottage at La Chalp to San Veran, a distance of only twelve miles.

The pastors who succeeded Neff had the same difficulties to encounter, and there were few to be found who could brave them. The want of proper domestic accommodation for the pastors was also felt to be a great hindrance. Accordingly, one of the first things to which the Rev. Mr. Freemantle directed his attention, when he entered upon his noble work of supplying the spiritual destitution of the French Vaudois, was to take steps not only to supply the poor people with more commodious temples, but also to provide dwelling-houses for the pastors. And in the course of a few years, helped by friends in England, he has been enabled really to accomplish a very great deal. The extensive parish of Neff is now divided into five sub-parishes—that of Fressinières, which includes Palons, Violins, and Dormilhouse, provided with three temples, a parsonage, and schools; Arvieux, with the hamlets of Brunissard (where worship was formerly conducted in a stable) and La Chalp, provided with two temples, a parsonage, and schools; San Veran, with Fongillarde and Pierre Grosse, provided with three temples, a parsonage, and a school; St. Laurent du Cros and Champsaur, in the valley of the Drac, provided with a temple, school, &c., principally through the liberality of Lord Monson; and Guillestre and Vars, provided with two temples, a parsonage, and a girls' school. A temple, with a residence for a pastor, has also of late years been provided at Briançon, with a meeting-place also at the village of Villeneuve.

Such are the agencies now at work in the district of the High Alps, helped on by a few zealous workers in England and abroad. While the object of the pastors, in the words of Mr. Freemantle, is "not to regard themselves as missionaries to proselytize Roman Catholics, but as ministers residing among their own people, whose faith, and love, and holiness they have to promote," they also endeavour to institute measures with the object of improving the social and domestic condition of the Vaudois. Thus, in one district—that of St. Laurent du Cros—a *banque de prévoyance*, or savings-bank, has been established; and though it was at first regarded with suspicion, it has gradually made its way and proved of great value, being made use of by the indigent Roman Catholics as well as Protestant families of the district. Such efforts and such agencies as these cannot fail to be followed by blessings, and to be greatly instrumental for good.

Our last night in France was spent in the miserable little town of Abries, situated immediately at the foot of the Alpine ridge which separates France from Italy. On reaching the principal hotel, or rather auberge, we found every bed taken; but a peep into the dark and dirty kitchen, which forms the entrance-hall of the place, made us almost glad that there was no room for us in that inn. We turned out into the wet streets to find a better; but though we succeeded in finding beds in a poor house in a back lane, little can be said in their praise. We were, however, supplied with a tolerable dinner, and contrived to pass the night in rest, and to start refreshed early on the following morning on our way to the Vaudois valleys of Piedmont.

CHAPTER VI.

THE VALLEY OF THE PELICE—LA TOUR—ANGROGNA— THE PRA DU TOUR.

THE village of Abries is situated close to the Alpine ridge, the summit of which marks the boundary between France and Italy. On the other side lie the valleys of Piedmont, in which the French Vaudois were accustomed to take refuge when persecution ravaged their own valleys, passing by the mountain-road we were now about to travel, as far as La Tour, in the valley of the Pelice.

Although there are occasional villages along the route, there is no good resting-place for travellers short of La Tour, some twenty-six miles distant from Abries; and as it was necessary that we should walk the distance, the greater part of the road being merely a track, scarcely practicable for mules, we were up betimes in the morning, and on our way. The sun had scarcely risen above the horizon. The mist was still hanging along the mountain-sides, and the stillness of the scene was only broken by the murmur of the Guil running in its rocky bed below. Passing through the hamlet of Monta, where the French douane has its last frontier station, we began the ascent; and soon, as the sun rose and the mists cleared away, we saw the profile of the mountain up which we were climbing cast boldly upon the range behind us on the further side of the valley. A little beyond the ravine of the Combe de la Croix, along the summit of which the road winds, we reached the last house within the French frontier—a hospice, not very inviting in appearance, for the accommodation of travellers. A little further is the Col, and passing a stone block carved with the fleur-de-lis and cross of Savoy, we crossed the frontier of France and entered Italy.

On turning a shoulder of the mountain, we looked down upon the head of the valley of the Pelice, a grand and savage scene. The majestic, snow-capped Monte Viso towers up on the right, at the head of the valley, amidst an assemblage of other great mountain masses. From its foot seems to steal the river Pelice, now a quiet rivulet, though in winter a raging torrent. Right in front, lower down the valley, is the rocky defile of Mirabouc, a singularly savage gorge, seemingly rent asunder by some tremendous convulsion of nature; beyond and over which extends the valley of the Pelice, expanding into that of the Po, and in the remote distance the plains of Piedmont; while immediately beneath our feet, as it were, but far below, lies a considerable breadth of green pasture, the Bergerie of Pra, enclosed on all sides by the mountains over which we look.

The descent from the Col down into the Pra is very difficult, in some places almost precipitous—far more abrupt than on the French side, where the incline up to the summit is comparatively easy.

The zigzag descends from one rock to another, along the face of a shelving slope, by a succession of notches (from which the footpath is not inappropriately termed *La Coche*) affording a very insecure footing for the few mules which occasionally cross the pass. Dr. Gilly crossed here from La Tour with Mrs. Gilly in 1829, when about to visit the French valleys; but he found the path so difficult and dangerous, that the lady had to walk nearly the whole way.

As we descended the mountain almost by a succession of leaps, we overtook M. Gariod, deputy judge of Gap, engaged in botanizing among the rocks; and he informed us that among the rarer specimens he had collected in the course of his journey on the summit were the *Polygonum alpinum* and *Silene vallesia*, above Monta; the *Leucanthemum alpinum*, near the Hospice; the *Linaria alpina* and *Cirsium spinosissimus* on the Col; while the *Lloydia serotina, Arabis alpina, Phyteuma hemisphericum*, and *Rhododendrum ferrugineum*, were found all over the face of the rocky descent to the Pra.

At the foot of the *Coche* we arrived at the first house in Italy, the little auberge of the Pra, a great resort of sportsmen, who come to hunt the chamois in the adjoining mountains during the season. Here is also the usual customs station, with a few officers of the Italian douane, to watch the passage of merchandise across the frontier.

The road from hence to la Tour is along the river Pelice, which is kept in sight nearly the whole way. A little below the Pra, where it enters the defile of

Mirabouc, the path merely follows what is the bed of the torrent in winter. The descent is down ledges and notches, from rock to rock, with rugged precipices overhanging the ravine for nearly a mile. At its narrowest part stand the ruins of the ancient fort of Mirabouc, built against the steep escarpments of the mountain, which, in ancient times, completely commanded and closed the defile against the passage of an enemy from that quarter. And difficult though the Col de la Croix is for the passage of an army, it has on more than one occasion been passed by French detachments in their invasion of Italy.

It is not until we reach Bobi, or Bobbio, several miles lower down the Pelice, that we at last feel we are in Italy. Here the valley opens out, the scenery is soft and inviting, the fields are well tilled, the vegetation is rich, and the clusters of chestnut-trees in magnificent foliage. We now begin to see the striking difference between the French and the Italian valleys. The former are precipitous and sterile, constant falls of slaty rock blocking up the defiles; while here the mountains lay aside their savage aspects, and are softened down into picturesquely wooded hills, green pastures, and fertile fields stretching along the river-sides, yielding a rich territory for the plough.

Yet, beautiful and peaceful though this valley of the Pelice now appears, there is scarcely a spot in it but has been consecrated by the blood of martyrs to the cause of liberty and religion. In the rugged defile of the Mirabouc, which we have just passed, is the site of a battle fought between the Piedmontese troops and the Vaudois peasants, at a place called the Pian-del-Mort, where the persecuted, turning upon the persecutors, drove them back, and made good their retreat to their mountain fastnesses. Bobi itself was the scene of many deadly struggles. A little above the village, on a rocky plateau, are the remains of an ancient fort, near the hamlet of Sibaud, where the Vaudois performed one of their bravest exploits under Henri Arnaud, after their "Glorious Return" from exile,—near which, on a stone still pointed out, they swore fidelity to each other, and that they would die to the last man rather than abandon their country and their religion.

Near Bobi is still to be seen a remarkable illustration of English interest long ago felt in the people of these valleys. This is the long embankment or breakwater, built by a grant from Oliver Cromwell, for the purpose of protecting the village against the inundations of the Pelice, by one of which it was nearly destroyed in the time of the Protectorate. It seems strange indeed that England should then have stretched out its hand so far, to help a people so poor and uninfluential as the Vaudois; but their sufferings had excited the sympathies of all Europe, and of Protestant England in particular, which not only sent them sympathy, but substantial succour. Cromwell also, through the influence of Cardinal Mazarin, compelled the Duke of Savoy to suspend for a time the persecution of his subjects,—though shortly after the Protector's death it waxed hotter than ever.

All down the valley of the Pelice, we come upon village after village—La Piante, Villar, and Cabriol— which have been the scenes sometimes of heroic combats, and sometimes of treacherous massacres. Yet all the cruelty of Grand Dukes and Popes during centuries did not avail in turning the people of the valley from their faith. For they continue to worship after the same primitive forms as they did a thousand years ago; and in the principal villages and hamlets, though Romanism has long been supported by the power of the State and the patronage of the Church, the Protestant Vaudois continue to constitute the majority of the population.

Rising up on the left of the road, between Villar and La Tour, are seen the bold and almost perpendicular rocks of Castelluzzo, terminating in the tower-like summit which has given to them their name. On the face of these rocks is one of the caverns in which the Vaudois were accustomed to hide their women and children when they themselves were forced to take the field. When Dr. Gilly first endeavoured to discover this famous cavern in 1829, he could not find any one who could guide him to it. Tradition said it was half way down the perpendicular face of the rock, and it was known to be very difficult to reach; but the doctor could not find any traces of it. Determined, however, not to be baffled, he made a second attempt a month later, and succeeded. He had to descend some fifty feet from the top of the cliff by a rope ladder, until a platform of rock was reached, from which the cavern was entered. It was found to consist of an irregular, rugged, sloping gallery in the face of the rock, of considerable extent, roofed in by a projecting crag. It is quite open to the south, but on all other sides it is secure; and it can only be entered from above. Such were the places to which the people of the valleys were driven for shelter in the dark days so happily passed away.

One of the best indications of the improved *régime* that now prevails, shortly presented itself in the handsome Vaudois church, situated at the western entrance of the town of La Tour, near to which is the college for the education of Vaudois pastors, together with residences for the clergy and professors. The founding of this establishment, as well as of the hospital for the poor and infirm Vaudois, is in a great measure due to the energetic zeal of the Dr. Gilly so often quoted above, whose writings on behalf of the faithful but destitute Protestants of the Piedmontese valleys, about forty years since, awakened an interest in their behalf in England, as well as in foreign countries, which has not yet subsided.

More enthusiastic, if possible, even than Dr. Gilly, was the late General Beckwith, who followed up, with extraordinary energy, the work which the other had so well begun. The general was an old Peninsular veteran, who had followed the late Duke of Wellington through most of his campaigns, and lost a leg while serving under him at the battle of Waterloo. Hence the designation of him by a Roman Catholic bishop in an article published by him in one of the Italian journals, as " the adventurer with the wooden leg."

The general's attention was first attracted to the subject of the Vaudois in the following curiously accidental way. Being a regular visitor at Apsley House, he called on the Duke one morning, and, finding him engaged, he strolled into the library to spend an idle half-hour among the books. The first he took up was Dr. Gilly's " Narrative," and what he read excited so lively an interest in his mind that he went direct to his bookseller and ordered all the publications relative to the Vaudois Church that could be procured.

The general's zeal being thus fired, he set out shortly after on a visit to the Piedmontese valleys. He returned to them again and again, and at length settled at La Tour, where he devoted the remainder of his life and a large portion of his fortune to the service of the

Vaudois Church and people. He organized a movement for the erection of schools, of which not fewer than one hundred and twenty were provided mainly through his instrumentality in different parts of the valleys, besides restoring and enlarging the collage at La Tour, erecting the present commodious dwellings for the professors, providing a superior school for the education of pastors' daughters, and contributing towards the erection of churches wherever churches were needed.

The general was so zealous a missionary, so eager for the propagation of the Gospel, that some of his friends asked him why he did not preach to the people. "No," said he; "men have their special gifts, and mine is *a brick-and-mortar gift.*" The general was satisfied to go on as he had begun, helping to build schools, colleges, and churches for the Vaudois, wherever most needed. His crowning work was the erection of the grand block of buildings on the Viale del Ré at Turin, which not only includes a handsome and commodious Vaudois church, but an English church, and a Vaudois hospital and schools, erected at a cost of about fourteen thousand pounds, principally at the cost of the general himself, generously aided by Mr. Brewin and other English contributors.

Nor were the people ungrateful to their benefactor. "Let the name of General Beckwith be blessed by all who pass this way," says an inscription placed upon one of the many schools opened through his efforts and generosity; and the whole country responds to the sentiment.

To return to La Tour. The style of the buildings at its western end—the church, college, residences, and adjoining cottages, with their pretty gardens in front, designed, as they have been, by English architects—

give one the idea of the best part of an English town. But this disappears as you enter the town itself, and proceed through the principal street, which is long, narrow, and thoroughly Italian. The situation of the town is exceedingly fine, at the foot of the Vandalin Mountain, near the confluence of the river Angrogna with the Pelice. The surrounding scenery is charming; and from the high grounds, north and south of the town, extensive views may be had in all directions—especially up the valley of the Pelice, and eastward over the plains of Piedmont—the whole country being, as it were, embroidered with vineyards, corn-fields, and meadows, here and there shaded with groves and thickets, spread over a surface varied by hills, and knolls, and undulating slopes.

The size, importance, industry, and central situation of La Tour have always caused it to be regarded as the capital of the valleys. One-half of the Vaudois population occupies the valley of the Pelice and the lateral valley of Angrogna; the remainder, more widely scattered, occupying the valleys of Perouse and Pragela, and the lateral valley of St. Martin—the entire number of the Protestant population in the several valleys amounting to about twenty thousand.

Although, as we have already said, there is scarcely a hamlet in the valleys but has been made famous by the resistance of its inhabitants in past times to the combined tyranny of the Popes of Rome and the Dukes of Savoy, perhaps the most interesting events of all have occurred in the neighbourhood of La Tour, but more especially in the valley of Angrogna, at whose entrance it stands.

The wonder is, that a scattered community of half-armed peasantry, without resources, without magazines, without fortresses, should have been able for any length of time to resist large bodies of regular troops—Italian, French, Spanish, and even Irish!—led by the most experienced commanders of the day, and abundantly supplied with arms, cannon, ammunition, and stores of all kinds. All that the people had on their side—and it compensated for much—was a good cause, great bravery, and a perfect knowledge of the country in which, and for which, they fought.

Though the Vaudois had no walled towns, their district was a natural fortress, every foot of which was known to them—every pass, every defile, every barricade, and every defensible position. Resistance in the open country, they knew, would be fatal to them. Accordingly, whenever assailed by their persecutors, they fled to their mountain strongholds, and there waited the attack of the enemy.

One of the strongest of such places—the Thermopylæ of the Vaudois—was the valley of Angrogna, up which the inhabitants of La Tour were accustomed to retreat on any sudden invasion by the army of Savoy. The valley is one of exquisite beauty, presenting a combination of mingled picturesqueness and sublimity, the like of which is rarely to be seen. It is hemmed in by mountains, in some places rounded and majestic, in others jagged and abrupt. The sides of the valley are in many places finely wooded, while in others well-tilled fields, pastures, and vineyards slope down to the river-side. Orchards are succeeded by pine-woods, and these again by farms and gardens. Sometimes a little cascade leaps from a rock on its way to the valley below; and little is heard around, save the rippling of water, and the occasional lowing of cattle in the pastures, mingled with the music of their bells.

Shortly after entering the valley, we passed the scene of several terrible struggles between the Vaudois and their persecutors. One of the most famous spots is the plateau of Rochemalan, where the heights of St. John abut upon the mountains of Angrogna. It was shortly after the fulmination of a bull of extermination against the Vaudois by Pope Innocent VIII., in 1486, that an army of eighteen thousand regular French and Piedmontese troops, accompanied by a horde of brigands to whom the remission of sins was promised on condition of their helping to slay the heretics, encircled the valleys and proceeded to assail the Vaudois in their fastnesses. The Papal legate, Albert Catanée, Archdeacon of Cremona, had his head-quarters at Pignerol, from whence he superintended the execution of the Pope's orders. First, he sent preaching monks up the valleys to attempt the conversion of the Vaudois before attacking them with arms. But the peasantry refused to be converted, and fled to their strongholds in the mountains.

Then Catanée took the field at the head of his army, advancing upon Angrogna. He extended his lines so as to enclose the entire body of heretics, with the object of cutting them off to a man. The Vaudois, however, defended themselves resolutely, though armed only with pikes, swords, and bows and arrows, and everywhere beat back the assailants. The severest struggle occurred at Rochemalan, which the crusaders attacked with great courage. But the Vaudois had the advantage of the higher ground, and, encouraged by the cries and prayers of the women, children, and old men whom they were defending, they impetuously rushed forward and drove the Papal troops down-hill in disorder, pursuing them into the very plain.

BATTLE OF ROCHEMALAN.

The next day the Papalini renewed the attack, ascending by the bottom of the valley, instead of by the plateau on which they had been defeated. But one of those dense mists, so common in the Alps, having settled down upon the valley, the troops became confused, broken up, and entangled in difficult paths; and in this state, marching apprehensively, they were fallen upon by the Vaudois and again completely defeated. Many of the soldiers slid over the rocks and were drowned in the torrent,—the chasm into which the captain of the detachment (Saquet de Planghère) fell, being still known as *Toumpi de Saquet*, or Saquet's Hole.

The resistance of the mountaineers at other points, in the valleys of Pragela and St. Martin, having been almost equally successful, Catanée withdrew the Papal army in disgust, and marched it back into France, to wreak his vengeance on the defenceless Vaudois of the Val Louise, in the manner described in a preceding chapter.

Less than a century later, a like attempt was made to force the entrance to the valley of Angrogna, by an army of Italians and Spaniards, under the command of the Count de la Trinité. A proclamation had been published, and put up in the villages of Angrogna, to the effect that all would be destroyed by fire and sword who did not forthwith return to the Church of Rome. And as the peasantry did not return, on the 2nd November, 1560, the Count advanced at the head of his army to extirpate the heretics. The Vaudois were provided with the rudest sort of weapons; many of them had only slings and cross-bows. But they felt strong in the goodness of their cause, and prepared to defend themselves to the death.

As the Count's army advanced, the Vaudois retired until they reached the high ground near Rochemalan, where they took their stand. The enemy followed, and halted in the valley beneath, lighting their bivouac fires, and intending to pass the night there. Before darkness fell, however, an accidental circumstance led to an engagement. A Vaudois boy, who had got hold of a drum, began beating it in a ravine close by. The soldiers, thinking a hostile troop had arrived, sprang up in disorder and seized their arms. The Vaudois, on their part, seeing the movement, and imagining that an attack was about to be made on them, rushed forward to repel it. The soldiers, surprised and confused, for the most part threw away their arms, and fled down the valley. Irritated by this disgraceful retreat of some twelve hundred soldiers before two hundred peasants, the Count advanced a second time, and was again repulsed by the little band of heroes, who charged his troops with loud shouts of "Viva Jesu Christo!" driving the invaders in confusion down the valley.

It may be mentioned that the object of the Savoy general, in making this attack, was to force the valley, and capture the strong position of the Pra du Tour, the celebrated stronghold of the Vaudois, from whence we shall afterwards find them again driven back, baffled and defeated.

A hundred years passed, and still the Vaudois remained unconverted and unexterminated. The Marquis of Pianesse now advanced upon Angrogna —always with the same object, "ad extirpandos hereticos," in obedience to the order of the Propaganda. On this occasion not only Italian and Spanish but Irish troops were engaged in a combined effort to exterminate the Vaudois. The Irish were known as "the assassins" by the people of the valleys, because of their almost exceptional ferocity; and the hatred they excited by their outrages on women and children was so great, that on the assault and capture of St. Legont by the Vaudois peasantry, an Irish regiment surprised in barracks was completely destroyed.

A combined attack was made on Angrogna on the 15th of June, 1655. On that day four separate bodies of troops advanced up the heights from different directions, thereby enclosing the little Vaudois army of three hundred men assembled there, and led by the heroic Javanel. This leader first threw himself upon the head of the column which advanced from Rocheplate, and drove it downhill. Then he drew off his little body towards Rochemalan, when he suddenly found himself opposed by the two bodies which had come up from St. John and La Tour. Retiring before them, he next found himself face to face with the fourth detachment, which had come up from Pramol. With the quick instinct of military genius, Javanel threw himself upon it before the beaten Rocheplate detachment were able to rally and assail him in flank; and he succeeded in cutting the Pramol force in two and passing through it, rushing up to the summit of the hill, on which he posted himself. And there he stood at bay.

This hill is precipitous on one side, but of comparatively easy ascent on the side up which the little band of heroes had ascended. At the foot of the slope the four detachments, three thousand against three hundred, drew up and attacked him; but firing from a distance, their aim was not very deadly. For five hours Javanel resisted them as he best could, and then, seeing signs of impatience and hesitation in the enemy's ranks, he called out to his men, "Forward, my friends!" and they rushed down-hill like an avalanche. The three thousand men recoiled, broke, and fled before the three hundred; and Javanel returned victorious to his entrenchments before Angrogna.

Yet, again, some eight years later, in 1663, was this neighbourhood the scene of another contest, and again was Javanel the hero. On this occasion, the Marquis de Fleury led the troops of the Duke of Savoy, whose object, as before, was to advance up the valley, and assail the Vaudois stronghold of Pra du Tour; and again the peasantry resisted them successfully, and drove them back into the plains. Javanel then went to rejoin a party of the men whom he had posted at the "Gates of Angrogna" to defend the pass up the valley; and again he fell upon the enemy engaged in attempting to force a passage there, and defeated them with heavy loss.

Such are among the exciting events which have occurred in this one locality in connection with the Vaudois struggle for country and liberty.

Let us now proceed up the valley of Angrogna, towards the famous stronghold of the Pra du Tour, the object of those repeated attacks of the enemy in the neighbourhood of Rochemalan. As we advance, the mountains gradually close in upon the valley, leaving a comparatively small width of pasture land by the river-side. At the hamlet of Serre the carriage road ends; and from thence the valley grows narrower, the mountains which enclose it become more rugged and abrupt, until there is room enough only for a footpath along a rocky ledge, and the torrent running in its deep bed alongside. This continues for a considerable distance, the path in some places being overhung by precipices, or encroached upon by rocks and boulders fallen from the heights, until at length we emerge from the defile, and find ourselves in a comparatively open space, the famous Pra du Tour; the defile we have passed, alongside the torrent and overhung by the rocks, being known as the Barricade.

The Pra du Tour, or Meadow of the Tower, is a little amphitheatre surrounded by rugged and almost inaccessible mountains, situated at the head of the valley of Angrogna. The steep slopes bring down into this deep dell the headwaters of the torrent, which escape among the rocks down the defile we have just ascended. The path up the defile forms the only approach to the Pra from the valley, but it is so narrow, tortuous, and difficult, that the labours of only a few men in blocking up the pathway with rocks and stones that lie ready at hand, might at any time so barricade the approach as to render it impracticable. The extremely secluded position of the place, its natural strength and inaccessibility, and its proximity to the principal Vaudois towns and villages, caused it to be regarded from the earliest times as their principal refuge. It was their fastness, their fortress, and often their home. It was more—it was their school and college; for in the depths of the Pra du Tour the pastors, or *barbas*,* educated young men for the ministry, and provided for the religious instruction of the Vaudois population.

It was the importance of the Pra du Tour as a stronghold that rendered it so often the object of attack through the valley of Angrogna. When the hostile troops of Savoy advanced upon La Tour, the

* *Barba*—a title of respect; in the Vaudois dialect literally signifying an *uncle*.

inhabitants of the neighbouring valleys at once fled to the Pra, into which they drove their cattle, and carried what provisions they could; there constructing mills, ovens, houses, and all that was requisite for subsistence, as in a fort. The men capable of bearing arms stood on their guard to defend the passes of the Vachére and Roussine, at the extreme heads of the valley, as well as the defile of the Barricade, while other bodies, stationed lower down, below the Barricade, prepared to resist the troops seeking to force an entrance up the valley; and hence the repeated battles in the neighbourhood of Rochemalan above described.

On the occasion of the defeat of the Count de la Trinité by the little Vaudois band near the village of Angrogna, in November, 1560, the general drew off, and waited the arrival of reinforcements. A large body of Spanish veterans having joined him, in the course of the following spring he again proceeded up the valley, determined, if possible, to force the Barricade—the royal forces now numbering some seven thousand men, all disciplined troops. The peasants, finding their first position no longer tenable in the face of such numbers, abandoned Angrogna and the lower villages, and retired, with the whole population, to the Pra du Tour. The Count followed them with his main army, at the same time directing two other bodies of troops to advance upon the place round by the mountains, one by the heights of the Vachére, and another by Les Fourests. The defenders of the Pra would thus be assailed from three sides at once, their forces divided, and victory rendered certain.

But the Count did not calculate upon the desperate bravery of the defenders. All three bodies were beaten back in succession. For four days the Count made every effort to force the defile, and failed. Two colonels, eight captains, and four hundred men fell in these desperate assaults, without gaining an inch of ground. On the fifth day a combined attack was made with the reserve, composed of Spanish companies, but this, too, failed; and the troops, when ordered to return to the charge, refused to obey. The Count, who commanded, is said to have wept as he sat on a rock and looked upon so many of his dead—the soldiers themselves exclaiming, "God fights for these people, and we do them wrong!"

About a hundred years later, the Marquis de Pianesse, who, like the Count de la Trinité, had been defeated at Rochemalan, made a similar attempt to surprise the Vaudois stronghold, with a like result. The peasants were commanded on this occasion by John Leger, the pastor and historian. Those who were unarmed hurled rocks and stones on the assailants from the heights; and the troops being thus thrown into confusion, the Vaudois rushed from behind their ramparts, and drove them in a state of total rout down the valley.

On entering the Pra du Tour, one of the most prominent objects that meets the eye is the Roman Catholic chapel recently erected there, though the few inhabitants of the district are still almost entirely Protestant. The Roman Catholic Church has, however, now done what the Roman Catholic armies failed to do—established itself in the midst of the Vaudois stronghold, though by no means in the hearts of the people.

Desirous of ascertaining, if possible, the site of the ancient college, we proceeded up the Pra, and hailed a young woman whom we observed crossing the rustic bridge over the Pêle, one of the mountain rivulets running into the torrent of Angrogna. Inquiring of her as to the site of the college, she told us we had already passed it, and led us back to the place—up the rocky side of the hill leading to the Vachère—past the cottage where she herself lived, and pointed to the site: "There," she said, "is where the ancient college of the Vaudois stood." The old building has, however, long since been removed, the present structure being merely part of a small farmsteading. Higher up the steep hill-side, on successive ledges of rock, are the ruins of various buildings, some of which may have been dwellings, and one, larger than the rest, on a broader plateau, with an elder-tree growing in the centre, may possibly have been the temple.

From the higher shelves on this mountain-side the view is extremely wild and grand. The acclivities which surround the head of the Pra seem as if battlemented walls; the mountain opposite throws its sombre shadow over the ravine in which the torrent runs; whilst, down the valley, rock seems piled on rock, and mountain on mountain. All is perfectly still, and the silence is only audible by the occasional tinkling of a sheep-bell, or the humming of a bee in search of flowers on the mountain-side. So peaceful and quiet is the place, that it is difficult to believe it could ever have been the scene of such deadly strife, and rung with the shouts of men thirsting for each other's blood.

After lingering about the place until the sun was far on his way towards the horizon, we returned by the road we had come, the valley seeming more beautiful than ever under the glow of evening, and arrived at our destination about dusk, to find the fireflies darting about the streets of La Tour.

The next day saw us at Turin, and our summer excursion at an end. Mr. Milsom, who had so pleasantly accompanied me through the valleys, had been summoned to attend the death-bed of a friend at Antibes, and he set out on the journey forthwith. While still there, he received a telegram intimating the death of his daughter at Allevard, near Grenoble, and he arrived only in time to attend her funeral. Two months later, he lost another dear daughter; shortly after, his mother-in-law died; and in the following December he himself died suddenly of heart disease, and followed them to the grave.

One could not but conceive a hearty liking for Edward Milsom—he was such a thoroughly good man. He was a native of London, but spent the greater part of his life at Lyons, in France, where he long since settled and married. He there carried on a large business as a silk merchant, but was always ready to give a portion of his time and money to help forward any good work. He was an "ancien," or elder, of the Evangelical church at Lyons, originally founded by Adolphe Monod, to whom he was also related by marriage.

Some years since he was very much interested by the perusal of Pastor Bost's account of his visit to the scene of Felix Neff's labours in the High Alps. He felt touched by the simple, faithful character of the people, and keenly sympathised with their destitute condition. "Here," said he, "is a field in which I may possibly be of some use." And he at once went to their help. He visited the district of Fressinières, including the hamlet of Dormilhouse, as well as the more distant villages of Arvieux and Sans Veran, up the vale of Queyras; and nearly every year thereafter he devoted a certain portion of his time in visiting the poorer congregations of the district, giving them such help and succour as lay in his power.

His repeated visits made him well known to the people of the valleys, who valued him as a friend, if they did not even love him as a brother. His visits were also greatly esteemed by the pastors, who stood much in need of encouragement and help. He cheered the wavering, strengthened the feeble-hearted, and stimulated all to renewed life and action. Wherever he went, a light seemed to shine in his path; and when he departed, he was followed by many blessings.

In one place he would arrange for the opening of a new place of worship; in another, for the opening of a boys' school; in a third, for the industrial employment of girls; and wherever there was any little heart-burning or jealousy to be allayed, he would set himself to remove it. His admirable tact, his unfailing temper, and excellent good sense, rendered him a wise counsellor and a most successful conciliator.

The last time Mr. Milsom visited England, towards the end of 1869, he was occupied, as usual, in collecting subscriptions for the poor Vaudois of the High Alps. Now that the good "merchant missionary" has rested from his labours, they will indeed feel the loss of their friend. Who is to assume his mantle?

CHAPTER VII

THE GLORIOUS RETURN:

AN EPISODE IN THE HISTORY OF THE ITALIAN VAUDOIS.

WHAT is known as The Glorious Return, or re-entry of the exiled Vaudois in 1689 to resume possession of the valleys from which they had been banished, will always stand out as one of the most remarkable events in history.

If ever a people fairly established their right to live in their own country, and to worship God after their own methods, the Vaudois had surely done so. They had held conscientiously and consistently to their religion for nearly five hundred years, during which they laboured under many disabilities and suffered much persecution. But the successive Dukes of Savoy were no better satisfied with them as subjects than before. They could not brook that any part of their people should be of a different form of religion from that professed by themselves; and they continued, at the instance of successive popes, to let slip the dogs of war upon the valleys, in the hopes of eventually compelling the Vaudois to "come in" and make their peace with the Church.

The result of these invasions was almost uniform. At the first sudden inroad of the troops, the people, taken by surprise, usually took to flight; on which their dwellings were burnt and their fields laid waste But when they had time to rally and collect their forces, the almost invariable result was that the Piedmontese were driven out of the valleys again with ignominy and loss. The Duke's invasion of 1655 was, however, attended with greater success than usual. His armies occupied the greater part of the valleys, though the Vaudois still held out, and made occasional successful sallies from their mountain fastnesses. At length, the Protestants of the Swiss Confederation, taking compassion on their co-religionists in Piedmont, sent ambassadors to the Duke of Savoy at Turin to intercede for their relief; and the result was the amnesty granted to them in that year under the title of the "Patents of Grace." The terms were very hard, but they were agreed to. The Vaudois were to be permitted to re-occupy their valleys, conditional on their rebuilding all the Catholic churches which had been destroyed, paying to the Duke an indemnity of fifty thousand francs, and ceding to him the richest lands in the valley of Luzerna—the last relics of their fortunes being thus taken from them to remunerate the barbarity of their persecutors.

It was also stipulated by this treaty, that the pastors of the Vaudois churches were to be natives of the district only, and that they were to be at liberty to administer religious instruction in their own manner in all the Vaudois parishes, excepting that of St. John, near La Tour, where their worship was interdicted. The only persons excepted from the terms of the amnesty were Javanel, the heroic old captain, and Jean Leger, the pastor-historian, the most prominent leaders of the Vaudois in the recent war, both of whom were declared to be banished the ducal dominions.

Under this treaty the Vaudois enjoyed peace for about thirty years, during which they restored the cultivation of the valleys, rebuilt the villages, and were acknowledged to be among the most loyal, peaceable, and industrious of the subjects of Savoy.

There were, however, certain parts of the valleys to which the amnesty granted by the Duke did not apply. Thus, it did not apply to the valleys of Pérouse and Pragela, which did not then form part of the dominions of Savoy, but were included within the French frontier. It was out of this circumstance that a difficulty arose with the French monarch, which issued in the revival of the persecution in the valleys, the banishment of the Vaudois into Switzerland, and their eventual "Glorious Return" in the manner we are about briefly to narrate.

When Louis XIV. of France revoked the Edict of Nantes in 1685, and interdicted all Protestant worship throughout his dominions, the law of course applied to the valleys of Pérouse and Pragela as to the other parts of France. The Vaudois pastors were banished, and the people were forbidden to profess any other religion than that prescribed by the King, under penalty of confiscation of their goods, imprisonment, or banishment. The Vaudois who desired to avoid these penalties while they still remained staunch to their faith, did what so many Frenchmen then did— they fled across the frontier and took refuge in foreign lands. Some of the inhabitants of the French valleys went northward into Switzerland, while others passed across the mountains towards the south, and took refuge in the valley of the Pelice, where the Vaudois religion continued to be tolerated under the terms of the amnesty above referred to, which had been granted by the Duke of Savoy.

The French king, when he found his Huguenot subjects flying in all directions rather than remain in France and be "converted" to Roman Catholicism, next tried to block up the various avenues of escape, and to prevent the rulers of the adjoining countries from giving the fugitives asylum. Great was his displeasure when he heard of the flight of the Vaudois of Pérouse and Pragela into the adjoining valleys. He directed the French ambassador at Turin to call upon the Duke of Savoy, and require him to prevent their settlement within his dominions. At the same time, he called upon the Duke to take steps to compel the conversion of his people from the pretended reformed faith, and offered the aid of his troops to enforce their submission, "at whatever cost."

The Duke was irritated at the manner in which he was approached. Louis XIV. was treating him as a vassal of France rather than as an independent sovereign. But he felt himself to be weak, and comparatively powerless to resent the insult. So he first temporised, then vacillated, and being again pressed by the French king, he eventually yielded. The amnesty was declared to be at an end, and the Vaudois were ordered forthwith to become members of the Church of Rome. An edict was issued on the 31st of January, 1686, forbidding the exercise by the Vaudois of their religion, abolishing their ancient privileges, and ordering the demolition of all their places of worship. Pastors and schoolmasters who refused to be converted were ordered to quit the country within fifteen days, on pain of death and confiscation of their goods. All refugee Protestants from France were ordered to leave under the same penalty. All children born of Protestant parents were to be compulsorily educated as Roman Catholics. This barbarous measure was merely a repetition by the Duke of Savoy in Piedmont of what his master Louis XIV. had already done in France.

The Vaudois expostulated with their sovereign, but in vain. They petitioned, but there was no reply. They requested the interposition of the Swiss Government as before, but the Duke took no notice of their memorial. The question of resistance was then discussed; but the people were without leaders. Javanel was living in banishment at Geneva—old and worn out, and unable to lead them. Besides, the Vaudois, before taking up arms, wished to exhaust every means of conciliation. Ambassadors next came from Switzerland, who urged them to submit to the clemency of the Duke, and suggested that they should petition him for permission to leave the country! The Vaudois were stupefied by the proposal. They were thus asked, without a contest, to submit to all the ignominy and punishment of defeat, and to terminate their very existence as a people! The ambassadors represented that resistance to the combined armies of Savoy, France, and Spain, without leaders, and with less than three thousand combatants, was little short of madness.

Nevertheless, a number of the Vaudois determined not to leave their valleys without an attempt to hold them, as they had so often successfully done before. The united armies of France and Savoy then advanced upon the valleys, and arrangements were made for a general attack upon the Vaudois position on Easter

Monday, 1686, at break of day,—the Duke of Savoy assailing the valley of Luzerna, while Catinat, commander of the French troops, advanced on St. Martin. Catinat made the first attack on the village of St. Germain, and was beaten back with heavy loss after six hours' fighting. Henry Arnaud, the Huguenot pastor from Die in Dauphiny, of which he was a native, particularly distinguished himself by his bravery in this affair, and from that time began to be regarded as one of the most promising of the Vaudois leaders.

Catinat renewed the attack on the following day with the assistance of fresh troops; and he eventually succeeded in overcoming the resistance of the handful of men who opposed him, and sweeping the valley of St. Martin. Men, women, and children were indiscriminately put to the sword. In some of the parishes no resistance was offered, the inhabitants submitting to the Duke's proclamation; but whether they submitted or not, made no difference in their treatment, which was barbarous in all cases.

Meanwhile, the Duke of Savoy's army advanced from the vale of Luzerna upon the celebrated heights of Angrogna, and assailed the Vaudois assembled there at all points. The resistance lasted for an entire day, and when night fell, both forces slept on the ground upon which they had fought, kindling their bivouac fires on both sides. On the following day the attack was renewed, and again the battle raged until night. Then Don Gabriel of Savoy, who was in command, resolved to employ the means which Catinat had found so successful: he sent forward messengers to inform the Vaudois that their brethren of the Val St. Martin had laid down their arms and been pardoned, inviting them to follow their example. The result of further parley was, that on the express promise of his Royal Highness that they should receive pardon, and that neither their persons nor those of their wives or children should be touched, the credulous Vaudois, still hoping for fair treatment, laid down their arms, and permitted the ducal troops to take possession of their entrenchments!

The same treacherous strategy proved equally successful against the defenders of the Pra du Tour. After beating back their assailants and firmly holding their ground for an entire day, they were told of the surrender of their compatriots, promised a full pardon, and assured of life and liberty, on condition of immediately ceasing further hostilities. They accordingly consented to lay down their arms, and the impregnable fastness of the Pra du Tour, which had never been taken by force, thus fell before falsehood and perfidy. "The defenders of this ancient sanctuary of the Church," says Dr. Muston, "were loaded with irons; their children were carried off and scattered through the Roman Catholic districts; their wives and daughters were violated, massacred, or made captives. As for those that still remained, all whom the enemy could seize became a prey devoted to carnage, spoliation, fire, excesses which cannot be told, and outrages which it would be impossible to describe."[*]

"All the valleys are now exterminated," wrote a French officer to his friends; "the people are all killed, hanged, or massacred." The Duke, Victor Amadeus, issued a decree, declaring the Vaudois to be guilty of high treason, and confiscating all their property. Arnaud says as many as eleven thousand persons were killed, or perished in prison, or died of want, in conse-

---

[*] Muston's "Israel of the Alps," translated by Montgomery; Glasgow, 1857; vol. i. p. 446.

quence of this horrible Easter festival of blood. Six thousand were taken prisoners, and the greater number of these died in gaol of hunger and disease. When the prisons were opened, and the wretched survivors were ordered to quit the country, forbidden to return to it on pain of death, only about two thousand six hundred contrived to struggle across the frontier into Switzerland.

And thus at last the Vaudois Church seemed utterly uprooted and destroyed. What the Dukes of Savoy had so often attempted in vain was now accomplished. A second St. Bartholomew had been achieved, and Rome rang with *Te Deums* in praise of the final dispersion of the Vaudois. The Pope sent to Victor Amadeus II. a special brief, congratulating him on the extirpation of heresy in his dominions; and Piedmontese and Savoyards, good Catholics, were presented with the lands from which the Vaudois had been driven. Those of them who remained in the country "unconverted" were as so many scattered fugitives in the mountains—sheep wandering about without a shepherd. Some of the Vaudois, for the sake of their families and homes, pretended conversion; but these are admitted to have been comparatively few in number. In short, the "Israel of the Alps" seemed to be no more, and its people utterly and for ever dispersed. Pierre Allix, the Huguenot refugee pastor in England, in his "History of the Ancient Churches of Piedmont," dedicated to William III., regarded the Vaudois Church as obliterated—"their present desolation seeming so universal, that the world looks upon them no otherwise than as irrecoverably lost, and finally destroyed."

Three years passed The expelled Vaudois reached

THE GLORIOUS RETURN. 501

Switzerland in greatly reduced numbers, many women and children having perished on their mountain journey. The inhabitants of Geneva received them with great hospitality, clothing and feeding them until they were able to proceed on their way northward. Some went into Brandenburg, some into Holland, while others settled to various branches of industry in different parts of Switzerland. Many of them, however, experienced great difficulty in obtaining a settlement. Those who had entered the Palatinate were driven thence by war, and those who had entered Wurtemburg were expelled by the Grand Duke, who feared incurring the ire of Louis XIV. by giving them shelter and protection. Hence many little bands of the Vaudois refugees long continued to wander along the valley of the Rhine, unable to find rest for their weary feet. There were others trying to earn a precarious living in Geneva and Lausanne, and along the shores of Lake Leman. Some of these were men who had fought under Javanel in his heroic combats with the Piedmontese; and they thought with bitter grief of the manner in which they had fallen into the trap of Catinat and the Duke of Savoy, and abandoned their country almost without a struggle.

Then it was that the thought occurred to them whether they might not yet strike a blow for the recovery of their valleys! The idea seemed chimerical in the extreme. A few hundred destitute men, however valiant, to think of recovering a country defended by the combined armies of France and Savoy! Javanel, the old Vaudois hero, disabled by age and wounds, was still alive—an exile at Geneva—and he was consulted on the subject. Javanel embraced the project with enthusiasm; and the invasion of the valleys was resolved upon! A more daring, and apparently more desperate enterprise, was never planned.

Who was to be their leader? Javanel himself was disabled. Though his mind was clear, and his patriotic ardour unquenched, his body was weak; and all that he could do was to encourage and advise. But he found a noble substitute in Henry Arnaud, the Huguenot refugee, who had already distinguished himself in his resistance to the troops of Savoy. And Arnaud was now ready to offer up his life for the recovery of the valleys.

The enterprise was kept as secret as possible, yet not so close as to prevent the authorities of Berne obtaining some inkling of their intentions. Three confidential messengers were first dispatched to the valleys to ascertain the disposition of the population, and more particularly to examine the best route by which an invasion might be made. On their return with the necessary information, the plan was settled by Javanel, as it was to be carried out by Arnaud. In the meantime, the magistrates of Geneva, having obtained information as to the intended movement, desirous of averting the hostility of France and Savoy, required Javanel to leave their city, and he at once retired to Ouchy, a little farther up the lake.

The greatest difficulty experienced by the Vaudois in carrying out their enterprise was the want of means. They were poor, destitute refugees, without arms, ammunition, or money to buy them. To obtain the requisite means, Arnaud made a journey into Holland, for the purpose of communicating the intended project to William of Orange. William entered cordially into the proposed plan, recommended Arnaud to several Huguenot officers, who afterwards took part in the expedition, supplied him with assistance in money, and encouraged him to carry out the design. Several private persons in Holland—amongst others the postmaster-general at Leyden—also largely contributed to the enterprise.

At length all was ready. The men who intended to take part in the expedition came together from various quarters. Some came from Brandenburg, others from Bavaria and distant parts of Switzerland; and among those who joined them was a body of French Huguenots, willing to share in their dangers and their glory. One of their number, Captain Turrel, like Arnaud, a native of Die in Dauphiny, was even elected as the general of the expedition. Their rendezvous was in the forest of Prangins, near Nyon, on the north bank of the Lake of Geneva; and there, on the night of the 16th of August, 1689, they met in the hollow recesses of the wood. Fifteen boats had been got together, and lay off the shore. After a fervent prayer by the pastor-general Arnaud, imploring a blessing upon the enterprise, as many of the men as could embark got into the boats. As the lake is there at its narrowest, they soon rowed across to the other side, near the town of Yvoirè, and disembarked on the shore of Savoy. Arnaud had posted sentinels in all directions, and the little body waited the arrival of the remainder of their comrades from the opposite shore. They had all crossed the lake by two o'clock in the morning; and about eight hundred men, divided into nineteen companies,* each provided with its captain, were now ready to march.

* Of the nineteen companies three were composed of the Vaudois of Angrogna; those of Bobi and St. John furnished two each; and those of La Tour, Villar, Prarustin, Prali, Macel, St. Germain, and Pramol, furnished one each. The remaining six companies were com

At the very commencement, however, they met with a misfortune. One of the pastors, having gone to seek a guide in the village near at hand, was seized as a prisoner by the local authorities, and carried off. On this, the Vaudois, seeing that they were treated as enemies, sent a party to summon Yvoirè to open its gates, and it obeyed. The lord of the manor and the receiver of taxes were taken as hostages, and made to accompany the troop until they reached the next commune, when they were set at liberty, and replaced by other hostages.

When it became known that the little army of Vaudois had set out on their march, troops were dispatched from all quarters to intercept them and cut them off; and it was believed that their destruction was inevitable. "What possible chance is there," asked the *Historic Mercury* of the day, "of this small body of men penetrating to their native country through the masses of French and Piedmontese troops accumulating from all sides, without being crushed and exterminated?" "It is impossible," wrote the *Leyden Gazette*, "notwithstanding whatever precautions they may take, that the Vaudois can extricate themselves without certain death, and the Court of Savoy may therefore regard itself safe so far as they are concerned."

No sooner had the boats left the shore at Nyon for the further side of the lake than the young seigneur of Prangins, who had been watching their movements,

posed of French Huguenot refugees from Dauphiny and Languedoc under their respective officers. Besides these, there were different smaller parties who constituted a volunteer company. The entire force of about eight hundred men was marshalled in three divisions— vanguard, main body, and rearguard—and this arrangement was strictly observed in the order of march.

rode off at full speed to inform the French resident at Geneva of the departure of the Vaudois; and orders were at once dispatched to Lyons for a strong body of cavalry to march immediately towards Savoy to cut them off. But the Vaudois had well matured their plans, and took care to keep out of reach of the advancing enemy. Their route at first lay up the valleys towards the mountains, whose crests they followed, from glacier to glacier, in places almost inaccessible to regular troops, and thus they eluded the combined forces of France and Savoy, which vainly endeavoured to bar their passage.

The first day's march led them into the valley of the Arve, by the Col de Voirons, from which they took their last view of the peaceful Lake of Geneva; thence they proceeded by the pyramidal mountain called the Mole to the little town of Viu, where they rested for two hours, starting again by moonlight, and passing through St. Joire, where the magistrates brought out a great cask of wine, and placed it in the middle of the street for their refreshment. The little army, however, did not halt there, but marched on to the bare hill of Carman, where, after solemn prayer, they encamped about midnight, sleeping on the bare ground. Next day found them in front of the small walled town of Cluse, in the rocky gorge of the Arve. The authorities shut the gates, on which the Vaudois threatened to storm the place, when the gates were opened, and they marched through the town, the inhabitants standing under arms along both sides of the street. Here the Vaudois purchased a store of food and wine, which they duly paid for.

They then proceeded on to Sallanches, where resistance was threatened. They found a body of men posted on the wooden bridge which there separated the village of St. Martin from Sallanches; but rushing forward, the defenders of the bridge fled, and the little army passed over and proceeded to range themselves in order of battle over against the town, which was defended by six hundred troops. The Vaudois having threatened to burn the town, and kill the hostages whom they had taken on the slightest show of resistance, the threat had its effect, and they were permitted to pass without further opposition, encamping for the night at a little village about a league further on. And thus closed the second day's march.

The third day they passed over the mountains of Lez Pras and Haute Luce, seven thousand feet above the sea-level, a long and fatiguing march. At one place the guide lost his way, and rain fell heavily, soaking the men to the skin. They spent a wretched night in some empty stables at the hamlet of St. Nicholas de Verose; and started earlier than usual on the following morning, addressing themselves to the formidable work of climbing the Col Bonhomme, which they passed with the snow up to their knees. They were now upon the crest of the Alps, looking down upon the valley of the Isère, into which they next descended. They traversed the valley without resistance, passing through St. Germain and Scez, turning aside at the last-mentioned place up the valley of Tignes, thereby avoiding the French troops lying in wait for them in the neighbourhood of Moutiers, lower down the valley of the Isère. Later in the evening they reached Laval, at the foot of Mont Iseran; and here Arnaud, for the first time during eight days, snatched a few hours' sleep on a bed in the village.

The sixth day saw the little army climbing the

steep slopes of Mont Iseran, where the shepherds gave them milk and wished them God-speed; but they warned them that a body of troops lay in their way at Mont Cenis. On they went—over the mountain, and along the crest of the chain, until they saw Bonneval in the valley beneath them, and there they descended, passing on to Bessant in the valley of the Arc, where they encamped for the night.

Next day they marched on Mont Cenis, which they ascended. As they were crossing the mountain a strange incident occurred. The Vaudois saw before them a large convoy of mules loaded with baggage. And shortly after there came up the carriage and equipage of some grand personage. It proved to be Cardinal Ranuzzi, on his way to Rome to take part in the election of Pope Alexander VIII. The Vaudois seized the mules carrying the baggage, which contained important documents compromising Louis XIV. with Victor Amadeus; and it is said that in consequence of their loss, the Cardinal, who himself aspired to the tiara, afterwards died of chagrin, crying in his last moments, "My papers! oh, my papers!"

The passage of the Great and Little Cenis was effected with great difficulty. The snow lay thick on the ground, though it was the month of August, and the travellers descended the mountain of Tourliers by a precipice rather than a road. When night fell, they were still scattered on the mountain, and lay down to snatch a brief sleep, overcome with hunger and fatigue. Next morning they gathered together again, and descended into the sterile valley of the Gaillon, and shortly after proceeded to ascend the mountain opposite.

They were now close upon the large towns. Susa

lay a little to the east, and Exilles was directly in their way. The garrison of the latter place came out to meet them, and from the crest of the mountain rolled large stones and flung grenades down upon the invaders. Here the Vaudois lost some men and prisoners, and finding the further ascent impracticable, they retreated into the valley from which they had come, and again ascended the steep slope of Tourliers in order to turn the heights on which the French troops were posted. At last, after great fatigue and peril, unable to proceed further, they gained the crest of the mountain, and sounded their clarions to summon the scattered body.

After a halt of two hours they proceeded along the ridge, and perceived through the mist a body of soldiers marching along with drums beating; it was the garrison of Exilles. The Vaudois were recognised and followed by the soldiers at a distance. Proceeding a little further, they came in sight of the long valley of the Doire, and looking down into it, not far from the bridge of Salabertrans, they discerned some thirty-six bivouac fires burning on the plain, indicating the presence of a large force. These were their enemies—a well-appointed army of some two thousand five hundred men—whom they were at last to meet in battle. Nothing discouraged, they descended into the valley, and the advanced guard shortly came in contact with the enemy's outposts. Firing between them went on for an hour and a half, and then night fell.

The Vaudois leaders held a council to determine what they should do; and the result was, that an immediate attack was resolved upon, in three bodies. The principal attack was made on the bridge, the passage of which was defended by a strong body of French soldiers, under the command of Colonel de Larrey.

On the advance of the Vaudois in the darkness, they were summoned to stand, but continued to advance, when the enemy fired a volley on them, killing three men. Then the Vaudois brigade rushed to the bridge, but seeing a strong body on the other side preparing to fire again, Arnaud called upon his men to lie down, and the volley went over their heads. Then Turrel, the Vaudois captain, calling out " Forward! the bridge is won!" the Vaudois jumped to their feet and rushed on. The two wings at the same time concentrated their fire on the defenders, who broke and retired, and the bridge was won. But at the further side, where the French were in overpowering numbers, they refused to give way, and poured down their fire on their assailants. The Vaudois boldly pressed on. They burst through the French force, cutting it in two; and fresh men pouring over, the battle was soon won. The French commander was especially chagrined at having been beaten by a parcel of cowherds. " Is it possible," he exclaimed, " that I have lost both the battle and my honour?"

The rising moon showed the ground strewed with about seven hundred dead; the Vaudois having lost only twenty-two killed and eight wounded. The victors filled their pouches with ammunition picked up on the field, took possession of as many arms and as much provisions as they could carry, and placing the remainder in a heap over some barrels of powder, they affixed a lighted match and withdrew. A tremendous explosion shook the mountains, and echoed along the valley, and the remains of the French camp were blown to atoms. The Vaudois then proceeded at once to climb the mountain of Sci, which had to be crossed in order to enter the valley of Pragelas.

It was early on a Sabbath morning, the ninth day of their march, that the Vaudois reached the crest of the mountain overlooking Fenestrelles, and saw spread out before them the beloved country which they had come to win. They halted for the stragglers, and when these had come up, Arnaud made them kneel down and thank God for permitting them again to see their native land; himself offering up an eloquent prayer, which cheered and strengthened them for further effort. And then they descended into the valley of Pragelas, passing the river Clusone, and halting to rest at the little village of La Traverse. They were now close to the Vaudois strongholds, and in a country every foot of which was familiar to most of them. But their danger was by no means over; for the valleys were swarming with dragoons and foot-soldiers; and when they had shaken off those of France, they had still to encounter the troops of Savoy.

Late in the afternoon the little army again set out for the valley of St. Martin, passing the night in the mountain hamlet of Jussand, the highest on the Col du Pis. Next day they descended the Col near Seras, and first came in contact with the troops of Savoy; but these having taken to flight, no collision occurred; and on the following day the Vaudois arrived, without further molestation, at the famous Balsille.

This celebrated stronghold is situated in front of the narrow defile of Macel, which leads into the valley of St. Martin. It is a rampart of rock, standing at the entrance to the pass, and is of such natural strength, that but little art was needed to make it secure against any force that could be brought against it. There is only one approach to it from the valley of St. Martin, which is very difficult; a portion of the way being in a deep wooded gorge, where a few men could easily arrest the progress of an army. The rock itself consists of three natural stages or terraces, the highest part rising steep as a wall, being surmounted by a natural platform. The mountain was well supplied with water, which gushed forth in several places. Caverns had been hollowed out in the sides of the rocks, which served as hiding-places during the persecutions which so often ravaged the valleys; and these were now available for storehouses and barracks.

The place was, indeed, so intimately identified with the past sufferings and triumphs of the Vaudois, and it was, besides, so centrally situated, and so secure, that they came to regard its possession as essential to the success of their enterprise. The aged Javanel, who drew up the plan of the invasion before the eight hundred set out on their march, attached the greatest importance to its early occupation. "Spare no labour nor pains," he said, in the memorandum of directions which he drew up, "in fortifying this post, which will be your most secure fortress. Do not quit it unless in the utmost extremity. . . . You will, of course, be told that you cannot hold it always, and that rather than not succeed in their object, all France and Italy will gather together against you. . . . But were it the whole world, and only yourselves against all, fear ye the Almighty alone, who is your protection."

On the arrival of the Vaudois at the Balsille, they discerned a small body of troops advancing towards them by the Col du Pis, higher up the valley. They proved to be Piedmontese, forty-six in number, sent to occupy the pass. They were surrounded, disarmed, and put to death, and their arms were hid away amongst the rocks. No quarter was given on either side during this war; the Vaudois had no prisons in which to place their captives; and they themselves, when taken, were treated not as soldiers, but as bandits, being instantly hung on the nearest trees. The Vaudois did not, however, yet take up their permanent position at the Balsille, being desirous of rousing the valleys towards the south. The day following, accordingly, they marched to Pralis, in the valley of the Germanasca, when, for the first time since their exile, they celebrated Divine worship in one of the temples of their ancestors.

They were now on their way towards the valley of the Pelice, to reach which it was necessary that they should pass over the Col Julian. An army of three thousand Piedmontese barred their way, but nothing daunted by the great disparity of force, the Vaudois, divided into three bodies, as at Salabertrans, mounted to the assault. As they advanced, the Piedmontese cried, "Come on, ye devil's Barbets, there are more than three thousand of us, and we occupy all the posts!" In less than half an hour the whole of the posts were carried, the pass was cleared, and the Piedmontese fled down the further side of the mountain, leaving all their stores behind them. On the following day the Vaudois reached Bobi, drove out the new settlers, and resumed possession of the lands of the commune. Thus, after the lapse of only fourteen days, this little band of heroes had marched from the shores of the Lake of Geneva, by difficult mountain-passes, through bands of hostile troops, which they had defeated in two severe fights, and at length reached the very centre of the Vaudois valleys, and entered into possession of the "Promised Land."

They resolved to celebrate their return to the country of their fathers by an act of solemn worship on the Sabbath following. The whole body assembled on the hill of Silaoud, commanding an extensive prospect of the valley, and with their arms piled, and resting under the shade of the chestnut-trees which crown the hill, they listened to an eloquent sermon from the pastor Montoux, who preached to them standing on a platform, consisting of a door resting upon two rocks, after which they chanted the 74th Psalm, to the clash of arms. They then proceeded to enter into a solemn covenant with each other, renewing the ancient oath of union of the valleys, and swearing never to rest from their enterprise, even if they should be reduced to only three or four in number, until they had "re-established in the valleys the kingdom of the Gospel." Shortly after, they proceeded to divide themselves into two bodies, for the purpose of occupying simultaneously, as recommended by Javanel, the two valleys of the Pelice and St. Martin.

But the trials and sufferings they had already endured were as nothing compared with those they were now about to experience. Armies concentrated on them from all points. They were pressed by the French on the north and west, and by the Piedmontese on the south and east. Encouraged by their success at Bobi, the Vaudois rashly attacked Villar, lower down the valley, and were repulsed with loss. From thence they retired up the valley of Rora, and laid it waste; the enemy, in like manner, destroying the town of Bobi and laying waste the neighbourhood.

The war now became one of reprisals and mutual devastation, the two parties seeking to deprive each other of shelter and the means of subsistence. The Vaudois could only obtain food by capturing the enemy's convoys, levying contributions from the plains, and making incursions into Dauphiny. The enterprise on which they had entered seemed to become more hopeless from day to day. This handful of men, half famished and clothed in rags, had now arrayed against them twenty-two thousand French and Sardinians, provided with all the munitions of war. That they should have been able to stand against them for two whole months, now fighting in one place, and perhaps the next day some twenty miles across the mountains in another, with almost invariable success, seems little short of a miracle. But flesh and blood could not endure such toil and privations much longer. No wonder that the faint-hearted began to despair. Turrel, the military commander, seeing no chance of a prosperous issue, withdrew across the French frontier, followed by the greater number of the Vaudois from Dauphiny;* and there remained only the Italian Vaudois, still unconquered in spirit, under the leadership of their pastor-general Arnaud, who never appeared greater than in times of difficulty and danger.

With his diminished forces, and the increasing numbers of the enemy, Arnaud found it impossible to hold both the valleys, as intended; besides, winter was approaching, and the men must think of shelter and provisions during that season, if resistance was to be prolonged. It was accordingly determined to concentrate their little force upon the Balsille, and all haste was made to reach that stronghold without further delay. Their knowledge of the mountain heights and passes enabled them to evade their enemies, who were watching for them along the valleys, and they passed

* The greater number of them, including Turrel, were taken prisoners and shot, or sent to the galleys, where they died. This last was the fate of Turrel.

from the heights of Rodoret to the summit of the Balsille by night, before it was known that they were in the neighbourhood. They immediately set to work to throw up entrenchments and erect barricades, so as to render the place as secure as possible. Foraging parties were sent out for provisions, to lay in for the winter, and they returned laden with corn from the valley of Pragelas. At the little hamlet of Balsille they repaired the mill, and set it a-going, the rivulet which flowed down from the mountain supplying abundance of water-power.

It was at the end of October that the little band of heroes took possession of the Balsille, and they held it firmly all through the winter. For more than six months they beat back every force that was sent against them. The first attack was made by the Marquis d'Ombrailles at the head of a French detachment; but though the enemy reached the village of Balsille, they were compelled to retire, partly by the bullets of the defenders, and partly by the snow, which was falling heavily. The Marquis de Parelles next advanced, and summoned the Vaudois to surrender; but in vain. "Our storms are still louder than your cannon," replied Arnaud, "and yet our rocks are not shaken." Winter having set in, the besiegers refrained for a time from further attacks, but strictly guarded all the passes leading to the fortress; while the garrison, availing themselves of their knowledge of the locality, made frequent sorties into the adjoining valleys, as well as into those of Dauphiny, for the purpose of collecting provisions, in which they were usually successful.

When the fine weather arrived, suitable for a mountain campaign, the French general, Catinat, assembled a strong force, and marched into the valley, determined to make short work of this little nest of bandits on the Balsille. On Sunday morning, the 30th of April, 1690, while Arnaud was preaching to his flock, the sentinels on the look-out discovered the enemy's forces swarming up the valley. Soon other bodies were seen approaching by the Col du Pis and the Col du Clapier, while a French regiment, supported by the Savoyard militia, climbed Mont Guinevert, and cut off all retreat in that quarter. In short, the Balsille was completely invested.

A general assault was made on the position on the 2nd of May, under the direction of General Catinat in person. Three French regiments, supported by a regiment of dragoons, opened the attack in front; Colonel de Parat, who commanded the leading regiment, saying to his soldiers as they advanced, " My friends, we must sleep to-night in that barrack," pointing to the rude Vaudois fort on the summit of the Balsille. They advanced with great bravery; but the barricade could not be surmounted, while they were assailed by a perfect storm of bullets from the defenders, securely posted above.

Catinat next ordered the troops stationed on the Guinevert to advance from that direction, so as to carry the position from behind. But the assailants found unexpected intrenchments in their way, from behind which the Vaudois maintained a heavy fire, that eventually drove them back, their retreat being accelerated by a shower of stones and a blinding fall of snow and hail. In the meantime, the attack on the bastion in front continued, and the Vaudois, seeing the French troops falling back in disorder, made a vigorous sortie, and destroyed the whole remaining force, excepting fifteen men, who fled, bare-headed and without arms, and carried to the camp the news of their total defeat.

A Savoyard officer thus briefly described the issue of the disastrous affair in a letter to a friend: "I have only time to tell you that the French have failed in their attack on the Balsille, and they have been obliged to retire after having lost one hundred and fifty soldiers, three captains, besides subalterns and wounded, including a colonel and a lieutenant-colonel who have been made prisoners, with the two sergeants who remained behind to help them. The lieutenant-colonel was surprised at finding in the fort some nineteen or twenty officers in gold and silver lace, who treated him as a prisoner of war and very humanely, even allowing him to go in search of the surgeon-major of his regiment for the purpose of bringing him into the place, and doing all that was necessary."

Catinat did not choose again to renew the attack in person, or to endanger his reputation by a further defeat at the hands of men whom he had described as a nest of paltry bandits, but entrusted the direction of further operations to the Marquis de Féuquières, who had his laurels still to win, while Catinat had his to lose. The Balsille was again completely invested by the 12th of May, according to the scheme of operations prepared by Catinat, and the Marquis received by anticipation the title of "Conqueror of the Barbets." The entire mountain was surrounded, all the passes were strongly guarded, guns were planted in positions which commanded the Vaudois fort, more particularly on the Guinevert; and the capture or extermination of the Vaudois was now regarded as a matter of certainty. The attacking army was divided into five corps. Each soldier was accompanied by a pioneer carrying a fascine, in order to form a cover against the Vaudois bullets as they advanced.

Several days elapsed before all the preliminaries for the grand attack were completed, and then the Marquis ordered a white flag to be hoisted, and a messenger was sent forward, inviting a parley with the defenders of the Balsille. The envoy was asked what he wanted. "Your immediate surrender!" was the reply. "You shall each of you receive five hundred louis d'or, and good passports for your retirement to a foreign country; but if you resist, you will be infallibly destroyed." "That is as the Lord shall will," replied the Vaudois messenger.

The defenders refused to capitulate on any terms. The Marquis himself then wrote to the Vaudois, offering them terms on the above basis, but threatening, in case of refusal, that every man of them would be hung. Arnaud's reply was heroic. "We are not subjects," he said, "of the King of France; and that monarch not being master of this country, we can enter into no treaty with his servants. We are in the heritage which our fathers have left to us, and we hope, with the help of the God of armies, to live and die in it, even though there may remain only ten of us to defend it." That same night the Vaudois made a vigorous sortie, and killed a number of the besiegers: this was their final answer to the summons to surrender.

On the 14th of May the battery on Mont Guinevert was opened, and the enemy's cannon began to play upon the little fort and bastions, which, being only of dry stones, were soon dismantled. The assault was then made simultaneously on three sides; and after a stout resistance, the Vaudois retired from their lower intrenchments, and retreated to those on the higher ledges of the mountain. They continued their resistance until night, and then, taking counsel together, and feeling that the place was no longer defensible in the face of so overpowering a force, commanded, as it was, at the same time by the cannon on the adjoining heights, they determined to evacuate the Balsille, after holding it for a period of nearly seven months.

A thick mist having risen up from the valley, the Vaudois set out, late at night, under the guidance of Captain Poulat, a native of the district, who well knew the paths in the mountains. They climbed up on to the heights above, over icy slopes, passing across gaping crevices and along almost perpendicular rocks, admitting of their passage only in single file, sometimes dragging themselves along on their bellies, clinging to the rocks or to the tufts of grass, occasionally resting and praying, but never despairing. At length they succeeded, after a long détour of the mountain crests, in gaining the northern slope of Guinevert. Here they came upon and surprised the enemy's outpost, which fled towards the main body; and the Vaudois passed on, panting and half dead with fatigue. When the morning broke, and the French proceeded to penetrate the last redoubt on the Balsille, lo, it was empty! The defenders had abandoned it, and they could scarcely believe their eyes when they saw the dangerous mountain escarpment by which they had escaped in the night. Looking across the valley, far off, they saw the fugitives, thrown into relief by the snow amidst which they marched, like a line of ants, apparently making for the mass of the central Alps.

For three days they wandered from place to place, gradually moving southwards, their object now being to take up their position at the Pra du Tour, the ancient fortress of the Barbas in the valley of Angrogna. Before, however, they could reach this stronghold, and while they were still at Pramol in the valley of Perosa, news of the most unexpected kind reached them, which opened up the prospect of their deliverance. The news was no other than this—Savoy had declared war against France!

A rupture between the two powers had for some time been imminent. Louis XIV. had become more and more exacting in his demands on the Duke of Savoy, until the latter felt himself in a position of oppressive vassalage. Louis had even intimated his intention of occupying Verrua and the citadel of Turin; and the Duke, having previously ascertained through his cousin, Prince Eugene, the willingness of the Emperor of Austria, pressed by William of Orange, to assist him in opposing the pretensions of France, he at length took up his stand and declared war against Louis.

The Vaudois were now a power in the state, and both parties alike appealed to them for help, promising them great favours. But the Vaudois, notwithstanding the treachery and cruelty of successive Dukes of Savoy, were true to their native prince. They pledged themselves to hold the valleys and defend the mountain passes against France.

In the first engagements which took place between the French and the Piedmontese, the latter were overpowered, and the Duke became a fugitive. Where did he find refuge? In the valleys of the Vaudois, in a secluded spot in the village of Rora, behind the Pelice, he found a safe asylum amidst the people whose fathers he had hunted, proscribed, and condemned to death.

But the tide of war turned, and the French were eventually driven out of Piedmont. Many of the Vaudois, who had settled in Brandenburg, Holland, and Switzerland, returned and settled in the valleys; and though the Dukes of Savoy, with their accustomed treachery, more than once allowed persecution to recommence, their descendants continue to enjoy the land, and to worship after the manner of their fathers down to the present day.

The Vaudois long laboured under disabilities, and continued to be deprived of many social and civil rights. But they patiently bided their time; and the time at length arrived. In 1848 their emancipation was one of the great questions of North Italy. It was taken up and advocated by the most advanced minds of Piedmont. The petition to Charles Albert in their favour was in a few days covered with the names of its greatest patriots, including those of Balbo, Cavour, and D'Azeglio. Their emancipation was at length granted, and the Vaudois now enjoy the same rights and liberties as the other subjects of Victor Emanuel.

Nor is the Vaudois Church any longer confined to the valleys, but it has become extended of late years all over Italy—to Milan, Florence, Brescia, Verona, Genoa, Leghorn, Naples, Palermo, Cataneo, Venice, and even to Rome itself. In most of these places there are day-schools and Sunday-schools, besides churches. The new church at Venice, held in the Cavagnis palace, seems to have proved especially successful, the Sunday services being regularly attended by from three to four hundred persons; while the day-schools in connection with the churches at Turin, Leghorn, Naples, and Cataneo have proved very successful.

Thus, in the course of a few years, thirty-three

Vaudois churches and stations, with about an equal number of schools, have been established in various parts of Italy. The missionaries report that the greatest difficulties they have to encounter arise from the incredulity and indifference which are the natural heritage of the Romish Church; but that, nevertheless, the work makes satisfactory progress—the good seed is being planted, and will yet bring forth its increase in God's due time.

Finally, it cannot but be acknowledged that the people of the valleys, in so tenaciously and conscientiously adhering to their faith, through good and through evil, during so many hundred years, have set a glorious example to Piedmont, and have possibly been in no small degree instrumental in establishing the reign of right and of liberty in Italy.

INDEX.

AIGUEMORTES, Huguenot prison at, 193, 273, 300
Albigenses, 75
Anabaptists of Munster, 282-3
Anduze, visit to, 125
Angrogna, valley of, 481; fighting in, 481-86, 498
Arnaud, Henry, 215, 512; leads back the Vaudois, 503-15; defends the Balsille, 515-19
Athlone, siege of, 349-50, 355-8

BALSILLE, the, 510; defence of, 515-19; given up, 519
Baridon, Etienne, 442-3
Barillon, M. de, 323, 330-1
Baville on the Protestants of Languedoc, 77, 86; occupies the Cevennes, 87; at Pont-de-Montvert, 92
Beauval, Basnage de, 364
Beauveau, Prince de, 273-4
Beckwith, General, 478
Berwick, Duke of, 310-11, 333, 351
Bibles, destruction and scarcity of, 215-16
Boileau, General, 351-2
Bonnafoux repulsed by Camisards, 142
Book-burning, 215, 235-6
Bordeille, Raphaël, 318
Bourg d'Oisans, 409-10
Boyne, battle of the, 341-7
Briançon, 414-16
Briset, Lieut., death of, 335
Broglie, Count, 143-4, 148; superseded, 149
Brousson, Claude, 30; advocate for Protestant church at Nismes, 31; meeting in house of, 34; petition by, 35; escape from Nismes, 42; at Lausanne, 43, 46; at Berlin, 44; in the Cevennes, 50-2, 54; reward offered for, 56; at Nismes, 57; preaching of, 58-9; to Lausanne, England, and Holland, 61-2; at Sedan, 64; through France, 66-7; portraiture of, 68 (note); to Nismes again, 69; taken, tried, and executed, 70-3
Browne, Col. Lyde, 380
Brueys on fanaticism in Languedoc, 91
Bull of Clement XI. against Camisards, 160

CAILLEMOTTE, Col., 339; death of, 345, 348
Calas, Jean, 257; executed, 258; case taken up by Voltaire, 259-62; reversal of judgment on, 262-3
Calvinism and race, 100 (note)
Calvinists, French and Scotch, compared, 100
Cambon, Col., 357
Camisards, the origin of name, 107; led by Laporte, 109; organization of, 112-13; encounter troops, 113-14, 117, war-song of, 115; organized by Roland, 123-4; successes of, 134-40, 142, 146-50; spread of insurrection of, 138-9; measures against, 139, 146-7; defeat of, at Vagnas, 150; defeat

of, near Pompignan, 152; success of, at Martinargues, 162-4; bull against, 160; success at Salindres, 164-5; defeated near Nismes, 168-9; reverses of, 170-1; success at Font-morte, 176-7; defeated at Pont-de-Montvert, and end of insurrection, 187-9
Camisards, White, 160-1
Carrickfergus, siege of, 335
Castanet, André, 111, 113, 118, 123, 189
Cavalier, John, joins insurgents, 108, 111; family of, 121; to Geneva, 121; to the Cevennes, 122; portrait of, 124; in Lower Languedoc, 133; defeats Royalists, 134-5; takes Château Servas, 136-7; repulses Bonnafoux, 142; at Nismes, 144-5; successes of, 148; winter campaign, 148-9; at Vagnas, 150-1, 153; betrayed at Tower of Belliot, 156-8; at Martinargues, 162-4; at Rosni, 169; his cave magazines, 170-1; his interview with Lalande, 173-6; attempts peace, 177; his interviews with Villars, 177-83; deserted by followers, 183-5; to England, and subsequent career, 186
Caves in the Cevennes, 125, 127-9; at La Tour, 477
Cazenove, Raoul de, 321, 367
Cevennes, the, persecutions in, 39, 52-3, 85; secret meetings in, 54, 84-8; executions in, 59, 67-8; description of, 79-82; arming of the people, 85-6; occupied by troops, 88; prophetic mania in, 88; encounter at Pont-de-Montvert, 92; outbreak against Du Chayla, 96-7; map of, 98; Protestants of, compared with Covenanters, 100-1; organization in, 123-5; caves in, 125, 127-9; visit to, 125-9; present inhabitants of, 129, 131-2; devastation of, 154-5
Champ Domergue, battle at, 114

Charlemont, capture of, 339
Château Queyras, 467
Chaumont, 271
Chayla, Du, 93-4, 97
Chenevix, 15 (note)
Choiseul, Duc de, 268
Claris, 237
Colognac, execution of, 59
Comiers, 407
Conderc, Salomon, 119, 123
"Conversions," rapid, 289
Converts, 19-23, 38-9
Cook, Captain, last voyage round the world, 371; cruel death, 371
Court profligacy, 275 (note)
Court, Antoine, 206-17; organizes school for preachers, 224; marriage of, 231; retires to Switzerland, 232; results of his work, 233-4; in Languedoc, 239
Covenanters compared with Protestants of the Cevennes, 100-2
Cromwell, 391-2, 476

D'Aguesseau's opinion of Protestants of Languedoc, 76-7
Dauphiny, map of, 382; aspect of, 383-4
Delada, Mdlle. de, 295
Denbeck, Abbé of, 322-3
Denèse, Rotolf de la, 364
Desert, assemblies in the, 83-8, 218-23
Desparvés, M., 297
Dormilhouse, 438, 443-54
Dortial, 238
Douglas, Lieut.-General, 349-51, 355
Dragonnades, 36-7, 42, 54-5, 288; horrors of, 291
Drogheda, surrender of, 349
Dumas, death of, 52
Dundalk, Schomberg's army at, 337-8
Durand, Pierre, 236

Easter massacre of the Vaudois, 390-92
England attempts to assist the Camisards, 166-7
Enniskilleners, the, 336

INDEX.

Evertzen, Vice-Admiral, 325
Execution of Pastors, 27

FABRE, JEAN, 265; sent to galleys, 266-9; obtains leave of absence, 269; exonerated, 270; life dramatized, and result, 270
Fermaud, Pastor, 407
Freemantle, Rev. Mr., visits of, to the Vaudois, 395, 450, 462
French labouring classes, present condition of, 397-400
Freney, gorge of, 411
Fusiliers, missionary, 293

GALLEY, description of, 197-8; use in war, 200-4
Galley-slaves, treatment of, 194-204; liberation of Protestants, 204, 264 (note), 271-3
Galway, Earl of, 360
Gilly, Dr., visit to the Vaudois, 393-4, 468, 477
Ginckel, Lieut.-General, 347, 354 et seq.
Glorious Return of the Vaudois, 493-5
Grace, Col. Richard, 351
Guarrison, Mdlle. de, 294
Guerin, death of, 67
Guignon betrays Cavalier, 156; executed, 159
Guil, valley of the, 466
Guillestre, 456-66
Guion executed, 57

HERBERT, Admiral, 325
Homel, tortures and death of, 40
Hood, Lord, 376
Huguenots, the (see *Camisards*); emigrations of, 43, 76-8, 83, 287, 316; persecution of, after Camisard insurrection, 190-204; as galley-slaves, 194-204; brought together by Court, 210-17; reorganization of, 218-228; outrages on, 228; great assemblies of, 239-40; last of the executions, 258; last of the galley-slaves, 265-273; character of, 274-5; later history of, 276-283; decrees against, 285-6;

in England, 309; foreign services of, 316-17

IRELAND and James II., 331 et seq.
Irish Brigade, 140-2, 359
Iron Boot, the, 102

JAMES II., flight of, 309, 329; lands with an army in Ireland, 309, 332; campaign against William III., 309 et seq., 333 et seq.; deserted, 328; taken prisoner, 329; his last proclamation, 330; at the French court, 331; cowardice, 337, 347-8; Catholic estimate of his character, 348
Joany, Nicholas, insurgent leader, 120, 123, 151
Johannot, 269
Julien, Brigadier, 147, 150-1

LAGIER, JEAN, 452, 453 (note)
Lajonquière defeated at Martinargues, 162-4
Lalande, his interview with Cavalier, 173-6
Languedoc (see *Cevennes*), early liberty in, 75; Albigenses in, 75; Protestants of, 76-7; industry of, 76; emigration from, after Revocation, 78, 289; arming of people of, 85-6; outbreak of fanaticism in, 88-92; present inhabitants of, 280-3
Laporte, leader of Camisards, 109-10; organizes insurgents, 112; at Collet, 113; at Champ Domergue, 114; killed at Molezon, 117
La Salette, 404; miracle of, 405-6
La Tour, 476-80
Laugier at Guillestre, 463; at Château Queyras, 464
Lausanne, school for preachers at, 224; Society of Help at, 224-5
Lauteret, Col de, 413
Lauzun, Count, 339, 358
Lesdiguières, Duc de, 402-3, 455
Limerick, siege of, 351-4, 359

Lintarde, Marie, imprisonment of, 54
Locke, John, on Protestants of Nismes, 31 (note)
Londonderry, siege of, 333
Louis XIV., 2, 10, 146, 205
Louis XV., 275
Louis XVI., 276; maxim of, 285; his decrees against Protestants, 285-6; his mode of stopping the emigration of Huguenots, 287-8; expulsion of Protestants, 316; assists James II., 332
Luttrell, Capt., brilliant naval achievement of, 372

MACKAY, Major-General, 355, 357
Marillac, Michel de, inventor of the dragonnades, 288
Marion on influence of Camisard prophets, 119
Marlborough, Earl of, 354
Marteilhe, autobiography of, 195, 201-4
Martinargues, battle at, 162-4
Massillon on Louis XIV., 10
Mazel, Abraham, 120, 123
Mialet, visit to, 127-8
Milsom, Edward, 395, 451, 490-92
Missionaries, booted, 288
Montandre, Marquis de, 314
Montauban, persecutions at, 289-90
Montpellier, Protestant Church at, 32-3; the Peyrou at, 72; execution of Brousson at, 73, 300
Montrevel, Marshal, in Languedoc, 149; at Pompignan, 152; adopts extermination, 153; at Tower of Belliot, 156-8; character of, 159; recalled, 167; defeats Cavalier, 168-9

NANTES, Revocation of Edict of, and its results, 1-19, 24, 44-5, 78; contemporary opinion upon, 1-10; enactments of Edict of Revocation, 12-15, 285-6
Neff, Felix, 427-32; life of, 394, 404; his account of winter at Dormilhouse, 447; his charge, 469
Nelson, Lord, eulogium on Capt. Riou, 368; at the battle of Copenhagen, 378-9
Ners, visit to, 131
Newton Butler, engagement at, 333
Nismes, Protestant Church at, 31; petition from, 41; Brousson at, 57, 69; Guion at, 57; country about, 81, 130-2; success of Camisards near, 143; Cavalier at, 144-5, 177-83; treaty of, 179-80; Huguenot meetings at, 265

ORMOND, Duke of, 349

PALONS, 433-6
Paulet, Mdlle., forgeries in name of, 32-4
Pechell, Augustus, 315
Pechell, Capt. William Cecil, 315
Pechell, Col. Jacob, 313
Pechell, Paul, 314
Pechell, Samuel, extraordinary probity of, 314
Pechell, Sir G. R. Brooke, 315
Pechell, Sir Thomas, 315
Péchels de la Boissonade, Samuel de, narrative of his persecutions, 291 et seq.; imprisonment, 296, 299-301; meeting with his wife, 297; condemned to banishment, 299; embarkation, 302; sails for America, 303; sufferings, 304-5; reaches the West Indies, 305; illness and arrival in London, 307; accepts a commission in the English army, 309; campaign in Ireland, 310; return to London, 311; removal with his wife and son to Dublin, 312; death of, 312; his descendants, 313
Péchels, family of, 290
Péchels, Madame de, inhumanity towards, 294-5; touching interview with her husband, 297; further trials, 297; escape to Geneva, 298; in London, 308; reunited to her husband, 311

INDEX.

Pelice, Valley of the, 472
Pélisson, 323
Pont-de-Montvert, outbreak at, 92-7; description of, 93-4; end of Camisard insurrection at, 187-9
Portland, Earl of, 361, 363
Portland Vase, 363
Poul, Captain, in Upper Cevennes, 108; at Champ Domergue, 114-16; takes Laporte at Molezon, 117; defeated and killed near Nismes, 143-4
Pra du Tour, 486-90, 499
Preachers, education of, 221-4; hardships of, 225-9, 236-8
Project, the, 34
"Protestant wind," the, 325
Protestantism in France, present chances of, 417

QUOITE, execution of, 53

RAPIN, Capt. Paul, birth and education, 321-2; emigrates to England, 322; embarks for Holland, 323; a cadet in the Dutch army, 324; sails for England, 325; encounters a storm, 326; with the army of William III., 335 *et seq.*; aide-de-camp, 350; wounded and promoted, 354; conciliatory spirit, 358-9; at Kinsale, 359; tutor to Lord Woodstock, 360; presented to the King, 371; makes the "grand tour" with his pupil, 362-3; secures the Portland Vase, 363; marriage, 363; at the Hague and Wesel, 364; his "Dissertation on the Origin and Nature of the English Constitution," 364; "History of England," 364-7; death of, 366
Rapin, Daniel de, 324
Rapin family, 317-21, 367
Rapin, Solomon, 354, 360
Ravanel, insurgent leader, defeats Royalists near Nismes, 143; near Bouquet, 145; supplants Cavalier, 182-5; death of, 189
Redothière, Isabeau, 53
Rességuerie, M. de la, 297

Rey, Fulcran, his preaching and death, 25-7
Riou, Capt., R.N., Lord Nelson's opinion of, 368; ancestry, 368-70; birth and education, 370; becomes a midshipman, 370; accompanies Capt. Cook in his last voyage, 371; witnesses the murder of the captain, 371; return to England and appointed lieutenant, 372; a sharer in the glory of Capt. Luttrell's brilliant achievement, 372; appointed to the command of the *Guardian*, 373; letters to his mother, 373, 377; his ship strikes upon an iceberg, 374; remains with the vessel, 375; letter to the Admiralty, 375; extract from his log, 376; rescued by Dutch whalers, and return to England, 376; receives the special thanks of the Admiralty, 377; commander of the royal yacht *Princess Augusta*, 378; at the battle of Copenhagen, 378-9; death of, 379; his character, 379-80; monument in St. Paul's Cathedral, 380
Rochemalan, Vaudois struggles at, 482-6
Roger, Jacques, 213
Roland, nephew of Laporte, 111; insurgent leader, 113; succeeds Laporte, 118; in Lower Cevennes, 122; organizes Camisards, 123-5; takes Sauvé, 137; at Pompignan, 152; at Salindres, 164-5; at Font-Morte, 176-7; at Pont-de-Montvert, 187; death of, 188
Romanche, Valley of the, 401, 408
Rosen, Count, 332; indignation against King James, 337
Rostan, Alpine missionary, 460 (note)
Rou, Jean, 363-4
Roussel, Alexandre, 232
Ruvigny, Major-General, 357

ST. BARTHOLOMEW, doubt thrown upon massacre of, 27

Saint-Etienne, Rabout, 276-7
St. Hypolite, meeting at, 35
Saint-Ruth, Marshal, 38; in Ireland, 38 (note), 354 *et seq.*
Saint-Simon on the treatment of converts, 23
Sands, Captain, 357
San Veran, 468
Sarsfield, General, 351-3, 356
Savoy and France, war declared, 520
Savoy, Duke of, takes refuge with the Vaudois, 520
Schomberg, Marshal, 309 *et seq.*, 317, 344 *et seq.*; death of, 345
Schomberg, Count, 348
Sedan, prosperity of, before Revocation, 64-5; Brousson at, 65-6
Seguier, Pierre, insurgent leader, 96, 103; at Frugères, 104; at Font-Morte, 106; taken, tried, and executed, 106-7
Sirven, 263; case of, taken up by Voltaire, 264
Society of Friends in Languedoc, 281-2
Souverain executed, 52
Squeezers, the, 101 (note)
Synod of French Protestant Church, 283

TALMASH, Major-General, 357
Telford, anecdote of, 82
Testart, Marie Anne, 363
Tetleau, Major-General, 357
Toleration, Edict of, 276
"Troopers' Lane," 310
Tyrconnel, Earl of, 331-2
Tyrconnel, Lady, retort to King James, 348

VAL Fressinières, 423-5, 432-43
Val Louise, 420; massacre at, 422
Vaudois, the country of, 385; early Christianity of, 385-6; early persecutions of, 388; Easter massacre of, 390-1; visits of Dr. Gilly to, 393-4, 468, 477; passiveness of, 420-1; massacre of, at Val Louise, 422; persecutions of, 424-6, 455, 481, 495-500, 513-20; refuges of, 459, 467, 475, 477, 481; struggles of, at Rochemalan, 482-6; flight at the Revocation, 495; apparently exterminated, 500; in Switzerland, 501; prepare to return, 502; Arnaud appointed leader, 502; assisted by William of Orange, 503; The Glorious Return of, 504-13; struggles of, at the Balsille, 515; assist Duke of Savoy, 520; emancipation of, 521-2
Venours, Marquis de, death of, 335
Vesson, 212, 214
Vidal, Isaac, preacher, 48
Villars, Marshal, on prophetic mania in Languedoc, 90; appointed to command in Languedoc, 167; at Nismes, 169; clemency of, 172-86; treats with Cavalier, 177, 185; suppresses insurrection of Camisards, 188
Vincent, Isabel, prophetess, 89, 90
Vivens, death of, 56
Voltaire, takes up case of Calas, 259-63; takes up case of Sirven, 264; case of Chaumont, 271

WALDENSES, the, 384
Walker, Dr. George, death of, 348
Waller, Sir James, 359
Wheel, punishment of the, 258 (note)
William of Orange lands in England, 308; proclaimed King, 309; campaign against James II., 309 *et seq.*, 340 *et seq.*; his fleet, 325-7; wounded, 342; death of, 364
Woodstock, Lord, 360-3
Wurtemberg, Duke of, 340, 357

www.ingramcontent.com/pod-product-compliance
Lightning Source LLC
Chambersburg PA
CBHW070524090426
42735CB00013B/2858